Praise for
VIRGINIA O'HARE DOCUMENTS
GOD'S LAW VS. MAN'S LAW

"This is the most amazing book I have ever read, besides the Holy Bible! *I have been deeply moved by Virginia's book, as she compares God's laws and His will for my life, to Man's laws. This moving, and divinely-inspired masterpiece is truly going to be the world's next Best Seller! She answers all my questions about God, prophesy, salvation, and eternal life through Jesus Christ.*

I have known Virginia for over 30 years and she is a remarkable woman with extraordinary visionary talents. She is a very successful business woman who has made a mark in the Ft. Lauderdale community, with an astounding amount of success and recognition for her honest, and godly dealings with the public. **I believe Virginia will receive a special crown in heaven for her endeavors!"**

Roger J. Light
Ministry of the Gospel
Ft. Lauderdale, FL

"I couldn't put the book down! *Virginia's writing is so skillful and knowledgeable, I think that she may have been hiding a law degree all these years. It is just captivating! You can feel her pain and suffering as she details her true circumstances in this book. She opens the eyes of the public on how our justice system is not there for us, but our Lord and Savior is!"*

Kathleen Dodd
Real Estate Broker
Lighthouse Point, FL

"Other than the Bible, this new book is the #1 MUST READ for every single American! I have never met anyone as intelligent, determined and dedicated as Virginia O'Hare. Her book will have a tremendous impact on all those who want to see our Civil and Constitutional Rights upheld by our Government. With her God-given strength, she will see that justice is served."

Brenda Spiwak
Charity Fundraiser
South Florida

"Virginia, I am carrying your book with me to Jerusalem. Ten of the most powerful Rabbis in Israel will lift a special prayer for you and your son, from the land where it all started! Your story is both a personal tragedy and a true travesty of justice. **You are His Angel, so have faith!** Those responsible WILL be punished and justice will prevail."

David de Beer
Real Estate Agent
Ft. Lauderdale, FL

"This is one of the most incredible things I have ever read! Your detailed documentation of God's Law Vs. Man's Law, answers so many questions I have had over the years. I truly had to stop reading every few pages to sit back and contemplate the information. This book is so amazing! I pray that it is published fast, so that all can see that the End-Times are approaching quickly!"

Betty Hensinger
Real Estate Agent
Mount Dora, FL

"I am thoroughly impressed with, 'Virginia O'Hare Documents God's Law vs Man's Law.' I have known Virginia professionally and personally for over the 30 years. She is a genuine God-fearing woman, so I'm not surprised with the God inspired contents of this amazing book. Her gift of *prophesy continues to amaze me.* **Virginia is 100% dedicated to saving souls for Jesus. I truly believe that 100,000,000 million souls will be saved through her,** *and I will be honored to be a part of her ministry forever."*

Rebecca "Becky" Norwood
Senior Vice President/Branch Manager
Local Community Bank

"Virginia, I just finished reading this amazing and powerful book! I am so deeply moved. **Just thinking of all you and your son have been through is unimaginable!** *I pray that your deep faith will continue to keep you strong. You and Robert are always in my thoughts."*

Lois A. Stoll
Vice President / Sr. Business Development Officer
Banking Industry

"This book is a very well documented account of our Creator's laws for mankind. **Virginia brilliantly summarizes the chronology of sin and its eventual punishment.** *I am not a book critic, nor am I a religious expert, however, I did enjoy reading the Law's history and the warnings about disobedience!"*

Dr. Kendra Orr
Tutoring Business Owner
Trust Fund Manager

Praise for Virginia's previous book, "Virginia O'Hare's Trials, Triumphs, and Vision from God"

"This book is a miracle! Everything in this book speaks directly to me, as a message directly from God. I am really blessed to have read this book. It changed me completely. It gave me both courage, and authority. It taught me not to be afraid. While reading this book, I could feel the power coming straight from God!

Pastor Dieuminfor
Haiti

God's Law vs MAN'S LAW

VIRGINIA O'HARE

For Robert

My only son,
Your heart of gold,
strength of character,
and the courage
of your convictions,
will see the day
where victory is yours.
For in you, Robert,
God is well pleased.

TABLE OF CONTENTS

SECTION THREE – ROBERT'S STORY

FOREWORD

When I read Virginia's first book, ***"Virginia O'Hare's Trials, Triumphs, and Vision from God,"*** I said that I could not put it down because it was so gripping, and it created a desire in me to see how it ended. Her new book, ***"Virginia O'Hare Documents God's Laws vs. Man's Laws,"*** affects me in a very different way. This book has kept me from being able to get the subject out of my conscience. No matter what I think or do, God's laws continue to pop-up in my mind.

This book is so important for those of us trying to cope with today's crazy world. It is a Biblical guide that is written with great clarity and Godly inspiration. This is a book that all Christians should read if they truly want to understand the difference between man's laws and God's laws.

Most of us have gone through life not fully understanding what influence the evil one has had on mankind's laws. The laws of government may have started out under the influence of God's laws, but they have been twisted and changed for man's purpose. As a student of history, the law, and the Bible, Virginia brings it all together by sharing her real-life experiences and her faith. I believe whoever reads this book will have similar feelings and their faith will be positively affected for the rest of their life.

Vincent J Vella CFPâ
Senior Vice President
Wealth Management Advisor

INTRODUCTION

Never before in world history have all biblical signs of the end of days converged together at the same time, with record-breaking disasters increasing with frequency and intensity. Our world is literally teetering on the brink of annihilation. Mankind is now facing the worst threat ever of an apocalyptic nuclear World War III. We are the final generation that is witnessing the fulfillment of all the biblical *"End of Days"* signs that includes: the preaching of the gospel of Jesus Christ throughout the whole world, explosion of knowledge, world travel by land, sea, and air, technological advancement to implement the soon coming Mark of the Beast (the antichrist), escalation of crime and corruption, sexual immorality, rise in spiritualism, mass animal deaths, wars and rumors of wars, countless natural and divine disasters with fires, floods, hurricanes, tsunamis, tornadoes, mudslides, and strange and ominous signs and wonders in the sky.

Israel becoming an independent nation on May 14, 1948, was a major prophetic sign of the last days, as foretold by prophets who lived thousands of years ago. No nation in world history has ever been resurrected after being out of existence for almost 2000 years! All these biblical signs, occurring at the same time signal the soon return of our Lord and Savior, Jesus Christ, and the end of our age. **Jesus warned: *"...when you see all these things, you know that it is near, right at the door. Truly I tell you, this generation will certainly not pass away until all these things have happened"*** (Matthew 24:33-34 NIV) [emphasis added].

Disasters are taking their toll on people's lives and property throughout the world, causing the hearts of many to fail them with fear and anxiety. These *End of*

Days, Biblical signs are recorded by God's prophets and are in the following books of the Bible: Isaiah, Jeremiah, Ezekiel, Daniel, Hosea, Joel, Amos, Micah, Nahum, Zechariah, and Malachi. The entire theme of Revelation is the prophetic account of the end of the age and the return of Jesus Christ who will establish God's kingdom here on earth. *"The revelation from Jesus Christ, which God gave him to show his servants what must soon take place...Look, he is coming with the clouds, and every eye will see him, even those who pierced him and all peoples on earth will mourn because of him."* (Revelation 1:1, 7 NIV)

These events are God's warning signs for all to wake up and be ready because the end of our world, as we know it, is only moments away from the doomsday clock striking midnight! When this occurs, God gives mankind two options, eternal salvation through His son Jesus Christ, or eternal damnation in the fires of hell if we do not repent of our sins and accept Jesus as our Lord and savior.

Our country is dealing with incredible challenges, with lawlessness, corruption, and terrorism at the top of the list. There are major internal problems growing by leaps and bounds in our government and are spreading throughout our entire political and judicial system.

Man's laws came into existence eleven years after the signing of our Declaration of Independence, which was formally declared on July 4, 1776. Our founding fathers wrote the U.S. Constitution, based on the principles of the Bible and God's Ten Commandments. This brought tremendous blessings, favor, prosperity, and growth to our nation

Today, our government has changed man's laws from compliance with the foundational principles of God's laws and are in fact, in opposition to God's Ten Commandments. This is bringing God's judgment on our country. To witness this fact, all we have to do is watch the daily news to see God's divine judgment pouring His wrath down on America. We see record-breaking disasters everywhere, including wildfires igniting and exploding randomly, floods that are destroying lives and properties, famines, incurable diseases, hurricanes, tornadoes, and tsunamis. God always shows His punishment on those who break His laws, with fire, floods, natural disasters, and death.

The Rule of Law is Mandatory for Democracy to Survive

Every American citizen has a legal entitlement to our civil and constitutional rights, which our government must honor. Abraham Lincoln, at his Gettysburg Address, enshrined the people's rule of law in the fervent pledge that, under God, this democracy shall not perish from the earth. Our government has a legal and moral responsibility to uphold, protect, and guarantee our democratic, civil and constitutional rights. We the people have the supreme power to vote into office those who will best represent our rights as American citizens.

Our democracy is a system of government by the entire population of all members of a state. It is a government by the people and for the people whereby the supreme power is vested in the people and exercised by them through a system of elected representatives. The very essence of democracy is that the majority rules on decisions made by a vote of more than one half of all who participate in an election. In a Constitutional Democracy, a majority rule is required for minority rights. These are normal individual rights that are applied to members of racial, ethnic, religious, linguistic, gender and sexual-orientation minorities and their collective rights accorded to minority groups, or to anyone who is not part of a majority decision.

Our democracy protects the rights of citizens, maintains order, and limits the power of the government. All citizens are equal under the law. No one is above the law, not even our president or an enforcement officer or any elected official. Our founding fathers created the Constitution to restrict government controls "over" the people. Those who came before us fought, and many died, for our unalienable God-given rights as documented in our Constitution. Their voices proclaimed, loud and clear in the Preamble: "We the people of the United States, in order to form a more perfect union, establish justice, insure domestic tranquility, provide for the common defense, promote the general welfare, and secure the blessings of liberty to ourselves and our posterity, do ordain and establish this Constitution for the United States of America." Our democratic government is a system that **"must"** treat everyone equally.

One of our constitutional rights is to seek justice in a court of law. This can be a very emotional and trying experience for the accused when those in power do not uphold the law or honor their constitutional rights. A major obstacle for American justice is when there is judicial misconduct due to bias, corruption, collusion, and politics. This causes those in the judicial system to rule unfairly and not always according to the law. Many of the accused facing such injustice will plead "no contest" and appeal, rather than gamble on the judicial system giving them a fair and impartial ruling. This plea is used in criminal proceedings as an alternative to a guilty or not guilty plea or going to trial. The defendant neither disputes or admits to doing the crime. This plea is also known as *"nolo contendere,"* which means, "I do not wish to contend." When there is a judicial misinterpretation of the law, a *de novo* appeal can be made. This is a standard appeal that can be applied on an appeal in which the appellate court uses the trial court's record but reviews the evidence and law without yielding to the trial court's rulings.

An Appellate Court is known as a finder of facts. There are three judges in an Appellate Court that have the power to overturn an incorrect ruling made in a lower court, as well as clarifying and interpreting the law. Appeals for either civil or criminal cases are based on errors made at the trial court level or errors made by a judge misinterpreting the law.

The highest court in the land is the Supreme Court, which was established by the U.S. Constitution in 1789. All other federal courts were created by Congress. A police officer is a government official, who plays a central role in the law enforcement system. Their primary duty is to focus on protecting people and property, to enforce the laws in areas they are assigned to patrol in, monitor criminal activity, respond to emergency calls, make arrests, issue citations, and testify in court cases.

The Constitution, which is the "Supreme" law of the land, requires all government officials, including police officers, to swear an oath to uphold the United States Constitution before taking office. Officers who violate the constitutional rights of the people in carrying out their duties should be held accountable because they take away the very essence of justice. Unfortunately, some enforcement officers, prosecutors, judges, appellate judges, and those who are pledged to uphold the peoples' civil and constitutional rights, have accused the guiltless of crimes they were innocent of committing. According to the Innocence Project's estimates, between 2.3 percent and as high as 5 percent of all US prisoners are innocent.[1]

The U.S. leads the world in the incarceration of its citizens with approximately 2,300,000 people today behind bars.[2] Everyone, regardless of the nature of their crime, is entitled to their civil and constitutional rights. Our government needs to affirm those rights, including our right to privacy. **Every American citizen has the legal right to feel secure in the privacy of their own home. No one should have their privacy violated by a corrupt or biased judicial system.**

This book documents the blessings and favor in obeying God's laws. We are seeing man's laws today that do not comply with God's Ten Commandments. This is bringing severe judgment upon those who choose to keep the traditions of man rather than the laws of God. Jesus said, *"...why do you break the command of God for the sake of your tradition? 'These people honor me with their lips, but their hearts are far from me. They worship me in vain; their teachings are merely human rules.'"* (Matthew 15:3, 8-9 NIV)

SECTION ONE

God's Law

FROM CREATION TO THE TEN COMMANDMENTS

IN THE BEGINNING...

God gave His Ten Commandments to Adam and Eve well before He codified them to Moses on Mt. Sinai. God's laws are the very essence of His being. God's Ten Commandments came before man's laws and will be in existence forever. If man's laws violate God's laws, we must honor God's laws! God's punishment for those who broke His laws are fully outlined in the bible. God defined transgression of the law or lawlessness as sin. *"Whoever commits sin also commits lawlessness, and **sin is lawlessness**"* (1 John 3:4 NIV) [emphasis added]. When we stand at the judgment seat of Christ, we will be judged according to God's laws and not man's laws. Each of us will answer to what we did in our bodies, whether it be good or bad: *"For we must all appear before the judgment seat of Christ, that each one may receive the things done in the body, according to what he has done, whether good or bad"* (2 Corinthians 5:10 NKJV).

Scripture attests to the presence of God's laws and the consequences of violating His Commandments from the time of creation to the writing of them on stone tablets with His own finger on Mt. Sinai.

In the very beginning of man's creation, God punishes Adam and Eve for breaking the 8th and 10th commandments, which are stealing and coveting.

Adam and Eve's first-born Cain killed his brother

Abel then lied to God about murdering his brother. God punished Cain for murder and lying as violations of the 6th and 9th Commandments.

"But the men of Sodom were exceedingly wicked and sinful against the Lord" (Genesis 13:13 NKJV). God destroyed them all by raining down fire from heaven for violation of the 1st and 7th Commandments.

Exactly one month after the Exodus, the Israelites ran out of food, and the entire camp was hungry and grumbling, so Moses appealed to the Lord. *"Then the Lord said to Moses, "Behold, I will rain bread from heaven for you. And the people shall go out and gather a certain quota every day, that I may test them, whether they will walk in My law or not. And it shall be on the sixth day that they shall prepare what they bring in, and it shall be twice as much as they gather daily"* (Exodus 16:4-5 NKJV). The Israelites violated the 4th commandment by disobeying God and working on the Sabbath.

In Leviticus 18, God condemned the practices of idolatry in the land of Canaan and all their filthy and degrading acts. They broke the 1st, 2nd, and 6th Commandments.

God gave Moses the Ten Commandments on Mount Sinai as the principles of moral behavior for the Israelites. God's laws should always be the foundation of mankind's moral code and the basis on which our legal system of justice should be based upon.

God's Law, the Ten Commandments, are Found in Exodus 20:2-17 NKJV

"I am the Lord your God, who brought you out of the land of Egypt, out of the house of bondage. You shall have no other gods before Me.

"You shall not make for yourself a carved image— any likeness of anything that is in heaven above, or that is in the earth beneath, or that is in the water under the earth; you shall not bow down to them nor serve them. For I, the Lord your God, am a jealous God, visiting the iniquity of the fathers upon the children to the third and fourth generations of those who hate Me, but showing mercy to thousands, to those who love Me and keep My commandments.

"You shall not take the name of the Lord your God in vain, for the Lord will not hold him guiltless who takes His name in vain.

"Remember the Sabbath day, to keep it holy. Six days you shall labor and do all your work, but the seventh day is the Sabbath of the Lord your God. In it you shall do no work: you, nor your son, nor your daughter, nor your male servant, nor your female servant, nor your cattle, nor your stranger who is within your gates. For in six days the Lord made the heavens and the earth, the sea, and all that is in them, and rested the seventh day. Therefore the Lord blessed the Sabbath day and hallowed it.

"Honor your father and your mother, that your days may be long upon the land which the Lord your God is giving you.

"You shall not murder.

"You shall not commit adultery.

"You shall not steal.

"You shall not bear false witness against your neighbor.

"You shall not covet your neighbor's house; you shall not covet your neighbor's wife, nor his male servant, nor his female servant, nor his ox, nor his donkey, nor anything that is your neighbor's."

The first four commandments show us how to love God. The last six commandments show us how to love our neighbor and live in harmony with each other.

When the Apostles asked Jesus, what was the most important commandment, He said, *"The first of all the commandments is, Hear, O Israel; the Lord our God is one Lord: And thou shalt love the Lord thy God with all thy heart, and with all thy soul, and with all thy mind, and with all thy strength: this is the first commandment.* (Commandments 1-4) *And the second is like, namely this, thou shalt love thy neighbor as thyself. There is none other commandment greater than these* (Commandments 5-10)" (Mark 12:29-31 NKJV) [commentary added].

God's laws never change. His Ten Commandments existed from the beginning and will last throughout all eternity. We need to walk in obedience to God's laws to be blessed and enjoy His countless favors. It pleases God to give us every provision necessary for our life. God wrote His laws on man's heart and mind and gave His Holy Spirit to empower believers to overcome temptation and to protect us from God's arch enemy, satan, and his demons.

Obedience to God's Ten Commandments brings blessings if we obey, and curses if we disobey. God gave the Israelites 613 commandments that were compiled in the first five books of the Bible, called the Torah. The Ten Commandments were included in the 613 commandments. When the law was transgressed by the Israelites, which was often, this broke their relationship with God. To restore this broken relationship, animal sacrifices were required, and penalties were given. God prescribed a sheep or goat be killed as their guilt offering as a temporary covering or atonement for their sins. This was to symbolize that sin brings death. *"This is to be a lasting ordinance for you: Atonement is to be made once a year for all the sins of the Israelites"* (Leviticus 16:34 NKJV). This was a foreshadow of the perfect and complete sacrifice of God's beloved son, Jesus. *"Without the shedding of blood, there is no forgiveness!"* (Hebrews 9:22 NKJV).

LEARNING GOD'S LAW

Every child growing up needs to learn first and foremost about God, His laws as outlined in the Ten Commandments, and that Jesus is our Lord and Savior who paid the price on the cross for our sins. Reading the Bible and praying keeps us in a spiritual connection with our Father. The Bible is the oldest and the longest standing "best-selling" book in the world. The Holy Spirit inspired its entire composition. The Bible gives a menu for instructions on how to live with God and man. **The Bible is not only historical and prophetic but is the most up-to-date-book in the entire world. It covers every issue in one's life, without exception and is the Rock of Reality.**

The writing of the Bible, authored by 40 inspired writers with an amazing collection of 66 books, has an "unbroken" continuity from Genesis to Revelation. The Bible was written over a period of 1400 to 1800 years.[3] It's divided into 39 books in the Old Testament and 27 books in the New Testament and was written under the inspiration of the Holy Spirit. *"All scripture is given by inspiration of God, and is profitable for doctrine, for reproof, for correction, for instruction in righteousness"* (2 Timothy 3:16 NKJV).

God inspired the first writing of the Holy Scriptures 2,500 years after creation and 1000 years after the flood.

The Bible has 11 chapters on the first 2000 years of human history and 1,178 chapters of the next 2000 years. The first five books of the old testament known as the Torah were written by Moses during 1450-1419 B.C. This was the period of time the children of Israel wandered in the wilderness for 40 years. The five books of the Torah consist of Genesis, Exodus, Leviticus, Numbers, and Deuteronomy. The last book written in the Old Testament was the book of Malachi, after which there were 400 years of scriptural silence by God.

The apostles of the Jewish Messiah, Jesus Christ, wrote the new testament many years after His resurrection. This included the gospels written by Matthew, Mark, Luke, and John. His apostles, wrote the events of our Savior's birth, life, death, His resurrection, and events that would occur prior to His Second Coming. They penned Jesus' prophetic messages that are exploding in fulfillment today in our generation. After Jesus' death on the cross, He appeared live to Paul, who became an avid disciple of Jesus and wrote 14 books of the Bible. Scholars have debated whether Paul wrote Hebrews.

The Bible is our guide to living life according to the will of God. It is our roadmap through the sometimes-perilous journey of life and teaches us how to turn our trials into triumphs. It is our anchor in times of trouble, and a refuge for all! We are the children of the Almighty God, made in His likeness and image. He is a loving eternal living God who loves us unconditionally. He gives each of us a purpose and a destiny and is our source of wisdom and everlasting life. The Bible shows us the standards for our conduct, knowing right from wrong. Our children need the Bible for instruction and inspiration, especially during their formative years. It shows them how to live in peace and harmony with each other and is essential for their spiritual growth as well as their intellectual and psychological development into adulthood. The Bible prepares our children for God's gift of eternal salvation through His son, Jesus Christ.

God's Ten Commandments are permanent and as valid today as they were when He wrote them with His own finger and gave them to Moses on Mt. Sinai, and to our first parents, Adam and Eve 6000 years ago. This shows how important God's laws are to Him. Throughout the pages of the Holy Bible, countless scriptures confirm the relevance of keeping God's laws. *"Do we then make void the law through faith? Certainly not! On the contrary, we establish the law"* (Romans 3:31 NKJV). On Judgment Day, believers, are going to be judged for our works, not our sins, because Jesus paid the price for our sins on the cross. Even so, this does not make void keeping God's Ten Commandments. *"So He said to him, 'Why do you call Me good? No one is good but One, that is, God. **But if you want to enter into life, keep the commandments**"* (Matthew 19:17 NKJV) [emphasis added].

Teaching the word of God, as outlined in the Holy Scriptures should be taught to everyone, young and old and should be the basis for molding and educating our children. Our students should be allowed to pray and read the Bible in our schools and have the awesome instructions for reading scriptures in the classroom. This is essential for the proper development of their mind, character, and the spiritual growth of our youth. We must prepare our children for their eternal salvation through Jesus Christ, from the very beginning of their ability to comprehend words. *"Train up a child in the way he should go: and when he is old, he will not depart from it."* (Proverbs 22:6 NKJV).

Our laws are wrong to disallow group prayers and the reading of the Bible in our classrooms. Our children are the future generation, who will contribute to the development and the Godly management of our country. If we do not fill their minds with spiritual knowledge and the proper moral values and behavior during their young, character building, and formative years, only the wrong things will be instilled instead.

After 50 years of taking the Bible and prayer out of our classrooms, our students are only allowed to pray if they do not disturb anyone. Our teachers are only allowed to pray privately or in a group and must do so outside the presence of students. The general rule of law is that organized prayer in the public school, in a classroom, or at a school-sponsored event, is unconstitutional. The only type of prayer that is constitutionally permissible is a private student prayer that does not interfere with the school's educational system.[4] Removing the Bible and prayer from our public schools has caused many negative and development issues for our students, including but not limited to a decrease in academic achievement, an increase in out of wedlock births, increase of illegal drug use, increase in juvenile crime, and the deterioration of school behavior.

The student's formative years for learning and developing moral principles for the rest of their life should be taught in the classroom as well as in the home. *"And that from childhood you have known the Holy Scriptures, which are able to make you wise for salvation through faith which is in Christ Jesus"* (2 Timothy 3:15 NKJV).

OBEDIENCE TO GOD'S TEN COMMANDMENTS IS NOT AN OPTION!

God's laws comply with His Holy character and are mandatory for all to keep in order to live in harmony with God and each other. We are commanded not to break any of God's Ten Commandments. In so doing, we alienate ourselves from God and each other, like Adam and Eve did when they disobeyed God and ate of the forbidden fruit. They broke their relationship with God. His blessings are on those who obey His commandments and curses on those who do not. God never changes; He is the same yesterday, today, and forever. He will not change His laws. They are eternal.

Man's laws now sanction same-sex marriages. The bible calls same-sex relationships sodomy. We have legalized abortions which the Bible calls murder. We have removed the Bible and prayers to God from our schools. Today, immorality is worse than it was in the days of Sodom and Gomorrah, and before the global flood in Noah's days. The only difference being we are legalizing sodomy, the murder of fetuses, taking the bible and prayers out of our schools, and removing the ten commandments from our Supreme Court building. Such acts lead people to moral corruptness.

These statistics are alarming and confirm what Jesus said two thousand years ago, that the end time generation would be like it was "in the days of Noah and Lot." God's most extreme judgments in the entire Old Testament were upon inhabitants who lived during Lot and Noah's days.

"But as the days of Noah were, so also will the coming of the Son of Man be. For as in the days before the flood, they were eating and drinking, marrying and giving in marriage, until the day that Noah entered the ark, and did not know until the flood came and took them all away, so also will the coming of the Son of Man be" (Matthew 24:37-39 NKJV).

"Likewise as it was also in the days of Lot: They ate, they drank, they bought, they sold, they planted, they built; but on the day that Lot went out of Sodom it rained fire and brimstone from heaven and destroyed them all. Even so will it be in the day when the Son of Man is revealed" (Luke 17:28-30 NKJV).

God's first created being was His only begotten son, Jesus Christ, who was with Him from the beginning. The Father, the Son, and the Holy Spirit are three in one who bear record in heaven. They are in total agreement with each other. *"For there are three that bear record in heaven, the Father, the Word, and the Holy Ghost: and these three are one"* 1 John 5:7 (NKJV). God's name is *Jehovah*, the one and only almighty and powerful god of the universe. He created all things through His only begotten son, Jesus Christ, and His Holy Spirit. Six thousand years ago, God formed the first man, Adam, from the dust of the ground and breathed into his nostrils the breath of life and made him into a living soul.

He is the God of the Old and New Testaments and judges sin with mercy, patience, and forgiveness. Through His prophets, Noah, Abraham, Lot, and Moses, He offered forgiveness of sins to all and provided eternal salvation and forgiveness of sins through His son, Jesus Christ. God offers abundant mercy and grace to those who love Him and keep His Ten Commandments. *"Showing mercy to thousands, to those who love Me and keep My commandments"* (Exodus 20:6 NKJV).

King David is an example of God's love, mercy, and grace. God forgave King David for his sin of taking another man's wife, Bathsheba, and then having her husband, Uriah, murdered. After David repented and poured out his heart to God to forgive him and restore his joy, God said David was a man after His own heart. We should love God with all our heart, mind and soul, and repent of our sins, and strive always to do His will. *"After removing Saul, he made David their king. God testified concerning him: 'I have found David son of Jesse, a man after my own heart; he will do everything I want him to do'"* (Acts 13:22 NIV).

Like King David, we all have come short of the Glory of God. From the moment we took our first breath, we inherited the original sin from our first parents, Adam and Eve. That's why God sacrificed His Son so we can be cleansed from the "original sin" of our first parents and every sin we ever committed thereafter, past present and future. It is only through Jesus that we become justified and are saved and free from the stain of sin and God's punishment. By repenting of our sins and accepting Jesus as our Lord and Savior, we are restored and made righteous in God's sight. *"For all have sinned and fall short of the glory of God, being justified freely by His grace through the redemption that is in Christ Jesus, whom God set forth as a propitiation by His blood, through faith, to demonstrate*

His righteousness, because in His forbearance God had passed over the sins that were previously committed, to demonstrate at the present time His righteousness, that He might be just and the justifier of the one who has faith in Jesus" (Romans 3:23-26 NKJV).

God's will for each of us is that we love Him, keep His Commandments, prosper, and be in good health. *"Beloved, I pray that you may prosper in all things and be in health, just as your soul prospers"* (3 John 1:2 NKJV). He wants us to love Him with all our heart, soul and might because He first loved us. Sickness, death, and sin came into the world after satan tempted our first parents to sin, which separated them from God. Jesus came to restore us back to God, give us eternal life, heal our bodies, and will destroy satan, sin, and death forever. Upon Jesus' Second Coming, we will be given a glorified body like his, which will be incorruptible.

God wants us to have an abundant life, and to live it to the fullest. He counsels us to meditate on only positive and good thoughts, and not to have negative thoughts, because as a man thinks in his heart, he is. He wants us to meditate on only good, honest, just, pure, lovely, and whatsoever things of good report. *"For as he thinks in his heart, so is he"* (Proverbs 23:7a NKJV). *"Finally, brethren, whatever things are true, whatever things are noble, whatever things are just, whatever things are pure, whatever things are lovely, whatever things are of good report, if there is any virtue and if there is anything praiseworthy—meditate on these things"* (Philippians 4:8 NKJV).

Everyone has trials and tribulations in this life. The Word of God tells us not to dwell on those things but think thoughts that are healthy and good for our body, soul, and spirit. He wants us to know that all things work together for good for those who love the lord. Whenever things go wrong, I always think of this scripture, and it gets me through every single trial with a good report. *"And we know that all things work together for good to those who love God, to those who are the called according to His purpose"* (Romans 8:28 NKJV).

Man's laws are always changing. God's laws never change and are forever. *"For I am the Lord, I do not change;"* (Malachi 3:6 NKJV). The Bible is clear. Those who keep the Commandments of God and their faith in Jesus Christ will enter into God's Kingdom and be joint heirs with Jesus, and rule and reign with Him over nations.

Through Adam and Eve's disobedience to God, death came to mankind. Man's "soul" is either lost forever by sin or saved forever through Jesus Christ. God said, *"Behold, all souls are Mine; The soul of the father as well as the soul of the son is Mine; The soul who sins shall die"* (Ezekiel 18:4 NKJV). The human soul needs atonement *"For the life of the flesh is in the blood, and I have given it to you upon the altar to make atonement for your souls; for it is the blood that makes atonement for the soul"* (Leviticus 17:11 NKJV). Jesus Christ is our atonement for our sins. He is the great shepherd of souls. Through His blood shed on the cross, we are cleansed from all our sins, healed of all our infirmities, and receive redemption from our sins and eternal life. *"In Him we have redemption through His blood, the forgiveness of sins, according to the riches of His grace"* (Ephesians 1:7 NKJV).

God wants us to meditate on His Word day and night, *"This Book of the Law shall not depart from your mouth, but you[a] shall meditate in it day and night, that you may observe to do according to all that is written in it. For then you will make your way prosperous, and then you will have good success"* (Joshua 1:8 NKJV).

When man's laws say it is okay to have same-sex marriage and it is okay to abort an unborn baby from a mother's womb, God's law commands us to obey Him and not man. Everyone will be judged by God's laws and not man's laws. Eternal salvation is far more important than the few moments we spend here on earth. Keeping God's Ten Commandments are beneficial to us and others. Those saved by grace are instructed to keep the law but are not under the law! If we sin, Jesus is our atonement, not the blood of some animal, nor is that sin accounted against us when we repent.

Holy Scripture confirms we are to keep God's Ten Commandments. In our Lord's own words are His instructions for obedience to the law. *"For assuredly, I say to you, till heaven and earth pass away, one jot or one tittle will by no means pass from the law till all is fulfilled. Whoever therefore breaks one of the least of these commandments, and teaches men so, shall be called least in the kingdom of heaven; but whoever does and teaches them, he shall be called great in the kingdom of heaven. For I say to you, that unless your righteousness exceeds the righteousness of the scribes and Pharisees, you will by no means enter the kingdom of heaven"* (Matthew 5:18-25 NKJV).

Clearly, the law of God, which is the very essence of His being and reflects His Holy and righteous nature, will be the standard for all eternity. *"You shall diligently keep the commandments of the LORD your God, His testimonies, and His statutes which He has commanded you"* (Deuteronomy 6:17 NKJV).

God rewards obedience to His laws. *"So you shall observe My statutes and keep My judgments, and perform them; and you will dwell in the land in safety. Then the land will yield its fruit, and you will eat your fill, and dwell there in safety. And if you say, 'What shall we eat in the seventh year, since we shall not sow nor gather in our produce?' Then I will command My blessing on you in the sixth year, and it will bring forth produce enough for three years. And you shall sow in the eighth year, and eat old produce until the ninth year; until its produce comes in, you shall eat of the old harvest"* (Leviticus 25:18-22 NKJV).

"Now, Israel, hear the decrees and laws I am about to teach you. Follow them so that you may live and may go in and take possession of the land the Lord, the God of your ancestors, is giving you. Do not add to what I command you and do not subtract from it, but keep the commands of the Lord your God that I give you. You saw with your own eyes what the Lord did at Baal Peor. The Lord your God destroyed from among you everyone who followed the Baal of Peor, but all of you who held fast to the Lord your God are still alive today. See, I have taught you decrees and laws as the Lord my God commanded me, so that you may follow them in the land you are entering to take possession of it. Observe them carefully, for this will show your wisdom and understanding to the nations, who will hear about all these decrees and say, "Surely this great nation is a wise and understanding people." What other nation is so great as to have their gods near them the way the Lord our God is near us whenever we pray to him? And what other nation is so great as to have such righteous decrees and laws as this body of laws I am setting before you today? Only be careful, and watch yourselves closely so that you do not forget the things your eyes have seen or let them fade from your heart as long as you live. Teach them to your children

and to their children after them. Remember the day you stood before the Lord your God at Horeb, when he said to me, "Assemble the people before me to hear my words so that they may learn to revere me as long as they live in the land and may teach them to their children." You came near and stood at the foot of the mountain while it blazed with fire to the very heavens, with black clouds and deep darkness. Then the Lord spoke to you out of the fire. You heard the sound of words but saw no form; there was only a voice. He declared to you his covenant, the Ten Commandments, which he commanded you to follow and then wrote them on two stone tablets. And the Lord directed me at that time to teach you the decrees and laws you are to follow in the land that you are crossing the Jordan to possess" (Deuteronomy 4:1-14 NIV).

"Now it shall come to pass, if you diligently obey the voice of the Lord your God, to observe carefully all His commandments which I command you today, that the Lord your God will set you high above all nations of the earth. And all these blessings shall come upon you and overtake you, because you obey the voice of the Lord your God: *Blessed shall you be in the city and blessed shall you be in the country. Blessed shall be the fruit of your body, the produce of your ground and the increase of your herds, the increase of your cattle and the offspring of your flocks. Blessed shall be your basket and your kneading bowl. Blessed shall you be when you come in and blessed shall you be when you go out. The Lord will cause your enemies who rise against you to be defeated before your face; they shall come out against you one way and flee before you seven ways. The Lord will command the blessing on you in your storehouses and in all to which you set your hand, and He will bless you in the land which the Lord your God is giving you. The Lord will* *establish you as a holy people to Himself, just as He has sworn to you, if you keep the commandments of the Lord your God and walk in His ways. Then all peoples of the earth shall see that you are called by the name of the Lord, and they shall be afraid of you. And the Lord will grant you plenty of goods, in the fruit of your body, in the increase of your livestock, and in the produce of your ground, in the land of which the Lord swore to your fathers to give you. The Lord will open to you His good treasure, the heavens, to give the rain to your land in its season, and to bless all the work of your hand. You shall lend to many nations, but you shall not borrow. And the Lord will make you the head and not the tail; you shall be above only, and not be beneath, if you heed the commandments of the Lord your God, which I command you today, and are careful to observe them. So you shall not turn aside from any of the words which I command you this day, to the right or the left, to go after other gods to serve them"* (Deuteronomy 28:1-14 NKJV).

And finally:

"Now all has been heard; here is the conclusion of the matter: Fear God and keep his commandments, *for this is the duty of all mankind"* (Ecclesiastes 12:13 NIV) [emphasis added].

GOD'S SEVEN BIBLICAL COVENANTS

Our eternal and living God not only is omnipotent, omnipresent, omniscient, omnibenevolent, but He is also mathematical. He created the Universe and everything in it, which is mathematically designed to function in perfect order and harmony. He does not do things just on a whim. He has a purpose and plan for everything He does. He has chosen to reveal that purpose through a series of covenants or testaments. God has one overall purpose for His creation. This single purpose is revealed in successive stages. Some Christians believe that God works in a disjointed way, with different plans for different people or eras. This is not true! There is only one plan for everyone. God's ultimate plan for mankind is salvation for everyone through His son, Jesus Christ. He wants each of us to spend an eternity with Him.

The word covenant is quite commonly used in legal, social (marriage), and religious and theological contexts.

The term is of Latin origin *"con venire,"* meaning a coming together. It presupposes two or more parties who come together to make a contract, agreeing on promises, stipulations, privileges, and responsibilities.[5]

Each of God's Seven Covenants is intimately linked

to the one before it. Even a quick reading of Scripture will show the importance of Covenants. The more a subject or word is used in the Bible, the more we know it is important. If God takes time to talk about a subject repeatedly, it reveals its value to God and it ought then to be a high priority for us. This word is used at least 26 times in the book of Genesis alone! "Covenant" is used 227 times in the rest of the Old Testament and 33 times in the New Testament.[6]

Seven Biblical Covenants[7]

Seven specific covenants are revealed in Scripture. These seven covenants fall into three categories—conditional, unconditional, and general. Conditional covenants are based on certain obligations and prerequisites; if the requirements are not fulfilled, the covenant is broken. Unconditional covenants are made with no strings attached and will be kept regardless of one party's fidelity or infidelity. General covenants are not specific to one people group and can involve a wide range of people.

The conditional covenant mentioned in Scripture is the Mosaic Covenant; the blessings it extends are contingent upon Israel's adherence to the Law. The unconditional covenants mentioned in the Bible are the Abrahamic, Palestinian, and Davidic Covenants; God promises to fulfill these regardless of other factors. The general covenants mentioned are the Adamic, Noahic, and New Covenants, which are global in scope. Each of these covenants is listed below in biblical order with a brief description:

1. Adamic Covenant. Found in Genesis 1:26-30 and 2:16-17, this covenant is general in nature. It included the command not to eat from the tree of the knowledge of good and evil, pronounced a curse for sin and spoke of a future provision for man's redemption (Genesis 3:15).

2. Noahic Covenant. This general covenant was made between God and Noah following the departure of Noah, his family, and the animals from the ark. Found in Genesis 9:11, *"I establish my covenant with you, that never again shall all flesh be cut off by the waters of the flood, and never again shall there be a flood to destroy the earth."* This covenant included a sign of God's faithfulness to keep it—the rainbow.

3. Abrahamic Covenant. This unconditional covenant first made to Abraham in Genesis 12:1-3, promised God's blessing upon Abraham, to make his name great and to make his progeny into a great nation. The covenant also promised to bless those who blessed Abraham and cursing to those who cursed him. Further, God vowed to bless the entire world through Abraham's seed. Circumcision was the sign that Abraham believed in the covenant (Romans 4:11). The fulfillment of this covenant is seen in the history of Abraham's descendants and in the creation of the nation of Israel. The worldwide blessing came through Jesus Christ, who was of Abraham's family line.

4. Palestinian Covenant. This unconditional covenant, found in Deuteronomy 30:1-10, noted God's promise to scatter Israel if they disobeyed God, then to restore them at a later time to their land. This covenant has been fulfilled twice, with the Babylonian Captivity in 586 B.C. and subsequent rebuilding of Jerusalem under Cyrus the Great; and with the destruction of Jerusalem in A.D. 70, followed by the reinstatement of the nation of Israel in 1948.

5. Mosaic Covenant. This conditional covenant, found in Deuteronomy 11 and elsewhere, promised the Israelites a blessing for obedience and a curse for disobedience. Much of the Old Testament chronicles the fulfillment of this cycle of judgment for sin and later blessing when God's people repented and returned to God.

6. Davidic Covenant. This unconditional covenant, found in 2 Samuel 7:8-16, promised to bless David's family line and assured an everlasting kingdom. Jesus is from the family line of David (Luke 1:32-33) and, as the Son of David (Mark 10:47), is the fulfillment of this covenant.

7. New Covenant. This covenant, found in Jeremiah 31:31-34, promised that God would forgive sin and have a close, unbroken relationship with His people. **The promise was first made to Israel and then extended to everyone who comes to Jesus Christ in faith (Matthew 26:28; Hebrews 9:15).**

While not all Bible scholars agree on every detail regarding these biblical covenants, it is clear that God has made certain promises. Some of His promises are to all people, and some are limited to Israel. **All of God's promises are based on who He is and His plan for the world. Under the New Covenant, which Jesus sealed with His own blood, everyone is offered salvation by grace through faith. *"And it shall come to pass that everyone who calls upon the name of the Lord shall be saved"* (Acts 2:21).**

THE CONSEQUENCE OF DISOBEYING GOD'S LAW IS DEATH

God created the first man, Adam and gave him dominion over the newly restored planet earth, with rules to follow. This included naming all the animals, dress and maintain the garden, and obey His commandments. One commandment was not to eat the fruit from the Tree of the Knowledge of Good and Evil. *"Then the Lord God took the man and put him in the garden of Eden to tend and keep it. And the Lord God commanded the man, saying, 'Of every tree of the garden you may freely eat; but of the tree of the knowledge of good and evil you shall not eat, for in the day that you eat of it you shall surely die'"* (Genesis 2:15-17 NKJV).

God was pleased with His creation of man in His likeness and image. He walked and talked with Adam in the Garden of Eden and enjoyed their fellowship. Adam was fully aware of what God wanted him to do and what He didn't want him to do. He knew he was not to eat the fruit from the Tree of the Knowledge of Good and Evil, so he refrained from even touching the tree.

As time went on, God saw that Adam was lonely. "And the Lord God said, 'It is not good that man should be alone; I will make him a helper comparable to him'" (Genesis 2:18 NKJV). God placed Adam in a deep sleep and performed the first surgical procedure mentioned in the Bible. He took one of Adam's ribs, which is the only bone in the body that is known medically to grow back. He covered over it, and formed a woman from Adam's rib, and gave her to Adam as his helpmate. Adam knew God removed the rib from his body to create the woman, and said, *"This is now bone of my bones and flesh of my flesh; She shall be called Woman, because she was taken out of Man"* (Genesis 2:23 NKJV). He named the woman, Eve, who became the mother of the human race.

The deceiver of mankind, the Devil, tempted Adam and Eve to disobey God and eat the forbidden fruit. One day when Eve was in the garden, she heard the voice of a talking serpent, who was satan in disguise, God's adversary. He beguiled her into eating the forbidden fruit from the Tree of the Knowledge of Good and Evil. He lied to Eve and told her she would not die if she ate the fruit but be like God. Believing the serpent, Eve ate the fruit then gave it to her husband who was with her. He, too, ate the fruit. Instantly, the judgment of death came upon them, and their seed and both were cast out of the Garden of Eden.

From the very beginning, God's judgment for sinning against His laws was death. God told Adam, "the day you eat of the fruit from the forbidden tree you will surely die." Although Adam lived 930 years, he died within God's one-day count because one day to our Lord is 1000 years to man. *"But, beloved, do not forget this one thing, that with the Lord one day is as a thousand years, and a thousand years as one day"* (2 Peter 3:8 NKJV).

God did not want Adam and Eve to eat the fruit from the Tree of the Knowledge of Good and Evil, because

He did not want them to partake of the knowledge of evil, and deal with the consequences of disobedience. He placed on them, His ultimate punishment of death. In obeying God's laws, we are prepared to live a triumphant life here on earth now and forever.

Out of jealousy of Adam and Eve's dominion over planet earth and not wanting to be subservient to them, satan caused our first parents to disobey God. In so doing, he caused Adam and Eve to lose their forever home in the Garden of Eden and have God's judgment of a death sentence on them and their seed. Through his evil plan, satan got dominion over planet earth and is still in control. That's why this world is in such a diabolical mess! His goal is to have everyone lose their eternal life in heaven because he lost his high position in heaven and of hovering over the throne of God. God's future judgment against satan, was by His son Jesus, who after the 1000-year millennium will consume him with fire.

Adam and Eve's judgment for disobedience meant they would be cast out of the Garden of Eden and death. God gives free will to His angels, and to mankind. He does not want us to be robots, but to have free will to choose either good or evil, life or death. Heaven is for those who choose life through Jesus, or the eternal fires of hell if we chose to disobey and follow satan. I pray all will choose God's amazing grace of salvation through His son, Jesus Christ, who is our one and only Savior. He is the only way to eternal life and heavenly bliss. *"Jesus said to him, "I am the way, the truth, and the life. No one comes to the Father except through Me"* (John 14:6 NKJV).

Today satan and his legion of demons are the driving force behind all the corruption, crime, and turmoil we see in our world today. Satanic influence is causing insurmountable problems that are escalating throughout our world. Daily we see breaking news of countless upheavals and disasters, with crime, corruption, and terrorism literally covering the globe. At the same time, there are natural and divine apocalyptic events, with record-breaking storms, flooding, earthquakes hurricanes, which are causing havoc around the world!

Satan, knowing he has a short time left, is causing world-wide atrocities to occur. We should pray always to escape the major effects from these end-time events that are accelerating unabated around the world.

Very soon World War III will commence, which will be worse than all previous wars put together. Shortly thereafter will commence the Battle of Armageddon, which will cause mankind to be on the brink of absolute annihilation. Before this happens, Jesus will rapture His elect from the four corners of the earth into heaven, then return to defeat satan and his demons in this great bloodbath Battle of Armageddon. Satan will be defeated then brought down to the bottomless abyss and chained there for 1000 years. Jesus Christ will take 100% control of all the nations and reign as King of Kings and Lord of Lords for 1000 years. This event will occur at the end of the 7-year tribulation, and the Battle of Armageddon.

PROPHETIC WARNINGS
OF PERILOUS TIMES

Our generation will experience horrific and perilous times right before the Second Coming of Jesus, which will commence at the beginning of the seven years of tribulation. This will be God's final judgment on planet earth before He sends His son to rapture all believers. The beginning of the seven years of tribulation will affect our entire planet. All the nations will gather their armies and fight in the region of the Euphrates River which will be dried up.

The end of the seven-year tribulation will commence the final war among the nations called the Battle of Armageddon. This will herald in the Second Coming of Jesus who will rapture His elect from the four corners of the earth and return to fight in the final Battle of Armageddon between God and satan. This war will destroy the lives of a quarter of all people on earth.

We are the final generation that will see the fulfillment of all these End-of-Days prophetic events and the Second Coming of our Lord and Savior, Jesus Christ. Jesus warns that prior to His coming, there would be "perilous times" with lawlessness, corruption, and mankind's immoral behavior would exist virtually everywhere. The very stability of our world is eroding rapidly.

We live daily with the existence of dangerous and terror-filled conditions that are affecting the very lives of people everywhere.

The following "end of days" bible scriptures are warnings of "perilous and dangerous times" that are now rapidly inundating our entire world:

"But mark this: **There will be terrible times in the last days.** *People will be lovers of themselves, lovers of money, boastful, proud, abusive, disobedient to their parents, ungrateful, unholy, without love, unforgiving, slanderous, without self-control, brutal, not lovers of the good, treacherous, rash, conceited, lovers of pleasure rather than lovers of God having a form of godliness but denying its power. Have nothing to do with such people"* (2 Timothy 3:1-5 NIV) [emphasis added].

"The coming of the lawless one is according to the working of satan, with all power, signs, and lying wonders, and with all unrighteous deception among those who perish, because they did not receive the love of the truth, that they might be saved. And for this reason, God will send them strong delusion, that they should believe the lie, that they all may be condemned who did not believe the truth but had pleasure in unrighteousness" (2 Thessalonians 2:9-12 NKJV).

"But the cowardly, unbelieving, abominable, murderers, sexually immoral, sorcerers, idolaters, and all liars shall have their part in the lake which burns with fire and brimstone, which is the second death" (Revelation 21:8NKJV).

"Knowing this first: that scoffers will come in the last days, walking according to their own lusts, and saying, "Where is the promise of His coming? For since the fathers

fell asleep, all things continue as they were from the beginning of creation" (2 Peter 3:3-4 NKJV).

The prophet Daniel was given God's prophetic message from Archangel Gabriel, over 2500 years ago, on conditions that would exist in the last days, just before the end of our age and the Second Coming of Jesus. Daniel could not understand or comprehend these visions that were given to him. He found them to be frightening and overwhelming. Daniel received some of the most sweeping prophecies in the Bible. His visions were from the days of the Babylonian captivity, which he was a part of, to the very end of our age. After giving Daniel these prophetic messages, God told him to seal up the book until the time of the end. *"But you, Daniel, shut up the words, and seal the book until the time of the end; many shall run to and fro, and knowledge shall increase"* (Daniel 12:4 NKJV).

Archangel Gabriel never explained to Daniel, the technology needed to be implemented in order to fulfill these incredible signs of the last days. Daniel could not comprehend his visions 2500 years ago, because it was not meant to be understood until the time of the end, which is in our generation. Today in the 21st century, the Book of Daniel is not only unsealed but understood. We are the generation that is seeing the fulfillment of Daniel's prophecies, that knowledge would increase. We are virtually living in the information age, where knowledge has increased exponentially and is doubling every two years. It is exploding in all directions. 80% percent of the world's total knowledge has been brought forth in the last decade, and 90% of all the scientists that ever lived are alive today[9]. We have access to the world-wide internet that holds tons of information, literally at our fingertips. Knowledge has increased within our current generation, which is beyond one's capacity to imagine.

At the end of World War II, knowledge doubled every 25 years. Today, nanotechnology ("nanotech" is manipulation of matter on an atomic, molecular, and supramolecular scale) is doubling every two years and clinical knowledge every 18 months. Human knowledge is doubling every 13 months. According to IBM, "the build-out of the internet of things" will lead to the doubling of knowledge every 12 hours.[9]

Daniel also predicted that man shall run to and fro. Today, we have the ability to travel from one part of the world to another, which is unlike anything seen before in history. Up until the 20th century, travel was by foot, horse, and boat. Today, we can fly anywhere in the world, and travel by car, truck or bus, on land, and across the seas by ships and giant mega ships for our goods and products and in the air by planes and jets. This was not the case when Daniel recorded his vision 2500 years ago. Our generation is seeing the fulfillment of Daniel's vision of the last days, which was written between 540 and 530 B.C.

Daniel's vision of the increase of knowledge brings blessings and curses. With the explosion of technological inventions, man has developed nuclear weapons and high-tech chemical, biological and sophisticated war machines that can now literally destroy mankind many times over. Our government officials are perplexed as to how to resolve and control these serious problems. Countries such as Russia, China, Iran, North Korea, Israel, Turkey, Syria, and countless other nations in the Middle East, continue to develop their weapons of mass destruction. This is causing volatility and fear in the world that is frightening and overwhelming to everyone.

During their life, God blessed our first parents with

many sons and daughters. Eve birthed children that grew into an incredible population throughout the centuries. Due to the wickedness of mankind, God destroyed all their seed, except for Noah and his family 4,359 years ago, or in 2348 B.C. All we know for sure is that eight (8) people were saved after the world-wide flood, Noah, his wife, their three sons, and their wives. Based on biblical records, the population count, from Adam to Noah, was over seven billion people. Noah and his family were left to repopulate the earth.

The most recent statistics on population estimates, since Noah, is 7.6 billion as of July 2018. This is according to the most recent United Nations, estimates elaborated by Worldometers.[10]

Bible prophecy warns, just before Jesus' Second Coming, the earth would again resemble the days of Noah. Those days are here now! Our world is covered in wickedness, lawlessness, and corruption. Unbelievers will be asleep during the 1000-year reign of Jesus. Believers in Christ will spend this time basking in the countless joys of heavenly bliss in God's kingdom, with their saved family members and loved ones.

Sadly, after the 1000-year millennium, the unbelievers will awake to face their final punishment at God's White Throne Judgment to pay for their own sins and be cast forever in the eternal fires of hell, which can never be quenched. To avoid this from happening, anyone who has not accepted Jesus as their Lord and Savior should do so right now! I cannot stress enough times in this book that time is running out, and there is no other way for mankind to be saved. Jesus said, *"I am the way, the truth, and the life. No one comes to the Father except through Me"* (John 14:6 NKJV).

Jesus said, *"Do not think that I came to destroy the Law or the Prophets. I did not come to destroy but to fulfill. For assuredly, I say to you, till heaven and earth pass away, one jot or one tittle will by no means pass from the law till all is fulfilled. Whoever therefore breaks one of the least of these commandments, and teaches men so, shall be called least in the kingdom of heaven; but whoever does and teaches them, he shall be called great in the kingdom of heaven. For I say to you, that unless your righteousness exceeds the righteousness of the scribes and Pharisees,* **you will by no means enter the kingdom of heaven"** (Matthew 5:17-20 NKJV) [emphasis added].

GOD'S TEN COMMANDMENTS ARE HIS LAWS FOREVER

God gave Moses His Ten Commandments. God instructs everyone to obey His Commandments. If we choose to break His laws, we put ourselves under God's judgment. After Adam and Eve sinned, their judgment was death. No good ever comes from breaking God's laws. Sin causes separation from God who is our source and breath of life. Sin adversely affects our mental, emotional, as well as our psychological capacity to function with our self and others. There is not enough space in this book to cover all the consequences sin causes in ones' life.

After our first parents sinned, they felt fear, shame, and nakedness for the first time since their creation. When God walked into the Garden of Eden, He called out to Adam, *"The Lord God called to the man, 'Where are you?' He answered, 'I heard you in the garden, and I was afraid because I was naked; so I hid'"* (Genesis 3:9-11 NIV). *"The Lord God made garments of skin for Adam and his wife and clothed them"* (Genesis 3:21 NIV). This was later symbolic of God's covenant with the Israelites and the shedding of blood to cover their sin. This practice was often repeated because the people kept on sinning against God's Commandments.

Two thousand years ago, God gave the Israelites His

final and perfect covenant, His son Jesus as the final sacrificial lamb. He replaced the former covenant of sacrificing animals and keeping the 613 *mitzvot*, which were commandments God required the Israelites to obey. The Ten Commandments were in the 613 *mitzvot* but were never abolished and will be valid forever. Believers in Jesus are no longer under the condemnation of the law but are saved by grace. *"Whoever calls on the name of the Lord shall be saved* (this is grace)" (Romans 10:13 NKJV) [commentary added].

Under the old covenant, God required an unblemished animal to be sacrificed, as a temporary covering for mankind's sins. *"Without the shedding of blood, there is no forgiveness"* (Hebrews 9:22 NIV). Two thousand years ago, God provided a more perfect and complete sacrifice for sin that would permanently erase all of mankind's' sins. This one and only perfect sacrifice, acceptable to God, was the life of His own son, Jesus. Jesus willingly became the unblemished sacrificial lamb, who paid the price for mankind's past present and future sins. To fulfill this covenant there had to be the shedding of blood to atone for man's sins. Jesus died on the cross, to fulfill this covenant. Therefore, no more animal sacrifices were necessary or required by God.

Jesus satisfied God's judgment of sin for everyone and saved humanity from being eternally damned in the fires of hell. God's decision to sacrifice His only begotten son, to save mankind from His judgment of sin, was the hardest thing He ever had to do. *"For God so loved the world that He gave His only begotten Son, that whoever believes in Him should not perish but have everlasting life"* (John 3:16 NKJV).

We all have a choice where we will spend eternity, either in heaven or hell. Your choice must be made prior to death. After you take your last breath in your mortal body, you will take your next breath on the other side. **Everyone's fate is sealed upon taking our last breath in this mortal body.** If we repent of our sins and make Jesus the Lord of our life, we will live forever in God's Kingdom. If no choice is made or one that rejects God's gift of salvation, that person will spend an eternity in the fires of hell. Everyone who passes on will be aware of where they are once they take their first breath on the other side. Then It will be too late to call upon Jesus to save you if you reject Him in this life. Jesus is the propitiation, the perfect sacrifice who willingly gave himself (cf. Galatians 1:4). His blood (i.e., His death) by which our sins may be forgiven. God ordained Jesus to take our punishment for our sin, in order to satisfy His judgment on sin. No one on earth was qualified because all are born in sin, which everyone inherited from our first parents. That is why Jesus had to be conceived in the womb of a virgin by God's Holy Spirit and not the seed of man with the stain of our first parent's original sin.

Here is the beautiful story of how God did this. He sent His Archangel Gabrielle to a young virgin named Mary, and gave her this breathtaking message:

"'And behold, you will conceive in your womb and bring forth a Son, and shall call His name Jesus. He will be great, and will be called the Son of the Highest; and the Lord God will give Him the throne of His father David. And He will reign over the house of Jacob forever, and of His kingdom there will be no end.' Then Mary said to the angel, "How can this be, since I do not know a man?' And the angel answered and said to her, 'The Holy Spirit will come upon you, and the power of the Highest will overshadow you; therefore, also, that Holy One who is to be born will be called the Son of God. Now indeed, Elizabeth your relative

has also conceived a son in her old age; and this is now the sixth month for her who was called barren. For with God nothing will be impossible.' Then Mary said, 'Behold the maidservant of the Lord! Let it be to me according to your word.' And the angel departed from her" (Luke 1:31-38 NKJV).

Jesus not only had to be conceived by the Holy Spirit, without the original sin from our first parents, but He also had to live a perfect, sinless life in our stead. Growing up, He knew His fate would be the cross. He allowed His persecutors to unmercifully and cruelly beat His body and nail Him to the cross at Calvary. He did this because He loves us more than His life. According to Mark's Gospel, Jesus hung on the cross and endured the torment of crucifixion for six hours from 9:00 am to 3:00 pm until He gave up His ghost. He suffered such excruciating and unbearable pain. To further scorn and mock Him, the Roman soldiers placed a crown of thorns on His head, puncturing His scalp and forehead, with blood pouring from each wound. His beaten body was covered in blood. His badly cut up and bloody face was not recognizable. His entire body had been whipped and tortured. He was in such excruciating pain as He hung for some six hours on the cross.

Jesus felt the feeling of sheer abandonment for the brief moment God turned away from Him. He cried out, *"My God, My God, why have You forsaken Me?"* (Matthew 27:46 NKJV)

God turned away for a moment because He, too, was in agony, watching His beloved son nailed to the cross bleeding in pain and suffering. Those deep and profound emotions were shared between them with both knowing this was for saving mankind from their sins and eternal damnation.

Because of Jesus's sacrifice on the cross, we, as believers in Christ, are no longer separated from God because of our sins. We can now come boldly to the Throne of God and obtain unmerited favor because our sins are now and forever washed away in the seas of His forgiveness. There's no other way for mankind to be saved, this includes good works, animal sacrifices, or good deeds. No one can save us from our sins and God's judgment of eternal damnation. Only the blood of Jesus Christ can and does.

Sin no longer reigns over mankind because Jesus Christ triumphed over and defeated sin on the cross. We are made righteous through Him. If we look at the history of mankind, as recorded in the Bible, the evidence of satan's influence to tempt mankind to sin and disobey God's laws are universal. It is only through Jesus' death on the cross that satan's power over sin and death was destroyed, and our relationship with God is restored.

I cannot stress enough in this book how close we are to His Second Coming, and how important it is for everyone to be ready. Jesus will soon rapture all believers to live eternally with Him and wipe away all our tears and fears. Every believer will receive their just rewards for their good works and have eternal life.

God's former covenant, with Abraham, Isaac, and Jacob, was abolished by the cross. Our penalty for breaking God's laws was paid for, in full, by Jesus' death at Calvary. No other sacrifice will ever be needed again. As believers, we become joint heirs with Christ with positions in the Kingdom. *"And if children, then heirs—heirs of God and joint heirs with Christ, if indeed we suffer with Him, that we may also be glorified together"* (Romans 8:17 NKJV).

God gives everyone free will. He wants us to honor Him and be first in our life. He wants us to love Him above everything else. Once we accept Jesus as our Lord and Savior, we inherit God's Holy Spirit that dwells in us here in this life and throughout all eternity. God's Holy Spirit empowers us to live a successful and triumphant Christian life. The only thing satan offers anyone who follows him is eternal damnation. When people say, "Hail satan," they are signing their eternal death certificate in the fires of hell, where their punishment will last forever.

When we repent of our sins and accept Jesus as our Lord and Savior, He 'pardons' all our sins, and restores us to a right relationship with God, our Father. That relationship was broken when our first parents sinned. Through Jesus, we now have our relationship with God restored and have the indwelling presence of God's Holy Spirit. The Holy Spirit brings us into harmony with God, His laws, and the guarantee of our eternal salvation through our Lord and Savior, Jesus Christ.

God does not change His laws but made provisions through His Son Jesus to change us, so we can keep His laws. *"For what the law could not do in that it was weak through the flesh, God did by sending His own Son in the likeness of sinful flesh, on account of sin: He condemned sin in the flesh, that the righteous requirement of the law might be fulfilled in us who do not walk according to the flesh but according to the Spirit"* (Romans 8:3-4 NKJV).

God is offering everyone an eternal life with Him in His Kingdom. Satan is offering everyone eternal damnation in the lake of fire. You choose where you want to spend your eternity. The right choice for everyone is to repent of all your sins and accept Jesus as Lord and Savior and obey God's Ten Commandments. This gives us eternal life with God's unconditional love, joy, peace, and unending happiness. Then we will reap all the benefits Christ died to give us including living forever with our saved loved ones, as well as being joint heirs with Him in the kingdom. In heaven, we will have God's love, wisdom, blessings, and favor forever.

Everyone needs to read, study, and meditate on the Holy Scriptures. It enriches our mind and spirit and prepares us for living our lives in the Lord. *"All Scripture is given by inspiration of God, and is profitable for doctrine, for reproof, for correction, for instruction in righteousness"* (2 Timothy 3:16 NKJV).

There is no greater love than God's amazing grace in giving His own son as atonement for our sins. I pray you will make your decision right now by choosing to repent of your sins and accept Jesus Christ as your lord and savior. In so doing, you will live forever in God's Kingdom where no eye has seen, no ear has heard, and no human mind has conceived the things God has prepared for those who love Him. (see 1 Corinthians 2:9 NIV)

FINAL THOUGHTS…

God gave Moses His Ten Commandments on two tablets of stone written by His own finger. These Commandments are God's spiritual and eternal laws. Because Moses found favor with God, he was the only prophet to see the image and presence of God face-to-face and live. *"So the Lord spoke to Moses face to face, as a man speaks to his friend"* Exodus 33:11 NKJV). *"Since then there has not arisen in Israel a prophet like Moses, whom the Lord knew face to face"* (Deuteronomy 34:10 NKJV)

Our government is changing our U.S. Constitution with man's laws that are far removed from the ones our founding fathers created based on God's Biblical principles and the Ten Commandments. Man's laws are demonically inspired, i.e., same-sex marriages, abortions, and removing prayers to God and the Bible out of our schools.

In the meantime, we all should unite and stand firm for our God-given rights, of life, liberty and the pursuit of happiness, and prepare for the soon coming of our Lord and Savior, Jesus Christ. He will rule over the nations of the world with equality and justice for all and re-establish paradise lost by our first parents.

When God appeared to me 38 years ago, I saw the image of His face in the sky, and audibly heard His astounding voice. I was standing in the very presence of

God. I wrote about this awesome and unforgettable visitation in my first book titled, ***Virginia O'Hare's Trials, Triumphs, and Vision From God.*** God's voice is beyond words and any sound I have ever heard! His prophetic messages to me are being fulfilled. As I was writing this second book, the Lord spoke to my spirit and said, *"Virginia as I called Moses out at 80 years of age to give my Ten Commandments to my people, I have chosen you at 80 years of age to confirm my Ten Commandments to the world."*

SECTION TWO

Man's Law

FROM THE FOUNDING FATHERS TO TODAY'S HEADLINES

WE THE PEOPLE…

Our founding fathers named our country the United States of America because the original colonists were 100% united on the Biblical principles of God, His Ten Commandments and the Bible. The major intention of our founding fathers was to secure every American's right to life, liberty, and the pursuit of happiness, and not be under the tyranny of a government. Those in office, are voted in by the people who expect their political leaders to uphold their solemn oath to protect, guide and move our nation forward and preserve every American's civil, constitutional and democratic rights. Our political leaders have a moral and legal obligation to protect the people and our great country from harm, destruction, and terrorists. Enemies of our democracy are seeking to annihilate the United States and will take every opportunity and advantage to do so. We must not let this happen! United we stand, divided we fall! Jesus first declared, *"Every kingdom divided against itself is brought to desolation, and every city or house divided against itself will not stand"* (Matthew 12:25 NKJV).

Our politicians are in a pernicious state of turmoil, with confusion, and internal non-stop warring among those who run our country. Elected officials are fighting and bickering, the clash of wills, egos, and unbridled dissension, does not do the American people one bit of good. Every citizen wants our Constitutional principles such as democracy, the rule of law, and separation of powers to prevail against all adversities.

The American people want our government to return to the rule of law that upholds every citizen's rights. These rights include: (1) Accountability laws that apply to everyone, and guarantee the privacy and security of persons, property and our human rights; (2) Open Government enacted, administered, and enforced in a fair and efficient manner; (3) Accessible and Impartial Dispute Resolution justice delivered by competent, ethical and independent representatives; and (4) Neutral Oversight with accessible and adequate resources and is reflective of the communities they serve. Every American citizen wants and demands our government to honor and uphold our civil and constitutional rights, not violate or diminish them by making new laws that give more rights to the government than to the people.

We are seeing the erosion of man's civil, and human rights, with changes to our Constitution being made by a few individuals, using man's interpretation of laws. Changes that do not always comply with our Constitution, nor God's Ten Commandments.

Corruption in our legal system, adds to the spiraling erosion of our legal, civil, and human rights. Establishing justice in our legal system, with man's own interpretation and distorted views of the law, is filling the cup of injustice for those seeking their legal rights and constitutional due process through our judicial system.

Judges, in their rulings, don't always uphold the constitutional rights of the accused. This is why there are countless appeals, so the accused can seek justice with the correct interpretation of the law. A lawless decision by those in authority, including judges and appellate judges, who can literally destroy the lives of the accused if judges do not follow the law in their rulings.

There are law enforcement officers, who take an oath to protect our citizens and honor our constitutional rights, yet they take the law into their own hands and violate the very rights of the people they pledge to protect. Today, the accused are often considered guilty until proven innocent. Many will take a plea rather than pay the high cost of defending their civil and constitutional rights or gamble on not receiving a fair and impartial trial in a court of law. Many of the accused, convicted unjustly, are now sitting in a cell for the rest of their lives because our justice system has failed them.

Nothing can wipe out all the corruption in our legal system before Jesus Christ comes and sets up His government here on earth. Then and only then will God's laws and justice prevail forever and for everyone. However, in the meantime, we should all strive for justice in our legal system and conform our lives and country to God's laws and His Ten Commandments. This will bring rich blessings on our nation and us, instead of His chastisement for disobedience. *"And the Lord commanded us to observe all these statutes, to fear the Lord our God, for our good always, that He might preserve us alive, as it is this day"* (Deuteronomy 6:24 NKJV).

THE CHARTERS OF FREEDOM

The three most significant documents to the American people are the Declaration of Independence, the United States Constitution, and the Bill of Rights. Together, they laid the groundwork for both the American government and the American way of life. The original parchment documents are now housed in the *Rotunda for the Charters of Freedom,* within the National Archives in Washington DC. Please note: The three documents were written with the words and spelling of the 18th Century "British English."

The Declaration of Independence

In 1761, fifteen years before the United States of America burst onto the world stage with the Declaration of Independence; the American colonists were loyal British subjects who celebrated the coronation of their new King, George III. The colonies that stretched from present-day Maine to Georgia were distinctly English in character although they had been settled by Scots, Welsh, Irish, Dutch, Swedes, Finns, Africans, French, Germans, and Swiss, as well as English.[11]

As English men and women, the American colonists were heirs to the thirteenth-century English document, the Magna Carta, which established the principles that no one is above the law (not even the King), and that no one can take away certain rights. So in 1763, when the King began to assert his authority over the colonies to make them share the cost of the Seven Years' War England had just fought and won, the English colonists protested by invoking their rights as free men and loyal subjects. It was only after a decade of repeated efforts on the part of the colonists to defend their rights that they resorted to armed conflict and, eventually, to the unthinkable–separation from the motherland.[12]

Drafted by Thomas Jefferson between June 11 and June 28, 1776, the Declaration of Independence became the nation's most cherished symbol of liberty and Jefferson's most enduring monument. Jefferson expressed the convictions in the minds and hearts of the American people. The political philosophy of the Declaration was not new; its ideals of individual liberty had already been expressed by earlier philosophers. What Jefferson did was to summarize this philosophy in "self-evident truths" and set forth a list of grievances against the King in order to justify before the world the breaking of ties between the colonies and the mother country.[13]

The Declaration of Independence was approved by Congress on July 4th, 1776.

The Declaration of Independence

When in the Course of human events, it becomes necessary for one people to dissolve the political bands which have connected them with another, and to assume among the powers of the earth, the separate and equal station to which the Laws of Nature and of Nature's God entitle them, a decent respect to the opinions of mankind requires that they should declare the causes which impel them to the separation.

We hold these truths to be self-evident, that all men are created equal, that they are endowed by their Creator with certain unalienable Rights, that among these are Life, Liberty and the pursuit of Happiness.—That to secure these rights, Governments are instituted among Men, deriving their just powers from the consent of the governed, —That whenever any Form of Government becomes destructive of these ends, it is the Right of the People to alter or to abolish it, and to institute new Government, laying its foundation on such principles and organizing its powers in such form, as to them shall seem most likely to effect their Safety and Happiness. Prudence, indeed, will dictate that Governments long established should not be changed for light and transient causes; and accordingly, all experience hath shewn, that mankind are more disposed to suffer, while evils are sufferable than to right themselves by abolishing the forms to which they are accustomed. But when a long train of abuses and usurpations, pursuing invariably the same Object evinces a design to reduce them under absolute Despotism, it is their right, it is their duty, to throw off such Government, and to provide new Guards for their future security. —Such has been the patient sufferance of these Colonies; and such is now the necessity which constrains them to alter their former Systems of Government. The history of the present King of Great Britain is a history of repeated injuries and usurpations, all having in direct object the establishment of an absolute Tyranny over these States. To prove this, let Facts be submitted to a candid world.

> He has refused his Assent to Laws, the most wholesome and necessary for the public good.

> He has forbidden his Governors to pass Laws of immediate and pressing importance unless suspended in their operation till his Assent should be obtained; and when so suspended, he has utterly neglected to attend to them.

He has refused to pass other Laws for the accommodation of large districts of people unless those people would relinquish the right of Representation in the Legislature, a right inestimable to them and formidable to tyrants only.

He has called together legislative bodies at places unusual, uncomfortable, and distant from the depository of their public Records, for the sole purpose of fatiguing them into compliance with his measures.

He has dissolved Representative Houses repeatedly, for opposing with manly firmness his invasions on the rights of the people.

He has refused for a long time, after such dissolutions, to cause others to be elected; whereby the Legislative powers, incapable of Annihilation, have returned to the People at large for their exercise; the State remaining in the mean time exposed to all the dangers of invasion from without, and convulsions within.

He has endeavoured to prevent the population of these States; for that purpose, obstructing the Laws for Naturalization of Foreigners; refusing to pass others to encourage their migrations hither, and raising the conditions of new Appropriations of Lands.

He has obstructed the Administration of Justice, by refusing his Assent to Laws for establishing Judiciary powers.

He has made Judges dependent on his Will alone, for the tenure of their offices, and the amount and payment of their salaries.

He has erected a multitude of New Offices, and sent

hither swarms of Officers to harrass our people, and eat out their substance.

He has kept among us, in times of peace, Standing Armies without the Consent of our legislatures.

He has affected to render the Military independent of and superior to the Civil power.

He has combined with others to subject us to a jurisdiction foreign to our constitution, and unacknowledged by our laws; giving his Assent to their Acts of pretended Legislation:

For Quartering large bodies of armed troops among us:

For protecting them, by a mock Trial, from punishment for any Murders which they should commit on the Inhabitants of these States:

For cutting off our Trade with all parts of the world: For imposing Taxes on us without our Consent:

For depriving us in many cases, of the benefits of Trial by Jury:

For transporting us beyond Seas to be tried for pretended offences

For abolishing the free System of English Laws in a neighbouring Province, establishing therein an Arbitrary government, and enlarging its Boundaries so as to render it at once an example and fit instrument for introducing the same absolute rule into these Colonies:

For taking away our Charters, abolishing our most valuable Laws, and altering fundamentally the Forms of our Governments:

For suspending our own Legislatures, and declaring themselves invested with power to legislate for us in all cases whatsoever.

He has abdicated Government here, by declaring us out of his Protection and waging War against us.

He has plundered our seas, ravaged our Coasts, burnt our towns, and destroyed the lives of our people.

He is at this time transporting large Armies of foreign Mercenaries to compleat the works of death, desolation and tyranny, already begun with circumstances of Cruelty & perfidy scarcely paralleled in the most barbarous ages, and totally unworthy the Head of a civilized nation.

He has constrained our fellow Citizens taken Captive on the high Seas to bear Arms against their Country, to become the executioners of their friends and Brethren, or to fall themselves by their Hands.

He has excited domestic insurrections amongst us, and has endeavoured to bring on the inhabitants of our frontiers, the merciless Indian Savages, whose known rule of warfare, is an undistinguished destruction of all ages, sexes and conditions.

In every stage of these Oppressions We have Petitioned for Redress in the most humble terms: Our repeated Petitions have been answered only by repeated injury. A Prince whose character is thus marked by every act which may define a Tyrant, is unfit to be the ruler of a free people.

Nor have We been wanting in attentions to our Brittish brethren. We have warned them from time to time of attempts by their legislature to extend an unwarrantable jurisdiction over us. We have reminded them of the circumstances of our emigration and settlement here. We have appealed to their native justice and magnanimity, and we have conjured them by the ties of our common kindred to disavow these usurpations, which, would inevitably interrupt our connections and correspondence. They too have been deaf to the voice of justice and of consanguinity. We must, therefore, acquiesce in the necessity, which denounces our Separation, and hold them, as we hold the rest of mankind, Enemies in War, in Peace Friends.

We, therefore, the Representatives of the United States of America, in General Congress, Assembled, appealing to the Supreme Judge of the world for the rectitude of our intentions, do, in the Name, and by Authority of the good People of these Colonies, solemnly publish and declare, That these United Colonies are, and of Right ought to be Free and Independent States; that they are Absolved from all Allegiance to the British Crown, and that all political connection between them and the State of Great Britain, is and ought to be totally dissolved; and that as Free and Independent States, they have full Power to levy War, conclude Peace, contract Alliances, establish Commerce, and to do all other Acts and Things which Independent States may of right do. And for the support of this Declaration, with a firm reliance on the protection of divine Providence, we mutually pledge to each other our Lives, our Fortunes and our sacred Honor

The 56 signatures on the Declaration of Independence:

Connecticut:
Roger Sherman
Samuel Huntington
William Williams
Oliver Wolcott

Delaware:
Caesar Rodney
George Read

Thomas McKean

Georgia:
Button Gwinnett
Lyman Hall
George Walton

Maryland:
Samuel Chase
William Paca
Thomas Stone
Charles Carroll of Carrollton

Massachusetts:
John Hancock
Samuel Adams
John Adams
Robert Treat Paine
Elbridge Gerry

New Hampshire:
Matthew Thornton
Josiah Bartlett
William Whipple

New Jersey:
Richard Stockton
John Witherspoon
Francis Hopkinson
John Hart
Abraham Clark

New York:
William Floyd
Philip Livingston
Francis Lewis
Lewis Morris

North Carolina:
William Hooper
Joseph Hewes

John Penn

Pennsylvania:
Robert Morris
Benjamin Rush
Benjamin Franklin
John Morton
George Clymer
James Smith
George Taylor
James Wilson
George Ross

Rhode Island:
Stephen Hopkins
William Ellery

South Carolina:
Edward Rutledge
Thomas Heyward, Jr.
Thomas Lynch, Jr.
Arthur Middleton

Virginia:
George Wythe
Richard Henry Lee
Thomas Jefferson
Benjamin Harrison
Thomas Nelson, Jr.
Francis Lightfoot Lee
Carter Braxton

The Constitution of the United States

The Federal Convention convened in the State House (Independence Hall) in Philadelphia on May 14, 1787, to revise the Articles of Confederation. Because the delegations from only two states were at first present, the members adjourned from day to day until a quorum of seven states was obtained on May 25. Through discussion and debate it became clear by mid-June that, rather than amend the existing Articles, the Convention would draft an entirely new frame of government. All through the summer, in closed sessions, the delegates debated and redrafted the articles of the new Constitution.[14] Among the chief points at issue was how much power to allow the central government, how many representatives in Congress to allow each state, and how these representatives should be elected—directly by the people or by the state legislators. The work of many minds, the Constitution stands as a model of cooperative statesmanship and the art of compromise.[15]

The Constitution of the United States

We the People of the United States, in order to form a more perfect Union, establish Justice, insure domestic Tranquility, provide for the common defence, promote the general Welfare, and secure the Blessings of Liberty to ourselves and our Posterity, do ordain and establish this Constitution for the United States of America.

Article I *(Legislative Powers)*

Section 1

All legislative Powers herein granted shall be vested in a Congress of the United States, which shall consist of a Senate and House of Representatives.

Section 2

1: The House of Representatives shall be composed of Members chosen every second Year by the People of the several States, and the Electors in each State shall have the Qualifications requisite for Electors of the most numerous Branch of the State Legislature.

2: No Person shall be a Representative who shall not have attained to the Age of twenty five Years, and been seven Years a Citizen of the United States, and who shall not, when elected, be an Inhabitant of that State in which he shall be chosen.

3: Representatives and direct Taxes shall be apportioned among the several States which may be included within this Union, according to their respective Numbers, which shall be determined by adding to the whole Number of free Persons, including those bound to Service for a Term of Years, and excluding Indians not taxed, three fifths of all other Persons. The actual Enumeration shall be made within three Years after the first Meeting of the Congress of the United States, and within every subsequent Term of ten Years, in such Manner as they shall by Law direct. The Number of Representatives shall not exceed one for every thirty Thousand, but each State shall have at Least one Representative; and until such enumeration shall be made, the State of New Hampshire shall be entitled to chuse three, Massachusetts eight, Rhode-Island and Providence Plantations one, Connecticut five, New-York six, New Jersey four, Pennsylvania eight, Delaware one, Maryland six, Virginia ten, North Carolina five, South Carolina five, and Georgia three.

4: When vacancies happen in the Representation from any State, the Executive Authority thereof shall issue Writs of Election to fill such Vacancies.

5: The House of Representatives shall chuse their Speaker and other Officers; and shall have the sole Power of Impeachment.

<u>Section 3</u>

1: The Senate of the United States shall be composed of two Senators from each State, chosen by the Legislature thereof, for six Years; and each Senator shall have one Vote.

2: Immediately after they shall be assembled in Consequence of the first Election, they shall be divided as equally as may be into three Classes. The Seats of the Senators of the first Class shall be vacated at the Expiration of the second Year, of the second Class at the Expiration of the fourth Year, and of the third Class at the Expiration of the sixth Year, so that one third may be chosen every second Year; and if Vacancies happen by Resignation, or otherwise, during the Recess of the Legislature of any State, the Executive thereof may make temporary Appointments until the next Meeting of the Legislature, which shall then fill such Vacancies.

3: No Person shall be a Senator who shall not have attained to the Age of thirty Years, and been nine Years a Citizen of the United States, and who shall not, when elected, be an Inhabitant of that State for which he shall be chosen.

4: The Vice President of the United States shall be President of the Senate, but shall have no Vote, unless they be equally divided.

5: The Senate shall chuse their other Officers, and also a President pro tempore, in the Absence of the Vice President, or when he shall exercise the Office of President of the United States.

6: The Senate shall have the sole Power to try all Impeachments. When sitting for that Purpose, they shall be on Oath or Affirmation. When the President of the United States is tried, the Chief Justice shall preside: And no Person shall be convicted without the Concurrence of two thirds of the Members present.

7: Judgment in Cases of impeachment shall not extend further than to removal from Office, and disqualification to hold and enjoy any Office of honor, Trust or Profit under the United States: but the Party convicted shall nevertheless be liable and subject to Indictment, Trial, Judgment and Punishment, according to Law.

<u>Section 4</u>

1: The Times, Places and Manner of holding Elections for Senators and Representatives, shall be prescribed in each State by the Legislature thereof; but the Congress may at any time by Law make or alter such Regulations, except as to the Places of chusing Senators.

2: The Congress shall assemble at least once in every Year, and such Meeting shall be on the first Monday in December,5 unless they shall by Law appoint a different Day.

<u>Section 5</u>

1: Each House shall be the Judge of the Elections, Returns and Qualifications of its own Members, and a Majority of each shall constitute a Quorum to do Business; but a smaller Number may adjourn from day to day, and may be authorized to compel the Attendance of absent Members, in such Manner, and under such Penalties as each House may provide.

2: Each House may determine the Rules of its Proceedings, punish its Members for disorderly Behaviour, and, with the Concurrence of two thirds, expel a Member.

3: Each House shall keep a Journal of its Proceedings, and from time to time publish the same, excepting such Parts as may in their Judgment require Secrecy; and the Yeas and Nays of the Members of either House on any question shall, at the Desire of one fifth of those Present, be entered on the Journal.

4: Neither House, during the Session of Congress, shall, without the Consent of the other, adjourn for more than three days, nor to any other Place than that in which the two Houses shall be sitting.

Section 6

1: The Senators and Representatives shall receive a Compensation for their Services, to be ascertained by Law, and paid out of the Treasury of the United States.6 They shall in all Cases, except Treason, Felony and Breach of the Peace, be privileged from Arrest during their Attendance at the Session of their respective Houses, and in going to and returning from the same; and for any Speech or Debate in either House, they shall not be questioned in any other Place.

2: No Senator or Representative shall, during the Time for which he was elected, be appointed to any civil Office under the Authority of the United States, which shall have been created, or the Emoluments whereof shall have been encreased during such time; and no Person holding any Office under the United States, shall be a Member of either House during his Continuance in Office.

Section 7

1: All Bills for raising Revenue shall originate in the House of Representatives; but the Senate may propose or concur with Amendments as on other Bills.

2: Every Bill which shall have passed the House of Representatives and the Senate, shall, before it become a Law, be presented to the President of the United States; If he approve he shall sign it, but if not he shall return it, with his Objections to that House in which it shall have originated, who shall enter the Objections at large on their Journal, and proceed to reconsider it. If after such Reconsideration two thirds of that House shall agree to pass the Bill, it shall be sent, together with the Objections, to the other House, by which it shall likewise be reconsidered, and if approved by two thirds of that House, it shall become a Law. But in all such Cases the Votes of both Houses shall be determined by yeas and Nays, and the

Names of the Persons voting for and against the Bill shall be entered on the Journal of each House respectively. If any Bill shall not be returned by the President within ten Days (Sundays excepted) after it shall have been presented to him, the Same shall be a Law, in like Manner as if he had signed it, unless the Congress by their Adjournment prevent its Return, in which Case it shall not be a Law.

3: Every Order, Resolution, or Vote to which the Concurrence of the Senate and House of Representatives may be necessary (except on a question of Adjournment) shall be presented to the President of the United States; and before the Same shall take Effect, shall be approved by him, or being disapproved by him, shall be repassed by two thirds of the Senate and House of Representatives, according to the Rules and Limitations prescribed in the Case of a Bill.

<u>Section 8</u>

1: The Congress shall have Power To lay and collect Taxes, Duties, Imposts and Excises, to pay the Debts and provide for the common Defence and general Welfare of the United States; but all Duties, Imposts and Excises shall be uniform throughout the United States;

2: To borrow Money on the credit of the United States;

3: To regulate Commerce with foreign Nations, and among the several States, and with the Indian Tribes;

4: To establish an uniform Rule of Naturalization, and uniform Laws on the subject of Bankruptcies throughout the United States;

5: To coin Money, regulate the Value thereof, and of foreign Coin, and fix the Standard of Weights and Measures;

6: To provide for the Punishment of counterfeiting the Securities and current Coin of the United States;

7: To establish Post Offices and post Roads;

8: To promote the Progress of Science and useful Arts, by securing for limited Times to Authors and Inventors the exclusive Right to their respective Writings and Discoveries;

9: To constitute Tribunals inferior to the Supreme Court;

10: To define and punish Piracies and Felonies committed on the high Seas, and Offences against the Law of Nations;

11: To declare War, grant Letters of Marque and Reprisal, and make Rules concerning Captures on Land and Water;

12: To raise and support Armies, but no Appropriation of Money to that Use shall be for a longer Term than two Years;

13: To provide and maintain a Navy;

14: To make Rules for the Government and Regulation of the land and naval Forces;

15: To provide for calling forth the Militia to execute the Laws of the Union, suppress Insurrections and repel Invasions;

16: To provide for organizing, arming, and disciplining, the Militia, and for governing such Part of them as may be employed in the Service of the United States, reserving to the States respectively, the Appointment of the Officers, and the Authority of training the Militia according to the discipline prescribed by Congress;

17: To exercise exclusive Legislation in all Cases whatsoever, over such District (not exceeding ten Miles square) as may, by Cession of particular States, and the Acceptance of Congress, become the Seat of the Government of the United States, and to exercise like Authority over all Places purchased by the Consent of the Legislature of the State in which the Same shall be, for the Erection of Forts,

Magazines, Arsenals, dock-Yards, and other needful Buildings;—And

18: To make all Laws which shall be necessary and proper for carrying into Execution the foregoing Powers, and all other Powers vested by this Constitution in the Government of the United States, or in any Department or Officer thereof.

Section 9

1: The Migration or Importation of such Persons as any of the States now existing shall think proper to admit, shall not be prohibited by the Congress prior to the Year one thousand eight hundred and eight, but a Tax or duty may be imposed on such Importation, not exceeding ten dollars for each Person.

2: The Privilege of the Writ of Habeas Corpus shall not be suspended, unless when in Cases of Rebellion or Invasion the public Safety may require it.

3: No Bill of Attainder or ex post facto Law shall be passed.

4: No Capitation, or other direct, Tax shall be laid, unless in Proportion to the Census or Enumeration herein before directed to be taken.7

5: No Tax or Duty shall be laid on Articles exported from any State.

6: No Preference shall be given by any Regulation of Commerce or Revenue to the Ports of one State over those of another: nor shall Vessels bound to, or from, one State, be obliged to enter, clear, or pay Duties in another.

7: No Money shall be drawn from the Treasury, but in Consequence of Appropriations made by Law; and a regular Statement and Account of the Receipts and Expenditures of all public Money shall be published from time to time.

8: No Title of Nobility shall be granted by the United States: And no Person holding any Office of Profit or Trust under them, shall, without the Consent of the Congress, accept of any present, Emolument, Office, or Title, of any kind whatever, from any King, Prince, or foreign State.

<u>Section 10</u>

1: No State shall enter into any Treaty, Alliance, or Confederation; grant Letters of Marque and Reprisal; coin Money; emit Bills of Credit; make any Thing but gold and silver Coin a Tender in Payment of Debts; pass any Bill of Attainder, ex post facto Law, or Law impairing the Obligation of Contracts, or grant any Title of Nobility.

2: No State shall, without the Consent of the Congress, lay any Imposts or Duties on Imports or Exports, except what may be absolutely necessary for executing it's inspection Laws: and the net Produce of all Duties and Imposts, laid by any State on Imports or Exports, shall be for the Use of the Treasury of the United States; and all such Laws shall be subject to the Revision and Control of the Congress.

3: No State shall, without the Consent of Congress, lay any Duty of Tonnage, keep Troops, or Ships of War in time of Peace, enter into any Agreement or Compact with another State, or with a foreign Power, or engage in War, unless actually invaded, or in such imminent Danger as will not admit of delay.

Article II *(Executive Power)*

<u>Section 1</u>

1: The executive Power shall be vested in a President of the United States of America. He shall hold his Office during the Term of four Years, and, together with the Vice President, chosen for the same Term, be elected, as follows

2: Each State shall appoint, in such Manner as the Legislature thereof may direct, a Number of Electors, equal to the whole Number of Senators and Representatives to which the State may be entitled in the Congress: but no Senator or Representative, or Person holding an Office of Trust or Profit under the United States, shall be appointed an Elector.

3: The Electors shall meet in their respective States, and vote by Ballot for two Persons, of whom one at least shall not be an Inhabitant of the same State with themselves. And they shall make a List of all the Persons voted for, and of the Number of Votes for each; which List they shall sign and certify, and transmit sealed to the Seat of the Government of the United States, directed to the President of the Senate. The President of the Senate shall, in the Presence of the Senate and House of Representatives, open all the Certificates, and the Votes shall then be counted. The Person having the greatest Number of Votes shall be the President, if such Number be a Majority of the whole Number of Electors appointed; and if there be more than one who have such Majority, and have an equal Number of Votes, then the House of Representatives shall immediately chuse by Ballot one of them for President; and if no Person have a Majority, then from the five highest on the List the said House shall in like Manner chuse the President. But in chusing the President, the Votes shall be taken by States, the Representation from each State having one Vote; A quorum for this Purpose shall consist of a Member or Members from two thirds of the States, and a Majority of all the States shall be necessary to a Choice. In every Case, after the Choice of the President, the Person having the greatest Number of Votes of the Electors shall be the Vice President. But if there should remain two or more who have equal Votes, the Senate shall chuse from them by Ballot the Vice President.

4: The Congress may determine the Time of chusing the

Electors, and the Day on which they shall give their Votes; which Day shall be the same throughout the United States.

5: No Person except a natural born Citizen, or a Citizen of the United States, at the time of the Adoption of this Constitution, shall be eligible to the Office of President; neither shall any Person be eligible to that Office who shall not have attained to the Age of thirty five Years, and been fourteen Years a Resident within the United States.

6: In Case of the Removal of the President from Office, or of his Death, Resignation, or Inability to discharge the Powers and Duties of the said Office,9 the Same shall devolve on the Vice President, and the Congress may by Law provide for the Case of Removal, Death, Resignation or Inability, both of the President and Vice President, declaring what Officer shall then act as President, and such Officer shall act accordingly, until the Disability be removed, or a President shall be elected.

7: The President shall, at stated Times, receive for his Services, a Compensation, which shall neither be encreased nor diminished during the Period for which he shall have been elected, and he shall not receive within that Period any other Emolument from the United States, or any of them.

8: Before he enter on the Execution of his Office, he shall take the following Oath or Affirmation:—"I do solemnly swear (or affirm) that I will faithfully execute the Office of President of the United States, and will to the best of my Ability, preserve, protect and defend the Constitution of the United States."

<u>Section 2</u>

1: The President shall be Commander in Chief of the Army and Navy of the United States, and of the Militia of the several States, when called into the actual Service of the

United States; he may require the Opinion, in writing, of the principal Officer in each of the executive Departments, upon any Subject relating to the Duties of their respective Offices, and he shall have Power to grant Reprieves and Pardons for Offences against the United States, except in Cases of Impeachment.

2: He shall have Power, by and with the Advice and Consent of the Senate, to make Treaties, provided two thirds of the Senators present concur; and he shall nominate, and by and with the Advice and Consent of the Senate, shall appoint Ambassadors, other public Ministers and Consuls, Judges of the Supreme Court, and all other Officers of the United States, whose Appointments are not herein otherwise provided for, and which shall be established by Law: but the Congress may by Law vest the Appointment of such inferior Officers, as they think proper, in the President alone, in the Courts of Law, or in the Heads of Departments.

3: The President shall have Power to fill up all Vacancies that may happen during the Recess of the Senate, by granting Commissions which shall expire at the End of their next Session.

<u>Section 3</u>

He shall from time to time give to the Congress Information of the State of the Union, and recommend to their Consideration such Measures as he shall judge necessary and expedient; he may, on extraordinary Occasions, convene both Houses, or either of them, and in Case of Disagreement between them, with Respect to the Time of Adjournment, he may adjourn them to such Time as he shall think proper; he shall receive Ambassadors and other public Ministers; he shall take Care that the Laws be faithfully executed, and shall Commission all the Officers of the United States.

<u>Section 4</u>

The President, Vice President and all civil Officers of the United States, shall be removed from Office on Impeachment for, and Conviction of, Treason, Bribery, or other high Crimes and Misdemeanors.

Article III *(Judicial Power)*

<u>Section 1</u>

The Judicial Power of the United States, shall be vested in one Supreme Court, and in such inferior Courts as the Congress may from time to time ordain and establish. The Judges, both of the supreme and inferior Courts, shall hold their Offices during good Behaviour, and shall, at stated Times, receive for their Services, a Compensation, which shall not be diminished during their Continuance in Office.

<u>Section 2</u>

1: The judicial Power shall extend to all Cases, in Law and Equity, arising under this Constitution, the Laws of the United States, and Treaties made, or which shall be made, under their Authority;—to all Cases affecting Ambassadors, other public Ministers and Consuls;—to all Cases of admiralty and maritime Jurisdiction;—to Controversies to which the United States shall be a Party;—to Controversies between two or more States;—between a State and Citizens of another State;10 —between Citizens of different States, —between Citizens of the same State claiming Lands under Grants of different States, and between a State, or the Citizens thereof, and foreign States, Citizens or Subjects.

2: In all Cases affecting Ambassadors, other public Ministers and Consuls, and those in which a State shall be Party, the Supreme Court shall have original Jurisdiction.

In all the other Cases before mentioned, the Supreme Court shall have appellate Jurisdiction, both as to Law and Fact, with such Exceptions, and under such Regulations as the Congress shall make.

3: The Trial of all Crimes, except in Cases of Impeachment, shall be by Jury; and such Trial shall be held in the State where the said Crimes shall have been committed; but when not committed within any State, the Trial shall be at such Place or Places as the Congress may by Law have directed.

<u>Section 3</u>

1: Treason against the United States, shall consist only in levying War against them, or in adhering to their Enemies, giving them Aid and Comfort. No Person shall be convicted of Treason unless on the Testimony of two Witnesses to the same overt Act, or on Confession in open Court.

2: The Congress shall have Power to declare the Punishment of Treason, but no Attainder of Treason shall work Corruption of Blood, or Forfeiture except during the Life of the Person attainted.

Article IV *(States' Relations)*

<u>Section 1</u>

Full Faith and Credit shall be given in each State to the public Acts, Records, and judicial Proceedings of every other State. And the Congress may by general Laws prescribe the Manner in which such Acts, Records and Proceedings shall be proved, and the Effect thereof.

<u>Section 2</u>

1: The Citizens of each State shall be entitled to all Privileges and Immunities of Citizens in the several States.

2: A Person charged in any State with Treason, Felony, or other Crime, who shall flee from Justice, and be found in another State, shall on Demand of the executive Authority of the State from which he fled, be delivered up, to be removed to the State having Jurisdiction of the Crime.

3: No Person held to Service or Labour in one State, under the Laws thereof, escaping into another, shall, in Consequence of any Law or Regulation therein, be discharged from such Service or Labour, but shall be delivered up on Claim of the Party to whom such Service or Labour may be due.

Section 3

1: New States may be admitted by the Congress into this Union; but no new State shall be formed or erected within the Jurisdiction of any other State; nor any State be formed by the Junction of two or more States, or Parts of States, without the Consent of the Legislatures of the States concerned as well as of the Congress.

2: The Congress shall have Power to dispose of and make all needful Rules and Regulations respecting the Territory or other Property belonging to the United States; and nothing in this Constitution shall be so construed as to Prejudice any Claims of the United States, or of any particular State.

Section 4

The United States shall guarantee to every State in this Union a Republican Form of Government, and shall protect each of them against Invasion; and on Application of the Legislature, or of the Executive (when the Legislature cannot be convened) against domestic Violence.

Article V *(Mode of Amendment)*

The Congress, whenever two thirds of both Houses shall

deem it necessary, shall propose Amendments to this Constitution, or, on the Application of the Legislatures of two thirds of the several States, shall call a Convention for proposing Amendments, which, in either Case, shall be valid to all Intents and Purposes, as Part of this Constitution, when ratified by the Legislatures of three fourths of the several States, or by Conventions in three fourths thereof, as the one or the other Mode of Ratification may be proposed by the Congress; Provided that no Amendment which may be made prior to the Year One thousand eight hundred and eight shall in any Manner affect the first and fourth Clauses in the Ninth Section of the first Article; and that no State, without its Consent, shall be deprived of its equal Suffrage in the Senate.

Article VI *(Prior Debts, National Supremacy, Oaths of Office)*

1: All Debts contracted and Engagements entered into, before the Adoption of this Constitution, shall be as valid against the United States under this Constitution, as under the Confederation.

2: This Constitution, and the Laws of the United States which shall be made in Pursuance thereof; and all Treaties made, or which shall be made, under the Authority of the United States, shall be the supreme Law of the Land; and the Judges in every State shall be bound thereby, any Thing in the Constitution or Laws of any State to the Contrary notwithstanding.

3: The Senators and Representatives before mentioned, and the Members of the several State Legislatures, and all executive and judicial Officers, both of the United States and of the several States, shall be bound by Oath or Affirmation, to support this Constitution; but no religious Test shall ever be required as a Qualification to any Office or public Trust under the United States.

Article VII *(Ratification)*

The Ratification of the Conventions of nine States, shall be sufficient for the Establishment of this Constitution between the States so ratifying the Same.

The 39 signatures on the Constitution of the United States:

George Washington
President and Deputy from Virginia

Connecticut
William Samuel Johnson
Roger Sherman

Delaware
George Read
Gunning Bedford, Jr.
John Dickinson
Richard Bassett
Jacob Broom

Georgia
William Few
Abraham Baldwin

Maryland
James McHenry
Daniel of St. Thomas Jenifer
Daniel Carroll

Massachusetts
Nathaniel Gorham
Rufus King

New Hampshire
John Langdon
Nicholas Gilman

New Jersey
William Livingston

David Brearley
William Paterson
Jonathan Dayton

New York
Alexander Hamilton

North Carolina
William Blount
Richard Dobbs Spaight, Sr.
Hugh Williamson

Pennsylvania
Benjamin Franklin
Thomas Mifflin
Robert Morris
George Clymer
Thomas Fitzsimons
Jared Ingersoll
James Wilson
Gouverneur Morris

South Carolina
John Rutledge
Charles Cotesworth Pinckney
Charles Pinckney
Pierce Butler

Virginia
John Blair
James Madison

The Bill of Rights

The first ten amendments to the Constitution make up the Bill of Rights. James Madison wrote the amendments, which list specific prohibitions on governmental power, in response to calls from several states for greater constitutional protection for individual liberties. For example, the Fourth Amendment safeguards citizens' right to be free from unreasonable government intrusion in their homes through the requirement of a warrant.[16]

One of the many points of contention between Federalists, who advocated a strong national government, and Anti-Federalists, who wanted the power to remain with state and local governments, was the Constitution's lack of a bill of rights that would place specific limits on government power. Federalists argued that the Constitution did not need a bill of rights, because the people and the states kept any powers not given to the federal government. Anti-Federalists held that a bill of rights was necessary to safeguard individual liberty.[17]

Madison, then a member of the U.S. House of Representatives, altered the Constitution's text where he thought appropriate. However, several representatives, led by Roger Sherman, objected, saying that Congress had no authority to change the wording of the Constitution. Therefore, Madison's changes were presented as a list of amendments that would follow Article VII.[18]

The House approved 17 amendments. Of these, the Senate approved 12, which were sent to the states for approval in August 1789. Ten amendments were approved (or ratified). Virginia's legislature was the final state legislature to ratify the amendments, approving them on December 15, 1791.[19]

The Bill of Rights

Congress of the United States begun and held at the City of New-York, on Wednesday the fourth of March, one thousand seven hundred and eighty nine.

The Conventions of a number of the States, having at the time of their adopting the Constitution, expressed a desire, in order to prevent misconstruction or abuse of its powers, that further declaratory and restrictive clauses should be added: And as extending the ground of public confidence in the Government, will best ensure the beneficent ends of its institution.

RESOLVED by the Senate and House of Representatives of the United States of America, in Congress assembled, two thirds of both Houses concurring, that the following Articles be proposed to the Legislatures of the several States, as amendments to the Constitution of the United States, all, or any of which Articles, when ratified by three fourths of the said Legislatures, to be valid to all intents and purposes, as part of the said Constitution.

ARTICLES in addition to, and Amendment of the Constitution of the United States of America, proposed by Congress, and ratified by the Legislatures of the several States, pursuant to the fifth Article of the original Constitution

Amendment I *(Freedom of religion, speech, press, assembly, and petition)*

Congress shall make no law respecting an establishment of religion, or prohibiting the free exercise thereof; or abridging the freedom of speech, or of the press; or the right of the people peaceably to assemble, and to petition the Government for a redress of grievances.

Amendment II *(Right to keep and bear arms)*

A well regulated Militia, being necessary to the security of a free State, the right of the people to keep and bear Arms, shall not be infringed.

Amendment III *(Soldiers cannot stay in people houses without their consent)*

No Soldier shall, in time of peace be quartered in any house, without the consent of the Owner, nor in time of war, but in a manner to be prescribed by law.

Amendment IV *(Freedom from unreasonable searches and seizures)*

The right of the people to be secure in their persons, houses, papers, and effects, against unreasonable searches and seizures, shall not be violated, and no Warrants shall issue, but upon probable cause, supported by Oath or affirmation, and particularly describing the place to be searched, and the persons or things to be seized.

Amendment V *(Right to due process of law, freedom from self-incrimination, double jeopardy. Private property cannot be taken away without compensation)*

No person shall be held to answer for a capital, or otherwise infamous crime, unless on a presentment or indictment of a Grand Jury, except in cases arising in the land or naval forces, or in the Militia, when in actual service in time of War or public danger; nor shall any person be subject for the same offence to be twice put in jeopardy of life or limb; nor shall be compelled in any criminal case to be a witness against himself, nor be deprived of life, liberty, or property, without due process of law; nor shall private property be taken for public use, without just compensation.

Amendment VI *(Rights of accused persons, e.g., right to a speedy and public trial)*

In all criminal prosecutions, the accused shall enjoy the right to a speedy and public trial, by an impartial jury of the State and district wherein the crime shall have been committed, which district shall have been previously ascertained by law, and to be informed of the nature and cause of the accusation; to be confronted with the witnesses against him; to have compulsory process for obtaining witnesses in his favor, and to have the Assistance of Counsel for his defence.

Amendment VII *(Trial by jury in certain civil cases)*

In Suits at common law, where the value in controversy shall exceed twenty dollars, the right of trial by jury shall be preserved, and no fact tried by a jury, shall be otherwise re-examined in any Court of the United States, then according to the rules of the common law.

Amendment VIII *(Prohibits excessive fines or bans. Prohibits cruel and unusual punishment)*

Excessive bail shall not be required, nor excessive fines imposed, nor cruel and unusual punishments inflicted.

Amendment IX *(Rights not specifically granted to the people in the Bill of Rights, still belong to the people)*

The enumeration in the Constitution, of certain rights, shall not be construed to deny or disparage others retained by the people.

Amendment X *(Any powers that aren't either given to the national government or denied to the state government belongs to the state)*

The powers not delegated to the United States by the Constitution, nor prohibited by it to the States, are reserved to the States respectively, or to the people.

In Conclusion

Our Declaration of Independence, the U.S. Constitution, and the Bill of Rights are for every American citizen, regardless of race, color or creed. The government must honor every American's rights as outlined in the Declaration of Independence which states, "We hold these truths to be self-evident, that all men are created equal, that they are endowed by their Creator with certain unalienable Rights, that among these are Life, Liberty and the Pursuit of Happiness."

Our forefathers based these foundational documents on God's Ten Commandments and the Bible. This is how our nation grew, prospered, and functioned successfully, under God, with his countless blessings and favor. In our Pledge of Allegiance, we affirm our American status: "I pledge allegiance to the flag of the United States of America and to the republic for which it stands, one nation, <u>under God</u>, indivisible, with liberty and justice for all.[20]" Yet, how can we now be <u>under God</u> if we violate His laws, and do away with prayers to Him in schools, do away with Bible reading in schools, remove His Ten Commandments from our Supreme Court buildings, and make laws that are against His Ten Commandments, i.e., Allowing same-sex marriage, abortions, and removing the Bible and prayer out of the classroom.

Today, more than 230 years since the Constitution was created, America has stretched across an entire continent, and its population and economy have expanded more than the document's framers likely ever could have envisioned. How far removed from the original U.S. Constitution has our government taken us. Man's personal input of what should be added, changed or subtracted, and making laws that alienate us from God and His laws, will certainly bring His judgment down on us. Man's sinful and lustful desires have found their way into the changes made to our Constitution. God will never sanction man changing or misinterpreting His laws to suit their sinful, and lustful desires. Man must live by God's laws in this life and in the next. *"Peter and the other apostles replied: "We must obey God rather than human beings!"* (Acts 5:29 NIV)

WHEN MAN'S LAW DISOBEYS GOD'S LAW

Since our Declaration of Independence from England, our country has prospered richly with God's blessings because we were established "in God we trust." Why are we now changing laws that are diametrically opposed to God's statutes? Our government is resorting back to exercising these same harsh laws today on the American people that England imposed on the original 13 colonies. With all the grievances we had against England and their abuse against our human and civil rights, why are we allowing history to repeat itself?

On June 25, 1962, the United States Supreme Court decided in Engel v. Vitale that a prayer approved by the New York Board of Regents for use in schools violated the First Amendment by constituting an establishment of religion. The following year, in Abington School District v. Schempp, the Court disallowed Bible readings in public schools for similar reasons.[21]

These rulings have had a huge negative effect upon our students and our society as a whole, which includes: a sharp drop in student's academic achievements, an increase of out of wedlock births, widespread use of illegal drugs, increase in juvenile crime, deterioration of school behavior, and confusion of one's belief in God, causing the increasing growth of atheism. These are only some of the results from removing the Bible and prayer from our schools. There are countless other negative effects this ruling has had on our society as a whole. Replacing God's laws with man's laws is bringing His divine judgment upon us as a nation. Just look at the record-breaking disasters "exploding" all around us.

In 2005, the Supreme Court barred the Ten Commandments from courthouse buildings. Their ruling was 5-4 that the Ten Commandments could not be displayed in court buildings or on government property. If we do not acknowledge a place for God, the Bible, prayer, and the Ten Commandments on our government buildings, in the courtroom, in our schools, where do we go from here? The Supreme Court justices are anything but unified or consistent in their views with each other. Inside the door of the Supreme Court are the symbols of the Roman numerals I-X, on two tablets of stone. They say this does not represent the Ten Commandments (as we know it does), but instead, it represents the 10 Amendments to the Bill of Rights.

Documented comments by justices on their ruling to remove the Ten Commandments from court buildings are as follows:

The justices ruled 5-4 that the Ten Commandments could not be displayed in court buildings or on government property. However, the Biblical laws could be displayed in a historical context, as they are in a frieze in the Supreme Court building. Notably, the first four commandments, which have to do with honoring God and the Sabbath, were obscured by the artist who designed the frieze.

Justice David H. Souter wrote in the majority opinion, citing previous court rulings. 'The touchstone for our analysis is the principle that the First Amendment mandates governmental neutrality between religion and religion, and between religion and nonreligion.'[22]

Justice Souter was joined by fellow liberal-leaning Justices John Paul Stevens, Ruth Bader Ginsburg, and Stephen G. Breyer, as well as moderate Republican and frequent swing voter Sandra Day O'Connor. Souter signaled an awareness of the intense passions surrounding the issue of religion in public life, which in several instances have been elevated to death threats. He wrote: 'Manifesting a purpose to favor one faith over another, or adherence to religion, generally, clashes with the 'understanding, reached...After decades of religious war, that liberty and social stability demand a religious tolerance that respects the religious views of all citizens.'[23]

Justice Sandra Day O'Connor, stated in her opinion, 'we are a religious people, but the separation between church and state was the very thing that freed Americans to practice their faiths. Our regard for constitutional boundaries has protected us from similar travails while allowing private religious exercise to flourish. At a time when we see around the world the violent consequences of the assumption of religious authority by government, Americans may count themselves fortunate.'[24]

Justice Antonin Scalia, who upheld the Christian values, and views of God's laws in his ruling, and the one leading the dissent, railed against the majority opinion inconsistency. He asked, 'with all of the reality staring in the face in which higher beings are invoked in public life, from so help me God, inaugural oaths to the prayer that opens the supreme court's sessions, how can the court possibly assert that the first amendment mandates government neutrality on religion?'[25]

Justice Antonin Scalia, who was joined in his dissent by Chief Justice William H. Rehnquist, Justices Anthony Kennedy, and Clarence Thomas, stated, 'the court's majority opinion ought to be voided because the court has not had the courage to apply the neutrality principle of consistently.'[26] He also wrote in his dissent that the changed displays of replacing the Ten Commandments with the Ten Bill of Rights had become constitutionally acceptable.

During oral arguments, Justice Scalia, trying to convince the court the displays of the two tablets of stone, had been stripped of religious intent. He said, 'it was idiotic to dress the (10) commandments in historical documents such as the Declaration of Independence.'[27] In further dispute, Justices Scalia, Rehnquist, and Thomas have all said, 'there is nothing wrong with government asserting God's supremacy.'[28] However, the other justices believe doing so would be to the exclusion of Americans of other faiths or no faith and is therefore unconstitutional.

Some of these same justices were disturbed by a resolution passed by McCreary County officials in reaction to a lower-court ruling, declared that American law was derived from the Ten Commandments. While revisions were made to the displays, that was left intact. In the resolutions, the county officials declared: 'The judicial laws of God, as they were delivered by Moses, should be a rule to all the courts in this jurisdiction.'[29]

Another Ten Commandments case, Van Orden v. Perry, involved a statue that had been donated to the government and placed on grounds outside the state capital states: 'A Texas court ruled that the replica, given by the Fraternal Order of Eagles in 1961 and placed among more than a dozen non-religious monuments, did not violate the Establishment clause.'[30]

This case brought by Thomas Van Orden, a former lawyer, stated during his interview with the Dallas Morning News, he predicted, 'the court would rule against him, but said winning or losing was almost beside the point. This was never a lawsuit at all; it was always a political question.'[31]

Justice Breyer sided for the display, giving opinion writer Rehnquist a 5-4 majority. Rehnquist said, 'Having religious significance does not mean the display automatically violates the Establishment clause. According to Judeo-Christian belief, the Ten Commandments were given to Moses by God on Mt. Sinai. But Moses was a lawgiver as well as a religious leader. And the Ten Commandments have an undeniable historical meaning.'[32] Rehnquist also said, 'the statue's placement on the grounds among secular monuments was 'passive,' rather than confrontational. Rehnquist was joined in his opinion by Justices Scalia, Kennedy, and Thomas. Justice Breyer wrote his opinion separately.'[33]

Justice Stevens, writing the dissent on behalf of O'-Connor, Souter, and Ginsburg, said there was nothing passive about the display. Having noted that the First Commandment — 'I am the Lord thy God' — is more boldly displayed than the other nine, he wrote, 'The message transmitted by Texas' chosen display is quite plain: This state endorses the divine code of the 'Judeo-Christian' God.'[34] Stevens also implied, 'the claim that the monument was on state grounds to honor history was disingenuous, because of the government's resistance to removing the display.'

Tony Perkins, president of the Family Research Council, told FOX News. 'This is not so much about neutrality toward religion, but a growing hostility by this court toward religion. This idea that somehow the Establishment Clause prohibits recognition of the Christian heritage of our nation is absurd,'[35]

Elliot Mincburg, Vice President of People for the American Way, told foxnews.com, 'Although we disagree on the facts of the Texas case and think the Supreme Court should have ruled that one unconstitutional as well, we're very pleased that what the clear majority of the court has done is reaffirm the principles behind church-state separation and religious liberty.'[36] He added, 'while the mixed rulings left some room for confusion, the religious displays issue would never be black and white. What most of the court is saying is this is not an area where there should be bright-line rules. After all, there's a Ten Commandments frieze in the Supreme Court building. This is an area where context is everything, You have to look more deeply at the fundamental purposes of the Constitution and the way in which all the justices eloquently said avoiding government promotion of religion is a critical way to ensure people are truly free to practice religion in any way they want to,'[37] he added.

Douglas Laycock, who has argued religious liberty cases before the Supreme Court, said, 'the mixed ruling means no end in sight to church-state litigation.'[38] He told foxnews.com, 'We will be litigating these cases one at a time for decades, The two rulings merely provided each side with some new arguments.'[39]

Douglas Laycock is perhaps the nation's leading authority on the law of religious liberty and also on the law of remedies. He has taught and written about these topics for four decades at the University of Chicago, the University of Texas, the University of Michigan, and now Virginia. HE STATES, 'There's a sort of road map for how to get away with putting these things up,' he said. 'On new displays, the lesson to politicians is to keep your mouth shut, don't talk about what you're really doing, pretend you're putting this up for secular reasons, put some secular stuff around it and swear to the judge it's all for secular purposes'" And, referring to Justice Breyer's observation that the monument had been up for 40 years before Van Orden complained, Laycock said, 'The lesson for the opponents is if anything new goes up, find your plaintiff and sue right away before it becomes historically grandfathered.'"[40]

Even the U. S. Supreme Court building reflects God's written laws. The architecture of the U. S. Supreme Court building reflects this biblical foundation. At the center of the sculpture over the east portico of the Supreme Court Building, there is the image of Moses holding the two tablets of the Ten Commandments;[41] which are also engraved over the chair of the Chief Justice and on the bronze doors of the Supreme Court.

The Ten Commandments are the Biblical principles that relate to ethics, worship, and law. God gave Moses the Ten Commandments on two tablets of stone on Mount Sinai in the Book of Exodus, which are the moral expression of the Sinai Covenant between God and His people the Israelites. Moses recounted the Ten Commandments of God to the Israelites in the Book of Deuteronomy. *"And He wrote on the tablets according to the first writing, the Ten Commandments, which the Lord had spoken to you in the mountain from the midst of the fire in the day of the assembly; and the Lord gave them to me"* (Deuteronomy 10:4 NKJV).

LAWLESSNESS WILL ABOUND UNTIL CHRIST RETURNS

On the Mount of Olives, almost 2000 years ago, Jesus Christ spoke a prophecy, which described "lawlessness" abounding in the last days. He gave this prophecy to His disciples, when they asked Him what to look for directly before His Return. Christ's said in Matthew 24:12 ***"...lawlessness will abound."*** Today, law enforcement officers are committing egregious crimes against their oath of office to uphold every citizen's 4th, 5th, and 6th Constitutional rights, and they are getting away with it. The increasing number of law enforcement officers who are committing serious violations of the American citizens are spreading their errors of lawlessness across our country. The Bureau of Labor outlines the common duties of a police officer which is to arrest individuals suspected of committing crimes, testifying in court, and conducting traffic stops.[42] The enforcement officer takes an oath to protect the people, their property, and honor their constitutional rights. Officers of the law are expected to carry out their duties and responsibilities without discrimination or inflicting any harm to the public.

Police officers are prohibited by law from using excessive brute force or participating in activities against anyone. They can face legal prosecution for their violations against the people. Officers are not legally allowed to discriminate because of race, color, creed or sexual orientation. An officer pledges to uphold the civil, and constitutional rights of the people. When an officer violates those rights, they should be held accountable and not be given immunity. An officer should not be given a free reign of taking the law into their own hands, especially when it conflicts with a citizen's constitutional rights. In our society today, such injustice is being served on the American people, who are victims of police brutality and their violations of the law. **Our government makes laws that give the police more rights over the people which our founding fathers would have thought were egregious and unlawful.**

Today, there are videos, cameras, cell phones, various electronic equipment, and DNA testing, as evidence exposing police officer's criminal acts. In most cases, our technology is so advanced; it can uncover evidence for or against either the suspect or an officer. Most importantly, it exposes the misconduct against the people's civil and constitutional rights. Top on the list are officer's use of excessive force, and inflicting bodily harm, lying on police reports, staging a crime scene against the suspect, and in some cases, killing the suspect. Unfortunately, the officer is frequently exonerated from such acts, or they are granted immunity. This is a travesty of justice against the victim and their civil and constitutional rights. Enforcement officers should be held accountable for their violations just like anyone else would be who commits the same criminal acts. Our laws should apply equally to everyone. **No one should be above the law regardless of their status.**

Among enforcement officers is a code known as the "brotherhood," which involves a "code of silence." In this brotherhood, officers cover up for each other's misconduct or violations of the law by doing the following: filing false police reports, staging a crime scene to make the suspect appear guilty, testifying falsely under oath in a court of law to protect themselves or their fellow officers from exposing their own criminal violations. Such a code of silence or covering up for each other's violations are not only illegal but makes a mockery of our justice system. Under this brotherhood code of silence, the innocent person suffers and can be convicted unjustly and spend years or even life in prison for being framed by an officer of the law.

The code of silence is an example of police corruption and misconduct in our country today. The police code of silence is also known as the blue wall of silence, the blue code, or the blue shield. This code of silence between police officers, who agree not to report on a colleague's errors, their misconduct or violations, also includes an officer's use of brutality. If an officer were questioned about an incident of alleged misconduct involving another officer during an official inquiry, the officer following the code would claim ignorance of another officer's wrongdoing or claim not to have seen anything. These officers who engage in discriminatory arrests, physical or verbal harassment and selective enforcement of the law are considered to be corrupt. The Supreme Court has stated repeatedly and unequivocally that discriminatory enforcement violates the equal protection clause of the fourteenth amendment.

Many officers who follow the brotherhood code participate in some form of these acts during their careers, either for personal reasons, or to protect and support their fellow officers. These illegal offenses are grounds for suspension or dismissal. Unfortunately, they are not prosecuted, as they should be.

The police slang for police perjury is called "testilying." This is when an officer gives false testimony in court. The police officers who honor the law and their badge and refuse to lie in court may be threatened or ostracized by their fellow officers. The officers who don't follow the law will falsify police reports, lie on their warrants, stage evidence against the accused, to cover up their own or fellow officer's criminal violations of breaking the law while performing their duties. Some officers will even jointly fabricate stories against the accused before a judge who will believe their "testilying" against the evidence of the accused, even when the accused has prima facie evidence. Prosecutors, in order to win their case, have been known to allow police perjury and will even encourage officer's "testilying" in a court of law in order to obtain a conviction.

The accused needs to be protected from such corruption, and conspiracy. If a prosecutor goes along with the enforcement officer's violations against the accused in order to win their case, they are guilty of prosecutorial misconduct. Guilty officers can be sued by the victim for damages caused by false arrest, imprisonment, malicious prosecution, wrongful death, and police brutality. It is often hard to convict an officer who follows the code or other forms of corruption because they are protected by the defense of immunity and are exempt from penalties and burdens that the law generally places on private citizens. In 2001 the U.S. Supreme Court reaffirmed, in Saucier v. Katz, 533 U.S. 194, that enforcement officers should be given the benefit of the doubt when accused of acting unlawfully in fulfilling their duties.

The U.S. Police Unions help many officers, who are fired for misconduct and violations, get back their jobs, often via secretive appeals to protect labor rights rather than public safety. Commanding officers often put unqualified officers back on the streets. They are impervious to termination and continue committing violations against the public because they can get away with it.

There are many officers dedicated to their badge who abide by the law and uphold their pledge to protect the citizen and honor their constitutional rights. Unfortunately, the officers who do abuse their authority are seldom prosecuted like anyone else would be, who was not wearing a police badge.

There are countless innocent people across our country who have spent time in prison for crimes they did not commit because of the acts of dishonest enforcement officers, state prosecutors, and bias judges, who go along with an officer's tainted evidence. This is robbing the accused of justice, liberty, relationships, families, finances, dignity, opportunities, and their time away from freedom. These wrongful convictions, orchestrated by the "brotherhood code" of enforcement officers, makes a mockery of our entire justice system.

I spoke to a retired Police Sergeant from the Broward County Sheriff's Department in Ft. Lauderdale, FL, who served for over 30 years. She confirmed that corruptness of officers exists among the Sheriff's Deputies on a large scale. She said, "The relationship between deputies is called 'The Brotherhood.' You stick up for each other regardless, because you don't know when you will need another officer to stick up for you. You even lie under oath for the 'Brotherhood.'" She said that she went to psychotherapy for a number of years because it bothered her so much to see innocent people convicted because of the 'Brotherhood' code.

Officers lying under oath causes unjust verdicts that send the falsely accused to years in captivity as a result of their falsely sworn testimony. An officer, who covers over his own violations and causes an innocent person to pay for *his* criminal acts with *their* life, is truly committing a travesty of justice. These wrongful convictions are caused mainly by the brotherhood and bad police procedures.

Coercing false confessions and suppressing important evidence for the defense are acts of misconduct by the prosecuting attorneys and police officers who jointly conspire to lie under oath against the accused. These egregious acts by law enforcement officers and state prosecutors increase wrongful convictions and can cause the innocent to pay for their misconduct and violations with their life.

In disputes between an officer's story and the accused, a lie detector analysis should be conducted on both. This will help to minimize false testimony. Telling the truth and seeking justice should always be our priority.

Law enforcement officers should be prosecuted for their violations of the law, and not treated like they are above the law or given state immunity. Bias judges who make rulings that are not according to the law should be held accountable. Every state should have compensation statutes that provide enough money for exonerees to put their lives back together.

The U.S. incarcerates 716 people for every 100,000 residents, more than any other country. In fact, our rate of incarceration is more than five times higher than most of the countries in the world.[43] There are 2.3 million prisoners behind bars in the United States, costing the federal government about $55 billion a year.[44] This cost is increasing as the number of incarcerations is growing daily. Unfortunately, a significant percentage of prisoners convicted are innocent of the crimes they have been accused of breaking.

In order to increase the integrity of our justice system, the following should be done: all defendants should be videotaped to protect against coercion and misconduct by enforcement officers, who are anxious to prove the guilt of the accused. **Our government should not give law enforcement officers the legal right to lie.** Every prosecutor should be held accountable for committing misconduct and undergo training in ethical practices to avoid causing wrongful convictions. The best forensic science practices should be used to decide guilt or innocence, and states must guarantee inmates access to crime scene DNA and preserve this evidence for the entire length of their prison term.

Several criminal defense lawyers I've spoken with about police misconduct said, "Police lying on a regular basis is something we have to deal with." I asked, "How does this protect the accused in seeking justice and having a fair trial?" They all admitted, "It doesn't, but there is nothing we can do about it." Unfortunately, enforcement officers "testilying" under oath is abounding throughout our entire judicial system at an alarming rate.

The accused does not always have the financial resources to defend their rights or fight for justice due to the exorbitant costs of legal fees and court costs. Some will take a plea, rather than gamble on the legal system giving them a fair and impartial trial when officers falsely testify against them. Lawyers have stated that justice can't be had when a police officer makes a false and damning statement in a court of law about their client. The judge will often believe the officer's lying testimony over defendant's evidence and will rule unjustly against the accused.

Violations against a citizen's civil and constitutional rights include officer's illegal searches and seizures, staging of a crime scene, false arrest charges, falsifying police reports, malicious prosecutions, and unjustified police shootings. The use of excessive physical and brutal police force is at the top of this list. Such egregious acts are growing at an alarming rate, with the innocent paying for such criminal acts with their life!

If ones' rights are violated by an officer using brutal police force, according to Federal Law 42 U.S.C. § 1983, a plaintiff, may collect state tort compensatory damages. This includes medical expenses, lost income, pain and suffering, emotional distress, reputational injury, etc. Punitive damages are also available against individuals, but not municipalities in cases involving reckless or callous disregard for the plaintiff's rights, as well as intentional violations of Federal Law (Smith vs. Wade, 1983). Reasonable attorney's fees and expert witness fees are also recoverable according to Federal Law 42 U.S.C. § 1983.

Lawsuits against law enforcement officer's misconduct can be directed either toward the individual officer involved in the incident or against the entire department when the conduct is unlawful. Civil rights cases are incredibly emotional, especially in cases brought by surviving family members of an individual who was killed without provocation by an officer. Since the discovery of DNA testing, and the latest advancement of technology, many wrongful convictions, based on newly discovered evidence, have been reversed.

Law firms, especially those specializing in constitutional and civil law, are filing lawsuits against police brutality and wrongful convictions. Settlements and jury awards are large in some cases, especially from those who have gone to prison for a crime they did not commit. Due to wrongful verdicts, some of those innocent men, have lost their families, friends, reputations, and careers, not to mention years or even decades of being incarcerated. They rightfully deserve the substantial compensation for all the injustice that was wrongfully served upon them by law enforcement officers. Prosecutors, who knowingly side with the false testimony given to them by officers of the law, will conceal evidence that is in favor of the accused, just to win a conviction. This pollutes our justice system to its core.

With today's electronic technology, one can uncover prima facie evidence to exonerate the innocent, and convict the guilty. People are in an uproar and are rioting in the streets against enforcement officers who violate their civil and constitutional rights.

A CULTURE OF POLICE BRUTALITY

The state of our legal system motivated me to expose the wide gap between justice and injustice. Included in this book are documented cases of the most egregious acts that have been committed by law enforcement officers. Those who commit such heinous crimes are either given immunity or exonerated by their superiors. One famous case was the inhumane beating of Rodney King on March 3, 1991, by Los Angeles police officers, following a high-speed chase. The fact that the officers in the Rodney King case were exonerated, caused rioting to break out on a mass scale throughout the city of Los Angeles. The rioters were crowds of people protesting the injustice of the officers being set free from all their criminal charges.

Today, such cases are proliferating all across our country with citizens demanding and crying out for justice and reform. Officers are not above the law and should not be treated differently than anyone else who breaks the law. Our government must uphold every citizen's civil and constitutional rights, without discrimination or bias. All should be treated equally. Everyone has the right to live under all the benefits given to us by our creator, and our founding fathers who created our civil and constitutional rights.

Laws that allow enforcement officers or any government employee immunity for committing crimes against the people should be abolished. Every officer of the law should be judged on the same standards as the general public, and not go unpunished for their violations or misconduct against the people. This includes judges, prosecutors, police officers, deputies, U.S. Marshals, federal agents, elected officials, and everyone who is employed by our government working for the American people. The law must apply to everyone regardless of race, gender, status or any other consideration. No one is above the law!

The Bible predicts that *"lawlessness will abound"* (Matthew 24:12 NKJV) in the last days, and the world, as we know it, will soon end with the Second Coming of our Lord and Savior, Jesus Christ. Under His rulership, there will be equality and justice for all (Psalm 72:1-20). Jesus will bring in world peace, which has been elusive in human governments throughout the centuries.

Shocking Police Brutality Cases Sweeping Across America

Police have a civic duty to protect and serve individuals, but like most people who hold a great deal of authority, their powers are sometimes abused. Unfortunately, police brutality is a common occurrence, and it's often accompanied by other examples of police misconduct. Out of the thousands of police brutality cases that have gone to court these are some of the worst cases in recent history:

Eric Garner – New York

The fatal arrest was partially captured on amateur video. Garner was killed after a New York police officer used a banned chokehold technique to restrain him, despite being unarmed. He was wrestled to the ground by several police officers after a complaint he was illegally selling loose cigarettes. In the video that went viral, the black 43-year-old said: "I can't breathe" which was soon adopted by protesters after Daniel Pantaleo, the only officer that was investigated by a grand jury, was not charged.[45]

Michael Brown - Ferguson, MO

Brown was an unarmed black teenager shot by Darren Wilson, a white police officer on the street Ferguson, Missouri. Some said he had his hands up in the air and the shooting led to protests and some violence for 10 days. A Grand Jury said the officer should not face criminal charges in the case that led to a nationwide discussion about the treatment of black people by white police officers.[46]

Tamir Rice – Cleveland, OH

Twelve-year-old Rice was shot and killed by police in a public park as he was playing with a BB gun. It was reported at the time that a man called police saying someone was brandishing a pistol but added it was "probably fake." The police claimed Rice reached into his waistband for the toy gun when the two officers ordered him to raise his hands.[47] A Cleveland grand jury declined to bring criminal charges against the two officers, Timothy Loehmann and Frank Garmback. Police said, "The suspect did not comply with officers' orders and reached to his waistband for the gun." Video puts doubt on that claim. In the infamous surveillance video of the shooting, Garmback arrives on the scene driving a police cruiser. As the car arrives, Loehmann exits the vehicle and shoots, fatally wounding Rice. The whole event took seconds, and, with no audio, there's no indication the officers warned

Rice or gave him a chance to respond. In explaining the grand jury's decision on Tuesday, Cuyahoga County prosecutor Timothy McGinty said it was "indisputable" that Rice was drawing the gun from his waistband when Loehmann shot him, citing a second, allegedly clearer video of the encounter. "It would be irresponsible and unreasonable to require a police officer to wait and see if the gun was real," he said, also noting that Rice was "big" for his age, and the officers mistook him for someone much older. "The actions of officers Garmback and Loehmann were not criminal," McGinty said. "The evidence did not indicate criminal conduct by police."[48]

Oscar Grant - Oakland, CA

Oscar Grant was shot dead by Bay Area Rapid Transit police officer Johannes Mehserle in 2009 in Oakland, California. Mehserle and other police officers had been responding to reports of a fight and arrested and handcuffed Grant and several others in a subway station. Grant was cuffed, unarmed and lying on the ground when Mehserle pulled out his gun and shot him in the back. In court, Mehserle claimed he thought his gun was his Taser. He was sentenced to two years in jail and let out on parole in June 2011.[49]

James Blake – New York

Blake who's biracial, was on his way to the 2015 U.S. Open when a white police officer dressed in plainclothes tackled and cuffed him in front of a Midtown Manhattan hotel, mistaking him for a suspect involved in a fraudulent credit-card scheme. Blake suffered cuts and bruises due to the force police used on him and eventually received apologies from NYC Mayor Bill de Blasio and NYPD Police Commissioner, William Bratton.[50]

Two years later, the cop who tackled Blake to the

ground during that notorious incident has received his punishment. But we don't know what it is. The New York Times reported that officer James Frascatore, 40, who was facing a dismissal following the Blake incident, reached a deal that allows him to escape a public disciplinary trial hearing on excessive force charges. The terms of Frascatore's agreement with the Civilian Complaint Review Board weren't disclosed.[51]

Jeremy McDole - Wilmington, DE

While responding to a call about McDole threatening to shoot himself, several Delaware police officers wound up fatally shooting the wheelchair-bound man. Wilmington Police said that he was "armed with a handgun." But in a bystander video that depicts McDole adjusting himself in his chair, he does not appear to have a weapon in his hands. Relatives of the deceased contend that he was sitting with his hands in his lap, and also dispute that he was suicidal. His death remains under investigation by officials from the Delaware Department of Justice's Office of Civil Rights and Public Trust.[52]

Keith McLeod - Reisterstown, MD

19-year-old Keith McLeod was fatally shot by an officer who claimed to have seen the victim reach around his back and pull out what seemed to be a handgun. The officer was responding to reports that McLeod tried to use a fake prescription. Baltimore County released a statement reporting that surveillance footage showed McLeod "abruptly whipping his hand around and pointing it toward the officer, as if with a weapon." Police confirmed the following day that no weapon was found at the scene. The incident occurred close to where 25-year-old Freddie Gray died of a spinal injury while in police custody.[53]

Unidentified Minor - Stockton, CA

A 16-year-old black teenager was tackled by multiple officers after allegedly jaywalking in a bus-only lane early one morning. A video of the arrest shows an unnamed officer pressing a baton against him, as the boy screams "get off me." The officer hits the boy twice with the baton and tells him to get on the ground. Seconds later, four more officers tackle the child to the ground and handcuff him. An investigation was launched after the attack and the boy's family filed an official complaint. The police department maintains that the officers' actions were justified.[54]

Unidentified Minor - Rancho Cordova, CA

In a scene that authorities described as a "chaotic situation," deputies shot and wounded an innocent bystander after mistaking his cellphone for a gun. Police arrived at the scene after neighbors reported hearing multiple rounds of gunshots. Ben Ledford, who was identified as the gunman, walked out of his home and surrendered to authorities. The wounded bystander had his hand stretched out while filming officers swarm the neighborhood, when two deputies then fired shots at him, striking him once in the leg. They later realized the bystander was not involved in the shooting.[55]

Dominic Fuller - Auburndale, FL

A Sheriff's deputy shot and killed a man armed with a stapler. Deputies were called to investigate suspicious activities and found Fuller sitting in a stolen car outside of a house. Fuller ran as the deputies approached him, which lead to a chaotic chase through the neighborhood. A witness reported hearing Fuller say he had a gun, and other witnesses reported him saying he was armed. According to the Sheriff's office, he was refusing command

and standing in a doorway with his right arm behind his back. When Fuller lifted his hand, the deputy saw a black and chrome object. Deputy Gabriel Reveron fired five times at Fuller. It was later confirmed that he was holding a stapler.[56]

Christopher Harris - Seattle, WA

Christopher Harris was walking home in 2009 in Seattle when sheriff's deputy Matthew Paul slammed him into a wall after mistaking him for an assault suspect. Paul was left in a coma and still requires massive medical care after suffering permanent head and spinal cord injuries. Paul escaped all charges in the incident and remains a police officer. A local police spokesman explained the incident by saying that sometimes " ... bad things happen to good people." 57

Walter Harvin - New York

Iraq war veteran Walter Harvin suffered a vicious 2010 beating at the hands of New York police officer David London. London had been closing the door to a building in a housing project when Harvin – who lived there – tried to slip in. An altercation began, in which London beat Harvin with his baton and then continued to hit and kick him after he was on the ground and not moving. London, who told the court Harvin had pushed him, was acquitted.[58]

Robert Davis - New Orleans, LA

Robert Davis, a retired school teacher, was beaten and arrested by four police in New Orleans on suspicion of public intoxication. On the night of Oct. 9, 2005, just a little over a month after Hurricane Katrina, Davis returned to New Orleans to check on his family's property and went to the French Quarter to buy cigarettes. There, he was attacked by four police officers who said he was belligerent and resisted arrest by not allowing them to handcuff him. One officer was fired over the incident, one was suspended, and another was acquitted of all charges. Davis said he was a teetotaler and had not had a drink for at least 25 years.[59]

Angela Garbarino - Shreveport, LA

Garbarino was severely beaten in 2008 by police officer, Wylie Willis in Shreveport, Louisiana after becoming angry in police booking room. Garbarino, who was drunk, got into an argument with Willis, who manhandled her to the floor. He then switched off a camera in the room. When it was turned on again, Garbarino was lying in a spreading pool of blood on the floor and was removed from the room on a hospital gurney. She suffered two black eyes, broken teeth, and a broken nose. Willis claimed the woman fell on her face while trying to leave the room. Garbarino settled out of court, and Willis was reinstated to his job.[60]

Frank Jude – Milwaukee, WI

In 2004, 26-year-old Frank Jude was viciously beaten by several off-duty Milwaukee police officers as he was leaving a party. The group of men attacked Jude and his friend, Lovell Harris, claiming they stole one of the officer's wallets that contained a police badge. Harris' face was cut with a knife, but he was able to get free and run away. Jude was repeatedly punched and kicked, as well as stabbed in the ears with a pen. Even the on-duty officer who was called to stop the fight began stomping on Jude's head. In the state trial, the jury acquitted the three officers charged. There was a great deal of community outrage and demand for a federal investigation. The federal grand jury convicted the three officers who were originally acquitted but did acquit the fourth officer.[62]

Sean Bell – New York

Bell was killed by NYPD detectives who fired 50 times at the car Bell, and his friends were riding in on Nov. 25, 2006. On the night of the shooting, a group of undercover officers was investigating a Queens, New York, strip club that was allegedly allowing prostitution. Bell was having his bachelor party at that club the same night. Following a confrontation that happened inside the club, one of the officers overheard Bell's friend talk about getting his gun. In order to stop a shooting from happening, the officer confronted Bell and his friends while they were in the car and ordered them to stop. Bell started to drive off, and the officer thought he saw a gun in the car, so he and the other police opened fire on the car. After the nonjury trial came to an end, the judge found all three detectives not guilty of manslaughter and assault.[63]

Timothy Thomas – Cincinnati, OH

Thomas was tragically shot and killed by a Cincinnati police officer, who followed the young man down a dark alley and opened fire because he thought Thomas had a gun. The 19-year-old man had 14 open warrants at the time of the shooting, and, according to Officer Roach, he was given verbal commands to stop running, but he did not comply. When Thomas began lowering his arms without instruction, Officer Roach opened fire and shot Thomas in the heart with a single bullet. There was no gun ever found on Thomas.[64]

Abner Louima – New York

Louima is a Haitian immigrant who was brutally attacked and tortured by a white New York police officer on Aug. 9, 1997. NYPD officer, Justin Volpe, took Louima into the restroom of the 70th Precinct station house in Brooklyn and sodomized the young man with a broken broomstick and then put it in his face. In court, Volpe said that he thought Louima punched him in the head during a scuffle outside of a nightclub but also admitted that he wanted to humiliate Louima regardless. Volpe left the police force and was sentenced to 30 years in prison, and Charles Schwarz was also sentenced to 15 years in prison for assisting Volpe in the assault. This incident brought greater awareness to the ongoing pattern of white New York police officers abusing black men and overstepping their authority.[65]

Robert Mitchell – Detroit, MI

Mitchell, a 16-year-old from Detroit, was tragically killed by police who said the teen was resisting arrest after a traffic stop. Police used a Taser on Mitchell who was running from his cousin's car and into an abandoned house. The Taser that killed Mitchell sent 50,000 volts of electricity into him. Police defended their use of the "non-lethal" weapon was because the teen was resisting an arrest.[66]

Amadou Diallo – New York

Diallo, an immigrant from Guinea, was shot and killed by New York police officers on the stoop of his apartment in February 1999. The four officers fired 41 times into the Bronx apartment building because they thought Diallo had a gun. The undercover officers said Diallo looked suspicious and thought he might have been assisting in a robbery or other criminal activity. Diallo didn't follow the officers' commands, and when he reached into his pocket, the officers began shooting only to find out that he was unarmed and was holding his wallet in his hand. A year later, the four officers who shot Diallo were acquitted of second-degree murder and other charges.[67]

Kathryn Johnston – Atlanta, GA

Johnston was tragically killed by two Atlanta police officers during a botched drug raid in 2006. The 92-year-old woman was alone inside her home when the officers burst in without warning. She fired at them with a handgun, injuring three of the men, and they fired back at Johnston, striking her five or six times. The officers were told by an undercover informant that he bought drugs from a dealer there named "Sam;" however, the man who claimed to be the informant said he never bought drugs at Johnston's house. The two police officers involved in the shooting pleaded guilty to manslaughter and several other charges, and a third officer was also indicted in the murder case.[68]

Kelly Thomas - Fullerton, CA

Thomas was a mentally ill and homeless man killed by police officers which sparked a nationwide outcry. His death came on July 10, five days after the 37-year-old was beaten by officers. In a video shown in court, he was seen lying on the ground being kicked and punched by the officers as he screamed for his father and help. In January, last year, Manuel Ramos was found not guilty of second-degree murder, and involuntary manslaughter and Jay Cicinelli was also acquitted of excessive force and involuntary manslaughter.[69]

Gil Collar - Mobile, AL

Collar was an 18-year-old student when he was killed by a University of South Alabama police officer, Trevis Austin. Austin was cleared of any wrongdoing after he shot the teenager who was under the influence of drugs. A grand jury in Mobile, Alabama concluded he acted in self-defense and did not bring charges.[70]

Andy Lopez Cruz - Sonoma County, CA

Cruz was a 13-year-old boy shot dead after a deputy sheriff in Santa Rosa, northern California, said he believed Cruz was carrying a real rifle. It was reported the boy was told to drop his gun as they crouched behind their patrol car. Cruz, only holding a replica of an assault rifle, turned with the gun still in his hand. Police said Erick Gelhaus then shot him "fearing for his life."[71]

Ezell Ford - Los Angeles, CA

Ford was shot by two Los Angeles police officers despite being unarmed. According to an LAPD statement, the officers tried to stop him, but there was a struggle. Police said the mentally ill 25-year-old then tried "to remove the officer's handgun from its holster." Charlie Beck, chief of LAPD, said the investigation was continuing after the release of the autopsy report.[72]

Antonio Martin - Berkeley MO

The black teenager was shot in Berkeley Missouri after police said he pointed a handgun at a white male police officer. The police added the suspect was "known to them," but in the aftermath of the shooting, protests took place as relations between the black community and police deteriorated further. Although videos were released, they did not show the moment of the shooting.[73]

Tremaine McMillan – Miami, FL

14-year-old Tremaine McMillan was feeding his puppy and playing on the beach with some friends when cops riding ATVs approached him and asked what he was doing. The officers say they saw McMillan roughhousing with another teenager, told him it was "unacceptable behavior," and asked where his mother was. When McMillan walked away, they chased him on ATVs, jumped out, pinned him to the ground and arrested him. Miami-Dade Police Detective Alvaro Zabaleta justified the use of force, saying McMillan was exhibiting threatening "body language," which includes "clenched fists."[74]

Jarmaine Darden - Fort Worth, TX

Fort Worth police entered the home of Jarmaine Darden in search of cocaine. The raid, which does not appear to have uncovered any cocaine, ended with the 34-year-old father died after he was tasered multiple times by police. Darden, a 350-pound man, who'd been asleep on the couch when police came in, couldn't drop to the ground on his stomach as officers commanded because he suffered from asthma. "They pulled him off the couch, and they tried to put him on his stomach. He can't breathe on his stomach. He doesn't even lie on the bed on his stomach," said Donna Randle, the mother of the victim.[75]

Cary Ball Jr. - St. Louis, MO

25-year-old Cary Ball Jr. was shot 25 times by police officers. Police say Ball refused to pull over for a traffic stop, eventually crashed into a parked car, and started running. According to police, Ball pointed a semi-automatic handgun at the officers, prompting them to open fire. Several witnesses, however, say Ball threw his gun on the ground and was walking toward police with his hands up to surrender when he was shot. Some unverified reports say 7 of the 25 shots hit him in the back. Police say there was no surveillance video in the area to verify exactly what happened. Ball was an honor student with a 3.86 GPA, majoring in human services at Forest Park Community College, where he had been celebrated as an "emerging scholar." According to family and friends, Ball was working to reform his life after being convicted of armed robbery when he was 17.[76]

Jamarion Robinson – Atlanta, GA

Atlanta law enforcement officers used excessive force when they shot a schizophrenic Georgia man at least 59 times in August 2016 and then tried to cover up their actions by tampering with evidence, lawyers for his mother assert in a federal civil rights lawsuit filed Wednesday. Officers serving an arrest warrant broke down the front door of an apartment in East Point and "without cause or provocation" began "spraying" the inside of an East Point apartment with bullets, killing 26-year-old Jamarion Rashad Robinson, lawyers for his mother, Monteria Najuda Robinson, wrote in the lawsuit. The officers were aware that Jamarion Robinson had been diagnosed with schizophrenia but failed to investigate his mental health status before trying to arrest him and weren't properly trained to arrest people with psychiatric conditions, the lawsuit says.[77]

The lawsuit says officers knocked loudly on the front door of the apartment multiple times and then broke the door down and began shooting without knowing how many people were inside. At least one officer then went up to a second-floor landing, where Robinson's body lay and took steps to cover up the officers' actions, including setting off a flash-bang grenade, firing two bullets into his body, handcuffing his body, putting an oxygen mask on his body and moving his body to the first floor. Those actions were taken to make it difficult or impossible to reconstruct the shooting accurately, the lawsuit says. The lawsuit was filed against eight named law enforcement officers from a number of different law enforcement agencies, as well as 11 unidentified officers. It alleges that the officers violated Robinson's constitutional rights, using excessive force, manipulating evidence and falsifying reports.[78]

Los Angeles County Sheriff's Department - Men's Central Jail

Sometimes, the corruption and violations of civil and constitutional rights become so widespread, entire law enforcement departments are swept up in the crime. In December 2013, 18 Los Angeles sheriff's deputies were arrested by Federal officials as part of an FBI investigation into allegations of civil rights abuses and corruption in the nation's largest jail system. The Grand Jury indictments allege unjustified beatings of jail inmates and visitors at downtown Los Angeles jail facilities, unjustified detentions and a conspiracy to obstruct a federal investigation into misconduct at the Men's Central Jail.[79]

In Summary

These documented cases of excessive police abuse are heart rendering and truly a travesty of justice. Law enforcement officers should be held accountable for their violations against the people and the laws they break. Such police brutality is rapidly skyrocketing throughout our country, with the looming threat that our government will allow law enforcement officers even more lawless activities on the general public. The increasing militarization of the police force is now becoming the norm in America and not the exception!

KNOW YOUR RIGHTS

Every American citizen **MUST** know and understand their rights! A civil right is an enforceable right or privilege, which if interfered with by another gives rise to an action for injury. Examples of civil rights are freedom of speech, press, and assembly; the right to vote; freedom from involuntary servitude; and the right to equality in public places.[80]

The most important expansions of civil rights in the United States occurred as a result of the enactment of the Thirteenth and Fourteenth Amendments to the U.S. Constitution. The Thirteenth Amendment abolished slavery throughout the United States. In response to the Thirteenth Amendment, various states enacted "black codes" that were intended to limit the civil rights of the newly freed slaves. In 1868 the Fourteenth Amendment countered these "black codes" by stating that no state "shall make or enforce any law which shall abridge the privileges or immunities of the citizens of the United States... [or] deprive any person of life, liberty, or property without due process of law, [or] deny to any person within its jurisdiction the equal protection of the laws."[81]

In more recent times, the most prominent civil rights legislation is the Civil Rights Act of 1964. Decisions of the Supreme Court at the time limited Congressional enforcement of the 14th Amendment to state actions, rather than individual actions. Therefore, in order to reach the actions of individuals, Congress, using its power to regulate interstate commerce, enacted the Civil Rights Act of 1964 under Title 42, Chapter 21 of the United States Code. Discrimination based on "race, color, religion, or national origin" in public establishments that have a connection to interstate commerce or are supported by the state is prohibited. Public establishments include places of public accommodation (e.g., hotels, motels, and trailer parks), restaurants, gas stations, bars, taverns, and places of entertainment in general. The Civil Rights Act of 1964 and subsequent legislation also declared a strong legislative policy against discrimination in public schools and colleges which aided in desegregation. Title VI of the Civil Rights Act prohibits discrimination in federally funded programs. Title VII of the Civil Rights Act prohibits employment discrimination where the employer is engaged in interstate commerce. Congress has passed numerous other laws dealing with employment discrimination.[82]

Civil rights ARE the protections and liberties enjoyed by EVERY American CITIZEN. These rights ensure that people are treated equally REGARDLESS OF their ethnicity, gender, or other such attributes. They guard against overly intrusive conduct by the government. Government AGENTS OF THE LAW are not permitted to make decisions arbitrarily, or to deprive individuals of their lives or property without affording them due process of law.

Every American citizen wants our government and our law enforcement officers to uphold their civil and constitutional rights! A law enforcement officer is required by law to protect and serve its citizens, not put them in danger, injure them or engage in offensive behavior. To properly protect the public, enforcement officers should be thoroughly trained in the rules, policies, and have the proper training and tools at their disposal. They must make encounters with citizens as safe as possible for themselves, the citizens and innocent bystanders.

When officers of the law violate, hurt, or kill the very people they are sworn to serve and protect; there must be accountability, not immunity or exoneration. Civil rights laws focus on protecting the constitutional rights of the people, which guarantees our bill of rights, as well as every amendment to our U.S. Constitution. Each person has the right to due process of law, and the right to be treated equality under the law. Every American citizen, as stated in our United States Declaration of Independence, has the unalienable rights given to us by our creator which are the right to life, liberty, and the pursuit of happiness.

When you encounter a police officer, sheriff, FBI or any federal agent, you are under no legal obligation to have a conversation with them without having your attorney being present. The 5th Amendment of the U.S. Constitution gives every American citizen the right not to answer questions asked by a police officer or government agency. You have the right to remain silent and refuse to answer any questions. When you say, "I am going to remain silent and want to contact my attorney," this automatically invokes your constitutional 5th Amendment rights, which protects you from police interrogation. The police officer is bound by law to stop questioning you.

If you are stopped, you should ask, "Am I free to go? Am I being arrested? Why am I being detained?" The 4th Amendment guarantees you the right to be free from "unreasonable searches and seizures," and protects your privacy from government intrusion. Police cannot search you, your possessions, your home, unless they have your consent, or obtain a search warrant. You must say to the police officer out loud "I do not consent to a search." If you don't say this, your silence waives your 4th Amendment rights.

Interacting with Police on the Street

Every American citizen should know their rights when interacting with a police or law enforcement officer. The most important thing to know is that you have civil and constitutional rights that have been put in place for your protection whenever you are interacting with an officer of the law. If you have a cell phone video, use it for evidence. The officer will be recording you as well in or outside their vehicle. Keep your hands visible at all times. Witnesses present are most helpful. Please know that whatever you say can and will be used against you. Therefore, stay calm and watch your words and actions.

Do not argue with the officer but assert your legal rights. Never run or resist an officer. When you do, you give your rights away. Ask if you are free to leave, if the officer says yes, then go. If you are required to provide identification, your name, address, and date of birth, do so. You are not required to say anything else. You have the right to ask the officer for his or her name, agency, and badge number. If the officer feels you pose a threat or serious physical injury, he or she can and will pat you down for any possessions within your reach, so keep your hands free of reaching for anything, and never, ever, give your consent to any searches! If an officer has probable cause, he can obtain a search warrant.

If an officer asks if he can search your car, you have the right to say, "No, I do not consent to a search of my car." Then remain silent. Do present your license, registration, and proof of insurance. You have the right to stay in your car. If you chose to get out of your car, be sure to take your license, insurance and video recorder with you. You can legally record your traffic stop by the officer. You have the right to close and lock your door. Make sure you have your keys with you if you lock your door.

The Supreme Court ruled that you must speak one time and say to the police officer "I'm going to remain silent." Don't answer any other questions from the police officer. Anything you say or do can and will be used against you by the police or the government. You can ask the officer, "Am I free to go?". If the police officer says, you're being detained or arrested tell the police officer "I'm going to remain silent."

The police officer needs your consent to search. The officer is allowed to do a pat down of your body for weapons, but not allowed to go inside your pockets. You do not have to remove anything in your purse or pocket. Always say "no" to police searches without a search warrant! You have every right not to talk to a police officer, and you should not talk to a police officer unless you have first consulted with a lawyer.

The government DOES allow the police to "pat down" your outer clothing. The law does allow the officer to go into your pockets ONLY if he feels a gun or what he believes is a weapon that can be used against him. Under any other set of circumstances, there is no law that requires you to empty your pockets or take off your shoes and socks.

Say nothing in the police car. They will be recording your conversation. Don't talk!!! If you are arrested, and your car is towed, the police are allowed to take an inventory of the items in your car. If they find anything that is illegal, i.e., drugs, stolen property, an unlicensed gun, the police will get a warrant from a judge then charge you with another crime.

Police officers need your permission to have a conversation. There is NO law that says you have to tell a police officer where you are going or where you have been, but you must tell the police officer "I'm going to remain silent." When dealing with a police officer in public, NEVER allow a conversation to start. If a police officer stops you and asks to speak with you, you're perfectly within your rights to say, "I do not wish to speak to you," then say good-bye. At this point, you should be free to leave, but the police officer might ask for your identification. If you have identification on you, tell the officer where it's at and ask permission to reach for it. In some states, you're not required to show an I.D. unless you're driving or after you've been arrested. Know the laws in your state!

If You are Placed Under Arrest

Don't answer any questions the police ask you, except for your name, address, and age once you're at the jail. Any other questions the police officer ask you, just say, "I want to talk to a lawyer."

Police officers don't always have to read you the Miranda Rights after you've been arrested if you "voluntarily" talk to a police officer. Talking to a police officer at any time can be very lethal to your case. Anything you say can and will be used against you.

Never talk to other jail inmates about your case, not even why you are incarcerated and what you have been charged with.

Within a reasonable amount of time, after you have been arrested and booked, the cops should allow you to make a local phone call to a lawyer, bail bondsman, relative or any other person you choose. The police cannot ever listen to your phone call if you're talking to your lawyer, and any and all correspondence to your lawyer from the jail is considered client-lawyer privilege.

The longest you can be held in jail is 72 hours. If you get arrested on a Friday night during a 3-day weekend, you won't see the judge until Tuesday morning. Usually, you will get out of jail within 4 to 24 hours if you can post a bond.

If you're on probation or parole, only tell your Parole Officer that you've been arrested and don't say anything else to anyone.

Interacting with Police at Your Home

Never open your door at home when a police officer knocks! There is no law that requires you to open your door to a police officer. If they have a search warrant, they will kick down your door before they knock. Don't even open your door with a chain-lock; the police officers will force their way in. Say nothing!

According to Supreme Court case law, Fernandez v. California on February 27, 2014, anyone in your residence can give permission for the police to search your home. This includes your children, spouse, neighbor, friend, or anyone that is in your residence because police officers need permission to come into your home. Teach your children they should not talk to the police officer if they are being questioned unless an adult is present because police do not need your permission to question a child.

A search warrant is the court's permission for an officer to search and seize evidence of a crime without permission or your presence. A warrantless search is permissible only if the police have your consent, probable cause that a crime was committed, or for any exigent circumstance. According to the "plain view doctrine," if an officer can see it, they can seize it.

The only exception to a warrantless search is in an emergency or exigent circumstance such as fire, smelling smoke; someone is screaming for help inside your home, police chase a suspect into your home, seeing a felony being committed, or someone inside your home called 911 for help! Only in these circumstances are police allowed to enter and search your home without a warrant. Under any other circumstances, it is unlawful for an enforcement officer to do a warrantless search of your premises.

The officer needs your consent to search your home or property. By giving consent, the person waives their 4th Amendment rights. Officers can and often do lie or use deception during the course of their investigations. However, there are some deceptions and lies that the Supreme Court ruled to be unlawful by an officer. One being **an officer is not allowed to make a false assertion that he/she possesses a search warrant when he/she doesn't. This is a material lie and is unlawful.**

The following case laws support the people's legal rights against officers who tell material lies, use deceit, makes misrepresentations, or uses trickery in order to gain access to a person's property, papers, or documents: Bumper v. North Carolina 391 U.S. 543 (1968); 42 U.S.C. 1983; Hadley v. Williams 368 F. 3d 747 (7th Cir. 2004); United States v. Bosse 898 F.2d 113 (9th Cir. 1990); United States v. Phillips 497 F. 2d 1131 (9th Cir. 1974); and United States v. Tweel, 550 F. 2d 297 (5th Cir. 1977).

Additional Rights

The 6th Amendment guarantees all defendants the right to the assistance of legal counsel in felony cases. If a person cannot afford to hire an attorney, the courts will appoint a lawyer, free of charge, not only for felony cases but also for misdemeanor charges that can result in incarceration. Appointed lawyers come from either a public defender's office or from a panel of local private lawyers approved by the court.

The 8th Amendment is just as relevant today as it was when it was ratified in the year 1791. It prohibits the federal government from imposing excessive bail, excessive fines, or cruel and unusual punishment. The U.S. Supreme Court has ruled that the Cruel and Unusual Punishment Clause also applies to the states.

Excessive police brutality is unlawful. According to Title 42, Section 1983 of the United States Code, which imposes liability on any person who, under "color of state law," deprives another individual of his or her federal civil rights. 1983 claims are lawsuits brought under this statute which allow victims to sue state and municipal government officials who violate federal civil rights laws.

Officers hiding behind their brotherhood code and agreeing to support each other in covering up their violations against the accused destroys the very essence of our judicial system. We must not allow such anarchy to exist. We need to stand up and make our voices heard and demand our government honors their legal responsibilities, to uphold our human, civil and constitutional rights, so the scales of justice can be balanced for every American citizen. Many victims of police corruption have lost their families, employment, reputation, and in some very sad cases, their lives.

Even as an inmate, you still have certain rights.

- The right to humane facilities and conditions

- The right to be free from sexual crimes

- The right to be free from racial segregation

- The right to express condition complaints

- The right to assert their rights under the Americans with Disabilities Act

- The right to medical care and attention as needed

- The right to appropriate mental health care

- The right to a hearing if they are to be moved to a mental health facility[83]

Inmates have the right to be free, under the Eighth Amendment of "cruel and unusual" punishment; the term noted by the Supreme Court is any punishment that can be considered inhumane treatment or that violates the basic concept of a person's dignity may be found to be cruel and unusual. For example, an inmate held in a 150-year-old prison infested with vermin, fire hazards, and a lack of toilets would exemplify a constitutional violation.[84]

The Government's "Right to Lie!"

The government allows police officers to lie to American citizens. For this reason alone, you have every reason not to trust the police or federal government who are the real threats to the innocent. Reports of enforcement officer's lying on a regular basis, staging crime scenes, and filing false police reports to cover up their criminal violations are running rampant in our country. Lawyers say this goes on all the time and they just have to deal with it. This is why the accused will often accept a plea bargain rather than fight for justice because they can't win against corruption in the judicial system.

Here are some ways a police officer is allowed to lie:

- Police can lie about having physical evidence.

- Police can trick you into giving up your DNA.

- Police can give fake tests to "prove you're guilty."

- Police may lie about having eyewitnesses.

- Police can lie about recording your conversation.

- Police can lie about having an accomplice confession.

- The police will try to imply that your refusal to cooperate will be damaging to your case.

- Police can lie about what will happen to other people.

- They will lie about wanting to help you out.

- Police may ignore your request for a lawyer.[85]

These are all lies! The bottom line is, don't trust the police! Their job is not to be your friend but someone who wants enough evidence to arrest you! That's their job!

Your best defense is always to remain silent and wait for a lawyer. Refusing to answer questions is not obstruction of justice. You will not talk yourself out of a jail cell. What most people don't realize is that the police do not charge you with a crime - only the district attorney can make that decision. The police are just supposed to hold you and get as much information as they can to convict you. That's it! That's their job. It is the DA's job to evaluate the evidence and decide whether even to issue a case. Often, a DA does not know anything about the case until the date of arraignment where they first pick up the file and read a police report. **If the officers lie on the Police Report as many of them do, this can cause the accused to pay a hefty price to prove their innocence.** Then the accused has to deal with the Judge who listens and, in many cases, believes the officer over the accused.

Most DA's simply read an intern's notes on the file. For the first time, one of the key pieces of evidence they are looking for is if you made any statements (that is the one thing that makes their job the easiest). United States v. Santos-Garcia (8th Cir.2002) 313 F.3d 1073, 1079 (noting that raised voices and suggestions on how to gain leniency do not render a confession involuntary).[86]

The hardest cases to prosecute are the ones where the Defendant has said NOTHING. The less you say to the Police, the better off you are at avoiding a charge. Talking to police only makes it more likely that charges will be filed.

The police will never help a suspect/person do anything but incriminate themselves. Their only job is to investigate a case.

There are many ways a police officer can LIE and trick you into talking. It's always safe to say the Magic Words: "Am I free to go? I'm going to remain silent."

Always remember, police officers are allowed to lie. Teach your children not to talk to a police officer, unless their parents are there with them. Imagine your child in a room with teachers, principal, assistant principal and police officers touching their gun and everyone demanding answers from your child without you being there or an attorney to represent your child. The child is so scared they will speak to the officer without knowing they have a choice.

Teach your children that they must call a parent for permission before they're allowed to talk to a police officer. Remember police officers are trained to put your child at ease and build trust. A police officers' job is to find, arrest, help convict a suspect, and that suspect could be your innocent child!

In Frazier v. Cupp, 394 U.S. 731 (1969), a United States Supreme Court case affirmed the legality of deceptive interrogation tactics. Police officers are trained at lying, twisting words and being manipulative. Police officers and other law enforcement agents are very skilled at getting information from people.[87]

Although police officers may seem nice and pretend to be on your side, they want to learn your habits, opinions, and affiliations of other people not suspected of wrongdoing. Don't try to answer a police officer's questions it can be very dangerous! You can never tell how a seemingly harmless bit of information that you give to a police officer might be used and misconstrued to hurt you, your family or someone else.

Overall, the vast majority of the law enforcement officers in this country perform their very difficult jobs with respect for their communities and in compliance with the law. Even so, there are incidents in which this is not the case.

Federal laws that address police misconduct include both criminal and civil statutes. These laws cover the actions of State, county, and local officers, including those who work in prisons and jails. In addition, several laws also apply to Federal law enforcement officers. The laws protect all persons in the United States (citizens and non-citizens).

FEDERAL LAW 42 U.S.C. § 1983

The Civil Rights Act of 1871 is a federal statute, numbered 42 U.S.C. § 1983, that allows people to sue the government for civil rights violations. It applies when someone acting "under color of" state-level or local law has deprived a person of rights created by the U.S. Constitution or federal statutes.[88]

Lawyers sometimes refer to cases brought under 42 U.S.C. § 1983 as "Section 1983" lawsuits. Section 1983 can apply in many scenarios, and claims under it don't have to involve violence. But it's often invoked when someone claims to be the victim of excessive police force.[89]

For Section 1983 to come into play, the person to be sued (the defendant) must have acted "under color of any statute, ordinance, regulation, custom, or usage, of any State or Territory or the District of Columbia."[90]

Courts have determined that the "under color of" clause requires that the wrongdoer qualify, at least in some sense, as a representative of the state when depriving the victim of civil rights. In a nutshell, the clause refers to people who misuse some kind of authority that they get from state law. Police officers who use excessive force generally fit this bill.[91]

Judges can consider a number of factors to decide whether, when violating someone's federal rights, an officer was acting under the color of state law. Among them is whether the officer:

- was on duty

- was wearing a police uniform

- used police equipment (like a squad car or hand-cuffs)

- flashed a badge or otherwise claimed to be an officer, or

- carried out an arrest.[92]

When a Section 1983 suit has to do with an arrest—a central police function—a court will normally consider the officer to have acted under color of state law.

History

Section 1983 didn't have much impact for nearly a hundred years when the United States Supreme Court stepped up to the plate in the watershed 1961 case of Monroe v. Pape. The case arose from events in Chicago. Cops broke into the home of an African-American man, Mr. Monroe. They ransacked his home and mistreated him in front of his family. Then they carted him off to jail and accused him of murder. No charges were brought against Monroe, but enough was enough. The Supreme Court agreed that Section 1983 gave Monroe the right to sue the cops for his damages.[93]

Section 1983 does not guarantee you will win your case. There are hurdles to overcome. But it gives you an additional chance to have your day in court.

A Section 1983 Case

You might have a U.S. Code Section 1983 case if a person acting "under color of" law deprives you of your constitutional rights. Here are a few examples:

- Shootings by law enforcement officers against unarmed citizens and other cases of police brutality and excessive force.

- False arrests by law enforcement officers and malicious prosecutions when there is no probable cause or evidence of criminal wrongdoing.

- State and federal law enforcement officers searching through your house and seizing your property without a valid warrant.

- If you are a prisoner and you are beaten and injured by guards or if guards deliberately ignore your medical needs.[94]

In the criminal justice area, Section 1983 covers the 4th Amendment constitutional right against unreasonable search and seizure and the 8th Amendment constitutional right against cruel and unusual punishment.

4th Amendment Example

The California case of Deorle v. Rutherford involved the 4th Amendment. In that case, Police Officer Greg Rutherford fired a "less lethal" lead-filled "bean bag round" into the face of Richard Leo Deorle, an emotionally disturbed resident of Butte County, California, who was walking at a "steady gait" in his direction. He did so although Deorle was unarmed, had not attacked or even touched anyone, had generally obeyed the instructions given him by various police officers, and had not committed any serious offense. Rutherford did not warn Deorle that he would be shot if he physically crossed an undisclosed line or order him to halt. Rutherford simply fired at Deorle when he arrived at a spot Rutherford had predetermined. The projectile Rutherford fired removed Deorle's eye and left lead shot implanted in his skull.[95]

The Ninth Circuit, an important federal court, looked at all the facts and circumstances of the case and concluded that the deputy violated Deorle's constitutional right against unreasonable seizure by using excessive force.

8th Amendment Example

"Another California case, Madrid v. Gomez, involved 8th Amendment violations at Pelican Bay State Prison. This case arose as a prisoner civil-rights class action challenging the conditions of confinement at the Pelican Bay State Prison in California. Plaintiffs-Appellees Madrid and others ("prisoners") alleged a multitude of constitutional violations, including a pattern and practice of excessive force against them, provision of inadequate medical and psychiatric care, and failure to maintain humane housing conditions. After a three-month trial, the district court verified many of the prisoners' complaints.[96]

As a result of the Madrid case and other Section 1983 cases federal courts now oversee major aspects of the California prison system.

Who Can You Sue?

This is a complicated area of law, but generally speaking, you might be able to sue any of the following:

- Police officers

- Sheriff's deputies

- Prison guards

- Police chiefs

- County sheriffs

- Prison wardens

- A city that employs offending officer

- A county that employs offending officer[97]

United States Code Section 1983 cases often involve multiple defendants. The prisoners in the Madrid case sued the warden, the chief deputy warden, the chief medical officer and the director of the entire corrections system.

States and judges are immune. Even though cases often have more than one defendant, you can't just sue anyone you feel like. You cannot sue a state under Section 1983 because of sovereign immunity and because the word "person" in Section 1983 does not include states.

You also can't sue certain kinds of professionals, like judges, because they have historically been immune from liability for performing their jobs.

Cities and Counties are not immune. You can sue cities and counties in what is called a "Monell Claim." It is a claim against the government entity that employed the individuals who committed the alleged civil rights violations.[98] To hold that entity liable, you need to show that your constitutional injury was caused by a policy or custom of the city or county.

The case of Chew v. Gates involved a "Monell Claim." The plaintiff brought suit after he was mauled by a K-9 police dog following a traffic stop.

The "Monell Claim" at issue stems from the policy of the Los Angeles Police Department ("LAPD") of using police dogs to search for, find and seize suspects, by biting if necessary. Chew claims that the manner in which the police dog was used during his arrest constituted excessive force in violation of his constitutional rights. He further alleges that his arresting officer carried out an LAPD policy of using police dogs to search for, find and seize suspects, by biting if necessary. Thus, part of Chew's Monell claim against the City is based on the argument that the use of the police dog to apprehend Chew by biting him violated his constitutional rights.[99]

In addition to the immunities described above, defenses such as lack of causation that come up in any civil case, a cop in a Section 1983 case might enjoy something called qualified immunity.

Qualified immunity is a presumption that a cop will be immune from liability for good faith performance of his or her discretionary duties. The plaintiff can overcome this presumption, and win his or her Section 1983 suit by showing that the offending officer's conduct was way out of bounds.

In the Deorle v. Rutherford case discussed above, the court concluded that the officer was not entitled to qualified immunity because Deorle had a clearly established right not to suffer excessive force like he did and no reasonable officer would have subjected him to it in such a way.[100]

But it's important to remember that not every case comes out like Deorle.

In Blandford v. Sacramento County, for example, a plaintiff who was paralyzed after being shot by cops lost his excessive force Section 1983 case even before it got to the jury. The plaintiff was wielding a sword when he was shot, and the court concluded that the cops acted reasonably under the circumstances.

Depending on the case, you might be able to get,

- Compensatory damages to reimburse you for expenses like medical bills and lost wages.

- Punitive damages to "punish" the wrongdoer.

- Equitable relief where a judge orders someone to do something or stop doing something.[101]

Damage awards in civil rights cases can be high. In 2007, a man won over three million dollars in damages he suffered from false arrest and other indignities by Oakland, California police officers. That award included punitive damages.

The inmates in the Madrid prison case got equitable relief. The judge ordered prison officials to work with the court to remedy the wide-ranging constitutional violations at Pelican Bay."

Winning a 1983 Suit is not easy. It is a civil case, not a criminal case. The burden is usually on the plaintiff to prove liability by a "preponderance of the evidence" (meaning "more likely than not").

But many states treat excessive force cases somewhat differently than typical lawsuits. In some jurisdictions, there is a presumption that the officer acted with the necessary level of force that the plaintiff must overcome. Additionally, some impose a higher burden of proof than "preponderance of the evidence," instead requiring the plaintiff to prove a claim of excessive force by "clear and convincing evidence" (a standard higher than "by a preponderance of evidence" but lower than "beyond a reasonable doubt").[102]

All states agree that the plaintiff being guilty of the crime for which the officer arrested him isn't a valid defense for the officer. But, by the same token, a plaintiff who can prove innocence is more likely to be able to show that the officer's use of force wasn't necessary.[103]

FINAL THOUGHTS…

Today lawmakers are making changes to our Constitution that are diminishing the rights of the people. Our Founding Fathers based the Constitution on the Bible and God's Ten Commandments. Some of these changes include:

- Taking away our privacy with increased government warrantless surveillance.

- Legalizing same-sex marriage and abortions.

- Eliminating God, prayers, and the Bible from our educational institutions, and from our judicial buildings.

Today we are dealing with too much government, too much surveillance, and not enough democratic justice for the people. Our republic was founded on biblical principles, with freedom, liberty, and justice for all. We are the first and perhaps the only nation that holds as self-evident truths that all men and women are created equal and are endowed by their creator with certain unalienable rights and that governments are instituted to protect those rights and derive their just powers from the consent of the governed. America was founded on the first principles of:

- The rule of law that mandates the law governs everyone.

- The first principle of unalienable rights that everyone is naturally endowed by our creator with certain rights of equality.

- The first principle that governments are instituted by the people and derive their just powers from the consent of the governed.

- The first principle of limited government which means the protection of unalienable rights is the legitimate purpose and limit of government to be strong enough to fulfill its purpose yet limited to that purpose.

- The final first principle is the right to declare revolution when the other first principles are being infringed by the government.[104]

Our Declaration of Independence explains that these foundational ideas were the philosophical underpinning of the American Revolution. Once independence was secured, the Founding Fathers labored to ensure that the Constitution became the living embodiment of a government based on these First Principles.

Today, we are witnessing the erosion of our democratic and constitutional rights. Just a few years ago, the Supreme Court ruled that the U.S. Government can seize a citizen's property for any reason and at any time they deem necessary. The civil asset forfeiture law allows government agencies like the IRS or the Department of Justice to confiscate anyone's property without FIRST obtaining criminal charges against them (18 U.S. Code § 981 - Civil forfeiture).

I have included in this book some of our nation's worst and most egregious criminal acts committed by law enforcement officers, who violate the rights of the American people. Unfortunately, some victims of false charges and arrests, who have been unjustly accused, are not financially able to pay for their adequate defense in order to prove their innocence. Many plead to a lesser sentence because they want to avoid an unjust ruling. They don't want to gamble on going to trial, where their testimony is challenged by lying officers, a biased judge, and a prosecutor who sides with the officers to win his case.

I pray that the best book in the world, *"The Holy Bible,"* be given to every single person in every single cell across the United States of America, along with a copy of this book. Everyone needs to know what their legal rights are, whether one is in or out of prison. Our government needs to uphold everyone's rights with no exception to race, color, or creed.

I pray this book will be a voice for those falsely accused, who are crying out for justice from imprisonment and to expose the acts of all government officials who violate their oath of office.

God will fight against all unjust charges and place His judgment on those judges who rule with bias and not according to the law. He will help everyone no matter how big or small their problem is. David fought Goliath with five smooth stones. *"If God is for us, who can be against us?"* (Romans 8:31 NKJV) *"No weapon formed against you shall prosper, And every tongue which rises against you in judgment You shall condemn. This is the heritage of the servants of the Lord, And their righteousness is from Me," Says the Lord"* (Isaiah 54:17 NKJV).

Before Jesus went to the cross, He endured false charges, an unjust trial, and paid the severe penalty of a guilty verdict with His life on the cross. He did this willingly to free all of mankind from sin. When Jesus took His last breath, he accomplished God's plan, which was to atone for mankind's sins. The cross gives everyone God's amazing gift of salvation. All we have to do is repent of our sins and say yes to Jesus, and our name is forever inscribed in the Lamb's Book of Life! Jesus now sits at the right hand of the Father, in power and glory. We, too, as believers will be joint heirs with Jesus in His kingdom.

Now that we are saved from our sins, we have God's promise of victory over every trial and unjust charge brought against us because God fights all our battles in this life, and he never loses.

Everyone deserves to have their civil and constitutional rights upheld, whether you are free or incarcerated. We need to rehabilitate the guilty, not destroy their life. Too often, no one hears their cries for help, nor for those who are unjustly charged for crimes they did not commit. Our legal system, unfortunately, is not perfect. Nevertheless, but we should provide justice and safeguard the rights of the accused. Throwing the key away after one is incarcerated is morally wrong. Our government must honor every American citizen's rights, whether one is in or out of prison.

Unfortunately, prisoners suffer cruel and inhuman treatment during their incarceration. There are countless prisoners housed in our penal system being denied their basic human and constitutional rights. They are considered just a number, that the penal system puts away in a locked cell, with several other inmates packed in like sardines. Too often, their basic human needs are ignored by the system.

Under God's Laws, humane treatment is needed for every single person. We are all His children!!! If God is no respecter of persons and what He does for one He will do for everyone, then we too must not discriminate one from another. We have all sinned and come short of the glory of God, with no exception. We need to start caring for and educating the hearts and minds of those incarcerated. They need to be cared for spiritually, and psychologically as well as physically in order to give them hope for today, and faith for all their tomorrows. We need to remember the golden rule, *"Do to others as you would have them do to you"* (Luke 6:31 NIV). We are only here for a short time compared to eternity, so each one can make a difference in someone else's life. Let's not ignore the needy, homeless, and those who need our support. Jesus said, *"Assuredly, I say to you, inasmuch as you did it to one of the least of these My brethren, you did it to Me"* (Matthew 25:40 NKJV).

What you are about to read in the next section of this book is the most heart-wrenching and difficult story I could ever imagine. It is the true story of my only son's horrific and unjust battle with each of the injustices discussed in this chapter. It is only through our faith in God that either of us has been able to live through such atrocities. I ask you to please keep my son in your prayers as you now read, Robert's Story...

SECTION THREE

Roberts Story

FROM BIRTH TO
HIS QUEST FOR JUSTICE

INTRODUCTION

Robert Anthony O'Hare was born at St. Joseph Hospital in Elmira, NY on November 1st, 1961. His birth completed our family with his two sisters Anne Marie 3 1/2, years old and Patty Lynne, 2 years old. When Robert was brought home from the hospital, I placed him in Patty's arms with her sister Anne Marie sitting right next to her on the red plaid sofa. I told the girls, "This is your baby brother, and you both are to take care of him." The look on their faces when they looked at their baby brother was priceless. From that moment forward, was created an unbroken bond that lasted throughout their life. Even after my husband and my two daughters went home to be with the Lord, their spirit is still with us.

My greatest earthly blessing was being their mother. When they were 9, 11, and 12 1/2 years of age, I became a single parent. This did not deter my being 100% dedicated to raising them and striving to give them the best possible life. I detailed this journey in my first book, ***"Virginia O'Hare's Trials, Triumphs, and Vision from God."*** I covered my troubled marriage, the challenges of motherhood, divorce, single life, remarriage to an awesome man, and my two very successful careers. The first career was as a self-employed Employment Consultant in Poughkeepsie, NY, licensed by the State of New York, and my second career was as a self-employed Owner-Broker of a very successful Real Estate Business in Ft. Lauderdale, FL, licensed in the State of Florida.

My first book gives a detailed account of my trials and triumphs, which includes a world-famous lawsuit I won in the New York Supreme Court, and my real-life vision from God. Included in the book are my trials living through a troubled marriage, raising three children as a single parent, and confronting all the challenges of being a single parent. Fortunately, Robert Anthony, Anne Marie, and Patty Lynne came out of all this as well adjusted, intelligent, happy, and very gifted children. Growing up, they loved life and lived it to its fullest. I began Bible studies at a very early age, which gave them a strong foundation during their formative years. We shared and did most things together as a family, which included vacations. One memorable family vacation was to Israel and being baptized together in the Jordon river and visiting all the awesome Biblical sights that we had studied about during our Bible studies.

Despite being a single parent, and working full time in my Employment Agency in Poughkeepsie, NY, their welfare and well-being was my number one priority. I instilled in them Biblical principles, to love God, obey His Ten Commandments, believe in Jesus as their Lord and Savior, and to pray always. After their passing I looked through Anne Marie and Patty Lynne's bibles and didn't find one page that wasn't read multiple times with their writing countless heartfelt notes over most of the bible pages. I truly treasure those bibles, and had the blessed assurance they were home with the Lord.

Celebrating holidays, and special occasions with our family, relatives, and friends was a normal occurrence for Robert, Anne, and Patty growing up. They loved getting together at Grandma's home in Elmira, N. Y. and visiting with all their cousins. Everyone enjoyed Grandma's home-cooked Italian meals and her freshly baked pastries on all those special occasions.

Despite the fact that Robert was the youngest sibling, and got a lot of attention, he wasn't spoiled. He was well adjusted, well liked, and very popular with his friends. Growing up he exhibited a great deal of common sense, wisdom, and leadership. He was independent with a very strong, and enduring character which we all admired. He was particular about how he lived his life. His standards, and principals were high due to his being a perfectionist. He never took drugs, drank or smoked. He took pride in living right and staying healthy.

After my divorce, I built a brand-new split-level home for my three children in Poughkeepsie, New York, which was within walking distance to their school. One day, a friend and her three children came to visit. Robert overheard me telling her I wanted to have the inside of my living and dining room walls repainted. He said, "Mom, I can paint the walls for you." My girlfriend said, "You can't let an 11-year-old paint this beautiful home, he'll ruin it!"

I looked at Robert's face, and without any hesitation said, "Yes Robert, you can paint the walls." His smile lit up his face because of my confidence in letting him paint our home. He not only did a perfect job, but was most careful masking around everything so no paint got on the windows, floors, or furniture. I was so proud of him, and the walls looked beautiful!

Seven years later, Robert began his painting career working with customers from our family's very successful Real Estate Business in Ft. Lauderdale, FL. He graduated into painting multi-million-dollar homes, and got referrals from former customers which kept him busy and in demand. I was amazed at how many jobs he acquired just through word of mouth, and he never had to advertise. To say I was proud of him and my two beautiful daughters would be an understatement. We always stayed together as a family and lived most of our lives under one roof. My second husband, Dan Ortung, blended well with our family and shared our same Christian values. We were together for 45 years until his passing.

From an early age, Robert had an interest in deciphering treasure codes and traveling across country, which he enjoyed very much. He did mining in the deserts of Arizona as a hobby and not for money. He explored the rough terrains in the deserts in Arizona, while enduring the sweltering weather. During his ventures, he encountered baby lions, snakes, and walked for miles in the harshness of the oppressively hot weather. He loved the vastness and serenity he found there. The scariest moment of his life was when he got lost in the desert and couldn't find his rented vehicle. He told me he had been walking all day in the hot sun and was following a code to a buried treasure when he lost track of time and darkness set in. He was hungry, thirsty, and exhausted. He had been traveling on foot all day through the harsh, barren land for a number of miles with very little signs of life around him other than the raw, dryness of the desert. He said he was so grateful, when he finally found his vehicle, and drove back to town. After filing claims, he would turn down offers to sell them. He said, "Mom, I didn't do this for the money, I did it for the challenge of breaking the codes and mining."

I told Robert, "All the riches of the world are the Lord's, and He disposes of them as He wills. God said, *'the gold and the silver is mine'* Haggai 2:8-9 (NKJV). He has paved the streets of Heaven in pure gold, and instructed the building of his temple to be in gold."

In addition to exploring for buried treasures, Robert experimented with turning water into fuel to run on any motor vehicle. He found great success with the development of this formula, and through trial and error perfected it. He tested his invention on his own vehicle, and it worked!

Robert never drank, smoked or took any drugs. Maintaining his mind, body, and spirit and staying in good physical health were always a priority to him. He's been extremely loyal and respectful to me, his family, and friends during his entire life.

After his two sisters and my husband went home to be with the Lord, within the span of one year and fifty-five days, Robert was truly an anchor for me. Two years after their passing, tragedy entered our life on October 5, 2015. This was the most devastating crisis we both had to go through and endure. It virtually catapulted our life into a dimension that I never thought existed. The holocaust that my son was put through by the corrupt Justice System in Lake County, FL, drove me to fight with every breath in my being to save his life and seek justice for him. It is this tragedy that gave birth to this book, ***"Virginia O'Hare Documents God's Laws vs. Man's Law."***

OCTOBER 5, 2015
SHERIFF'S DEPUTIES VIOLATE
THEIR OATH OF OFFICE

The day began with Robert and I going through our usual morning routine in our Colonial waterfront home in quaint Mt. Dora Florida. I was listening to my Bible tapes when I heard the most blood-curdling cries, coming from inside our home. I rushed into the living room and witnessed three Lake County Sheriff's Deputies brutally assaulting my son as he laid defenseless on the floor crying out with pain from their savage beating to his entire body. They were thrusting blunt and brutal blows to his body, head, face, and eyes and repeatedly kicking, and punching Robert as he laid in a submissive position on the floor. I was in total shock, thinking this must be a nightmare. The three Deputies ignored my pleas to stop beating my son and continued assaulting him as he was crying out in pain from their sadistic and brutal assault.

After their unlawful entry, Robert told me that the three Lake County Sheriff's Deputies had come to our front door and asked if they could come into our home to search for a computer, they allege may have child pornography downloaded, and said they did not have a search warrant. Robert told me his friend, and our neighbor in Ft. Lauderdale had given him his used laptop, and said he was not aware what was downloaded on the hard drive was illegal. So, he told the officers to get a search warrant, and he would call his attorney.

The following conversation was recorded on one of the Sheriff's Deputy's body-worn camcorder and was played at the Motion to Suppress Proceedings:

Sheriff's Deputy: "Anyone else here with you?"

Robert: "My Mother, can I call my lawyer?"

Sheriff's Deputy: "No."

Robert: "What did I do wrong?"

Sheriff's Deputy: "Asked for consent to come in and search the home."

Robert: "No, I want you to get a warrant!"

Sheriff's Deputy: "Step outside!"

Robert: "No."

As Robert was closing the door, the Corporal forcefully pushed open the door and stepped over the threshold of our home, with the other two Deputies following him. They physically overpowered Robert and commenced hitting, kicking, and punching him while he laid defenseless on the floor. That's when I walked into the room and yelled for them to stop. When they wouldn't, I ran into my bedroom and got my cell phone and began video recording them for 35 minutes until it stopped recording. The Deputies lied on their Police Report and stated a completely different story other than what I witnessed while they were unlawfully in our home.

I watched with over whelming fear as one Deputy laid bodily over Robert's legs, while the other two deputies, one on each side, were both repeatedly kicking, hitting, and punching Robert non-stop. I kept yelling, "Please stop beating my son!" The Sheriff's Deputy on Robert's left side kept kicking Robert repeatedly to his ribs and abdomen, soccer ball style, 10-12 times with his heavy, beige colored work shoes. At the same time, another Deputy, kneeling on one knee on Robert's right side, kept hitting him repeatedly in the head, face, and eyes. His multiple blunt blows to Robert's eyes caused a buckle, (also known as a drum), that had been surgically implanted a year earlier to secure a torn retina, to become dislodged. This caused Robert a severe amount of immediate pain and blindness. He was in constant pain until he had the buckle surgically removed months later. His blindness was difficult for him to deal with.

The second Deputy, who kicked Robert repeatedly, and maliciously tore his t-shirt down to below his chest, drew blood on his own fist and on Robert's face and body. I later read in the Police Report where this Deputy lied and said Robert was running towards the kitchen and that's why he tore his shirt. My cell phone video proved otherwise. Robert was down on the floor just a few feet from the front entrance facing in the opposite direction to the kitchen with his t-shirt torn below his chest, exposing the bruise marks on his neck from the tear and the punch marks and cuts on his upper torso. **This tear was on the front of his t-shirt, not on the back, further proof that Robert was NOT running towards the kitchen.**

When the Deputies saw that I was recording them with my cell phone, they stopped their assault, and abruptly sat Robert upright and tightly handcuffed his wrists behind his back. He never once resisted. Robert said the handcuffs were too tight and hurting him. I told the Deputy that his wrists and hands were turning red. The officer clicked the handcuffs to a tighter notch out of spite, which cut off the blood circulation to his hands even more.

Three other law enforcement officers entered our home during this altercation. One, with the rank of Captain, who claimed my son was in a Tea Shop in downtown Mt. Dora, with a laptop they thought had child pornography downloaded. They wanted to search the home for the laptop in order to inspect it. I recorded the Captain admitting **HE HAD NO SEARCH WARRANT AND NO PROBABLE CAUSE!**

They left my son sitting on the floor, his hands tightly handcuffed behind his back, cutting off the blood circulation to his hands and wrists, while they commenced searching the home for the laptop.

After searching the entire home, opening doors and drawers, and not finding the laptop, the Captain became angry. He stated, as recorded on my 35-minute cell phone video, "Even if we don't find the laptop we are still going to arrest your son anyway."

I asked, "On what charge?"

He said, "For resisting an officer without violence."

I said, "Resisting an officer when you forced your way into our home without a search warrant?"

Then he said, "We are going to draw up a search warrant. If we don't find the laptop, after our search, this is a free country, we will leave, but we are going to charge your son anyway with resisting an officer without violence."

The only place they did not look for the laptop was in my son's locked bedroom closet. As Robert sat on the floor, with his hands tightly handcuffed behind his back and in a beaten, traumatic and painful state, the Captain made an unlawful command to Robert, "If you don't tell us where the key is to your locked bedroom closet by the count of 10, we will kick the door off its hinges." He started counting out loud, 1, 2, 3, 4, 5, 6, 7, 8, etc. Without giving his consent, Robert, in fear of reprisal, and the six Deputies hovering over him, told the Captain where the key was.

The Deputies unlocked the bedroom closet door without a search warrant, without consent, without probable cause, and without any exigent circumstances, and found the laptop. They removed the laptop from the closet, unzipped the case and staged the laptop as a crime scene to justify the "Plain View Doctrine." They placed the laptop on the floor and the case on the bed, then called CSI to take pictures of their "staged" crime scene.

The proof of this and their criminal violations were recorded on the Corporal's body-worn camcorder video, which recorded the Deputies talking to each other about finding the laptop in the locked bedroom closet. The video time-stamped their conversation as being on October 5, 2015, at 11:37 a.m. The warrant was not signed until several hours later at 5:44 pm.

My deceased husband's firearms were in Robert's locked bedroom closet. Prior to his demise, he was licensed as a Florida Private Investigator and Licensed to carry firearms. Robert was charged with possession of a short-barrel rifle which the Deputies removed from his locked bedroom closet. The Detective falsely stated in the Police Report that the rifle was in "plain view."

Later, under oath, this same Deputy testified at the

Bond Hearing that he had to move clothes around the back of the locked bedroom closet to get to the short barrel rifle. He contradicted his Police Report which stated the rifle was in "plain view."

Witnessing my son's brutal beating, and seeing his face and body bloodied and bruised, caused my blood pressure to rise to a very dangerous level. At almost 79 years of age, I was physically and emotionally feeling the adverse effects of being terrorized by the Deputies. The officers recognized how distraught I was and called the Emergency Medical Technicians.

When they arrived, the Deputy who punched and kicked my son repeatedly to his ribs and abdomen was the first one to meet the EMT'S at the front door asking for a band-aid for the open wound on *his* fist!

One EMT warned me repeatedly that my blood pressure was at a dangerously high level of 222 over 102, and said I should be immediately transported to the hospital. She gave me the tape of my blood pressure reading and stated my blood pressure was dangerously high and kept urging me to go to the hospital or I could go into shock and die.

However, hiring a criminal defense attorney for my son and safeguarding my cell phone video of the Deputies' violations took priority over dying. My fear intensified with the thought that the Deputies would take my cell phone and erase all the evidence I had of their criminal violations. This cell phone video was the only proof I had of their brutal beating to my son and conducting an unlawful warrantless search and seizure of the laptop. In addition to all their violations, I recorded the Captain's admission that he didn't have a warrant, or probable cause when they entered our home. Also recorded was the Corporal, who blinded my son, admitting, "This happened to your son because he wouldn't let us come in and search your home."

Robert said, **"Mom, they didn't have a warrant."**

I answered the Corporal, "Without a warrant, I don't blame him for not letting you in." With all this evidence on my cell phone, I could not afford to have them take it from me and erase such legally damning evidence against all of them.

I could feel my blood pressure rising to a dangerous level and was feeling very ill. I told the Deputies I was going to drive myself to the hospital as suggested by the EMT. As I was leaving our home, I looked over at Robert, who was now sitting on the chair only several feet from the front entrance, traumatized by the Deputies' beating and the shock of their invasion into our home. My heart broke to leave him beaten and alone with these officers. I had to leave and drive to the hospital with my cell phone before they took it away from me. I could have died right there with a stroke just from fear alone. I needed to stay alive and focus on saving my son's life! They could have killed him with their brutal assault. Thank God, he was still alive!

While driving to the nearby Waterman Hospital, in Eustis, Florida, I focused on staying calm while praying for Robert. I needed to get him legal help as soon as possible. I left voice messages to three criminal lawyers I found on the internet. One lawyer called back immediately and said he had 30 years' experience in Lake County as a criminal defense attorney. After telling him what happened, he said, "Those Deputies are doing this ass backward. Let them take whatever they want, and I'll have it thrown out." Being told that the Deputies broke the law, I asked if he could sue them for their criminal violations. He said, "I know these Lake County Deputies personally. If I sue them, they'll plant drugs in my car. But I can get someone who can sue them for you. You are very lucky they didn't take your cell phone from you and erase the video." This attorney confirmed the Deputies' reputation in the community of creating their own standards and not following the law.

After he confirmed that the Deputies could take my cell phone and erase it, I detoured from going to the hospital and drove directly to Radio Shack to store my cell phone video to the cloud. On my way to Radio Shack, the second lawyer returned my call. She was from Clermont, Florida, and was a former State Prosecuting Attorney for 3 years and now working 3 years as a criminal defense attorney in her own practice. She said, "The Deputies violated your son's 4th Amendment Rights, and their acts were 100% illegal." Many months later I met her as I was leaving the courthouse after one of my son's hearings. She remembered our conversation and reconfirmed that the acts of the Deputies were against my son's 4th Amendment Rights and were 100% illegal.

I arrived at Radio Shack and had the clerk save my video to the cloud. The third lawyer called, while I was there, and said he was nearby and would meet me at Radio Shack. He confirmed what the other two attorneys said, "The Deputies violated your son's 4th Amendment Rights and this was an illegal search and seizure." All three attorneys said the Deputies could not use any of the evidence they found in my son's closet because it was "Fruit from a poisonous tree." The "fruit of the poisonous tree" doctrine is an extension of the exclusionary rule, which, subject to some exceptions, prevents evidence obtained in violation of the Fourth Amendment from being admitted in a criminal trial. Like the exclusionary rule, the fruit of the poisonous tree doctrine is intended to deter police from using illegal means to obtain evidence.

The third Attorney wanted to come back to the house with me and speak with Robert. When we arrived, Robert was still sitting in the chair by the front door, handcuffed, while still in a frightened and traumatic state from his beating. He was covered with open wounds, cuts and bruises, with his face and both eyes swollen and bruised. He said he couldn't see out of his left eye, and his abdomen and ribs were hurting him badly. He said he was in severe pain. "Mom, I'm thirsty." The officers objected to me going into the kitchen to get him water. Even so, I returned with the glass of water and held it up to my son's mouth, wiped his bloody wounds with several wet paper towels to clean off the blood that was still oozing from his open wounds. Robert said, "Mom while you were away, they called CSI to take pictures of my bedroom, and they are still in there." As one of the CSI photographers was leaving, I asked her to take pictures of my son's bruised body and face for further evidence of their brutal beating. I lifted Robert's torn t-shirt, so the CSI photographer could take pictures of his wounds on his upper body, back and chest as well as his face and eyes that were now badly swollen, bloody and bruised.

For the next 10 hours, they had Robert sitting on a straight chair, next to the front entrance, with his hands still tightly handcuffed, while waiting for the search warrant to be drawn up. The search warrant was signed at 5:44 p.m. and delivered to our home about 6:45 p.m. Then two other Lake County Deputies arrived at around 10:00 pm to drive Robert to the Lake County Detention Center for booking. One of the deputies called, happened to be

Robert's long-time friend. He asked to be replaced as he could not be a part of Robert's arrest.

I not only had to endure watching my son's vicious beating by the three Deputies, I now had to witness his being taken from our home handcuffed and with chains around his waist and ankles, and brought to the Lake County Detention Center. Robert later told me he was crammed into the back seat of their vehicle fetus style and sped away at over 80 miles per hour to the Lake County Detention Center.

Prior to this day, Robert never had any legal problems before these Deputies forced their way into our home, and literally tore our lives apart.

After Robert left, the Captain went into my son's bedroom and came out holding the laptop in his hands, like it was his new-found trophy. He stated twice while holding the laptop towards me and in front of the forensic people who were sitting around the kitchen table examining the electronics, "Here look at the child porn on your son's laptop." I steadfastly refused to look at the laptop. He raised his voice and again demanded, "Here look at the child porn on your son's laptop." He was upset that I wouldn't look at the pictures on the laptop, then shouted sarcastically, "Mrs. O'Hare You bother me!" Such disrespectful behavior coming from a Captain of the Lake County Sheriff's office was appalling. His asking me to look at child pornography was absolutely repulsive.

After the Captain completed the investigation with the Forensic people, they all left. I later read in the Police Report that they charged my son with, "Resisting an officer without violence." A Use-Of-Force Report was never filed by the Lake County Sheriff's office. This Use-Of-Force

Report is required whenever the use of force is used by an officer or officers who are involved. This documentation should include a written report, photographs, a collection of evidence, and recorded statements.

The U.S. Supreme Court has ruled that the Fourth Amendment to the U. S. Constitution prohibits the use of excessive force to effect an arrest or prevent the escape of a suspect unless the police officer reasonably believes that the suspect committed or attempted to commit crimes involving the infliction or threatened infliction of serious physical injury. (Tennessee v. Garner, 471 U.S. 1 (1985).

In my son's case, he was not a threat. He was lying flat on the floor when the Deputies continued to use substantial and excessive police force. This led to the Deputies' criminal liability because Robert was in a prone position and had submitted to handcuffing. In the Rodney King case, officers used substantial force to compel King into a prone position, only the last few blows lead to criminal liability because King had complied with the order to assume a prone position and submit to handcuffing (United States v. Koon, 833 F.Supp. 769, C.D. Cal. 1993, aff'd in part, 518 U.S. 81, 1996).

The Deputies filing a false charge against Robert for resisting an officer without violence in our own home was a false arrest charge. According to Florida State law and Florida Supreme Court Precedent: "A law enforcement officer may not enter a person's home to arrest them for resisting an officer without violence, even if the crime is committed in his presence, regardless of whether the suspect is in the residence when he commits that crime or commits the crime outside the residence and then flees inside." The following case laws support this Florida Supreme Court doctrine: M.J.R. v. State, 715 So.2d 1103

(Fla. 5th DCA 1998), Markus v. State, 160 So.3d 488 (Fla. 5th DCA 2015); Rodriguez v. State, 964 So.2d 833 (Fla. 2d DCA 2007), Connor v. State, 641 So.2d 143 (Fla. 4th DCA 1994), and Jackson v. State, 192 So.3d 541 (Fla. 4th DCA 2016).

In addition to the above, and just as important, the Fourth Amendment to the U.S. Constitution provides that the "Right of the people to be secure in their persons, houses, papers, and effects, against unreasonable searches and seizures, shall not be violated." Robert's 4th Amendment rights were clearly violated. The following U.S. Supreme Court case law supports this: United States v. Allen (U.S. App. Lexis 1467 2d Cir. Jan. 29, 2016). The majority opinion found that "Officers stepping across the threshold to arrest without a warrant violated the Fourth Amendment, and one's civil, and Constitutional rights as well."

By midnight everyone left. Those 12 hours were literally like going through the fires of hell. I was impacted with deep and profound emotional pain that gripped my whole entire being. Not only did I lose my husband and two daughters, just two years earlier, but now seeing my son, the only living member of my family, being led off in handcuffs and chains after being beaten and in the state of shock, was absolutely gut-wrenching. This left my heart literally pounding, aching, and broken. I went to bed, but sleep was not possible. I went back into the living room looking at the floor reliving the terrifying nightmare of seeing my son lying there, crying out with each painful blow to his face, head, and body. To this very day, the memory of witnessing my son's beating is painfully etched in my mind and heart. I was now all alone, with dead silence surrounded me, and completely engulfed in the state of shock. I could not stop crying and praying to God, when suddenly I heard God's powerful voice in my spirit saying, "Virginia, that's how I felt when they crucified My son and nailed Him to the cross." Prior to this moment, I never imagined the depth of God's pain and suffering as he witnessed his own son's brutal assault and crucifixion.

This scene will never diminish until I see justice for my son's life and his constitutional rights being upheld by our Federal Government. I know by the Grace of God, I will see His victory over all this evil and corruption against my son perpetrated by the Lake County Deputies, and the Lake County Judicial System in Tavares, Florida, for violating their **Oath of Office**.

In the State of Florida, ALL Sheriff Deputies, are required to raise their right hand and affirm the following oath. **"I do solemnly swear (or affirm) that I will support, protect, and defend the Constitution and Government of the United States and of the State of Florida; that I am duly qualified to hold office under the Constitution of the State, and that I will well and faithfully perform the duties of (Title of Office) on which I am now about to enter, so help me God."** U.S. Code § 951 - Oath of Office.

OCTOBER 6-9, 2015
ROBERT'S RELEASE ON BOND

The following morning, I spoke with the Clermont lawyer again and told her what the Captain did. She said, "It was illegal for him to want you to look at child pornography. He should know better." Later that night, at around 9:00 p.m., my doorbell rang. I looked through the shutters and saw a tall black man standing outside my front door. Not opening the door, I asked, "Who are you?"

He identified himself as being a news reporter from a local television station. I asked, "How did you get in here; this is a gated community?"

He said, "I can't say."

I told him to put his card through the mail slot in the garage door and leave.

Being alone, my heart pounding with fear, I was too afraid to call the police, after seeing what they did to my son. I feared the police more than I did the tall black man standing outside my front door at 9:00 p.m. at night!

My husband of 45 years was a Real Estate Broker, and a Florida State Licensed Private Investigator. He was also licensed to carry a concealed weapon or firearm. After he passed away, my son kept all his firearms, expensive surveillance equipment, cameras, tripods, etc. in his closet. My husband, Dan Ortung, passed away on September 30, 2013, my daughter Patricia Lynne passed away 55 days later on November 25, 2013. My eldest daughter Anne Marie passed away one year earlier on September 17, 2012. My husband and both my daughters were a total joy to my heart, as my son is and always will be.

The Lake County Detention Center said the only way I could see my son was to write him a letter asking him to give them permission for me to visit him. I did this immediately and sent it out overnight.

On the fourth day of Robert's incarceration, a bail bondsman called and said, "Mrs. O'Hare, I'm here with your son. He is worried about you." He said he could have Robert out on bail and asked if he could come to my home for the payment of $13,500. I said, "Yes, come right over."

When he arrived, he said, "I have an attorney you can hire for your son. He is one of the ten best criminal attorneys in the state of Florida." I told him I was hiring a former prosecutor, who was coming to my home that evening. He said, "No, I'll call him right now, and he will come to your home today to see you."

A few hours later, the Bail Bondsman brought the Attorney to my home. He confirmed what the other three attorneys had said, "The Deputies' forcing their way into your home was a violation of your son's 4th Amendment Rights, and their search and seizure without a warrant was illegal. Whatever they get, will be 'fruit from a poisonous tree.' They cannot use it, because there was no legal reason for them to force their way into your home. There were no exigent circumstances present of any crime they could see, hear, or smell, and there was no contraband in plain view. Therefore, I'm confident they will be defeated on their violating your son's 4th Amendment Rights."

Several months later, the Corporal who stepped over the threshold of our home without a search warrant testified during a deposition that he could not view the inside of our home on October 5, 2015, because he could not see through the shutters on the front door and windows. This confirmed what the Lawyer said that the Deputies had no exigent circumstances to justify forcing their way into our home without a search warrant.

Both the Attorney and the Bail Bondsman promised they could have my son home that evening. On his representation that my son would be home that evening, I hired the Attorney. At 11:00 p.m. on October 9, 2015, the Attorney brought my son home and said, "I feel better about this case after meeting your son. He looks wholesome and is good looking and well mannered. He doesn't look anything like the charges the Deputies made against him!"

I was more than elated to see my son after his being brutally beaten by the Deputies and in jail for 4 days. This was the first time in his 54 years he had ever been in jail. He had no prior criminal record, lived his life as a God-fearing Christian, and was self-employed as a house painter and also worked in our family's real estate business. He never drank, smoked, or taken any drugs. My friends often told me how lucky I was to have such a close-knit family. I was proud of all three of my children. When Robert came home from the Lake County Detention Center, he said, "Mom, I prayed to God repeatedly for hours to let me come home and sleep in my own bed by 11:30 p.m." God answered my son's prayers, he was home and in his own bed by 11:30 p.m.

After bringing Robert home, our attorney advised us to leave Mt. Dora immediately and go to our other home in Ft. Lauderdale, to be safe and away from any further harm from the Lake County Deputies. He said he knew of their reputation and wanted me to leave as soon as possible.

We stayed at our home in Ft. Lauderdale for five months, before returning to our home in Mt. Dora to pursue a criminal complaint against the Lake County Sheriff's Deputies with the Internal Affairs Bureau.

BLINDNESS
TRAGEDY AT THE HANDS
OF A SHERIFF'S DEPUTY

Soon after Robert was released on bond, we were able to see a Retina Macula specialist. The doctor surgically removed a scleral buckle in Robert's left eye. This buckle had been surgically implanted one year earlier to secure a torn retina. The Corporal's beating to his head and face with repeated blunt blows to his eyes, caused the buckle around the retina to dislodge and wrinkle, leaving him not only blind but in unending pain from the dislodged buckle.

The removal of the scleral buckle relieved some of the excruciating pain Robert was experiencing, but he was still without his vision in his left eye.

After several weeks of healing from his eye surgery, Robert visited the Miami Eye Institute for the second surgical procedure to attempt to restore his vision. Unfortunately, the surgeon was unable to restore any vision to his left eye. The surgical report indicated that "Robert O'Hare's blindness was caused by a 'trauma' to his left eye." That trauma occurred during his beating by the Corporal from the Lake County Sheriff's Office. A third surgery was to take place in the next ninety days. Due to a legal curve-ball that no one could have foreseen, the third surgery was never performed.

During this same ten-month period, of his being on Bail, Robert's 6th Amendment Right to a Speedy Trial was continually blocked by the State's Prosecutor. I hired two additional lawyers for Robert to combat the corruption Robert was facing in the Lake County Judicial System. They filed a Motion to Compel States' Discovery. In a criminal trial, the prosecution MUST release any and all evidence that it has against the defendant, to his attorney. Failure to do so is a violation of the law, but unfortunately, it is a common tactic used by corrupt Prosecutors to stall the proceedings. This led Robert's Lawyers to file a second Motion to Compel Discovery. A Motion to Compel Discovery is used to ask the court to order the non-complying party to produce the documentation or information requested, and/or to sanction the non-complying party for their failure to comply with the discovery requests.

In Robert's case, the Prosecutor conspired with the Sheriff's Department for 300 days before the Judge issued the second Order to Compel. This delay was an obvious violation of Robert's 6th Amendment Rights. The Judge never sanctioned the Prosecutor's failure to comply with the first Motion to Compel.

INTERNAL AFFAIRS
THE CRIMINAL COMPLAINT AGAINST
THE SHERIFF'S DEPUTIES

Five months after leaving our Mt. Dora home, and witnessing daily Robert's suffering from the Deputies' beating, I felt compelled to make a formal criminal complaint against the Sheriff's Deputies to the Lake County Internal Affairs Department in Tavares, Florida. I spoke with the Internal Affairs Investigator who was anxious to hear the details of my complaint against the Deputies. He wanted to see me as soon as possible. I met with him and his Supervisor, at their office the following day. After our meeting, they both wanted to interview my son, which was on the following day.

The next morning, the two Investigators arrived at our home to meet with Robert. They asked him to tell them exactly what happened. Robert stated, "Three Deputies came to our front door and asked if they could search our home. I asked if they had a search warrant? The deputy said, 'No, we do not have a search warrant.' I told them, to get a search warrant and I'll call my lawyer. As I was closing the door, the three deputies forced the door open, entered our home, punched me in the stomach, knocked me to the floor. Then one officer started kicking me repeatedly 10-12 times to my ribs and stomach on my left side, while the other officer, on my right side, on one knee, was repeatedly cuffing me to my head, face, and eyes. I could not see out of my left eye. He blinded me! The third deputy was bodily holding down my ankles while the other two officers, on each side of me, kept beating me. I was in terrible pain. My mother walked into the room and was yelling at them to stop beating me. They wouldn't stop hitting and kicking me." My son asked if they would take a lie detector's test on him and the Deputies because he said, "I'm telling the truth." They never took a lie detector's test on the Lake County Sheriff's Deputies.

The Internal Affairs Department continued to investigate my criminal complaint and eventually interviewed all the Deputies that were in our home on October 5, 2015. In the official Internal Affairs report, one of the Deputies swore under oath, "We thought going into defendant's home (O'Hare) without a warrant would work like it did all the other times." In other words, these Lake County Sheriff's Deputies made it a practice to violate the law anytime they could get away with it.

A full investigative Lake County Internal Affairs report was given to the Prosecutor for his review. Instead of acknowledging the evidence in the report of the Deputies' criminal violations to Robert's 4th Amendment rights and Federal Statute 42 U.S.C. § 1983, he conspired with the Deputies to create more damning lies, false allegations, and bogus charges against Robert.

The State Prosecutor was given a copy of this Internal Affairs criminal report and failed to act on the Deputies' violations. He and the Lake County Sherriff dismissed the criminal complaint as being "unfounded."

AUGUST 17, 2016
THE PROSECUTOR'S SECOND SET OF CHARGES

Wednesday, August 17, 2016, started out the same way most days did. Robert had been out on bond for a little over 10 months, and we were living in our second home in Bay Colony, an upscale, gated waterfront community in Ft. Lauderdale, FL. We left our home around noon to run a few errands and have lunch. We were about to pull on to the street when I noticed a large, dark blue, SUV starting to tailgate us very closely. We had no idea who this was, and I feared that they might hit our vehicle.

I told Robert to drive down the next dead-end street to see if the vehicle would follow us. It not only followed us but drove past us and made a U-turn at the end of the cul-de-sac street, then sped head on towards our car. To avoid a head-on collision, Robert immediately turned our car to the right side of the road and stopped just over the swale of our neighbor's lawn, to avoid a head-on collision. Just then, another vehicle came speeding down the street towards our stopped car and smashed his large SUV into the passenger's side of our vehicle. The driver jumped out of his vehicle, pointed his gun at us with his arms shaking nervously back and forth. Then, for no reason, he used a sharp iron instrument and smashed the rear window of our parked car, splattering glass all over the inside of the car.

Just then several other cars came onto the street, also unmarked with no lights or sirens. Then a voice command came from the first vehicle that was tailgating us, "Put your hands up in the air!" Robert immediately put up his left hand up over his head, at the officer's command, while keeping his right hand on the stick shift, trying to put it in a park position. The stick shift was stuck and difficult to put into the park position due to the impact of the officer's large SUV driving onto the back wheel on the passenger's side of our vehicle. I was later informed by a mechanic that the vehicle smashing into the rear tire bent the axle, which made it difficult for Robert to move the stick shift to the park position. Robert said, "The stick shift is stuck!" After several tries, Robert finally got it into the park position.

The U. S. Marshal told Robert to get out of the car and lie flat on the pavement. Robert unfastened his seat belt and laid face down on the hot pavement. When he did this, one of the Police Officers abruptly pulled Robert's right arm up in the air, lifting him bodily off the pavement, then dropped him flat on his face on the concrete pavement. From this officer's brutal act, Robert landed face down, scratching his face, arms, and knees on the hot pavement with his left arm underneath his chest. Just then the officer who smashed his SUV into our vehicle, laid across Robert's left shoulder and said, "Put your hands behind your back." Robert put his right hand behind his back, but with the officer's full body weight laying on Robert's left shoulder, and his left arm underneath his chest it was difficult to do this. I heard this officer yelling, for no reason, "Stop resisting, stop resisting." Robert was not resisting! He was lying flat on the pavement in a submissive, prone position ready to be handcuffed.

Despite the pain he was in, Robert forced his left

hand from underneath his chest, with the weight of the officer still on his shoulder, causing his arm and hand to be scratched and bloodied from the abrasive concrete pavement. He did this to comply with the officer's command. I took pictures on my cell phone that shows cuts and bruises with blood on his arm, face, hand, and knees while complying with the officers' command to put his left arm behind his back. He never once resisted the officer without violence as the Officers falsely charged.

Instantly, my mind flashed back to the scene of the Lake County Deputies brutally beating my son, on October 5, 2015, and falsely accusing him of resisting an officer without violence. Now, watching another incident of brutal police force being used on him again, ten months later, was heart wrenching. I yelled and said, "He is not resisting! He cannot get his hand behind his back with your 200 lbs. of body weight laying on his shoulder. I'm going to sue you for using excessive force on my son and crashing into my parked car." This Officer filed a false Resisting an Officer Charge against Robert to justify smashing his SUV into our parked car. When I lodged an Internal Affairs complaint against him, I was told this was his first week on the job.

The U.S. Marshal said he had a warrant from Lake County. I asked him for a copy of the warrant. He replied, "I don't have a copy of the warrant."

I immediately called Robert's Attorney on my cell phone and had him speak with the U.S. Marshal in charge. He told our attorney, "We are charging Robert with resisting an officer without violence because we used force." The officer admitted they were the ones who used force, not Robert, yet they charged him with resisting an officer. They filed the false charge of resisting an officer without violence, to justify their using excessive police force on my son, and smashing into my car, then breaking out the back window.

We later received a sworn affidavit from the U.S. Marshal stating that the fact they used force during the arrest is enough of a reason to charge Robert with "Resisting an officer without violence." This fabricated charge invalidated my son's $25,000 bond in Lake County, which I had just paid for only four days earlier.

As they were putting Robert into their vehicle, he informed them that he was experiencing extreme intestinal pain, and was suffering from painful intestinal bleeding problems. The U.S. Marshals took my son to the Emergency Room at the Broward Health Medical Center in Ft. Lauderdale, Florida for observation. The Broward Health Medical Report stated that my son had pre-cancerous bleeding polyps and should be seen by a Gastro-Intestinal (GI) Doctor within three days and must have a colonoscopy.

Upon being released from the Broward Health Medical Center, Robert was transported back to the Lake County Detention Center.

PROSECUTORIAL MISCONDUCT
A NIGHTMARE WORSENS

At this point, the corruption and the violations of Robert's civil and constitutional rights created a travesty of justice that Robert, or no other human being, should have to live through.

First, Robert's second arrest charges on August 17, 2016, were based on Broward County and the U.S. Marshal's false charge of resisting an officer without violence.

Second, the Lake County Prosecutor deliberately stalled Robert's Forensic Attorney for five months before allowing him to examine any of the State's Forensic evidence.

Third, the Prosecutor delayed producing Discovery Files to the Defense Attorney for ten months. He ignored the first Motion to Compel order from the Judge, and it was only with a second Motion to Compel issued by the Judge, that the State Attorney's office finally turned over the required documents to the Defense Attorney, which was after 300 days from the first request. **The Prosecutor was NEVER sanctioned by the Judge for his non-compliance to the first Motion to Compel!**

Fourth, the new charges of "Resisting an officer

without violence" filed by the U.S. Marshals Service in Broward County, triggered the revocation of his Bond in Lake County. This caused Robert to be incarcerated without the benefit of medical treatment for his impaired vision or his malignant colon cancer. Plus, there were additional legal fees for Robert's representation of these new bogus charges.

Robert's second arrest charges, made by the Lake County Prosecutor, falsely stated that Robert delivered two "toy" Jukeboxes to a neighbor in 2011 or 2012 with lenses in them for spying. The Prosecutor admitted to a news reporter that he assumed Robert delivered two toy Jukeboxes to the wrong neighbor thinking the wrong neighbor would deliver the Jukeboxes to the right neighbor. The Prosecutor released this bogus story to the news media, which was spread worldwide, and is forever posted on the Internet!

In order to give his Jukebox story credibility, the Lake County Prosecutor conspired with the Detective from the Lake County Sheriff's Cyber Sex Unit to falsely state, under oath during Robert's Bond Hearing, that he received information from a Broward County Officer, who told him that Robert O'Hare had delivered two empty Jukeboxes to a family in Broward County in 2016. This Broward County Officer was the same one who smashed into my vehicle and filed a false resisting charge against my son. I immediately filed another complaint against the Broward County Officer with Broward County Internal Affairs. The Investigator confirmed that the Officer never stated this Jukebox story to the Lake County Detective, and offered their Police Report as further proof that no Jukeboxes were EVER mentioned on the Police Report.

Prior to Robert's trial in Broward County for the resisting charges, his Attorney was in pre-trial negotiations with the Broward County Prosecutor to drop the resisting charges. He said they were making headway towards the charges being dropped so Robert's bond could be reinstated in Lake County. The Lake County Prosecutor, who conspired with the Lake County Detective to lie about the Broward Officer now was trying to vindictively sabotage my son's chance for having the false resisting charges dropped in Broward County. He called the Broward County Prosecutor and told her that Robert was a flight risk and a danger to the community and he sent her an audio recording of one of my conversations with my son during one of our monitored jail calls.

Upon receiving this audio, the Broward County Prosecutor said she wanted to meet with me before making her decision. Knowing the reinstatement of my son's bond was predicated upon her dropping those resisting charges in Broward County, I was more than pleased to have the opportunity to meet with her and give her my eyewitness account of the events of the U.S. Marshals' false resisting charges.

During this meeting, she told me about the call she had received from the Lake County Prosecutor. She said after she listened to his audio, she would let my attorney know of her decision.

She said, "I heard you read part of the new book you're writing while you spoke to your son on the jail phone. I wanted you to continue reading more of it. It sounded very interesting. You must have done a lot of research for the book. I want to purchase it when it comes out."

She asked what the name of the book would be. I

told her, ***"Virginia O'Hare Documents God's Laws vs. Man's Laws."*** She also wanted the name of the first book I had published a year earlier. I told her, ***"Virginia O'Hare's Trials, Triumphs, and Vision from God."*** She said she wanted to purchase that book as well. I told her both books were written and inspired by God's Holy Spirit, with Divine warnings of disasters coming upon our generation, with the end of days just around the corner!

On the audio she was given by the Lake County Prosecutor, I was recorded as saying, "Robert, when this is over, we are going to travel around the world."

Robert's response was, "My preference is to ride my motorbike through the Blue Ridge Mountains."

That recording was taken completely out of context. However, the Broward County Prosecutor opted to ignore all the evidence submitted to her during her pre-trial negotiations with Robert's Attorney and went with the Lake County Prosecutor's false characterization of Robert being a flight risk and a danger to the community. **I told her, through tears, "You will lose this case when it goes to trial!"**

Her decision meant that Robert would be denied bail on the "resisting" charges and remain in custody at the Lake County Detention Center. This would result in Robert's first bond for $13,500, stemming from the original arrest on October 5, 2015, being revoked, and Robert's 2nd bond for $25,000 for the 2nd charge on August 17, 2016, being revoked as well.

On November 9, 2016, Robert was transported back to Ft. Lauderdale for his scheduled trial date set in Broward County for the "Resisting an officer without violence charge."

The Jury Trial in Broward County

During the Jury Selection Process, both the Prosecutor and Robert's Attorney found the prospective jurors to be totally unacceptable and blocked all the jurors. The new trial date was rescheduled for November 29th, 2016 to pick a new set of jurors. This meant that Robert would return to the Paul Rein Detention Center, in Pompano Beach, FL for the next three weeks awaiting the new trial date. For the first time in his 55 years, Robert would spend Thanksgiving in a jail cell. For his Thanksgiving meal, Robert was given 4 slices of white bread with baloney. This was one of the regular meals on the inmate's lunch menu.

On the morning of November 29, 2016, I drove to the Broward County Courthouse, anxious to see my son for the first time since he was incarcerated on August 25, 2016. I was blessed with a parking space right next to the courthouse building and had only a few minutes to get to the courtroom on the 4th floor before the trial began. When I stepped out of my car onto the sidewalk in front of the courthouse, I accidentally tripped on a broken protruding edge of the sidewalk and fell on my hands and knees with copies of legal documents for my son's trial flying in all directions from the gusty winds. Retrieving all the documents alone was impossible. The papers were blown in all directions. Hurting badly from the fall, I got up and tried to get as many of the documents as I could. A lady and a man came to my rescue and gathered up every one of the documents.

I hurried into the courthouse with my papers all disarranged, but back in my folder. I stopped in the restroom to clean and bandage my wounds before going into the courtroom. The Broward County Prosecutor came into the restroom and said, "Did your attorney call and tell you the trial has been canceled again and rescheduled." My heart sank, as I was trying to catch my breath after the fall and rushing to be on time for Robert's trial.

Disappointed, I asked, "To when?"

She said, "I don't want to tell you."

I asked, "Please!"

She said, "To January 24, 2017."

I asked, "Why?"

She said, "Because your attorney was too sick with the flu to try your son's case."

I thought, "This cannot be happening!" I was bloody with bruises on my hands and knees, trying hard to hold back the sadness of not being able to see my son and dealing with the pain from the fall.

The Prosecutor said, "Let's sit on a bench, in the hallway." We spoke for about a half hour.

I asked her, "Why are you doing this to my son? You have all the evidence you need to prove he was not resisting those officers. Those lying officers have caused my son to lose his bond!"

Her answer was, "I'm just doing my job."

This delay meant I would spend Christmas and New Year's Eve alone without my son, the only living member left of my family. Fortunately, friends invited me to celebrate the holidays with their family for lunch, and other friends invited me to dinner with their family members.

I spoke almost daily to my son during the ten weeks

he was incarcerated at the Paul Rein Detention Center while waiting for his new trial date. On a positive note, the Paul Rein Detention Center is a far superior facility, and more humane than the Lake County Detention Center. It has no bars, only doors on the dorm-like rooms that housed the inmates. This facility offered sports activities, bible studies, and Robert was allowed to go outside daily in the fenced yard. It is a very well operated facility. I met three times with the nursing administrator, to let her know of my son's pre-cancerous bleeding polyps to coordinate his medical treatments. She said their facility scored 100% by the State of Florida for the operation of their facility. After reviewing Robert's medical reports from the Broward Health Medical Center Report and two letters from two GI specialists, she said she would do everything she could to get Robert a GI Doctor as soon as possible.

I prayed with my son daily during our monitored jail calls. I put extra money in his account for commissary orders, so he could buy what he needed and give to the other inmates who were not so fortunate. He did this on a regular basis. He told me how much they appreciated this because they did not have the funds to buy from the commissary, and were tired of eating the same meals, with no variations in the menu. He said, "Mom, the younger inmates call me Pops."

One night at 8:00 p.m., Robert called me and said, "Mom, put on your bathrobe, we're going for a walk down our street as we used to every night when I was home." Surprised and happy, I put my bathrobe over my nightgown and walked outside while talking with my son on my cell phone. I was blessed with our ongoing conversations, which were always on world events, especially current breaking news, and how they related to Bible prophecy. Even though I walked alone down the street then back to our two-story colonial home, I could actually feel his presence being there with me even though we were only talking on the phone. Thereafter, we did this on a regular basis. Those walks were truly a blessing and a joy for me to take while talking with my son on the jail phone.

I used to take walks with my husband and my daughters before they passed away. We never ran out of conversations. We all loved keeping abreast of world affairs and tying them together with Bible prophecy. One evening while we were talking on the phone, and I was walking alone down our street, Robert asked me, "Mom, look up at the stars in the sky. Do you see the moon and the three bright stars next to it?"

I said, "Yes, Rob, I do."

"That's good because I can see the same from my third-floor cell window, the moon, and the three stars." Then he said, "Because it is New Year's Eve, I want you to go to the Pompano Isles Buffet tomorrow." My husband, Rob, and my daughters and I dined at that restaurant for years. Coincidentally, friends invited me to join their family to celebrate New Year's Day with them at Pompano Isles Buffet. Other dear friends invited me to their home that evening for a home cooked dinner. My son was happy to hear I was going to our favorite restaurant and we both knew that God orchestrated the entire holiday. Robert said, "Just because I'm suffering in here doesn't mean you have to as well."

The third rescheduled jury trial in Broward County commenced on January 24, 2017. Seeing my son for the first time, since his arrest on August 25, 2016, was heart-wrenching. He was led into the courtroom with chains around his hands, waist, and ankles. His body looked thin, frail, and sickly. His cheekbones protruding from his face showed the excessive amount of weight he lost during his first and only time in his life of being incarcerated. As a mother, witnessing all this ongoing corruption in the Lake County Judicial System, and now my son facing these false charges made against him by Broward County Officers was disturbing to the core of my being.

During the two-day jury trial in Broward County, the three U.S. Marshals nervously testified with inconsistent stories to support their false charges of "Resisting an officer without violence." The Broward County Prosecutor, without any credible evidence tried to defend and support the three lying U.S. Marshals' testimony. She was sorely losing the battle to convince the Jurors and the Judge. This Broward County Judge was honorable, decent and fair. He followed the law to the "T." The Lake County Judge was just the opposite. He was biased, unfair in his rulings and did not follow the law. This fact was confirmed by Robert's four Lawyers in Central Florida, who found it difficult to deal with all the corruption in the Lake County Judicial System.

When I took the stand and testified as an eyewitness that my son was not resisting the officer, and was submissive and compliant. The Prosecutor tried in vain to "impeach" my testimony. She took the evidence she had received during the pre-trial negotiations with Robert's lawyer and tried to present it to the Judge. Robert's Attorney objected, saying that according to the rule of law, it is not permissible to take evidence submitted during pretrial negotiations into a court of law. He added, "I'm surprised that she would do such a thing, she knows better."

The Judge overruled her Motion to Impeach my testimony. Despite overruling her and allowing my testimony to stand as an eyewitness for my son, she kept insisting I be impeached. She wanted the Judge to hear my taped conversation with my son that was provided to her by the Lake County Prosecutor which was taken completely out of context. The Judge dismissed the jurors and me from the courtroom and listened to the taped conversation. My son later told me that after the Judge heard the taped conversation, he scolded the Prosecutor and said, "Did you not hear what I said, 'Overruled!' Stop badgering this 80-year-old woman. I'm not changing my ruling. You are not going to impeach her as a witness!"

I went back into the courtroom and finished my testimony as an eyewitness to the U.S. Marshal's false charge that my son resisted an officer during their arrest. Thereafter, my son testified and told the Jurors exactly what happened, which was supported by all the prima facie evidence. Shortly thereafter, the jurors left the courtroom for deliberation.

During the two-day trial, the jurors listened carefully and reviewed all the evidence presented to them: (1) Testimony of the three U.S. Marshals, (2) Robert's testimony (3) My eyewitness testimony (4) Pictures of the police inflicted wounds on my son's face, neck, arms hands, and body (5) Pictures of the Broward County Officer's SUV after smashing into my car on the passenger's side, and breaking the back window for no apparent reason (6) The cost of repairs and replacement for my damaged vehicle, and (7) Robert's Attorney's sworn statement from the U.S. Marshal's admission to him stating, "Because we used force, that's why we charged Robert with resisting an officer without violence." With all this evidence, the jury returned after less than 10 minutes of deliberation, with a verdict in favor of my son, "Not guilty."

After the Broward County Jury came back with a "not guilty" verdict, the Prosecutor came over to me and said, "Congratulations! I wish you and your son peace; I know you both have been put through hell!" I deeply appreciated her kind and heartfelt words.

My son and I were elated over the verdict. I thanked God and complemented our Broward Attorney for a job well done. He said, "Don't thank me, I didn't win this case for your son. Your son won his own case by telling the whole truth most thoroughly with all the details that were supported by the evidence. Your son was most eloquent!" I, too, was impressed and proud of Robert's testimony, his incredible strength of character, and living through and triumphing over the false charge made by the three U.S. Marshals.

Only God could give such strength and endurance for Robert to live through all these serious violations committed against him by Law Enforcement Officers in both Lake County and Broward County Florida. Fortunately, my son had his day in court, and the Judge and Jury ruled in his favor against the lying U.S. Marshals.

Several months later, I was in a restaurant located by the Ft. Lauderdale Intercoastal Waterway. I was having lunch with my friend, a Senior Vice President of a local bank. We were enjoying our meal and celebrating our 30-year-old friendship, when the former Broward County Prosecutor, came over to our table. She hugged me and said, "You don't know how often I think of you. In fact, I think about you all the time. I'm a mother of a son and can identify with what you are going through."

She wanted to know how my son and I were doing. I told her, "Keeping our faith in God!"

She said, "I don't hug anyone, but I am hugging you."

I reminded her, "I told you my son was going to win his case."

My friend said, "Virginia was born with a gift of seeing things before they happen and is 100% accurate."

We wished each other well. The meeting was a fine moment of closure for both of us.

The U.S. Marshal's false charges of resisting an officer without violence, caused my son to go through all these dreadful experiences including being ostracized from our upscale gated community. The U.S. Marshal's arrest of Robert on August 17, 2016, was made in Bay Colony, an upscale, gated community on the waterfront in Ft. Lauderdale, FL where we had maintained a second residence since 2011.

The U.S. Marshal filing of the false charges led the lawyer for the homeowner's association to forbid my son to reside in our community because his arrest was considered a "nuisance," which is not allowed in the By-Laws.

This issue faded away immediately when my son was found innocent of the charges by a Broward County Jury. In fact, the Captain of the Guards, said to me, "Virginia, with your faith in God, I know that Robert will be free and home with you soon. I'm praying for you both." The Association asked me to run for one of their offices. I declined in lieu of spending my time exonerating my son from those horrible and false charges in Lake County, Florida.

The financial expense to defend Robert against the U. S. Marshal's false charge of "Resisting an officer without violence," was not only costly but damning to my son's case in Lake County. It gave the Lake County Prosecutor a foothold to keep my son unjustly incarcerated without his constitutional due process rights and medical treatment for his stage 3 or 4 malignant colon cancer.

After winning a "Not Guilty" jury verdict in Broward County on January 26, 2017, Robert's lawyers were hopeful that the Lake County Judge would now reinstate his $25,000 bond in Lake County because he had no LEGAL reason not to.

Robert was transported back to the Lake County Detention Center, to await his Motion to Reinstate his bond. This was the day before he was scheduled to see the GI Doctor at the Paul Rein Pompano Beach Detention Center.

The Bond Hearing

During my son's Bond Hearing on February 24, 2017, the Lake County Prosecutor lied to the Judge and said Robert was a danger to the community and a flight risk, and his bond should not be reinstated.

The Judge ignored the fact that Robert had been out on bail for 10 months and was not a flight risk or a threat to any community. When the Judge asked me about Robert being a flight risk. I said, "Your honor, I told my son, when this is all over, I want us to travel around the world. This is something that I've always wanted to do but never did in my 80 years of life. Those were not Robert's words, but mine. I was trying to comfort my son with having this to look forward to. He is not a flight risk, or a risk to any community."

The Prosecutor purposefully had taken our monitored jail calls completely out of context in front of the Judge and never produced any evidence to support his false allegations not even an audio CD of that conversation.

The Prosecutor didn't stop there with his character assassination on my son. He called as his "star" witness, the Deputy who brutally and viciously assaulted my son during his unlawful warrantless entry into our home on October 5, 2015.

When the Prosecutor questioned this Deputy about listening to my conversations with my son on our monitored jail calls, and giving his opinion of our calls, Robert's trial Lawyer immediately objected to the Deputy giving a third-party hearsay testimony, without first producing an audio CD of the jail phone calls. The Judge ordered the Prosecutor to give a copy of the phone calls between my son and me to Robert's attorney. The hearing was canceled and rescheduled for the following month. This delay caused my son to have to wait another month without any medical treatment for his pain and suffering from malignant colon cancer. He was dealing with the constant issues of dealing with intestinal bleeding and severe bowel problems as a result of the 70% blockage in his colon. I looked over to my son, who was pale and sickly looking having lost over 40 lbs. This showed on his face and entire body. He took a deep breath of disappointment that this would delay his medical treatment for yet another month.

As this Deputy exited the courtroom, he walked past me with a smirk on his face. He was wearing the same beige shoes, he wore when he brutally and repeatedly kicked my son in his stomach and ribs, while Robert laid defenseless in a prone, submissive position on the floor. I thought, "Dear God, how do we fight against all this corruption, conspiracy, bias, and injustice against my son?" God's powerful words to my spirit were, "Virginia, no weapons forged against your son will prosper, and there will be judgment on those who did this to him."

Prior to the next Bond Hearing on March 20, 2017, the Lake County Prosecutor told Robert's lead Attorney, "I'm going to put your client away for life." After the Bond hearing, the Lead Attorney told me, **"Virginia, your son was set up at the Bond Hearing by the Prosecutor and Deputies. You need to immediately hire a Civil Rights Attorney to save your son's life."**

At the rescheduled Bond Hearing, the Prosecutor never brought up the taped jail phone conversations between my son and me. He knew he took those conversations out of context and with the taped conversation, he could not prove his false allegations. He didn't have his Star witness, the Deputy who beat my son testify either. However, he did have two neighbors from our Loch Leven community testify.

The first neighbor said, "I saw Robert taking walks at 9:00 p.m. with his mother on the street in front of their home." These walks were something I did with my family on a regular basis.

The other neighbor said, "I close my shades at night for privacy."

With these two statements, the Lake County Prosecutor tried to convince the Judge that my son was a "danger" to our neighborhood, where we lived for 17 years with no problems whatsoever. Later, the Prosecutor told Robert's Lead Attorney, "I let Mrs. O'Hare's neighbors listen to her jail calls with her son."

The Prosecutor could see that the hearsay evidence presented a month earlier, and the testimony of these two neighbors was not going to be enough to convince the Judge to continue to deny bail. He needed something "big" to keep Robert from being released on bond. This entire case had become a "personal crusade" for this Prosecutor. He wanted to prevent any evidence about the illegal, warrantless search by the Deputies and the excessive, brutal force they used on Robert from coming out, which would destroy his entire case against convicting Robert.

The Prosecution's next witness was a Lake County Sheriff's Detective from their Cyber Sex Unit. The Prosecutor had conspired with this witness to lie under oath and create a story that would paint Robert as a danger to the community. During his testimony, the Detective falsely stated, "I was told by a Broward County Officer that Robert O'Hare delivered two empty jukeboxes to a family in Broward County, FL In 2016." I saw Robert, shaking his head in total disbelief at this false statement coming from the Detective.

Ironically, this Broward County Officer was the one I previously filed an Internal Affairs Complaint against for smashing into my parked car during Robert's arrest on August 17, 2016, and the same one who falsely accused Robert of Resisting an Officer without Violence. Fortunately, a Broward County Jury found Robert "Not Guilty" of those bogus charges.

The main purpose of the Prosecutor's collusion with this Detective to make this false statement, under oath, at the Bond Hearing, was to support his own bogus charges made seven months earlier. The Prosecutor knowingly alleged that Robert delivered two jukeboxes to a family in our Mt. Dora subdivision in 2011 or 2012, with lenses in them for spying. He gave this ridiculous story to the news media stating it was his assumption that Robert delivered two jukeboxes to the wrong neighbor thinking the wrong neighbor would deliver the jukeboxes to the right neighbor. His "assumption theory," was spread all over the country and is now permanently recorded on the internet.

During a court recess, I asked Robert's Trial Attorney, "If I can prove the Detective lied under oath about the Broward County Officer telling him that Robert gave two jukeboxes to a family in Broward County in 2016, what would that do?"

The Attorney said, "If he lied about something like that under oath, that would be lethal against the Detective."

That was all I needed to hear. I immediately phoned the Broward County Officer's Supervisor, who I had spoken to previously. He denied that any such statement was ever made by his Officer, to the Lake County Detective, of Robert giving two jukeboxes to a family in Broward County in 2016. He further added, "We don't have any jukeboxes on our police report as proof of this. You have a copy of that Police Report, you can see for yourself there are no jukeboxes reported. If that jukebox story was true, it would have to be put on the Police Report. We just don't make up stories like that and put them in the Police Report."

I have a copy of the Broward County Police Report, and it confirms what the Broward County Sergeant and the Investigator of Internal affairs stated. There was no mention whatsoever of any Jukeboxes being given by Robert to a Broward County family on the police report.

The Broward County Internal Affairs Investigator confirmed, "The Officer did not say anything to the Lake County Detective about two Jukeboxes being delivered to a family in Broward County by Robert O'Hare."

Unfortunately, the conspiracy between the Prosecutor and the Detective worked, because the Lake County Judge, on March 20, 2017, denied reinstating my son's $25,000 bond, and wrote on his Order that Robert would be a danger to the Loch Leven community if released on Bond. The Judge stated in his ruling; he used witness evidence submitted to him at the Bond Hearing.

Robert's defense team continued with its preparation to fight the original charges stemming from the unlawful warrantless entry and search of our home. This case against the Deputies' criminal violations to Robert's 4th Amendment rights and Federal Statute 42 U.S.C. § 1983, was established by law. Therefore, according to Robert's 4th Amendment Rights, any evidence discovered during the Deputies illegal search could not be used against Robert in a trial.

All that was needed was for the Judge to rule in favor of Robert's Motion to Suppress, which was based solely on the Deputies violation of Robert's 4th Amendment Rights, as fully outlined in the U.S. Constitution and Supreme Court case law. A Motion to Suppress is simply a formal request by a defendant that the judge exclude certain evidence from trial. In addition to the 4th Amendment violation, the Deputies' brutal beating violated Federal Statute 42 U.S.C. § 1983.

The Lake County Prosecutor knew, based on the facts at hand, that the Motion to Suppress was likely to be granted. He knew that all evidence from the illegal search of our home could not be used and that he would have to dismiss the charges against Robert and my son would be set free. This was when he began the highly unethical practice of postponing this inevitable Motion to Suppress Hearing from occurring. Listening to all my monitored telephone calls with my son and hearing first hand that he could die at any moment with his stage three or four malignant colon cancer advancing, he stalled five Motions to Suppress Hearing dates for a period close to eight months: The original Hearing date was set on April 2017 then canceled and rescheduled for June 2017; then canceled and rescheduled for August 10, 2017; then canceled and rescheduled for September 5, 2017; then canceled and rescheduled for October 4, 2017; then canceled and rescheduled on November 8, 2017.

On November 8, 2017, his prosecutorial misconduct continued. The live video taken from my cell phone of the Deputies' violations, was given to the Prosecutor to give to the Judge pre-hearing and for him to bring it to the Hearing. There was no logistical reason for this not occurring because his office was next door to the Judge's office in the Court House Building.

However, upon reviewing the video, the Prosecutor knew this was damning evidence to his case, which showed the deputies' unlawful entry, illegal search and seizure, and the aftermath of their severe beating to Robert. The Prosecutor intentionally showed up at the Motion to Suppress without it. This was not only an egregious act of prosecutorial misconduct, but it was 100% intentional.

Fortunately, Robert's Trial Attorney suspected that the Prosecutor would not bring the video to the hearing as he promised, and had a copy of the video file to present to the Judge. This left the Judge little or no chance to ignore the horrendous unlawful acts of the deputies.

We had to wait another month to receive the Judge's ruling on the Suppression Hearing. On December 4, 2017, the Judge wrote, "The court observes that no justification was offered as to why police did not seek a warrant prior to approaching defendant's house for the knock and talk. Multiple search warrants had already been granted in the course of the investigation, nor does there appear to have been any particular time constraint. Had officers simply sought a warrant before entering the defendant's residence instead of afterward, they would have avoided an entirely unnecessary expenditure of both judicial and police resources. Separately from whether the tactics employed by police were legal, they were clearly unwise and unnecessary."

However, despite all this evidence, the Judge added to his Order, in error, a Doctrine of Inevitable Discovery, that does not exist in the Florida Supreme Court Case Law, Rodriguez vs. State of Florida. This non-lawful Doctrine of Inevitable Discovery exonerated the deputies warrantless search and seizure and caused Robert to lose his Motion to Suppress unjustly.

During the proceedings, Robert's Trial Attorney had given the Judge a copy of Florida Supreme Court case law Rodriguez vs. State of Florida which clearly states in black and white that a Doctrine of Inevitable Discovery does not exist in the circumstances surrounding the Deputies warrantless search of our home. The Judge's bias against my son and for the Deputies caused him to ignore the law and add a non-existent Doctrine of Inevitable Discovery to his Order. Robert's defense team, knowing this could happen, had already prepared a Motion for Reconsideration to allow the Judge the opportunity to correct his error. Instead of correcting his error, the Judge denied the motion without adding any legal explanation, because there was none.

Robert losing the Motion to Suppress meant that he would remain incarcerated without receiving any medical treatment for his malignant colon cancer. Ironically, it did give Robert the legal foothold to pursue an appeal and have his Motion to Suppress ruling reviewed by a higher court without the shadow of corruption that blanketed the Lake County Criminal Justice System.

This level of corruption caused me to sell our beautiful Mt. Dora, FL home on November 16, 2017, and permanently move away from Lake County.

CANCER
A LIFE-THREATENING DIAGNOSIS

Immediately following Robert's severe beating at the hands and feet of the Lake County Sheriff's Deputies on October 5, 2015, he suffered debilitating health issues which included: severe pain with blindness in his left eye, chronic pain on the left side of his ribs, abdominal pain with rectal bleeding, and difficulty in eliminating bowel movements. He had to take stool softeners or enemas on a regular basis.

Robert's abdominal issues were exacerbated by the excessive force used on him during the second arrest on August 17, 2016, in Ft. Lauderdale, FL, by the U.S. Marshals.

Their brutal assault caused increased trauma to Robert's abdominal area. As the U.S. Marshals were putting Robert into their vehicle, he informed them that he was experiencing extreme intestinal pain. They took my son to the Emergency Room at the Broward Health Medical Center in Ft. Lauderdale, FL for observation. The Broward Health's medical report, dated August 25, 2016, stated that my son had pre-cancerous bleeding polyps and should be seen by a Gastro-Intestinal (GI) Doctor within three days and must have a colonoscopy.

In addition to feeling nauseous and tired all the time, Robert lost a lot of weight in the Lake County

Detention Center. For the first 2 1/2 months, he was incarcerated in a cell 24/7 and only allowed out of his cell for a total of 3 hours a week. Shortly thereafter, he weighed in at 145 pounds, down from his original weight of 190 pounds. While on lockdown, Robert said he drank unfiltered water from his cell that had a horrible taste and a foul odor. These conditions exacerbated his bowel and intestinal problems considerably.

During Robert's first thirteen months of incarceration, the Lake County Detention Center refused to give him any medical treatment from a GI doctor for his pre-cancerous bleeding polyps as medically prescribed. Countless notifications were given thereafter of Robert's pre-cancerous bleeding polyps and his need for immediate medical treatment. The Medical Report from the Broward Health Medical Center, dated August 25, 2016, instructed Robert to see a Gastroenterologist within three days and have a colonoscopy because his pre-cancerous bleeding polyps were the beginning stages of colon cancer. Copies of this report and letters from two GI Doctors stating my son has life-threatening cancerous symptoms were given to the Lake County Detention Center, the Lake County Sheriff, the Lake County Warden, the Lake County State Attorney.

Robert's Lead Attorney visited him at the Lake County Detention Center and witnessed how ill he was. Fearing for his life, he made another emergency motion to the Lake County Judge for an outside medical furlough in September 2017. This time, the Judge allowed Robert one outside exam, with a Doctor in Leesburg, FL., for which I was asked to pay the bill. Robert was accompanied to this medical appointment by two armed guards from the Lake County Detention Center. This was his first examination in the thirteen months since his incarceration on August 25, 2016.

This Doctor medically diagnosed Robert with colon cancer and inflammation of the pancreas and stated this injury was caused by an injury to his abdomen. This injury was caused by the Lake County Deputy who repeatedly kicked Robert 10-12 times in his ribs and abdomen on October 5, 2015. The ill-effects of this beating were ongoing to Robert, which also included blindness, pain, colon bleeding, severe bowel problems, nausea, weakness, and a loss of 40 lbs.

Upon receiving the Doctor's medical report, the Lake County Detention Center called his Leesburg, Florida office to terminate all medical care on Robert because they were going to have their own Doctor from the Detention Center treat him for his colon cancer. I was informed of this by the GI Doctor's Head Nurse.

Days later, on September 5, 2017, Robert was examined by the Detention Center's Oncologist, who gave Robert a colonoscopy. This test confirmed Robert has stage 3 or 4 malignant colon cancer with a 70% blockage in his colon. The doctor was not sure which stage the colon cancer was in without taking further tests, but told Robert he thought it was stage 4. The Detention Center failed to conduct any of those required tests, allowing Robert to suffer for the entire year. This was confirmed by the Doctor who stated to Robert and also put this in his Medical Report, **"This cancer was present in your body for one year."** He told Robert, the cancerous growth was so large in his colon, he could not safely remove it without first using chemotherapy to shrink it. He needed an MRI to see the size of the cancer. The Detention Center said they would only allow him to have outside chemotherapy without hospitalization and wanted him to sign a waiver, freeing the Detention Center from any liability. Robert refused to sign their waiver.

On October 4th, 2017, our attorney made another emergency motion for a Medical Furlough to the Lake County Judge to get outside medical treatment. His ruling came immediately, "I deny your motion. You can come back in another month to see if the Detention Center can supply your cancer treatments." The Judge made this ruling with full knowledge that the Detention Center had not given Robert any care or treatment for his cancer for over one year, and now wants Robert to wait still another month with his current health crisis. His bias and unjust rulings were unconscionable.

After more than thirteen months of incarceration, the Lake County Judge had only allowed Robert one single outside visit to a GI Doctor, and then only after he became critically ill. The only thing my son was receiving at the Lake County Detention Center up to that date was one iron pill per day for anemia due to his constant colon bleeding, and a stool softener so he could move his bowels, which often took up to 4 days. Robert told me he has to walk daily within the facility to be able to move his bowels as well as taking the stool softener.

The following day, October 5, 2017, the original, Leesburg, Florida GI Doctor's surgical coordinator informed me of the following: "The doctor requested an MRI for Robert over one month ago, to see how large the cancerous growth was, so he could either operate or do chemotherapy. The MRI will show the size of the cancer to either surgically remove it or to immediately commence chemotherapy to reduce the size of the growth prior to surgery. If it's too large, the doctor can't operate unless the growth can be reduced in size." She added, "The Lake County Detention Center has dropped the ball."

She gave me the name of the Medical Treatment Coordinator for the Lake County Detention Center. She reiterated again, "Your son needs this taken care of immediately. Your son needs tests and an MRI to see the size of the cancer. This must be done immediately! **No judge in the world will deny a person with your son's medical condition, a Medical Furlough.**"

Unfortunately, the Lake County Judge handling Robert's case was the one Judge in the world who did deny my son his Motion for a Medical Furlough for his urgently needed outside cancer treatment. He did this with the full documented medical report as to the urgency for Robert's medical treatment.

During his continued incarceration at the Lake County Detention Center, Robert fell on his face repeatedly during his showers from being faint and weak due to anemia. On one occasion, a guard asked Robert as he exited the shower area if he had fallen again because his face was all red. Robert simply answered, "Yes."

Other inmates told Robert, "You look really bad, you look like you're dying. You have no color to your face; your skin is all gray." His Attorney told him the same thing, "Robert, you look God awful." Fearing for Robert's life, the Attorney made multiple emergency motions to the Lake County Judge for Robert to receive urgently needed, outside medical treatment. The Lake County Judge denied all motions for outside medical treatment.

The Lake County Detention Center did not give Robert any further tests or treatment for five months. It wasn't until January 28th, 2018, almost eighteen months after his incarceration date, that Robert was finally given five radiation treatments. The radiation treatments caused around the clock pain, suffering and diarrhea. Robert couldn't hold his bowel movements and was confined 24/7 in a lock-down cell, and only allowed out three hours a week with no medical care or follow up treatment from a doctor. This mistreatment goes beyond being egregious against any human being, especially one who is critically ill and not being properly medically treated for stage 3 or 4 malignant colon cancer!

THE QUEST FOR JUSTICE

On January 16, 2018, the same Deputy who had repeatedly kicked Robert in the stomach 10-12 times on October 5, 2015, and lied under oath about him at his Bond Hearing, came to see him at the Lake County Detention Center. He told Robert he wanted to talk to him and ask some questions. He asked Robert, "Where are you going to live when you get out?" Robert refused to talk with him without his lawyers being present. This made the Deputy very angry. He ordered Robert into his cell, and searched everything Robert had. He left with two bags of Robert's commissary food and one cookie. The guard on duty later came over to Robert and said, "I've been a guard here for 12 years, and I have never seen anything like this happen before to anyone. This Deputy was really pissed at you Robert!"

Four days prior to the Deputy's visit to my son, he came to my home, which is a four-hour drive from the Sheriff's office in Tavares, Florida. He banged his fist repeatedly on my front door for three hours then called multiple times on my cell phone from 3:45 pm to 6:45 pm before finally leaving. I phoned Robert's Lead Attorney, who looked up the number I gave him on my caller ID. He confirmed the cell number was registered to this Deputy. I had that same overwhelming feeling of terror upon witnessing the three Lake County Deputies beating my son. Now, two years later, this same Deputy was at my front door in Fort Lauderdale, Florida!

Following these incidents, Robert's lawyers counseled him not to go to trial with a biased Judge. They strongly advised Robert to plead "No Contest," and Appeal the Judge's Order on the basis of his misrepresenting Florida Supreme Court Law, Rodriguez vs. State of Florida. The Judge, in error, added the Doctrine of Inevitable Discovery which does not exist in this Supreme Court Case law. **When a Motion for Reconsideration was filed, the Judge refused to correct his error, with NO LEGAL EXPLANATION!**

In pleading "No Contest," Robert would finally be free from the Lake County Judge's bias, dirty politics, and his unjust rulings, and the Prosecutor's misconduct, conspiracy, and collusion, with the Deputies. He decided to take a plea because he has malignant colon cancer and wants to clear his name and win the appeal before anything happens to him. The Lawyers all agreed that the Appeal could get Robert the much-needed Justice he is legally entitled to as a US citizen.

Upon pleading "No Contest," the Lake County Judge immediately sentenced Robert to 20 years in a Florida State Correctional Facility. This sentence proved not only the Judge's bias but his unfair and harsh ruling against Robert's legal rights.

Robert's lawyers had already started preparing their Appeal Brief, and once the Judge entered the "No Contest" plea, they were able to file for a Supersedeas Bond Hearing. This is a legal instrument that prevents a judgment from being executed while the defendant is appealing the decision.

On January 29, 2018, the eve of Robert's supersedeas bond hearing, the Lake County Prosecutor sank to a level of prosecutorial misconduct that I could never have imagined, even from someone with his past record! Another false charge was being filed against Robert. He was falsely accused of solicitation to kill the Lake County Judge! This new charge was based on an alleged conversation between Robert and me on a monitored jail call. This false and outlandish charge was made up, in my opinion, because the Prosecutor knows that the Lake County Judge's Order to deny the Motion to Suppress will be reversed by the Appellate Court and he will have no choice but to dismiss all charges against Robert and set him free.

The same Deputy who beat up my son and kicked him multiple times in the ribs and stomach on his forced entry into our home on October 5, 2015, is the one who did the investigation of these new charges against Robert. He publicly alleged to the news media, the falsehood that Robert used a "secret code" to ask me to hire a long-time family friend to kill the Lake County Judge. This never happened!!!

This family friend is a 75-year-old senior citizen, blind in one eye and cataracts in the other eye with cancer in his body. He vehemently denies any affiliation with any such allegations made up by the Lake County Prosecutor and stated so to this Deputy, who assaulted Robert, when he came to his home to question him. He also said he told the Deputy, "You are not going to do to my life what you did to Robert O'Hare. You Deputies have a very bad reputation in this community and are the ones that should be locked up, not the innocent people you go after." He also stated this to Robert's Attorney and to the news media. He said he told the Deputy, "I was never solicited to kill a judge. I have known Virginia and Robert for 35 years, and they wouldn't hurt anyone." He told me he wants to sue the Deputy and the Lake County Sheriff's office for smearing his name all over the news media.

These new false charges by the Sheriff's Office and the State Attorney's office are their final attempt to try to wash away their own criminal violations by falsely accusing Robert of such a bogus charge on the eve of his supersedes bond hearing. This new charge kept my son from being released on a new bond while keeping him incarcerated now for two years without any urgently needed medical treatment for his malignant colon cancer.

Fear of my son being set free and the repercussions this could cause them is the sole reason for these latest charges, as well as the Deputy's visit to my home in Fort Lauderdale on January 11, 2018, and his visit to Robert's cell at the Lake County Detention Center on January 16, 2018. He wanted to know where Robert was going to live when he gets out. This was the first question he asked Robert which shows his concern over Robert being free, and his fear of potential civil and legal charges.

I met with Robert's legal defense team, and they believe this new charge is in retribution to the fact that Robert will be free upon his appeal.

Every American citizen has their Civil and Constitutional Rights from the moment we take our first breath when we come out of the birth canal until we take our last breath when our spirit returns to God who gave it. No American citizen, rich or poor, black or white, young or old should ever settle for injustice, corruption, conspiracy, and bias, from anyone employed by our Government that works in our Criminal Justice System. Our constitutional rights are expressed in our Fifth Amendment guarantees that: "No person shall be deprived of life, liberty, or property, without due process of law." This applies to all states by the 14th Amendment.

Robert's lawyers had enough with dealing with the corruption, conspiracy, and bias from the Lake County Judicial System. One of Robert's Attorneys said, "I have never seen a case like this before in my entire career. With all this corruption, we will file a Motion to Recuse the entire Lake County Judicial System and defend these latest charges against Robert outside of the Lake County Judicial System."

In early February 2018, this motion was granted, and the Lake County State Attorney recused the Lake County Judge and their entire Judicial System from my son's case.

In June 2018, an Appellate Brief was filed in the District Court of Appeal of Florida, Fifth District. The Appellate Brief can be read in its entirety, in Appendix – B of this book.

Writing this book was gut-wrenching as I detailed all the corruption I witnessed in the Lake County Judicial System against my son. I only got through the heart rendering details of the travesty of justice my son suffered through thus far, by being 100% inspired by God's Holy Spirit. My son and I believe God is using what he is going through, for me to write this book, ***"Virginia O'Hare Documents God's Laws vs. Man's Laws."*** God's message rings loud and clear from the pages of this book. He wants the world to know that His Ten Commandments are forever, and man's laws are not!

MY DEEPEST THOUGHTS AND FERVENT PRAYERS

"Virginia O'Hare Documents God's Laws vs. Man's Laws" was a time-consuming quest that embraced my every waking hour. I wanted to seek justice not only for my son but for everyone! Our Founding Fathers birthed Man's Laws in the U.S. Constitution based on God's Ten Commandments and the Bible. Since then, man has failed to create, amend, and enforce laws that conform to God's laws

I included in this book, an account of my son's quest for justice in a corrupt legal system. I've also included three letters to President Donald Trump, United States Attorney General Jeff Sessions at the U.S. Department of Justice, and the Federal Bureau of Investigation. I am requesting a criminal investigation into the corrupt legal system that has unjustly denied my son his civil, constitutional, and prisoner's rights.

Jesus said that in the last days, *"lawlessness will abound"* (Matthew 24:12 NKJV). Major prophetic signs of the last days are now increasing with frequency and intensity. *"I looked when He opened the sixth seal, and behold, there was a great earthquake; and the sun became black as sackcloth of hair, and the moon became like blood. And the stars of heaven fell to the earth, as a fig tree drops its late figs when it is shaken by a mighty wind. Then the sky receded as a scroll when it is rolled up, and every mountain and island was moved out of its place. And the kings of the earth, the great men, the rich men, the commanders, the mighty men, every slave and every free man, hid themselves in the caves and in the rocks of the mountains, and said to the mountains and rocks, "Fall on us and hide us from the face of Him who sits on the throne and from the wrath of the Lamb! For the great day of His wrath has come, and who is able to stand?"* (Revelation 6:12-17 NKJV).

We are the generation that is seeing such record-breaking events that are unfolding in every facet of our life. This includes: economic, scientific, technologic, ecologic, moral, cultural, geopolitical, and spiritual. These signs are all converging together at the same time and bringing our world, which is already teetering over the edge, to the point of no return. Jesus said. *"Now when these things begin to happen, look up and lift up your heads, because your redemption draws near"* (Luke 21:28 NKJV).

Jesus' Second Coming is now on the horizon. He will rapture all believers and set up His millennial kingdom here on earth where total justice will reign for everyone. All our fears and tears will be wiped away. We will live in a world dominated by goodness, and kindness. A world where there is no injustice, where no court ever renders an unjust verdict, where everyone is treated fairly and equally without any bias. A world that has total peace, where joy abounds, good health prevails, and where no one ages or is sick. The curse of death is removed, we will live in the pristine purity of Heaven on Earth which God has created for all who love Him and keep His Commandments. The kingdom will be ruled by our glorious King,

Jesus Christ where utopia will be a reality, and death will be swallowed up in victory. *"He will swallow up death forever, And the Lord God will wipe away tears from all faces; The rebuke of His people. He will take away from all the earth; For the Lord has spoken"* (Isaiah 25:8 NKJV).

Never again will we be separated from our saved loved ones. The sting of sin and death shall be swallowed up in victory forever. *"So when this corruptible has put on incorruption, and this mortal has put on immortality, then shall be brought to pass the saying that is written: 'Death is swallowed up in victory'"* (1 Corinthians 15:54 NKJV).

To be guaranteed this eternal bliss, everyone must repent of their sins and accept Jesus as their Lord and Savior. By saying this life-saving prayer of repentance for eternal salvation, your name will be immediately written in the Lamb's Book of Life.

Dear Jesus,

I am truly sorry for all my sins. Please forgive me. I believe you died on the cross for all my sins. Come into my heart as my Lord and Savior to rule and reign from this day forward.

I embrace the power of your Holy Spirit to live in me, to guide and direct me always to do the will of the Father.

Thank you, Jesus, for forgiving me all my sins. I believe I am now saved and look forward to your soon return!

Amen

I pray a blessing over everyone who reads this book, and for all to know how special you are to God. He created us in His likeness and image and loves us unconditionally. He gives eternal life to those who repent of their sins and accepts Jesus as their Lord and Savior. We are required to keep God's Ten Commandments, which are as valid today as they were 6000 years ago. We are counseled to do good, seek justice, and help the oppressed. *"Learn to do good; Seek justice, Rebuke the oppressor"* (Isaiah 1:17 NKJV).

Our eternal abode awaits all who put their faith and trust in God. He created us to have fellowship with Him. Adam and Eve broke that fellowship by sinning. To restore us to Him, He allowed His only begotten son, Jesus, to pay the penalty for our sins so we can have eternal life and fellowship with Him again in His kingdom. So, now that we are saved through the atoning blood of Jesus we can walk with God, talk with God and have His enduring love forever.

"This is love: not that we loved God, but that He loved us and sent his Son as an atoning sacrifice for our sins" (1 John 4:10 NIV). Let us praise and worship God and proclaim His greatness. In so doing we will have an enriching life here in this life and in the next, which is soon to come.

The content of this fully documented book on God's laws vs. Man's laws is a wealth of knowledge, with a judicious and spiritual perspective for everyone. Our legal system must serve every American citizen with equality and justice. Every American citizen must know what their legal rights are. We must stand together to enforce our constitutional rights. **United we stand divided we fall!**

Obedience to God's Ten Commandments is essential for our life here on earth and our eternal life to come.

God's blessings and favor are upon all who embrace Him and His son, Jesus Christ, with our love, faith, and hope. In so doing, God's Holy Spirit will dwell in us and give us His special gifts as needed. These gifts are love, joy, peace, patience, kindness, goodness, knowledge and wisdom. His gifts will get us through all the trials and tribulations in this life with good measure and success.

It is my prayer that this book will richly bless everyone with the knowledge of God's Word, His laws, His unconditional love, and His salvation for all who accept His son Jesus as their Lord and Savior.

I pray everyone will embrace God's truth and stand up for preserving our God-given rights, and our civil and constitutional rights as American citizens. Please share this inspired and documented book with others.

***"Go therefore and make disciples of all the nations, baptizing them in the name of the Father and of the Son and of the Holy Spirit, teaching them to observe all things that I have commanded you; and lo, I am with you always, even to the end of the age. Amen"* (Matthew 28:19-20 NKJV).**

ENDNOTES

1 Why Are There Up to 120,000 Innocent People in US Prisons?, https://news.vice.com/article/why-are-there-up-to-120000-innocent-people-in-us-prisons

2 Ibid.

3 When Was The Bible Written?, https://www.allabout-truth.org/when-was-the-bible-written-faq.htm

4 Prayer in Public Schools, https://www.adl.org/education/resources/tools-and-strategies/religion-in-public-schools/prayer

5 What Is A Covenant? Bible Definition And Meaning, https://www.biblestudytools.com/dictionary/covenant/

6 The Seven Covenants God Made With Mankind, https://www.free-bible-study-lessons.com/covenants.html

7 What Are The Different Covenants In The Bible?, https://www.compellingtruth.org/covenants-in-the-Bible.html

8 Increase of Knowledge, https://www.bibleuniverse.com/articles/second-coming-prophecies-fulfilled/id/1950/increase-of-knowledge

9 Knowledge Doubling Every 12 Months, Soon to be Every 12 Hours, http://www.industrytap.com/knowledge-doubling-every-12-months-soon-to-be-every-12-hours/3950

10 World Population: Past, Present, and Future, http://www.worldometers.info/world-population/

11 The Road To Independence | Military.com, https://www.military.com/independence-day/road-to-independence.html

12 Ibid.

13 The Declaration Of Independence | Military.com, https://www.military.com/independence-day/the-declaration-independence.html

14 Why We Celebrate The 4th Of July In America - Wall Street, https://wall-street.com/4th-why-we-celebrate/

15 Hampton University - Office Of Financial Aid, http://www.hamptonu.edu/studentservices/financialaid/gen_info/dloans_news.cfm

16 Bill Of Rights - Bill Of Rights Institute, http://billofrightsinstitute.org/founding-documents/bill-of-rights/

17 Ibid.

18 Ibid.

19 Ibid.

20 The American Flag | Usagov, https://www.usa.gov/flag

21 When the Court Took on Prayer and the Bible in Public Schools, https://religionandpolitics.org/2012/06/25/when-the-court-took-on-prayer-the-bible-and-public-schools/

22 Supreme Court Bars Commandments From Courthouses | Fox News, http://http://www.foxnews.com/story/2005/06/28/supreme-court-bars-commandments-from-courthouses.html

23 Ibid.

24 Ibid.

25 Ibid.

26 Ibid.

27 Ibid.

28 Ibid.

29 Ibid.

30 Ibid.

31 Ibid.

32 Ibid.

33 Ibid.

34 Ibid.

35 Ibid.

36 Ibid.

37 Ibid.

38 Ibid.

39 Ibid.

40 Ibid.

41 The Ten Commandments Of God - Biblescripture.net, http://biblescripture.net/Commandments.html

42 Occupational Outlook Handbook, https://www.bls.gov/ooh/protective-service/police-and-detectives.htm#tab-1

43 States of Incarceration: The Global Context, https://www.prisonpolicy.org/global/

44 Top 5 Secrets of the Private Prison Industry | Yahoo Finance, https://finance.yahoo.com/blogs/daily-ticker/top-5-secrets-private-prison-industry-163005314.html

45 A Timeline Of Police Attacks In The USA - Telegraph, https://www.telegraph.co.uk/news/worldnews/northa

merica/usa/11446472/A-timeline-of-police-attacks-in-the-USA.html

46 Ibid.

47 Ibid.

48 Tamir Rice Death Is What Happens When Police Aren't Required To Accept Risk, https://static-ssl.businessinsider.com/tamir-rice-death-is-what-happens-when-police-arent-required-to-accept-risk-2016-1

49 US Police Brutality: The Five Worst Examples, https://www.theguardian.com/world/2011/oct/24/us-police-brutality-worst-examples

50 Here's What Happened to the Cop Who Racially Profiled and Tackled Tennis Player James Blake, https://www.bet.com/news/sports/2017/05/16/the-cop-who-tackled-tennis-player-james-blake.html

51 Ibid.

52 The Worst Cases of Police Brutality In September, https://thinkprogress.org/the-worst-cases-of-police-brutality-in-september-a45130915451/

53 Ibid.

54 Ibid.

55 Ibid.

56 Ibid.

57 US Police Brutality: The Five Worst Examples, https://www.theguardian.com/world/2011/oct/24/us-police-brutality-worst-examples

58 Five Cases of Brutality Before the Anaheim One, https://insomniacs2.wordpress.com/category/nwo/page/12/

59 Police Brutality By Johanna Ruiz On Prezi,

https://prezi.com/wmzfchx-aw5g/police-brutality/

60 US Police Brutality: The Five Worst Examples, https://www.theguardian.com/world/2011/oct/24/us-police-brutality-worst-examples

61 Police Brutality By Johanna Ruiz On Prezi, https://prezi.com/wmzfchx-aw5g/police-brutality/

62 Ibid.

63 Ibid.

64 Ibid.

65 Ibid.

66 Ibid.

67 Ibid.

68 Ibid.

69 A Timeline Of Police Attacks In The USA - Telegraph, https://www.telegraph.co.uk/news/worldnews/northamerica/usa/11446472/A-timeline-of-police-attacks-in-the-USA.html

70 Ibid.

71 Ibid.

72 Ibid.

73 Ibid.

74 Fourteen-year-old Tremaine Mcmillan Was Feeding His Puppy, http://unstablecopsinamerica.blogspot.com/2013/06/fourteen-year-old-tremaine-mcmillan-was.html

75 12 Shocking Examples of Police Brutality...Just This Month, https://www.alternet.org/police-brutality

76 Ibid.

77 Suit claims excessive force, cover-up in Georgia police shooting, http://www.onlineathens.com/local-news/2018-01-10/suit-claims-excessive-force-cover-georgia-police-shooting

78 Lawsuit: Officers used excessive force, attempted cover-up, http://www.wrdw.com/content/news/Lawsuit-Officers-used-excessive-force-attempted-cover-up-468662743.html

79 18 Los Angeles sheriff's deputies arrested in federal jail investigation | Fox News, http://www.foxnews.com/us/2013/12/09/7-los-angeles-sheriff-deputies-arrested-in-jail-investigation.html

80 Civil Rights - Corporate.findlaw.com, https://corporate.findlaw.com/litigation-disputes/civil-litigation/civil-rights.

81 Civil Rights Attorney | Dallas Labor Law, http://www.laborassociates.com/civil-rights-attorney-dallas/

82 Ibid.

83 Rights Of Inmates - Findlaw, https://civilrights.findlaw.com/other-constitutional-rights/rights-of-inmates.html

84 Ibid.

85 Ten Ways Police Can Legally Lie to You, https://www.njmoorelaw.com/10-ways-police-can-lie-to-you

86 Ibid.

87 What To Do If Stopped By Police – Policecrimes.com, http://policecrimes.com/police-html/

88 What Is a "Section 1983" Lawsuit Against the Police?, https://www.nolo.com/legal-encyclopedia/what-is-a-section-1983-lawsuit-against-the-police.html

89 Ibid.

90 Ibid.

91 Ibid.

92 Ibid.

93 United States Code Section 1983 & Civil Rights Litigation California Civil Rights Lawyers, https://www.shouselaw.com/1983.html

94 Ibid.

95 Richard Lee Deorle V. Greg Rutherford, Et Al, http://www.morelaw.com/verdicts/case.asp?s=CA&d=1 8272

96 Madrid V. Gomez | Findlaw, https://caselaw.findlaw.com/us-9th-circuit/1011426.html

97 United States Code Section 1983 & Civil Rights Litigation California Civil Rights Lawyers, https://www.shouselaw.com/1983.html

98 What Is A Monell Claim? - Q&A - Avvo, https://www.avvo.com/legal-answers/what-is-a-monell-claim—2306447.html

99 Chew v. Gates, 744 F. Supp. 952 (C.D. Cal. 1990), https://law.justia.com/cases/federal/district-courts/FSupp/744/952/1797069/

100 United States Code Section 1983 & Civil Rights Litigation California Civil Rights Lawyers, https://www.shouselaw.com/1983.html

101 Ibid.

102 Suing The Police For Excessive Force | Nolo.com, https://www.nolo.com/legal-encyclopedia/suing-the-police-excessive-force.html

103 Ibid.

104 America's First Principles, http://www.americas-survivalguide.com/americas-first-principles.php

APPENDIX - A

OFFICIAL CORRESPONDENCE WITH THE FEDERAL GOVERNMENT

CORRESPONDENCE TO AND FROM THE PRESIDENT OF THE UNITED STATES

April 2, 2018

President Donald J. Trump
The White House
1600 Pennsylvania Ave. NW
Washington, DC. 20500

Dear President Trump,

Please add this updated letter to the formal complaint sent to you on February 16, 2018., which was also sent to Attorney General, Jeff Sessions. This civil and criminal complaint is to attest to the continuing violations committed by the Lake County Judicial System in Tavares, Florida against my son, Robert A. O'Hare's human, civil, constitutional, and prisoner's rights.

I was informed by a member of the Attorney General, Jeff Sessions' staff that my complaint was turned over to their criminal unit for investigation.

The civil and constitutional violations against my son began on October 5, 2015, when three Lake County Sheriff's Deputies from Tavares, Florida, forced their way into our home, without a search warrant, and immediately commenced brutally and maliciously assaulting my son, which caused permanent harm and disability.

Lake County Deputy Sheriff's Corporal XXXXXX blinded my son in his left eye with his blunt blows to his head, face, and eyes. The 2nd Deputy. XXXXXX, repeatedly kicked my son in the ribs and abdomen, soccer ball style, as my son laid helpless on the floor in our home. The third Deputy, XXXXXX, bodily suppressed my son's legs while the other two deputies severely beat him into a trauma state. This beating not only caused Robert's blindness in his left eye but internal intestinal damage, with bleeding and serious health issues that led to my son's current illness. He now has stage three or four malignant colon cancer with a 70% blockage in his sigmoid colon. One major health issue caused after their beating was his inability to move his bowels without stool softeners or enemas.

Upon making a criminal complaint against the deputies to the Lake County Sheriff's office, through internal affairs, resulted in the Lake County Sheriff dismissing the criminal complaint as being "unfounded."

On December 4, 2018, Lake County Judge, XXXXXX made an order to Robert's Motion to Suppress, which was based on the deputies violating his 4th amendment rights. Judge XXXXXX confirmed that the deputies' warrantless search and seizure were unlawful. However, Judge XXXXXX exonerated their unlawful warrantless entry into our home, by giving the deputies a doctrine of Inevitable Discovery that does not exist in the Supreme Court Case Law, Rodriguez vs. State of Florida. This case law was used in Robert's Motion to Suppress. According to this Supreme Court case law, **a warrantless entry is unlawful and violates one's' 4th amendment rights.**

Robert's lawyers immediately filed a Motion for Reconsideration for Judge XXXXXX to correct his error in misinterpreting this supreme court case law. Judge XXXXXX denied this Motion for Reconsideration and refused to correct his error in misinterpreting the Supreme Court case law. Robert's attorneys were disappointed that Judge XXXXXX did not follow the law with his ruling. This prompted them to advise Robert not to go to trial with a biased judge because he would not receive a fair trial. They based their opinion on all the motions Judge XXXXXX should have granted to Robert but didn't. These motions included Judge XXXXXX denial to reinstate Robert's bond, which he was legally entitled to, his motions for urgently needed outside medical treatment, which he wasn't receiving at the Lake County Detention Center, his Motion to Suppress, which was based solely on the law, and his Motion for Reconsideration. The lawyers filed a Motion for Reconsideration for Judge XXXXXX to correct his error. He denied this motion as well with no legal explanation. With all this corruption Robert was going through with the judicial system, his lawyers recommended Robert plead no contest and appeal on the basis of Judge XXXXXX misinterpreting the Supreme Court case law, Rodriguez vs. State of Florida. Robert took their advice and entered a plea of "no contest" and filed a "De Nova Appeal" based solely on Judge XXXXXX misinterpretation of the law. **Exhibit A.**

A Lake County Detention Center guard told my son, that he worked in Judge XXXXXX' chamber prior to their trials, and said, "The judge and the prosecutor decide before going into the courtroom what his ruling will be. The people don't have a chance for justice in the Lake County courtroom. The judge always rules in favor of the deputies and the prosecutor. There is no justice in their courtroom. The people always lose against the prosecutor and deputies." For verification of this conversation with my son, this call was recorded on the monitored jail calls.

Unfortunately, Judge XXXXXX making up a doctrine of Inevitable Discovery that does not exist in Supreme Court case law exonerated the deputies in their unlawful warrantless entry and illegal search and seizure in our home. By misrepresenting the law in his ruling in my son's Motion to Suppress Judge XXXXXX caused Robert to lose the motion and further exposed the judge's bias against him.

For sixteen months of Robert's incarceration, the Lake County Judicial System denied his due process of law, his urgently needed medical care and treatment for his bleeding pre-cancerous polyps as diagnosed by the Broward County Health Hospital on August 25, 2016. Without giving Robert any medical treatment, this condition developed into stage three or four malignant colon cancer and was diagnosed by the detention center's medical doctor on September 5, 2017. The Doctor stated in his Medical Report that Robert had this malignant colon cancer for one year. He told Robert, "I don't know why the Detention Center didn't treat this cancer before now." I submitted to the Lake County Judicial System a copy of Robert's original medical report from Broward County Health Hospital, on August 25, 2016, which instructed Robert to see a GI doctor within three (3) days and have a colonoscopy for his pre-cancerous bleeding polyps. A copy of this medical report was submitted to your office in this correspondence as **Exhibit B.**

The Lake County Judicial System kept Robert incarcerated for sixteen (16) months without a trial, canceled five (5) of his pre-hearing dates for his Motion to Suppress for close to eight (8) months. This violated Robert's due process of law and is against his 5th and 14th amendment rights.

The deputies who assaulted Robert made false statements against Robert under oath which influenced Judge XXXXXX's rulings to deny Robert's bond motion, medical furloughs, Motion to Suppress, and Motion for Reconsideration. The Lake County Detention Center continued to deny Robert urgently needed medical care and treatment for his intestinal bleeding, pain, and suffering for seventeen (17) months.

Upon becoming critically ill on September 5, 2017,

the Lake County Detention Center, had Dr. XXXXXX examine Robert and gave him a colonoscopy. Robert was diagnosed with stage three (3) or stage four (4) malignant colon cancer. The doctor told Robert he was not sure which stage his cancer was in without taking more tests. The Detention Center has not allowed Robert to have these tests as to the date of this letter. Dr. XXXXXX told Robert to have an MRI, radiation, then surgery immediately. This was the first medical examination given by the Lake County Detention Center to Robert since his incarceration on August 25, 2016. See Dr. XXXXXX's medical report: **Exhibit C.**

Since Robert's September 5, 2017, medical diagnoses by Dr. XXXXXX, he has not received any medical treatment or medical care for his malignant colon cancer until almost five months later. On or about January 28, 2018, Robert was given five (5) radiation treatments. The after-effects of the radiation treatments were painful and debilitating. The doctor's nurse explained to me, "the doctor cannot remove the 70% blockage in Robert's colon surgically because it is too large in size and is too dangerous to remove surgically. Your son needs an MRI, chemotherapy, radiation or both to reduce the size of the tumor before it can be surgically removed safely. This should be done immediately." After months of this not being done, **she told me, "the detention center has dropped the ball by not having this done sooner."** Dr. XXXXXX informed Robert, "this blockage has been in your colon for over one year."

The Lake County Detention Center is legally responsible for Robert's medical care and treatment during his incarceration. Their refusal to give Robert the proper medical care and treatment has allowed his precancerous bleeding polyps to grow into a 70% blockage in his colon, which possibly may have metastasized to other parts of his body. Without further tests, the doctor said this is an unknown. This neglect to give Robert proper medical treatment with the proper tests taken is a violation to his 8th amendment rights and has caused him unending pain and suffering for seventeen (17) months, and the real possibility of losing his life!

On February 16, 2018, during our monitored jail phone call, Robert said, "Mom, if they gave me treatment when I first got here, I wouldn't be going through this stage 3 or stage 4 cancer now. The doctor told me he was concerned it could be stage 4, but he wasn't sure. The detention center has not given me any follow up visits with this doctor or any doctor other than this radiation. **They are slowly murdering me.** When I get out, the first thing I want to do is go to the hospital and take blood tests and find out where this cancer has traveled to in my body." This monitored phone call with Robert on February 16, 2018, can be verified by the monitored jail calls at the Lake County Detention Center.

On January 28, 2018, the Lake County Detention Center placed Robert in a closet-sized cell in lockdown and refuse to give him any follow up medical care, tests, or treatment after his five (5) radiation treatments in his colon. It is a known medical fact that the colon is the most painful area to have radiation treatments, and follow up care is medically mandatory.

Robert said he is suffering from the after-effects of the radiation treatment and has to empty his bowels every five minutes. He is losing weight and still has colon bleeding and pain. He is only allowed out of his cell three hours a week, one hour on Monday, one hour on Wednesday, and one hour on Friday. He said he is so weak and can't hold his bowel movements. Such inhuman treatment for a critically ill inmate being denied medical care and treatment with his life-threatening illness is a severe violation of his civil, constitutional, prisoner's, and 8th amendment rights.

For the record, as of the date of this letter, April 2, 2018, Robert is still not receiving the mandatory medical care or treatment required for his colon cancer. He has had no follow up medical treatment, tests, or a doctor's visit since receiving the five radiation treatments on January 28, 2018.

Without medical treatment, Robert said he doesn't know how long he can hold on. I pray with him each time we speak for his healing and exoneration from all these bogus charges. My prayer is for Robert to receive his constitutional rights and justice, not the corrupt injustice he has received to date. The deputies conspiring with the prosecutor making false and damning allegations against Robert to cover over their own criminal violations should all be held accountable to the full extent of the law. If everyone were to be treated by a judicial system across our country as my son has been, we would have a rule of anarchy and mobocracy instead of democracy and justice.

President Trump, I am putting you on notice of this serious deprivation to my son's human, civil and constitutional rights. If this were your son, Barron, what would you want a president to do?

The Lake County prosecutor has just placed another bogus charge against my son. He is being accused of soliciting a longtime family friend of 35 years through me on one of my jail calls with Robert to kill the judge. **This never happened!!!** This longtime family friend, XXXXXX, is 75 years old, has cancer, blind in one eye and his other eye is covered with cataracts. He was approached by Lake County Deputy XXXXXX, who was the one who kicked and beat Robert in our home on October 5, 2015. The Deputy XXXXXX asked him if he were a Rabbi and did Robert slip him a note from his mother to kill the judge. He said he told Deputy XXXXXX, "I've known Virginia and Robert for over 35 years, they wouldn't hurt anyone! This is all bull shit! She never gave me any slip of paper, and I hadn't spoken to her or Robert since November 13, 2017, when I took Virginia out to lunch to celebrate her 81st birthday."

Deputy XXXXXX spread his name all over the news media as the rabbi that was solicited to kill the judge. He told me he was going to sue the Lake County sheriff's office for defamation of his character. He said he told Deputy XXXXXX, "I saw what you all did to Robert's life. You are not going to do the same thing to mine, what I have left of it. You deputies have a very bad reputation in this Lake County community for doing things like this. You even pulled a woman from her wheelchair. You are the criminals that should be prosecuted, not the innocent people you go after. I am getting calls from everyone about this lying story of being the rabbi solicited to kill a judge. They have this lying story all over the news media and tv."

Attorney XXXXXX texted me and said, "Virginia the state wants you as their star witness against your son." These deputies will stop at nothing to hide their violations of the law and avoid being judged and prosecuted with all the evidence there is against them.

This Deputy XXXXXX went to see my son on January 16, 2018, at 12:00 noon at the detention center and wanted to talk with him. Deputy XXXXXX asked Robert, "where are you going to live when you get out?" My son refused to talk to him without his lawyers being present. Mad at my son not talking with him, Deputy

XXXXXX demanded my son go into his cell and ransacked through all his belongings. He left taking Robert's two bags of commissary food and one cookie. The guard who witnessed this, Officer XXXXXX, came over to Robert's cell and said, "I've been a guard here for 12 years and have never seen anything like this happen before to anyone, that deputy was really pissed at you Robert." This guard can give his eyewitness account of what Deputy XXXXXX said and did to my son.

On January 11, 2018, Deputy XXXXXX also came to my home in Ft. Lauderdale and banged on my front door for three hours before leaving. He called me repeatedly on my cell phone from 3:35 pm to 6:45 pm. I called Attorney XXXXXX and gave him the cell number on my caller id. He said it was registered to this Deputy.

It was fear for my life and my son's life that caused me to sell our home, which we owned for 17 years, in Mt. Dora, FL on November 16, 2017. Close friends cautioned me to be out of range from these deputies in Lake County because they are dangerous to both my son and me. I never dreamed in a million years; this Deputy would come to my home in Ft. Lauderdale, which is a 3 1/2 hour drive from his office.

This latest bogus charge by the Lake County Prosecutor is their last-ditch effort to whitewash their own criminal violations. Evidence of this is in my criminal complaint to Attorney General, Jeff Sessions. I have submitted exhibits A-Q which fully document the deputies' conspiracy with the Lake County Prosecutor, XXXXXX, and rulings made by Judge XXXXXX that do not comply with the law.

The deputies' unlawful entry, planting a bogus crime scene in our home, filing a false police report, lying under oath in a court of law, and using the news media against Robert are all substantiated with evidence I have submitted, to the U.S. Dept. of Justice to Attorney General Jeff Sessions.

Further proof of the deputies' criminal violations is a live video I took during their unlawful warrantless entry into our home. This video showed the aftermath of their brutal beating to my son, holding both of us hostage, (which lasted for close to 11 hours) and doing an illegal warrantless search and seizure. They compounded their violations by mutually staging a crime scene with my son's laptop computer that was locked in his bedroom closet, then calling CSI to take pictures of their staged crime scene. This fact was evidenced, during the Motion to Suppress hearing, by Corporal XXXXXX's body-worn camera/recorder video. The deputies were recorded talking about finding the laptop in the locked bedroom closet hours before they got a warrant. Their police report falsely stated the laptop was on the floor and the case on the bed in "plain view" with pictures from CSI of this staged crime scene.

Multiple violations were committed when the deputies did the following: (1) removed the laptop computer from the locked bedroom closet without a warrant. (2) unzipped its case and staged the laptop on the floor and placed the case on the bed. (3) called in CSI to take pictures of their staged crime scene. (4) falsified their police report to line up their staging the laptop as being in "plain view to comply with the plain view doctrine. (5) the plain view doctrine allows an officer to confiscate the laptop if it is in plain view. (6) in this case, there was undeniable evidence the laptop was in a locked bedroom closet and not in plain view.

During Corporal XXXXXX's testimony at the Motion to Suppress hearing, his body cam recorder video proved they found the laptop in the closet several hours before they even got the warrant. All the above evidence proved the deputies staged the crime scene to justify their unlawful warrantless entry into our home. The deputies staging of the laptop is a conscious criminal act. Judge XXXXXX exonerated these criminal acts by the deputies by adding a doctrine of Inevitable Discovery in his ruling on Robert's Motion to Suppress that is not in the law.

During the suppression hearing, Attorney XXXXXX in his Motion to Suppress submitted proof with an expert witness that Deputy XXXXXX omitted pertinent facts on the search warrant and had a magistrate judge sign it without making full disclosure. This lethal evidence against Deputy XXXXXX's warrant was immediately denied by Judge XXXXXX.

If all that wasn't enough police corruption placed on my son, they falsely charged him with resisting an officer without violence then stating under oath he was a flight risk and a danger to the Loch Leven community. We lived in Loch Leven community for 17 years with absolutely no problems whatsoever.

See Robert's picture immediately after the deputies beating. Deputy XXXXXX who had kicked Robert repeatedly in his ribs and stomach also tore Robert's shirt down his back and lied under oath stating Robert was running toward the kitchen, that was 500' away, and that's why he tore his shirt. I took a video of Robert lying face down on the floor only a few feet from the front entrance facing the opposite direction from the kitchen, as further proof of the Deputy lying.

Upon the deputies' unlawful entry to our home on October 5, 2015, I videotaped Robert's beaten body, his eyes swollen shut, blinded in his left eye by Corporal

XXXXXX, and his face bloodied and bruised from their beating. I submitted two pictures of my son's face right after the deputies' beating in my prior letter: **Exhibit D.**

During Robert's 17 months of incarceration, the deputies continued to violate Robert's civil, constitutional and prisoner's rights, by openly lying under oath with made up outrageous stories against my son, which are documented in the court's electronic transcriptions. Judge XXXXXX and Prosecutor XXXXXX never questioned the Deputies veracity.

I have detailed all the evidence of their violations in my letter to Jeff Session, which was sent to you by Federal Express on February 16, 2018, along with all the court documents of the entire Motion to Suppress hearing. In those documents are the false sworn testimonies of the deputies, and prosecutor XXXXXX, lying to both Judge XXXXXX and Attorney XXXXXX during the court proceedings. This is evidenced in the Court electronic transcriptions.

These violations committed by the Lake County Judicial System against my son are covered in close to 100 pages sent to Jeff Sessions. I detailed and documented every violation with evidence, pictures, video, depositions, internal affairs reports, police body cam recorded video, and witnesses to the Lake County judicial system's criminal violations against my son. Robert's three lawyers witnessed overwhelming corruption and conspiracy, which they had to deal with while defending my son's legal, civil, and constitutional rights.

This is a horror story of major proportions of police abuse, corruption, and physical brutality by three Lake County deputies and corruption in the Lake County's Judicial System. The Lake County Detention Center, the Warden, Sheriff, Judge XXXXXX, Prosecutor

XXXXXX, and State Attorney XXXXXX, have all ignored the seriousness of this criminal complaint and have done nothing to correct the egregious ongoing violations against my son that are being committed under their direct supervision.

On October 4, 2017, my Ft. Lauderdale maid, XXXXXX called and said, her son, XXXXXX, was in the Lake County Detention Center for two weeks for a traffic ticket violation. She said, her son was in the same pod, as my son. When her son came home, he told his mother about my son's pain and suffering, and the detention center's refusal to give him any medical treatment. Below is his notarized statement from XXXXXX:

"I hear Robert cry at night with pain. They refuse to give him any medicine for the pain from his cancer. Robert looks sickly and is very skinny. His hair has turned all white. I feel very sorry for him they are killing him. He has cancer and is very ill. He is dying, and they are doing nothing to help him. He asks for medicine, and they refuse to give him medicine. That place is horrible! Robert is a kind person and asked me when I left to give my mattress to one of his cellmates that sleeps above him on just an iron mattress. Even though Robert is very ill, he still thinks about helping others. He is a very kind and a very good person."

My maid showed her son a picture of my son before he was incarcerated and asked him, "is this Robert?" He said, "yes." But he looks really bad now, skinny, and sickly; his hair is all white."

Another cellmate of Robert, a homeless man, brought Robert a peanut butter sandwich because he was too sick to raise his head off the bed. My son told me about this heart rendering event. He said, "Mom, here is this man who is homeless and was brought in for panhandling and he is helping me because I was too sick even to raise my head off the bed to eat. He fed me his peanut butter sandwich. Here, I had an affluent life, and this man sleeps under bridges and gives me his peanut butter sandwich. His deed got to my heart." I said, "Robert God is watching over you, and he will exonerate you and see you through all these unjust and bogus charges." This monitored jail call from the detention center can be verified.

In my soon to be published book, ***"Virginia O'Hare Documents God's Laws vs. Man's Laws,"*** will be a chapter on the corruption, injustice, bias, that my son has been subjected to by the Lake County Judicial System in Tavares, Florida, with indisputable evidence. See the attached book cover with a synopsis of the criminal violations committed against my son: **Exhibit E.**

On January 29, 2018, the eve of Robert's supersedes bond hearing in front of Judge XXXXXXs, the Lake County Sheriff's office came up with another bogus charge against my chronically ill son by an investigation conducted by the Deputy who kicked and beat him in our home, Deputy XXXXXX. This time, Robert was falsely accused of solicitation to kill Judge XXXXXX with a longtime family friend, XXXXXX, who also was investigated by this Deputy. This family friend stated to the news media, "this is all bull shit. I was never solicited by Robert or Virginia to kill anybody. I've known them both for 35 years they wouldn't hurt anyone. The criminals here are the deputies who are a threat to the community. They are known for lying and making up stories like this to innocent people who live here in this community. I hadn't seen or talked to either one since November 13, 2017, when I took Virginia out to celebrate her 81st birthday and haven't seen or talked with her or Robert since."

This false and outlandish charge was made up by Lake County officials whose violations against my son's 4th amendment, civil, and constitutional rights was confirmed by Judge XXXXXX in his order to my son's Motion to Suppress, dated December 4, 2018.

See **Judge XXXXXX' order** on page 3 of 6 at the bottom of the page #2 which reads as follows:

"The court observes that no justification was offered as to why police did not seek a warrant prior to approaching defendant's house for the knock and talk. Had officers simply sought a warrant before entering the defendant's residence instead of afterward, they would have avoided an entirely unnecessary expenditure of both judicial and police resources. Separately from whether the tactics employed by police were legal, they were clearly unwise and unnecessary." Exhibit F.

My son said he was very pleased and stated so on our jail phone monitored call, "Judge XXXXXX did me a big favor in my Motion to Suppress. If he were here, I would hug him and give him a kiss. He gave me 95% of what I asked for in my Motion to Suppress. He only misinterpreted the law, which I can win on the appeal."

These new false charges by the Lake County sheriff's office and the state prosecutor are their final attempt to destroy my son's life so their criminal acts can be washed away. I am praying you do not give these corrupt lawbreakers a license to destroy the life of my son and get away with their criminal violations.

On or about January 2018, the Lake County State Attorney recused Judge XXXXXX from my son's case.

Robert's lawyers have had enough with dealing

with the corruption, conspiracy, and bias from the Lake County Judicial System and have filed the appropriate Motion to Recuse the entire Lake County Judicial System. They will defend their latest charges against my son outside of the Lake County Judicial System.

Today, my son is chronically ill, living under the inhuman maltreatment from the Lake County Detention Center and their neglect in not giving him medical treatment for his malignant colon cancer. I have statements from cellmates who witnessed the Lake County Detention Center's ignoring his pain and suffering and denying him urgently needed medical care and treatment. These witnesses are documented in my letter to Jeff Sessions, with one notarized witness who heard my son crying out with pain and suffering nightly while being denied urgently needed medical care and treatment.

After Robert's malignant colon cancer stage three or four was diagnosed by Dr. XXXXXX on September 5, 2017, Robert did not receive any medical care or treatment until almost five months later. He received his first five radiation treatments starting around January 28, 2018. During these five radiation treatments, the Lake County Detention Center put Robert in medical lockdown in a closet-sized cell 7' x 14', and only him let out 3 hours a week. He was never given any medical follow up care to oversee the adverse symptoms from the radiation treatments. The Detention Center placed him in a medical psych ward with mentally ill cellmates. This barbaric treatment is beyond being maltreatment. My son's civil, constitutional, prisoner's, and 8th amendment right, are being egregiously violated by the Lake County Judicial System.

My son called me and said, "Mom, they have me in lockdown, and I am only allowed out 3 hours a week, I can't even walk around in my cell it's so small. I am without any medical care. I have to go to empty my bowels every five (5) minutes. They are not giving me any medical treatment at all. They are slowly murdering me." Robert told me this on our monitored jail call on February 16, 2018. For close to seventeen (17) months, Judge XXXXXX denied all my son's motions. If he wasn't recused the day before my sons supersedes bond hearing, Robert's lawyers told him they were prepared for Judge XXXXXX to rule against his bond.

Robert lost over 40 lbs. of his body weight and is slowing being murdered by this corrupt criminal justice system. I lost my husband and two daughters in 2012 and 2013. Robert is my only living family member. Seeing him go through this inhuman pain and suffering and slowly slipping away without the proper medical treatment or any form of justice, is 100% against our united states civil and constitutional rights. This is more than devastating for me to watch, as they are slowly murdering my son.

I have reported all of this to the Lake County State Attorney, XXXXXX, who has not taken any action or honored my son's constitutional rights under his supervision.

President Trump, please treat my son like you would want your son, Barron, to be treated if he were going through the same thing. I have all the evidence needed for you to immediately intercede: sworn affidavits, police body cam recording video, court documents, sworn affidavits, reports from the Lake County Internal Affairs, live video, pictures, and witnesses, which I can produce upon request, including Robert's three lawyers who witnessed all the above violations to date.

Mr. President, please uphold my son's civil, consti-tutional, and prisoner's rights. Time is of the essence for you to do so now!

Respectfully submitted,

____

VIRGINIA O'HARE

THE WHITE HOUSE

WASHINGTON

April 11, 2018

Ms. Virginia M. O'Hare
XXXXXXXXXXXXXXX
XXXXXXXXXXXXXX

Dear Ms. O'Hare,

Thank you for taking the time to write and share your story with President Donald J. Trump. He is honored by the opportunity to serve you and the American people.

White House staff reviewed your correspondence and forwarded it to the appropriate Federal agency for further action. For additional information about the Federal government in the meantime, please visit www.USA.gov or call 1-800-FED-INFO.

Respectfully,

The Office of Presidential Correspondence

CORRESPONDENCE TO AND FROM THE U.S. DEPARTMENT OF JUSTICE

Attorney General Jeff Sessions
Civil Rights Division
U.S. Department of Justice
950 Pennsylvania Avenue, NW
Washington, DC 20530-0001

From: Virginia O'Hare

Date: May 8, 2018 (update to ID #XXXXXXXX)

Re: Robert O'Hare

Dear Mr. Jeff Sessions,

Herein is another update to my criminal complaint, Case ID #XXXXXXXX that was originally submitted to you with critical updates on: XXXXXXX, XXXXXX, XXXXXXXX, XXXXXXXXX, XXXXXXXXX, XXXXXXXXX,XXXXXXXX.

My son, Robert A. O'Hare was physically beaten by three Lake County Sheriff's Deputies who entered our home unlawfully without a warrant on October 5, 2015. Their brutal beating caused Robert's current disability of a life-threatening stage 3 or 4 malignant colon cancer. To date, the Lake County Detention Center has failed to provide the mandatory medical treatment, care, and tests needed for his stage 3 or 4 colon cancer.

Prior to his incarceration at the Lake County Detention Center in Tavares, FL., on August 25, 2016, Robert was medically diagnosed on that same day during his ER visit to Broward Health Hospital in Ft. Lauderdale, FL with pre-cancerous bleeding polyps. This medical report stated Robert should be seen by a GI doctor within three (3) days and must have a colonoscopy. Robert's medical report was given immediately, upon his incarceration, to the Lake County Detention Center, the Lake County Sheriff, the Lake County Prosecutor, and multiple times thereafter, to Judge XXXXXXX for a Medical treatment and Furlough. Judge XXXXXX ruled against all of Robert's Emergency Medical treatment and Furlough Motions.

On October 4, 2017, after being incarcerated for over thirteen months and not receiving any medical treatment from the Lake County Detention Center, other than his medical diagnosis on September 5, 2017, Judge XXXXXX again denied my son's emergency motion for a Medical Furlough for outside chemotherapy, radiation, MRI, and surgery. The only thing my son was receiving at the Lake County Detention Center up to that date was one (1) iron pill per day for anemia due to his constant colon bleeding, and a stool softener so he could move his bowels, which often took up to 4 days. Robert told me he has to walk daily within the facility to be able even to move his bowels as well as taking the stool softener.

It wasn't until January 28th, 2018, almost eighteen (18) months from his incarceration date, that Robert was finally given five radiation treatments with absolutely no follow-up exam by a medical doctor from January 28th, 2018 to several months thereafter. The radiation treatments caused around the clock pain, suffering and diarrhea. Robert couldn't hold his bowel movements and was incontinent while he was confined 24/7 in a lock-down cell, and only allowed out three (3) hours a week with no medical care or follow up treatment from a doctor. This mistreatment goes beyond being egregious against any human being, especially one who is critically ill and not being properly medically treated for stage 3 or 4 malignant colon cancer!

After Attorney XXXXXX, visited Robert and witnessed how ill he was, he feared for his life and made another emergency motion to Judge XXXXXX for an outside furlough in September 2017. This time, the Judge allowed Robert one outside exam, which I paid for, with Dr. XXXXXX in Leesburg, FL. Robert was accompanied to this medical appointment by two armed guards from the Lake County Detention Center. This was his first and only examination in one year since his incarceration on August 25, 2016.

Doctor XXXXXX medically diagnosed Robert with colon cancer and inflammation of the pancreas and stated this injury was caused by an injury to his abdomen. This injury was caused by the Lake County Deputy, XXXXXX who repeatedly kicked Robert 10-12 times in his ribs and abdomen on October 5, 2015, when he unlawfully entered our home without a search warrant. The symptoms of this beating were ongoing to Robert, which included blindness, pain, colon bleeding, nausea, weakness, and a loss of 40 lbs.

Upon receiving Dr. XXXXXX's medical report, the Lake County Detention Center called Doctor XXXXXX to terminate any medical care on Robert because they were going to have their own doctor from the Detention Center examine him for his colon cancer. On September 5, 2017, Robert was examined by the Detention Center's Oncologist, Dr. XXXXXX who gave Robert a colonoscopy. This test confirmed Robert has stage 3 or 4 malignant colon cancer with a 70% blockage in his colon. The doctor was not sure which stage the colon cancer was in without taking further tests, but thought it was stage 4. The Detention Center failed to provide any of those required tests.

The doctor further stated to Robert, **"this cancer was present in your body for one year."** Since this doctor's diagnosis, two months went by with no further treatment, hospitalization, surgery, chemotherapy or radiation. The Detention Center said they would only allow him to have outside chemotherapy without hospitalization and wanted him to sign a waiver, freeing the Detention Center from any liability. Robert refused to sign their waiver. The doctor told Robert his cancerous growth was so large in his colon he could not safely remove it without first using chemotherapy to shrink it, and said he needed an MRI to see the size of the cancer.

The Lake County Detention Center failure to medically treat Robert for his pre-cancerous bleeding polyps for 13 months, caused his cancer to worsen and spread from pre-cancerous bleeding polyps, as diagnosed by Broward Health Hospital on August 25, 2016, to malignant colon cancer, as diagnosed on September 5, 2017, by Dr. XXXXXX. Dr. XXXXXX recommended Dr. XXXXXX for Robert to immediately have an MRI.

At Robert's October 4th, 2017 Hearing for an Emergency Medical Furlough, Judge XXXXX said to his Attorney, XXXXXX, "I deny your motion. You can come back in another month to see if the Detention Center can supply his cancer treatments." Judge XXXXXX, made this ruling with full knowledge that the Detention Center had not given Robert any care or treatment for his cancer for over one year, and now wants Robert to wait still another month with his current health crisis. His bias and unjust rulings were unconscionable.

On October 5, 2017, Dr. XXXXXX's surgical coordinator, XXXXXX informed me of the following: "The doctor requested an MRI for Robert over one month ago, to see how large the cancerous growth was, so he could either operate or do chemotherapy. The MRI will show the size of the cancer to either surgically remove it or to immediately commence chemotherapy to reduce the size of the growth prior to surgery. If it's too large, the doctor can't operate unless the growth can be reduced in size." She added, "The Lake County Detention Center has dropped the ball, and so have your attorneys for not getting our records before the judge for a furlough for your son for outside medical treatment. We can't give you your son's medical records, but we can give them to your son's lawyers. We do this all the time. They know what they have to do to get the records. That's what you are paying them for. This is not your responsibility to get our records; it's theirs." I told her that Attorney XXXXXX said the ball was in my court to get the surgical schedule for Robert's surgery and treatment in writing, so he could go back to Judge XXXXXX in one month with this additional information.

She gave me the name of XXXXXX who coordinates medical treatment for the Lake County Detention Center. She reiterated again and said. "Your son needs this taken care of immediately, and both the detention center and your attorneys are dropping the ball. You need to call XXXXXX, the Case Manager who coordinates the tests for the Detention Center. Your son needs tests and an MRI to see the size of the cancer. This must be done immediately! You have been bombarding our office with calls, and we feel sorry for what you and your son are going through, but we cannot give you any of the information you need in writing. Have your attorneys do their job and get on the ball and contact us for our records. Your lawyers know what they have to do, that's what you are paying them for. **No judge in the world with your son's medical condition will deny him a medical furlough."**

Unfortunately, Judge XXXXXX was the one Judge in the world who did deny my son his Motion for a Medical Furlough for his urgently needed outside cancer treatment. He did this with the full documented medical report from Dr. XXXXXX as to the urgency for Robert's medical treatment. Judge XXXXXX was also informed of the Detention Center's failure to provide medical treatment for 13 months. The court records will confirm Judge XXXXXX denying Robert's motions to receive urgently needed outside medical treatment, hospitalization, surgery, and chemotherapy. As of January 27, 2018, Robert had not received any hospitalization, surgery, or chemotherapy

On January 16, 2018, Deputy XXXXXX, the deputy who repeatedly kicked Robert in the stomach 10-12 times on October 5, 2015, and lied under oath about him at his hearings, came to see him at the Lake County Detention Center. He told Robert he wanted to talk to him and ask some questions. He asked Robert, "where are you going to live when you get out?" Robert refused to talk with him without his lawyers being present. This made Det. XXXXXX very angry. He ordered Robert into his cell and searched everything he had. He left with two bags of Robert's commissary food and one cookie. The guard on duty, Officer XXXXXX, came over to Robert and said, "I've been a guard here for 12 years, and I have never seen anything like this happen before to any-one. This Deputy was really pissed at you Robert!"

Four days prior to Dep. XXXXXX's visit to my son, he came to my home in Ft. Lauderdale and banged on my front door for three hours and called me repeatedly on my cell phone from 3:34 pm to 6:45 pm until he fi-nally left. Due to fear of this Deputy banging on my door and repeatedly calling me, I phoned Attorney XXXXXX who looked up the number I gave him that was on my caller ID. He confirmed the number was registered to this Deputy. The fear for my son's life and mine, from the ongoing criminal and violent acts committed by the three Lake County Deputies, including their lying under oath at my son's hearings, caused me to sell our home in Mt. Dora, FL, on November 16, 2017, where we lived since 1999.

The Lake County Prosecutor, XXXXXX, having the Deputies testify under oath with statements he knew were false against my son at hearings, was responsible for Robert not receiving reinstatement of his Bond, and a Medical Furlough for outside medical treatment for his cancer treatment. The Deputies prodded by the Prosecu-tor, and the Prosecutor himself falsely stating to Judge

XXXXXX that Robert was a flight risk and a danger to the community during the hearing motions, is what contributed to the adverse rulings by Judge XXXXXX. For the record, my family and I lived in Loch Leven for 17 years. We were the original homeowners in that waterfront community, which was our 2nd home. We never had any problems in our community whatsoever or any community we ever lived in for that matter.

The Prosecutor, XXXXXX canceled Robert's Motion to Suppress Hearings five (5) times over a period of almost eight months. He knew what a burden this was on Robert's health because he listened to all our monitored jail phone calls daily. He knew Robert was in severe pain and suffering with malignant colon cancer while the Prosecutor lied at the Hearings to keep Robert from receiving urgently needed medical treatment. A guard told Robert, "legally they can't keep you incarcerated for more than six months without a trial, they have kept you in here longer than they are supposed to." Upon investigation, I learned this was correct. Robert's Motion to Suppress should have been granted sooner than eight months.

The sixth Motion to Suppress was scheduled for November 8th, 2017. Prior to this Hearing, Attorney XXXXXX gave the Prosecutor the defense evidence of a live Video to give to Judge XXXXXX pre-hearing. The Video I took of the deputies when they were in our home on October 5, 2015, was vitally important evidence for my son's defense, which showed the egregious acts of the Deputies violations against his 4th Amendment Rights, and Federal Law Section 1983. **The Prosecutor failed to give this video to Judge XXXXXX prehearing and did not bring it to the Motion to Suppress Hearing as he promised Robert's Attorney he would.** By law, the Prosecutor was legally required to submit to the court the Defense's evidence. Unfortunately, Judge

XXXXXX did not get to see my son's video prior to the Motion to Suppress Hearing. However, suspecting the Prosecutor would not give this video to Judge XXXXXX, because it was lethal evidence against the Prosecution's case and against the unlawful acts of the Deputies, Attorney XXXXXX brought an extra copy of the video to court and showed his copy on his laptop computer to Judge XXXXXX. This video was powerful evidence for my son's case, showing the 4th Amendment violations committed by the Deputies, which his Motion to Suppress was based on.

At all previous Hearings, including this Motion to Suppress Hearing, Prosecutor, XXXXXX, repeatedly lied to Judge XXXXXX, stating my son was a flight risk and a danger to the community and said he should not be free on bond, and not have an outside medical furlough. These false stories were impregnated into Judge XXXXXX mind who came to the Motion to Suppress with his mind made up to rule against Robert's motion. The Prosecutor had no basis or any evidence whatsoever that Robert would be a flight risk or a danger to the Loch Leven neighborhood. However, the Prosecutor convinced Judge XXXXXX he was. Judge XXXXXX denied Robert's bond motion stating on his Order that Robert was a danger to the neighborhood. The prosecutor's influence over Judge XXXXXX with his bogus lies and false statements took priority over my son's prima facie evidence and justice.

When Robert was out on bond for 10 months from October 9, 2015, to August 17, 2016, on the Prosecutor's first bogus charges, he was not a flight risk or a danger to any community we lived in. He was out on bond for the Prosecutor's first bogus charges of resisting an officer without violence and their illegal confiscation of Robert's personal belongings without having a search warrant. The Police Report stated Robert had a laptop that had child porn on it but said he was not viewing or using his laptop at the tea shop but was merely in possession of the laptop. They stated the laptop was in a black zipper case. This used laptop was given to Robert by a friend in Ft. Lauderdale and he did not know it was illegal. Robert was not a flight risk then, nor is he now. All my son wants, and needs is medical treatment for his life-threatening and painful malignant colon cancer, and his legal rights upheld in a court of law.

Because Robert has a 70% blockage in his colon, due to the malignant colon cancer growth, he could not move his bowels normally. With this death sentence of malignant colon cancer, which to date is untreated by the Detention Center, he can hardly move about let alone be a flight risk, as falsely stated by the Prosecutor. Believing this lie and being 100% bias, Judge XXXXXX denied all of Robert's Motions for Reinstatement of his Bond and urgently needed Medical Furlough for treatment of his stage 3 or 4 malignant colon cancer.

For 55 years of his life, Robert never once had any legal problems, no police record, never drank or smoked, never took drugs, was never a threat to anyone, or any community as he is wrongfully and unjustly being accused of by this Prosecutor. His health is rapidly deteriorating without any medical treatment by the Lake County Detention Center for close to eighteen (18) months, which is well over the six-month time limit of being incarcerated without a trial or his due process of law. These violations of his civil, constitutional and prisoner's rights are egregious and unlawful. His three lawyers, XXXXXX, XXXXXX, XXXXXX, failed to get the mandatory medical care or justice for my son from the Lake County Judicial System. This is why Robert's attorneys counseled me to hire a civil rights lawyer to sue the Detention Center to save my son's life. Right now, time is of the essence to get my son his urgently needed medical care to treat his malignant colon cancer.

Judge XXXXX's rulings have overruled any form of justice for my son. The Prosecutor is treating his case against Robert like he is already guilty of the charges he has unjustly amassed against him, without having a trial or his Motion to Suppress Hearing which the Prosecutor canceled five times! I pray your investigation into the severe criminal violations to my son's Civil, Constitutional, and Prisoner's Rights, will be timely, to save his life. This is why I am making this complaint to the Department of Justice in order for my son to obtain Justice.

The following prosecutorial misconduct was committed by Prosecutor XXXXXX:

He refused to give the State's Discovery to my son's Attorneys for 300 days. He only turned over the State's Discovery after charging my son with his 2nd bogus arrest charges, and only after two motions to Judge XXXXXX were made to compel him to do so.

I was informed by Internal Affairs Investigator, XXXXXX that Prosecutor XXXXXX, used the same evidence he had on the first charges, to make his 2nd arrest charges, and that there was no new evidence against my son. I was charged $25,000 for a bond on the 2nd charges for my son on the same evidence the Prosecutor used for his 1st arrest charges, which I had already paid $13,500 for the first bond. This is a violation against Robert's 8th Amendment Rights, to be charged excessive bail on bogus charges.

Prosecutor XXXXXX made our Forensic Attorney, XXXXXX wait five months (150 days) before allowing him to examine the State's Forensic Report. During which time, my son was being denied his due process of law and suffering in severe pain without any medical treatment from the Detention Center. Waiting close to eight months for his Motion to Suppress Hearing and being denied medical treatment was violating his Constitutional rights.

Prosecutor XXXXXX gave false and damning information against Robert to Judge XXXXXX so reactivation of his $25,000 bond would be denied. His repeatedly telling Judge XXXXXX that Robert was a flight risk and a danger to the community, was without any viable evidence whatsoever. The Prosecutor based his case against my son on lies and bogus charges. **He kept Robert unjustly incarcerated to cover over his and the deputy's severe violations of the law.**

The Prosecutor canceling Robert's Motion to Suppress Hearing dates five times over a period of eight (8) months, ignored his Constitutional and due process of law rights.

After making his 2nd bogus arrest charges against my son, the Prosecutor gave false and damning information to the news media that went viral all over the country. He told the news media he based his 2nd arrest charges against Robert on his "assumption" that my son delivered two (2) jukeboxes with lenses in them in either 2011 or 2012 to the wrong neighbor thinking the wrong neighbor would deliver the jukeboxes to the right neighbor. He based his entire criminal charges against my son on his illogical "assumption" theory which was 100% false! The Prosecutor had my son arrested on August 17, 2016, with no proof whatsoever of any delivery of two jukeboxes in 2011 or 2012, because there was none.

The Prosecutor's false arrest charge resulted in the U. S. Marshals making their false charge against Robert of resisting an officer without violence. The U.S. Marshal admitted to Robert's Attorney they made this charge against Robert because they used Police Force in their arrest. Due to this bogus charge, Prosecutor XXXXXX immediately had Judge XXXXXX revoke my son's bond, on August 25, 2016, which I had just paid $25,000 to Lake County only 4 days earlier. Attorney XXXXX told me my son must have those charges removed in Broward County in order to reactivate Robert's 2nd bond in Lake County.

Prior to Robert going to trial for the resisting an officer charge in Broward County, the Prosecutor, contacted the Broward County Prosecutor XXXXXX and told her Robert was a flight risk and a danger to the community and she should not release Robert from the resisting charges. He sent her one audio of my jail phone conversation with my son, which was taken out of context. After speaking with the Lake County Prosecutor, she opted not to drop the "resisting an officer charge, "and my son went to trial. Robert had his case tried in front of six jurors and one alternate juror. After a 2-day trial, and less than 10 minutes of deliberation, the six jurors found Robert "Not Guilty," of the U. S. Marshal's false resisting an officer charge. The alternate 7th juror, came over to Robert after the verdict was read and said, "if I were still on the jury, I would have voted not guilty for you as well. Those officers were lying through their teeth." He told me the same thing as we were leaving the courtroom.

Prosecutor XXXXXX vindictively informed Robert's lead Attorney, XXXXXX, "I'm going to put your client away for life!" He made this statement without Robert having a trial by jury. XXXXXX's prosecutorial misconduct, and the Deputies lying under oath, with the bias shown in Judge XXXXXX's rulings, caused my son to be denied his constitutional due process of law and justice.

Prosecutor XXXXXX told Attorney XXXXXX that he allowed our neighbors in Loch Leven, and the Lake County Deputies, to listen to my son's monitored jail calls with me.

Prosecutor XXXXXX intentionally failed to bring to court Robert's vitally important live video evidence for his November 8, 2017 Motion to Suppress Hearing. This live video showed the Lake County Deputies' violations and criminal acts against my son's 4th Amendment Rights, and Federal Law Section 1983, Article 1 Section 8 of the U. S. Constitution. Their violations included: Deputies unlawful warrantless entry into our home on October 5, 2015, their illegal search and seizure, and their brutal physical assault causing permanent bodily harm to Robert. Also recorded on the live video was Captain XXXXXX's unlawful command to Robert threatening to kick down his bedroom closet door off its hinges if he didn't tell him where the key was. The Lake County Deputies committed all the above violations without a search warrant.

At the Motion to Suppress Hearing, on November 8, 2017, the Prosecutor lied to Attorney XXXXXX, and to Judge XXXXXX. In one instance he intentionally gave the wrong interpretation of the Supreme Court case law Rodriguez vs. State of Florida (2015) to Judge XXXXXX. He lied multiple times to support the Deputies illegal warrantless entry and search and seizure into our home on October 5, 2015. His lies caused Attorney

XXXXXX to go over to him in front of Judge XXXXXX and state, "XXXXXX, if you lie to me one more time in court I will go after your bar license." The Attorney also heard Judge XXXXXX say to Prosecutor XXXXXX, "you put me in a bad situation." The Attorney, XXXXXX can verify both these statements.

In Judge XXXXXX Order dated December 4, 2017, to my son's Motion to Suppress, he confirmed the warrantless violations committed by the Lake County Deputies were unlawful. The video showing the Deputies violations was clear prima facie evidence without question to support the Judge's statement. However, Judge XXXXXX put in his Order a Doctrine of Inevitable Discovery, which does not exist in the Supreme Court case law Rodriguez vs. State of Florida on a warrantless search. Robert's lawyers filed a Motion for Reconsideration, for Judge XXXXXX to correct his error in misinterpreting the Supreme Court case law, Rodriguez vs. State of Florida. Judge XXXXXX declined to correct his error in misinterpreting the law and gave no legal comment whatsoever for denying the Motion for Reconsideration.

I made a formal criminal complaint to Florida State Attorney, XXXXXX, and the Lake County Sheriff, regarding the Deputies violations to my son's 4th Amendment Rights. I included the following evidence with prima facie proof of the Deputies unlawful warrantless entry, their illegal search and seizure, their use of excessive physical, brutal force, which is in violation of Federal Law Section 1983, and Prosecutor XXXXXX's misconduct. Neither the Lake County Sheriff nor the Lake County State Attorney XXXXXX took any action on my complaint.

Due to all the corruption in the Lake County Judicial system, Robert's lawyers said the only viable option for him to seek justice was to plea "No Contest" and appeal. They said even though Judge XXXXXX ruled against the Deputies violations to Robert's 4th Amendment Rights it was still in my son's favor, stating Judge XXXXXX error in misinterpretation the Supreme Court case law, Rodriguez vs. State of Florida, by adding a doctrine of Inevitable Discovery that doesn't exist in the law opened the door for Robert to Appeal on the grounds that Judge XXXXXX misinterpreted the law.

Robert's lawyers agreed that Judge XXXXXX's error in misinterpreting this Supreme Court case law should be overruled by the 5th DCA Court on an Appeal. In order to do this, they recommended Robert Plea "No Contest" and appeal. They said he wouldn't get a just ruling from the Corrupt Lake County Justice System if he went to trial but would through his appeal because the Judge clearly misinterpreted the Supreme Court case law.

I am requesting herein an immediate expedited investigation, because time is of the essence, due to my son's critical health issues. All this delay of going 18 months without the necessary medical treatment for his malignant colon cancer is life-threatening. In addition, he is living with severe pain, suffering, and going without the proper medical care and treatment. His stage three or four malignant colon cancer is obstructing 70% of his colon. He not only has to deal with painful health issues but also with injustice his constitutional and prisoner's rights being violated.

During their unlawful warrantless entry on October 5, 2015, the three Lake County Deputies committed the following violations to Robert's 4th amendment rights and federal law section 1983:

Deputy XXXXXX Repeatedly kicked Robert in the stomach and ribs 10-12 times, which caused immediate internal intestinal health issues. He and the other two Deputies violated Federal Law Section 1983 with his brutal beating while being unlawfully in our home without a warrant, which violated Robert's 4th Amendment Rights.

Corporal XXXXXX repeatedly hitting Robert with blunt blows to his face, head, and eyes, caused him to go blind in his left eye. Corporal XXXXXX admitted on my cell phone video, "this happened to your son (their beating him) because he wouldn't let us come in and search your home."

Deputy XXXXXX is also guilty of forcefully entering our home without a Search Warrant with Deputy XXXXXX and Corporal XXXXXX and physically holding down my son while the other two Deputies brutally assaulted him.

During his first seventeen months of incarceration, Robert's pain and suffering continued daily while being caged in an 8 x 14 cell, packed in with up to 5-6 other cellmates, at one time, without any medical care of treatment. The malignant colon cancer growing inside his colon was ignored and untreated by the Lake County Detention Center during his first 17 months of incarceration. The Deputies brutal assault, resulted in Robert's unending pain while suffering from constant pain and bleeding like diarrhea from his colon, with nausea, fatigue, and a loss of over 40 pounds, and permanent blindness to his left eye.

Robert was denied a speedy trial while his constitutional rights and due process of law were severely violated. He often slept on the concrete floor, when a bottom bunk was not available because he couldn't climb on to a top bunk due to severe abdominal pain and bleeding from his colon cancer. Robert told me on one of our monitored jail calls, "climbing to the top bunk was too painful for me, so I sleep on the floor."

Robert's lawyers made ongoing requests to the Lake County Detention Center, the Lake County Sheriff, with motions to Judge XXXXXX for medical furloughs and medical treatment for Robert, all of which were denied. As of October 7, 2017, Robert's cancer was at stage three or four; the Doctor wasn't sure which stage it was in without having more tests taken, which the Detention Center failed to order as of the date of this letter.

Attorney XXXXXX told me on October 4, 2017, after Judge XXXXXX denied Robert's Motion for an Emergency Medical Furlough, "You need to hire a civil rights lawyer for Robert, to commence an immediate civil suit against Lake County Detention Center because he is in their care. His life depends upon it!"

I called a Civil Rights Lawyer in Ocala, Fl., who spoke to State Attorney, XXXXXX's head counsel, Attorney XXXXXX, who stated to him, "he is not as ill as his mother thinks he is." This Civil Rights Attorney said, "let's sue them all now, we have to give them a six-month notice!"

Summary of violations committed by the Lake County Prosecutor, the Lake County Deputies, and the Lake County Judge:

In Judge XXXXXX' Order to my son's Motion to Suppress, held on November 8, 2017, he confirmed the Deputies violated Robert's 4th Amendment Rights.

Judge XXXXXX' Order on addendum #2 on the bottom of page 3 of 6:

"The court observes that no justification was offered as to why police did not seek a warrant prior to approaching defendant's house for the knock and talk.

Had officers simply sought a warrant before entering the defendant's residence instead of afterward, they would have avoided an entirely unnecessary expenditure of both judicial and police resources. Separately from whether the tactics employed by police were legal, they were clearly unwise and unnecessary."

Judge XXXXXX added a Doctrine of Inevitable Discovery to his Order which did not exist in Supreme Court case law, Rodriguez vs. State of Florida. This doctrine reversed the unlawful violations of the Deputies. Judge XXXXXX misinterpretation of this Supreme Court Law allowed the illegal acts of the Deputies to override the law.

In order for Judge XXXXXX to correct his error on his Order, Robert's lawyers filed a Motion for Reconsideration, which he also denied with no legal explanation. This opened the door to the only justice available to my son now was an appeal. The lawyers told Robert the only way to be free from all this corruption is to plea "no contest" and appeal on the basis of Judge XXXXXX error in misinterpretation of the law. They said with the Judge's bias and the Prosecutor and Deputies conspiring with bogus testimony against Robert; this collusion would be difficult to overcome if Robert went to trial. Their opinion was based on all the motions Judge XXXXXX denied that should have been legally granted, and the ongoing conspiracy and collusion between the Prosecutor and Deputies during prior hearings. They further outlined their continued corruption that occurred during the Motion to Suppress Hearing when the following occurred:

Prosecutor, XXXXXX gave the wrong interpretation of case law and lied during the Hearing in front of Judge XXXXXX, which protected the violations committed by the Deputies. His lying in Court caused Attorney XXXXXX to approach him in front of Judge XXXXXX and state, "XXXXXX if you lie to me one more time in Court I will go after your Bar License." Attorney then gave the correct interpretation of the law to Judge XXXXXX a copy of the Supreme Court Law for his review as proof that the Prosecutor was lying.

Corporal XXXXXX's false sworn testimony was revealed by his body worn camcorder video which was played during the court proceedings. His sworn testimony was riddled with lies that were proven by the overwhelming evidence against his false testimony. Corporal XXXXXX did admit to his unlawful warrantless entry, search and seizure because of proof from the live video, and his body worn camcorder video. The transcribed Court Proceedings were previously submitted to your office of the Motion to Suppress Hearing.

Herein is a detailed summary report with Exhibits A-Q of criminal violations committed by the Lake County Deputies, Prosecutor, Judge, and the Lake County Detention Center in Tavares Florida:

On October 5, 2015, around 11:20 am three Lake County Sheriff's Deputies, Deputy XXXXXX, Deputy XXXXXX, and Corporal XXXXXX made an unlawful entry over the threshold of our home without a warrant, without consent, without probable cause, and without any exigent circumstances. They violated Robert's 4th amendment rights, by their unlawful entry, and their illegal search and seizure. Their brutally beating Robert was in violation of Federal Law Section 1983.

Upon the deputies being informed by my son, they needed the warrant to search our home, the three (3) officers immediately and forcefully entered our home and commenced using physical and brutal "POLICE FORCE." Their assault on my son caused life-threatening and permanent bodily injury and disability from their malicious beating. The Medical reports confirm Robert's injuries and disability from their beating. A Live Video of the aftermath of their beating and pictures of their violations were submitted to your office with all my Exhibits A-Q, on May 25, 2017.

Corporal XXXXXX's repeated blunt blows to Robert's face, head, and eyes, permanently blinded him in his left eye. Dep. XXXXXX kicking Robert repeatedly with his work shoes to his ribs and stomach caused life-threatening intestinal bleeding which being UNTREATED BY THE LAKE COUNTY DETENTION CENTER developed into pre-cancerous bleeding polyps, to malignant colon cancer, with a 70% blockage in his colon.

Deputy Corporal XXXXXX was recorded on my cell phone video admitting: "This (beating) happened to your son because he would not let us come in and search your home." My answer was, "without a warrant; I don't blame him!" Corporal XXXXXX repeated blows to Robert's eyes caused the drum that was surgically implanted in his left eye one year earlier, to secure a torn retina, to become wrinkled. This caused the blindness and a great amount of ongoing pain. The medical report, pictures, and video show the aftermath effect of this brutal beating.

During their unlawful entry, the Deputies kept Robert tightly handcuffed and in a trauma state for ten (10) hours, with no medical care while they roamed around our home looking for the laptop. At 10:00 pm, Robert was put in the back-seat of a police vehicle fetus style, without a seat belt and driven at a high speed of 80 mph, to the Lake County Detention Center.

I recorded on my cell phone video the following: Deputies' unlawful entry in our home, the aftermath results of their beating to my son, Deputies illegal search and seizure, Captain XXXXXX's unlawful command for the key to the locked bedroom closet, Capt. XXXXXX and Corp. XXXXXX's admission they had no search warrant and no probable cause, and Corporal XXXXXX's admission they beat up Robert because he would not allow them to do a warrantless search. In order to cover over their criminal violations, the Deputies created a false charge against Robert of resisting an officer without violence and proceeded to stage a crime scene. This was proven by Corporal XXXXXX's body-worn camcorder video.

After their unsuccessful warrantless search for the laptop, Captain XXXXXX deducted it must be in the locked bedroom closet, which was the only place they had not searched in our home. Captain XXXXXX threatened Robert with an unlawful command and said, "If you don't give us the key to your locked bedroom closet, we will kick the door off its hinges by the count of 10." Robert, in fear of reprisal and without giving his consent, told Captain XXXXXX where the key was.

The Deputies removed the laptop from the locked bedroom closet, unzipped the laptop's case, placed the laptop on the floor and put the case on the bed. The Master Deputy, who was in charge, Detective XXXXXX called CSI to take pictures of this "staged crime scene," and stated on his Police Report the laptop and case were in "plain view." He did this to cover up their illegal entry, search and seizure and to qualify their unlawful search under the plain view doctrine, "if an officer can see it, they can seize it." However, the plain view doctrine does not apply to a warrantless search on the doctrine of Inevitable Discovery in Rodriguez vs. State of Florida. Detective XXXXXX filed a false charge against Robert for resisting an officer without violence, in order to further justify their illegal entry, brutal beating, and illegal search and seizure, prior to obtaining the search warrant, which was signed several hours later.

Lake County Deputy XXXXXX only obtained his Search Warrant at 5:44 pm after their unlawful entry at 11:30 am. He had a Magistrate Judge sign the warrant leaving out important omissions on his warrant. These omissions were noted by Attorney XXXXXX in his Motion to Suppress and was 100% factual and documented during the Hearing with an expert witness who testified against the validity of the Search Warrant. Judge XXXXXX immediately denied this important evidence against the validity of the warrant even after an expert witness, Forensic Attorney, XXXXXX testified against its validity. (see Exhibit M).

Deputy XXXXXX not only falsified a police report with bogus statements to justify their criminal acts but lied under oath to cover up their violations, which I have documented with evidence, as outlined in Exhibits A-Q. Evidence includes pictures, video, police body worn video camera/recorder, court transcripts, depositions, and the court transcription of proceedings at the November 8, 2017 Motion to Suppress Hearing. Exhibits A-Q were mailed to your office on May 25, 2017, and the transcription of the Suppression Hearing was faxed to your office on February 6, 2018. Your assistant, XXXXXX, who was most helpful, was trying to search for these exhibits, which may have been lost in your system. Upon request, all Exhibits can be resubmitted.

The Live Video and documents were submitted with my April 5, 2018, updated letter. I received your confirmation of this letter with an assigned ID # XXXXXXX on April 9, 2018.

Five months after the initial charge was made against my son, on October 5, 2015, I made a formal criminal complaint against the Sheriff's Deputies to the Lake County Internal Affairs Department in March 2016. During Detective XXXXXX's Internal Affairs investigation of Captain XXXXXX and the Deputies, they gave this sworn recorded statement: "We thought going into defendant's home (O'Hare) without a warrant would work like it did all the other times." In other words, these Lake County Sheriff's Deputies made it a practice to violate the law anytime they could get away with it.

In 2016 case law United States v. Allen (U.S. App. Lexis 1467 2d Cir. Jan. 29, 2016) states: **"Officers stepping across the threshold to arrest without a warrant violated the Fourth Amendment and one's civil, and constitutional rights as well."**

In 2015, the Supreme Court ruled in Case Law Rodriguez vs. State of Florida that **warrantless searches by Police officers are unlawful.** This case law was used in Robert's Motion to Suppress. The Suppression hearing for this motion was held on November 8, 2018. Two witnesses in the Courtroom XXXXXX and XXXXXX both stated Judge XXXXXX appeared to be appalled upon viewing the unjustified acts of the deputies on the live video. They both said prior to viewing this video Judge XXXXXX appeared to have made up his mind against my son's case when he first entered the Courtroom, but his demeanor changed dramatically after seeing the video.

Judge XXXXXX did acknowledge in his Order to my son's Motion to Suppress, that the Deputies had no justification to come into our home without a warrant. Their doing so was unlawful and against my son's 4th Amendment Rights. It was Judge XXXXXX's error in adding a Doctrine of "Inevitable Discovery, "that does not exist in the Supreme Court Case, Rodriguez vs. State of Florida. Robert's Attorney XXXXXX filed a Motion for Reconsideration to give Judge XXXXXX the opportunity to correct his error of misinterpreting this case law. Judge XXXXXX declined to correct his error which opened the door for Robert to Appeal.

All four of Robert's lawyers confirmed that Judge XXXXXX error in his Order in misrepresenting the law and adding a doctrine that doesn't exist in the law was a clear indication Robert should not go to trial with this Judge. Robert's lawyers again warned him, "this judge is so biased against you Robert he is not following the law. You should not go to trial with a biased judge and the prosecutor conspiring against you with the deputies. This would be lethal. You will lose! We recommend you enter a Plea of No Contest and Appeal in order to find justice and freedom."

A central Florida Judge who took an interest in my son's case read all the documents of his Motions to Suppress and advised the same. They all agreed that the Judge left the door wide open for an Appeal on the Basis of his misrepresentation of the law which gave Robert an excellent chance to win the appeal and be set free. This left Robert no legal recourse but to Plea "no contest," and take Judge XXXXXX's stiff sentence of 20 years, and file the Appeal, while my son was still alive. The appeal was filed with the 5th DCA on February 8, 2018. Our hopes are high for this appeal to be granted because it is based solely on Supreme Court Case Law Rodriguez vs. State of Florida.

At the Motion to Suppress, Judge XXXXXX was given positive proof of the Deputies violations against Robert's 4th Amendment Rights. With the evidence of the live video, pictures, depositions, Police body-camcorder video, false police reports, and witnesses, the Deputies' violations were undeniable.

Even with all the above evidence, it was overridden by bias, corruption, collusion, and politics. An immediate investigation is sorely needed on this complaint. This form of Judicial Governing is dangerous not only to my son but anyone seeking their constitutional rights and justice in the Lake County's Judicial system. Corruption, bias, and politics undermine the very essence of civil and constitutional rights of the people and causes an absence of due process of law for anyone who has the misfortune to try their case in a Court of Law that doesn't honor one's constitutional rights or the law.

Lake County Prosecutor, XXXXXX's major prosecutorial misconduct, includes perverting justice by lying in a court of law, conspiring with the Lake County Sheriff's Deputies, giving false testimony at Robert's Bond Hearing, and at the Medical Furlough Hearing, then lying during the Motion to Suppress Hearing to the Judge.

The Prosecutor's failure to bring the defense's evidence to Judge XXXXXX prehearing and to the Motion to Suppress Hearing on November 8, 2017, was a major violation of his prosecutorial misconduct. He purposefully kept the defense's Live Video evidence from Judge XXXXXX because it exposed the deputies' illegal entry, evidence of their physical assault on my son, searching our home without a warrant, Captain XXXXXX making an unlawful warrantless demand for a key to a locked bedroom closet, and proof of their staging a crime scene with the laptop and case.

Proof of the above was evidenced at the Suppression Hearing with the live video and Corporal XXXXXX's body-worn camcorder video, which was evidence of the Deputies talking about retrieving the laptop from the locked closet, several hours before they obtained their search warrant. Their placing the laptop on the floor and the case on the bed was verified on Detective XXXXXX's police report, and his calling CSI to take pictures of their "staged" laptop and case being in "plain view." He did this to comply with the Plain View Doctrine to justify their unlawful warrantless search and seizure.

Fortunately, Attorney XXXXXX, suspecting the

Prosecutor would not bring the video to Judge XXXXXX at the Hearing, had an extra video with him to present to Judge XXXXXX. This Video was prima facie evidence of the Sheriff's Deputies violations against Robert's 4th Amendment Rights. If Attorney XXXXXX did not have an extra copy of the Live Video with him at the Hearing, all the above evidence for my son against the Deputies would have been lost! This would have been a true travesty of justice. This was the sole intent of this Prosecutor to keep my son's vitally important evidence from Judge XXXXXX. Fortunately, Judge XXXXXX did get to view the video of the Deputies warrantless search and seizure and did acknowledge their violations in his Order to Robert's Motion to Suppress, dated December 4, 2017, and did state their entry was unlawful.

The Prosecutor's prosecutorial misconduct includes issuing still another 2nd bogus arrest charge against Robert, 10 months after his first charges. He admitted to the news media his 2nd charges were based solely on his "assumption," that Robert delivered two jukeboxes with lenses in them in 2011 or 2012 to one of our Mt. Dora neighbors thinking that neighbor would deliver the two jukeboxes to the correct neighbor. The Prosecutor wasn't sure which year this was in. He had no evidence whatsoever of Robert making any such delivery, just his "assumption."

Despite not having any such evidence of Robert delivering two jukeboxes, in 2011 or 2012 the Prosecutor had the Broward County Police Officers and the U. S. Marshals in Ft. Lauderdale, Florida, arrest him anyway on August 17, 2016

During Robert's arrest by the Broward County Police Officers, they committed the following violations: (1) They used excessive physical force on my son, (2) smashed into our parked car with their SUV, (3) broke the back window on the passenger's side on our parked car, (4) pointed a loaded gun towards our head as we were sitting in the front seat of our parked car, (5) filed a false charge on my son of resisting an officer without violence, (6) and falsified their police report to justify their violations. During a jury trial in Broward County, my son was found "Not Guilty" of all those bogus charges made up by the U.S. Marshals and Broward County Officers in Ft. Lauderdale, FL.

Prosecutor XXXXXX continued on with his conspiracy and prosecutorial misconduct by having A Detective from the Sheriff's office in their cybersex unit testify under oath, at Robert's Bond Motion Hearing, that he was told by Broward County Officer XXXXXX that Robert delivered two (2) Jukeboxes to a family in Ft. Lauderdale in 2016. This lie was denied by the Broward Officer XXXXXX to his Supervisor Sargent XXXXXX and Internal Affairs Investigator, XXXXXX. Both confirmed that "Officer XXXXXX never stated to the Lake County Detective XXXXXX that Robert delivered two jute boxes to a family in Broward County, and as further proof, this Jukebox story was not put on officer's XXXXXX's Police Report (#XXXXXX)."

Exhibit A: Broward County-Ft. Lauderdale Police Report #XXXXXX; Internal Affairs Case #XXXXXX.

Note: There are no two (2) Jukeboxes mentioned anywhere on this Report, as Lake County Detective XXXXXX falsely testified to, under oath at the Bond Hearing.

Prosecutor XXXXXX's prosecutorial misconduct includes but is not limited to: lying in a court of law, not producing states evidence to defense counsel timely, not being neutral, conspiring with the Lake County Deputies, not producing evidence at a hearing that would exonerate the defendant, giving false and damning evidence to the news media, and being 100% vindictive.

Prosecutor XXXXXX canceled five hearings for Robert's Motion to Suppress for eight (8) months while keeping him incarcerated and objecting to his receiving urgently needed medical care. He made vindictive and threatening statements against my son to Attorney XXXXXX. He lied to Judge XXXXXX during all the hearings, with intent to have my son's Motions for Reinstatement of his Bond denied, for his urgently needed medical furlough, his Motion to Suppress and his Motion for Reconsideration. He falsely stated my son was a flight risk and a danger to the neighborhood with no such evidence. These are all major acts of prosecutorial misconduct and prosecutorial vindictiveness.

After 13 months of pain and suffering, the Detention Center allowed Robert to see one Medical Doctor, XXXXXX, who told Robert he had inflammation to his pancreas, from an injury to his abdomen, and colon cancer. This injury was caused by Det. XXXXXX punching and kicking Robert 10-12 times in the ribs and abdominal area, on his illegal warrantless entry to our home on October 5, 2015.

Upon receiving the Medical Report from the GI Doctor, Dr. XXXXXX, the Lake County Detention Center called the Doctor and said not to treat Robert any further because they were going to have their own Doctor take over Robert's care. I was informed of this by the Doctor's Assistant. Finally, after one year of incarceration, the Detention Center hired an Oncologist, who did a colonoscopy and diagnosed my son with malignant colon cancer with a 70% blockage to his colon.

This Doctor informed Robert he must have an immediate MRI, surgery, and chemotherapy. Since this diagnosis on September 5, 2017, the Detention Center procrastinated giving him the prescribed MRI or any chemotherapy or hospitalization for his life-threatening malignant colon cancer. Four months later, on January

28, 2018, Robert was given 5 radiation treatments after 17 months of incarceration. Since his 5 radiation treatments to date, he has not been seen by a medical doctor or given any follow up medical treatment or care by a Doctor to the date of this updated letter on April 24, 2018. During and after his 5 radiation treatments, they put Robert in locked down 24/7 Psyche Ward and only allowed him out of his cell for a total of 3 hours a week on Monday, Wednesday, and Friday.

On December 15, 2017, my son said, "Mom, I don't want to scare you, I'm bleeding every day, etc." These monitored jail calls can be reviewed in your investigation as evidence he is not being given any necessary medical treatment for his life-threatening illness.

The three Lake County Deputies who I am making this formal criminal complaint against are:

Corporal XXXXXX, who blinded my son in his left eye with repeated blunt blows with his fist to Robert's face, head, and eyes. An Eye Doctor's Report, an exhibit which is added to this complaint, states Robert's blindness was caused by a blunt blow to his left eye. This eye had a drum surgically implanted a year earlier, to secure the torn retina. Pictures, I took right after Robert's beating shows his beaten, bloody face, swollen eyes, with punch marks on his face, head, and eyes. His eyes were swollen shut, his face bloody, only moments after the deputies illegally entered our home and brutally beat him. These pictures were included in the Exhibits A-Q that were sent to DOJ in May 2017.

Deputy XXXXXX, who held my son down bodily on the floor, while Dep. XXXXXX and Corporal XXXXXX were severely and brutally assaulting him, cooperated 100% with the assault and their unlawful search and seizure.

Deputy XXXXXX, who I witnessed beating and repeatedly kicking my son in the stomach and ribs, and punching him with his fists, and tearing his t-shirt down below his chest as he was on all fours. His beating caused severe pain and damage to my son's pancreas, intestines, and ribs. Robert has had unending pain and ongoing intestinal bleeding issues ever since, which has been, medically untreated by the Lake County Detention Center. This was later diagnosed as life-threatening malignant colon cancer with a 70% blockage. Robert is still bleeding from his bowel movements. I reported all this to the State Attorney, XXXXXX, who, to date, is non-responsive to giving my son any urgently needed treatment for his malignant cancerous growth in his colon or taken any actions against the criminal violations of the Deputies that are under his direct supervision. He is culpable for such neglect.

In addition to making a formal Criminal complaint against the three Lake County Deputies named above, I am making a Formal complaint against the Lake County Detention Center for violations of my son's, 8th Amendment, and Prisoner's Rights. The Detention Center never gave my son any medical treatment for over one year. It was only on September 7, 2017, that Robert was seen for the first time by a medical doctor, since his incarceration on August 25, 2016. He never received any medical treatment from the Doctor only a diagnosis. There was never any follow up care until January 28, 2018, when he was given 5 radiation treatments.

The Oncologist from the detention center, Dr. XXXXXX, confirmed the diagnoses made by Dr. XXXXXX. Dr. XXXXXX informed Robert he had malignant colon cancer with a mass that is blocking his colon 70% and **needs immediate surgery and chemother-**

apy. Dr. XXXXXX confirmed on his report that my son had this cancer growth in him for one year! He told Robert, "I don't know why the Detention Center didn't do something about this sooner." His report was submitted to your office. He stated in his medical report: "Mr. O'Hare is a pleasant 55-year-old gentleman."

Each time my son complained of his abdominal pain and rectal bleeding to the Detention Center Guards, he was threatened by one guard that told him, "Go to your cell, or I'll put you in the box." My son informed me of this and all the above conversations we had during our monitored jail phone conversations. All these calls can be verified in your investigation.

I include in this formal criminal complaint the following names of the four additional Deputies because they entered our home during the ensuing brutal assault, by the three Deputies XXXXXX, XXXXXX, and XXXXXX. They all violated my son's 4th Amendment Rights as well, and are culpable for assisting the three Deputies in their unlawful criminal violations to my son's 4th Amendment Rights in their illegal search and seizure:

Captain XXXXXX, who threatened my son with an unlawful warrantless command: "If you don't give me the key to your locked bedroom closet, I'll kick the door off its hinges at the count of 10." His threat to kick the door off its hinges was recorded on my cell phone video

Detective XXXXXX, the officer who falsely testified, under oath at the March 20, 2017 bond hearing, stated: "Broward County Officer, XXXXXX, told me Robert O'Hare gave two (2) Jukeboxes to a Broward family in 2016." The Broward Officer XXXXXX's supervisor, Sargent XXXXXX said no such jukebox story was ever stated by Officer XXXXXX to Lake County Detective XXXXXX, and as further proof, it was not on his police report. (see Exhibit A) Broward County Internal Affairs Investigator, XXXXXX, also stated the same, "No jukebox story was ever stated by Officer XXXXXX to Detective XXXXXX."

This false statement of two (2) Jukeboxes made up by Detective XXXXXX, under oath, caused two things to happen. Judge XXXXXX denied reactivating my son's $25,000 bond, so he could not get outside medical treatment for his malignant colon cancer, and this lie was meant to support the Prosecutor XXXXXX's bogus 2nd charges of Robert delivering two (2) Jukeboxes to a neighbor in 2011-2012, which the prosecutor based solely on his "assumption" theory with no delivery evidence whatsoever.

Both the Prosecutor and Detective XXXXXX conspired together to implant this falsehood to Judge XXXXXX by stating Robert would be a threat to the community and a flight risk if he were to receive reactivation of his bond or a Medical furlough so he could receive outside urgently needed medical treatment. This conspiracy between Detective XXXXXX and Prosecutor, XXXXXX worked! My son's $25,000 Bond was permanently revoked by Judge XXXXXX who put on his ruling stated that from the witness testimony that Robert was a threat to the Loch Leven subdivision we lived in. Unfortunately for my son, conspiracy, collusion, bias, and corruption reigned over Justice in the Lake County Judicial System, and violated his civil, constitutional and prisoner's rights!

In 2012, this same Detective XXXXXX was arrested in Baltimore for indecent exposure, of his private parts, and rehired again by the Lake County Sheriff's Office to work in their Cyber "Sex" Crime Unit. The article of his arrest is attached to this letter, along with other articles defining the questionable reputation of the Lake County Deputies and their Judicial System. Due to Det. XXXXXX making a false and damaging testimony at the Bond Hearing against my son, I submitted a formal complaint to the Lake County Sheriff's Internal Affairs Dept. and included the article of Detective XXXXXX's arrest in 2012. My complaint was flatly denied, and I was informed that no action would be taken against Detective XXXXXX. The Investigator of Internal Affairs was the same investigator for Detective XXXXXX's arrest charges in 2012 as well as this criminal complaint.

Master Deputy XXXXXX made several "major" false statements on his police report and lied under oath during the hearings. One false statement made was that he went into the front door by the garage of our home while the three (3) deputies, XXXXXX, XXXXXX, and XXXXXX, were assaulting my son inside the house, he said he yelled, "Sheriff's Office." Then wrote in his police report he heard the officers say twice, "stop resisting, stop resisting." He made this bogus statement on his Police Report to justify their false charges against my son of resisting an officer without violence, and to justify their unlawful entry, beating, and searching in our home, without a warrant.

The truth being, I personally saw Master Deputy XXXXXX coming through the front entry door, while the 3 Deputies were assaulting my son. I recorded him on my cell phone video camera talking to me and then laying sideways across my son's legs after he was beaten by the three deputies. The front door by the garage was padlocked, and no one could come through that door unless they physically broke it down. Master Deputy XXXXXX never thought I would be the one reading and reporting herein his falsifying his Police Report. See page 8 of 30 in the Police Report #XXXXXXX.

To support their staged crime scene, CSI was called in to take pictures of the laptop and case which the Deputies placed in the bedroom, staging the case on the bed and the laptop on the floor. The false documentation of the crime scene was filed in their Police Report as being in "plain view."

During the Motion to Suppress Hearing held on November 8, 2017, Attorney XXXXXX substantiated this damning evidence of the Body Worn Camcorder Video in his cross-examination of Corporal XXXXXX. A transcript of this Hearing verifies all the above evidence that was previously submitted to this criminal complaint, ID #XXXXXXX, and updated ID #XXXXXXX.

This intentional conspiracy to jointly stage this crime scene to cover over the Deputies illegal search and seizure, are serious criminal violations that went unpunished by the Lake County Sheriff and the State Attorney, XXXXXX.

The following is another recorded conversation on Corporal XXXXXX's Body Worn-Camcorder Video of their initial contact with Robert at the front entry door on October 5, 2015, in which Corporal XXXXXX told him he couldn't call his lawyer:

XXXXXX: "Anyone else here with you?"

Robert: "My Mother, can I call my lawyer?"

XXXXXX: "No."

Robert: "What did I do wrong?"

XXXXXX: "Asked for consent to come in and search the home."

Robert: "No, I want you to get a warrant!"

XXXXXX: "Step outside!"

Robert: "No."

As Robert was closing the door, the three deputies forcefully stepped over the threshold of our home and physically overpowered and brutally assaulted Robert. This became an instant violation to my son's 4th Amendment Rights, and Federal Law Section 1983. The Deputies committed these serious acts of violence and criminal violations against my son and his constitutional rights. You have been given more than enough evidence in this criminal complaint with Exhibits A-Q to prosecute them all.

Our Government and our Supreme Court Laws demand that Enforcement Officers must abide by the law or will be prosecuted for poisoning the very essence of our democracy. Enforcement Officers take a pledge to uphold the people's 4th, 5th, and 6th Amendment Rights in our Constitution. The Deputies made a false arrest charge against my son for "resisting an officer without violence," to justify their own unlawful entry, search and seizure, and brutally beating Robert. Using their badge to cover over their criminal violations is fully documented in detail with prima facie evidence in this formal complaint.

Exhibit B: Lake County Incident Report #XXXXXXXX posts a false charge against my son of resisting an officer without violence.

The deputies staging a crime scene with the laptop is 100% illegal. Master Deputy XXXXXX's filing of a bogus police report to justify their illegal search and seizure of the laptop is also 100% illegal. Police Reports are supposed to be based on true and accurate facts, not fabricated lies made up by Law Enforcement Officers to cover over their violations. An Officer writing up a detailed and accurate report is important evidence. A well-written incident report gives a thorough account of what actually happened, and the officer must stick to the facts. Detective XXXXXX lied on his Police Report, primarily to cover over his and the other deputies' violations. The Law Enforcement Officer's Brotherhood of conspiracy, collusion, and lying under oath is 100% illegal! Police Officers who commit such unlawful acts should be prosecuted and not given immunity.

In the Broward County police report, there was no mention of Robert giving two (2) jukeboxes to a family in Broward County. The Prosecutor, XXXXXX conspiring with Detective XXXXXX to falsely testify under oath about their made-up Jukebox story is a major form of prosecutorial misconduct. When I brought this to the Lake County Internal Affairs attention in a Formal Complaint, they found nothing wrong with Detective XXXXXX lying under oath about this Jukebox Story even with all the proof I gave them that he lied. Internal Affairs took no action against him, choosing to ignore all the positive evidence I submitted to them that included Sargent XXXXXX and Internal Affairs Investigator XXXXXX's statement that Officer XXXXXX never told this jukebox story to Lake County Detective XXXXXX. The Broward County Police Report #XXXXXXX filed by Officer XXXXXX confirms this as well as the Broward County Internal Affairs Report #XXXXXXX.

I informed Lake County State Attorney, XXXXXX of the Prosecutor's false arrest charges made up about

Robert delivering two (2) Jukeboxes in 2011 or 2012 to a family in Lake County, and all the proof I have of his public statements to the news media, where he stated, "I assume Robert O'Hare delivered two (2) Jukeboxes in 2011 or 2012 to the wrong neighbor thinking the wrong neighbor would deliver the two (2) Jukeboxes to the correct neighbor." **The State Attorney was silent about the Prosecutor's misconduct, and took no action.**

Without any evidence against Robert, only his assumption, the Prosecutor, XXXXXX, chose to publish his false allegations all over the news media to try his false arrest charges against Robert using public condemnation rather than reserving his assumptions in a court of law. Prosecutor XXXXXX giving false and damning information to the news media based on his "assumption," theory is a very dangerous and lethal way for a Lake County State Prosecutor to execute unsubstantiated charges against my son or anyone.

Previously, several lawyers I interviewed for my son revealed, the Judges in Lake County rules in favor of the Deputies and the Prosecutor, over the accused. Even one of the guards at the Detention Center told Robert he was a guard in Judge XXXXXX' chambers and heard both the Judge and the Prosecutor discussing their cases before entering the courtroom. He said the Judge would make his ruling about cases before they enter the courtroom, and not during court proceedings, as it should be. He said the people don't have a chance. **No Judicial System in our Country should function in this manner.**

The following "summarizes" all the details of violations that were previously stated in the prior correspondence with Exhibits A-Q.

On October 5, 2015, around 11:15 am, Robert and I were in our home on XXXXXX, Mt. Dora, FL., going through our usual morning routine. I was listening to my bible tapes when I heard blood-curdling cries coming from inside our home. I rushed into the living room and saw three (3) Lake County Sheriff's Deputies brutally assaulting my son, in powerful unison. They were thrusting blunt and brutal blows to Robert's body, head, face, and eyes. Two of the Deputies were repeatedly kicking, and punching Robert, as he lay defenseless and helpless on the floor. I was in total shock, thinking this must be a nightmare. These three men ignored my pleas and continued assaulting Robert as he was crying out in pain from their beating.

During this assault, Deputy XXXXXX was bodily suppressing my son's legs, while the other two deputies, one on each side, were repeatedly kicking, hitting, and punching Robert, non-stop. Deputy XXXXXX was standing over my son's body kicking him repeatedly on his left side, to his ribs and abdomen, soccer ball style, 10-12 times with his heavy beige colored work shoes. The other Deputy, Corporal XXXXXX, kneeling on one knee on Robert's right side, was hitting my son to his head, face, and eyes, with multiple blunt blows with his fist. Corporal XXXXXX blinded Robert in his left eye. Deputy XXXXXX caused intestinal bleeding that developed into severe bowel problems to bleeding polyps to malignant colon cancer.

Exhibit C: Pictures of Robert's bloody face and injuries to his body after his severe beating by the three (3) Lake County Sheriff's Deputies.

The Deputies only stopped their assault after I started to videotape them with my cell phone. They abruptly sat Robert upright and tightly handcuffed his wrists behind his back. Robert said the handcuffs were too tight. I told the deputy his wrists were instantly turning red. The officers clicked the handcuffs to even a tighter notch out of spite, which cut off his blood circulation even more to his hands. The other deputies who had entered our home during this altercation were Deputy XXXXXX, Captain XXXXXX, and Detective XXXXXX. They said my son was in a tea shop in downtown Mt. Dora, called XXXXXX, with a laptop they allege may have child porn downloaded on it. They wanted to search the home for the laptop, admitting on my cell phone they had no search warrant or probable cause.

After searching the entire home, opening doors and drawers, and not finding the laptop, Captain XXXXXX became angry and was recorded on my 35-minute cell phone video as saying, "Even if we don't find the laptop we are still going to arrest your son anyway." I asked, "On what charge?" He said, "For resisting an officer without violence." I said, "Resisting an officer when you forced your way into our home without a search warrant?" Then he said, "We are going to draw up a search warrant." "If we don't find the laptop, after our search, this is a free Country, we will leave, but we are going to charge your son anyway with resisting an officer without violence." **This false resisting charge was filed against my son by the Lake County Sherriff's Deputies.**

My son was still on the floor, his hands tightly handcuffed behind his back, cutting off his blood circulation to his hands, and in a great deal of pain from their beating. The Deputies commenced searching our home for the laptop. The only place they did not look for the laptop was in my son's locked bedroom closet. Captain XXXXXX said to Robert, "If you don't tell us where the key is to your locked bedroom closet, I'll kick the door off its hinges." Out of fear, my son told him where the key was but did not give his consent to Captain XXXXXX's unlawful command. The deputy unlocked the closet door and came back into the living room several minutes later while talking with each other. They were pleased they had found the laptop that Robert had with him at the teahouse, called XXXXXX in Mt. Dora, Florida on October 5, 2015.

Thereafter, for a total of 10 hours, they had Robert sitting on a chair, next to the front entrance, with his hands still tightly handcuffed. They kept him sitting there while waiting for the search warrant to be drawn up and signed by the magistrate. The search warrant was signed at 5:44 pm and delivered to our home about 6:45 pm. This was several hours after their forced entry and the completion of their illegal search and seizure of the laptop. At around 10:00 pm Robert was taken to the Lake County Detention Center by two officers who crammed him into the back seat of their vehicle, fetus style because it was loaded with stuff. The Deputy sped over 80 miles per hour to the Lake County Detention Center where Robert was booked into the facility.

The Lake County Sheriff's Deputies, used harmful and deadly brutal force on Robert while keeping him tightly handcuffed for 10 hours, during which time it took them six hours to obtain a search warrant. The Deputies' actions were unlawful and against all acceptable police protocol. They severely violated Robert's 4th Amendment Rights, which prohibits searches and seizures without a valid search warrant or probable cause. They also violated Federal Law Section 1983 by using excessive brutal police force. The Deputies admitted they did not have a judicially sanctioned warrant, nor was one in place when they unlawfully entered our home. **Neither was a mandatory Use-of-Force Incident Report ever filed by the Sheriff's Deputies.**

Master Deputy XXXXXX stated in his police report the following:

1 Robert O'Hare was **in a restaurant** called, XXXXXX, with his laptop zipped in his black case, and **he was not using the laptop.**

2　Even though there were 20 other people using the Wi-Fi in the area on that day, Robert was singled out because he was a regular customer at the tea shop.

3　Master Deputy XXXXXX's Police Report stated falsely they found the Toshiba laptop on the floor in Robert's bedroom and the case for the laptop on the bed. When, all the while, **the laptop was in a locked bedroom closet zipped in its case.**

4　Corporal XXXXXX's body-worn camcorder video recorded his conversation with the other deputies, talking about finding the Toshiba laptop in a locked bedroom closet, which was several hours before obtaining the search warrant.

5　The Deputies staged their own crime scene to cover up their unlawful and forceful entry over the threshold of our home, and their illegal search and seizure without a search warrant.

6　This warrantless search was confirmed by the Deputies, who swore under oath to Detective XXXXXX, of Lake County Internal Affairs, stating, "We thought this would work like it did all the other times, (warrantless search) and that O'Hare would let us in and search his home."

On my cell phone video, I recorded Captain XXXXXX's admission that the only probable cause they had when they forcefully entered our home was one they created, which was to accuse my son of resisting an officer without violence. This was after they assaulted him and were in our home without a warrant. The Deputies' forced entry into our home was not only a violation of my son's 4th Amendment Rights but brutally beating him was against "Federal law U.S. Code, title 42 chapter 21, subchapter 1, 1983. In Section 1983: This law provides a federal cause of action against any person who, acting under color of state law, deprives another of his federal rights, and uses excessive police force."

Countless case laws support our civil and constitutional rights, which the three (3) Lake County deputies egregiously violated. Corporal XXXXXX admitted, as recorded on my cell phone video, "This happened to your son (Deputies' beating Robert) because he wouldn't let us come in and search the property." They not only beat my son close to death but restrained him in handcuffs in his beaten traumatic state for close to 10 hours. During which time, it took the deputy in charge, Detective XXXXXX six (6) hours to obtain a search warrant.

Any excuse of doing a protective sweep was not applicable in this instance, as my son and I were the only known occupants in the home, as confirmed on Corporal XXXXXX's Body-Worn Camcorder Video, and in Master Deputy's XXXXXX's police report. The Deputies knew this fact when they first knocked on the door and asked Robert if anyone else was in the house. Robert answered, as recorded on Corporal XXXXXX's Body-Worn Camcorder Video, "my mother." It does not take several armed men several hours to do a protective sweep of a home when they know there was no other occupant in our home. The Deputies warrantless search of opening up doors, drawers and a privately locked bedroom closet door, without a search warrant, consent, or any exigent circumstances, were clearly unlawful. (Rodriguez vs. State of Florida, 2015)

In Corporal XXXXXX's testimony at the Motion to Suppress, he states, "We couldn't see through the front door because there were shutters, so I put my foot over the threshold." By Corporal XXXXXX's own sworn admission, this was an illegal entry without a warrant. He admits he could not see into the home because there were shutters on the doors and windows in front of the home. Therefore, no exigent circumstances existed, to justify their illegal entry. The Deputies illegal entry was further confirmed by Judge XXXXXX in his Order to Robert's Motion to Suppress. **Judge XXXXXX states in his Order: "The Court observes that no justification was offered as to why police did not seek a warrant prior to approaching Defendant's house for the knock and talk."**

However, in his Order, Judge XXXXXX in error rewarded the Deputies criminal violations with a doctrine of Inevitable Discovery that does not exist in the Supreme Court case, Rodriguez vs. State of Florida, without a search warrant being first in place. In my son's case, the Deputies had no warrant in place or even one on the way.

Exhibit D: The Search Warrant, issued at 5:44 pm, was six hours after deputies forced entry, and their conducting an illegal search, and seizure of the laptop. This was confirmed on Corporal XXXXXX's Body Worn Camcorder Video with date and time registered at 11:37 am on October 5, 2015.

Exhibit E: The "Live Video," showing the "aftermath" of the Lake County Deputies' savage and brutal assault on Robert, and their violations committed while in our home against Robert's 4th Amendment Rights, and Federal Law, Section 1983.

After Robert was brutally assaulted and blinded in his left eye by Corporal XXXXXX, I wiped the blood dripping down my son's face and upper body, as he sat on the chair in a great deal of pain. Deputy XXXXXX had maliciously ripped my son's t-shirt down below his chest, which exposed the deep wounds and bruise marks from the Deputies' beating. He falsely stated in his police report that Robert was running towards the kitchen and that's why he tore his shirt. My video shows Robert on the floor only a few feet from the front entry door, facing the opposite direction from the kitchen, with his t-shirt torn down his back. He was not running towards the kitchen, which was 50' away, as Deputy XXXXXX falsely stated in his police report. He did this to justify the brutal force he used on my son. Corporal XXXXXX, falsely stated under oath at the Motion to Suppress Hearing on November 8, 2017, that he was the one who tore Robert's shirt when he stepped over the threshold of the front entry door. Robert confirmed, "it was not Corporal XXXXXX who tore my shirt. It was Deputy XXXXXX, the one who kept kicking me in my stomach."

This cell phone video was my only proof of their illegal presence in our home without a warrant. The video also shows their roaming freely throughout our 5000-sq. Ft. Mt. Dora residence while unlawfully searching for the laptop. After searching the home and not finding the laptop, Captain XXXXXX deducted it must be in the only place they didn't look in, and that was my son's locked bedroom closet. Captain XXXXXX made an unlawful command to Robert, "give me the key to your locked bedroom door, or I'll kick the door off its hinges at the count of 10." He started counting 10, 9, 8, 7, 6, 5, 4....! That's when Robert, without giving his consent, and in fear of further violence, told him where the key was.

The Deputies opened the closet, found the laptop, unzipped the black case, placed the laptop on the floor and the case on the bed. Then called CSI to take pictures of the "staged" laptop and case and stated in their Police Report it was in "plain view." My deceased husband's firearms were also in Robert's locked bedroom closet. Robert was charged with his short barrel rifle in his locked bedroom closet. Mater Deputy XXXXXX stated in his Police Report that the rifle was in "plain view. They staged the crime scene of those items as well in order to justify the "plain view doctrine. The firearm and laptop were both stored in the locked bedroom closet. They were not in plain view. During his testimony at the Bond Motion, Master Deputy XXXXXX testified he had to move clothes from the back of the closet to find the short barrel riffle.

Witnessing my son's brutal and vicious beating, and seeing his face and body bloodied and bruised, caused my blood pressure to rise to a very dangerous level. At almost 79 years of age, I was physically and emotionally feeling the adverse effects of being terrorized by the Deputies. Captain XXXXXX, knowing how distraught we were, called the Emergency Medical Technicians. When they arrived, Deputy XXXXXX, who kicked and punched my son repeatedly to his ribs and abdomen with soccer ball kicks, was the first one to meet the EMT at the front door asking for a band-aid to cover the open wound on his fist. The Emergency Medical Technician warned me several times that my blood pressure was at a dangerously high level of 222 over 102, and said I should be immediately transported to the hospital. She gave me the tape of my blood pressure reading and said for the third time, my blood pressure was dangerously high and urged me to go immediately to the hospital or I could go into shock and die. This was recorded on my cell phone video.

Hiring a criminal defense attorney for my son and safeguarding my cell phone video of the Deputies' violations, took priority, over dying. What good would that do my son? My fear intensified thinking they would take my cell phone video from me and erase it. This cell phone video was the only proof I had of their horrendous acts and their criminal violations. The video recorded Deputies conducting an illegal search and seizure of the laptop without a warrant. All their violations were recorded on my Live Cell Phone Video. In addition to this were pictures I had taken of their illegal entry and search, Deputies Depositions, Corporal XXXXXX's Body

Worn Camcorder Video confirming their staging of a crime scene with the laptop and case, then falsifying their Police Reports to cover up their violation, and the Internal Affairs report of their sworn taped statements.

My cell phone video also recorded Corporal XXXXXX and Captain XXXXXX's admission they didn't have a warrant, or probable cause when they entered our home. It also recorded Corporal XXXXXX admitting they beat up my son because he would not give them his consent to search our home without a warrant. With all this evidence on my cell phone video, I could not afford to have them take it from me and erase such legally damning evidence against them.

I could feel my blood pressure rising to a dangerous level and was feeling very ill. I told the deputies I was going to drive myself to the hospital as suggested by the EMT. One deputy said, "You can't take your car." I said, "Then I'll drive my son's truck." As I was leaving our home, I looked over at Robert, who was now sitting on the chair only several feet from the front entrance, traumatized by the Deputies' beating and the shock of their invasion into our home. My heart broke to leave him alone with these officers. I had no choice but to leave and drive to the hospital with my cell phone before they confiscated it. I could have died right there with a stroke from fear alone. I needed to stay alive and focus on saving my son's life! They could have killed him with their brutal assault. Thank God, he was still alive!

While driving to the nearby Waterman Hospital, in Eustis, Fl. I focused on staying calm praying for Robert and getting him legal help. I left three voice messages to criminal lawyers I found on the internet. One lawyer called back immediately and said he had 30 years' experience in Lake County as a criminal defense attorney. After telling him what happened, he said, "Those deputies are doing this ass backward. Let them take whatever they want, and I'll have it thrown out." Being told that the deputies broke the law, I asked if he could sue them for their criminal violations. He said, "I know these Lake County Deputies personally if I sue them, they'll plant drugs in my car. But I can get someone who can sue them for you. You are very lucky they didn't take your cell phone from you and erase the video." This attorney confirmed the Deputies' reputation in the community of creating their own standards and not following the law.

After this Attorney confirmed that the deputies could take my cell phone and erase it, I detoured from going to the hospital and drove directly to Radio Shack to store my cell phone video to the cloud. On my way to Radio Shack, the 2nd lawyer called and said she was from Clermont, Fl., and was a former State Prosecuting Attorney for 3 years and now working 3 years as a criminal defense attorney in her own practice. She said, "The Deputies violated your son's 4th Amendment Rights, and their acts were 100% illegal." Many months later I met her as I was leaving the courthouse after one of my son's Hearings. She confirmed again, the acts of the Deputies were 100% illegal.

I arrived at Radio Shack and had the clerk save my video to the cloud. The third lawyer called, while I was there, and said he was nearby and would meet me at Radio Shack. He confirmed what the other attorneys said, "the Deputies violated your son's 4th Amendment Rights and this was an illegal search and seizure." All three attorneys said the Deputies could not use any of the evidence they found in my son's closet because it was fruit from a poisonous tree." I later found out this was supported by a 2015 Supreme Court case law, Rodriguez vs. State of Florida, which was passed on December 10, 2015.

This 3rd Attorney wanted to come back to the

house with me and speak with Robert. When we arrived, Robert was still sitting in the chair by the front door, handcuffed, still in a frightened and traumatic state from his beating, covered with cuts and bruises, with face and both eyes swollen and bruised. He said he couldn't see out of his left eye, and his abdomen and ribs were hurting him badly. He said he was in severe pain. He said, "Mom, I'm thirsty." The officers objected to me going into the kitchen to get him water. Even so, I returned with the glass of water and held it up to my son's mouth, wiped his bloody wounds with several wet paper towels to clean off the blood that was still oozing from his open wounds. He said, "mom while you were away, they called CSI to take pictures of my bedroom, and they are still in there." As one of the CSI photographers was leaving, I asked her to take pictures of my son's bruised body and face for further evidence of their brutal beating. I lifted Robert's torn t-shirt, so the CSI photographer could take pictures of his wounds on his upper body, back and chest as well as his face and eyes that were swollen, bloody and bruised.

After 10:00 pm that evening, they took Robert to the Lake County Detention Center. Robert had never had any legal problems before these Deputies forced their way into our home and literally tore our lives apart. I not only had the punishment of watching my son's vicious beating, but I had to see him bruised and battered being taken away in handcuffs to the Lake County Detention Center.

After Robert left, Captain XXXXXX went into my son's bedroom and came out holding the laptop in his hands, like it was his new-found trophy. He stated twice while holding the laptop up in front of me and in front of the forensic people who were sitting around the kitchen table examining the electronics, "Here look at the child porn on your son's laptop." I steadfastly refused to look at the laptop. He raised his voice and again demanded, "Here look at the child porn on your son's laptop." He was upset that I wouldn't look at the pictures, then shouted sarcastically, "You bother me!" Such disrespectful behavior from a Captain from the Lake County Sheriff's office was appalling. Then asking me to look at child porn was repulsive.

By midnight everyone left. During those 12 hours of literally going through the fires of hell, impacted me with deep and profound hurtful feelings. Not only did I lose my husband and two daughters two years earlier, all within one year and 55 days apart, but now seeing my son, the only living member of my family, being led off to a detention center handcuffed, beaten and in the state of shock, was gut-wrenching. This left my heart literally pounding, aching, and broken. I went to bed, but sleep was not possible. I went back into the living room looking at the floor reliving the terrifying nightmare of seeing my son lying there, crying out with each painful blow to his face, head, and body.

To this very day, the picture of my son's beating is painfully etched in my mind and heart. I was crying and praying to God, when I heard God's powerful voice in my spirit say, **"Virginia, that's how I felt when they crucified my son and nailed him to the cross."** I never imagined the depth of God's suffering, until I witnessed my own son's brutal assault. This scene will never diminish until I see justice for my son's life and his constitutional rights being honored by our judicial system. By the Grace of God, I will see His victory over all this evil and corruption committed by these Lake County Deputies, in Tavares, Florida.

The following morning, I spoke with the Clermont Lawyer and told her what Captain XXXXXX did. She said, "It was illegal for the Captain to want you to look at child pornography. He should know better." The 2nd night, at around 9:00 p.m. My doorbell rang. I looked through the shutters and saw a tall black man standing outside my front door. Not opening the door, I asked, "Who are you?" He said XXXXXX, from XXXXXX-TV. I asked, "How did you get in here; this is a gated community?" He said, "I can't say." I told him to put his card through the mail slot in the garage door and leave. Alone, with my heart pounding with fear, I was too afraid to call the police, after seeing what they did to my son. I feared the police more than I did the tall black man standing outside my front door at 9:00 at night!

My husband of 45 years was a Real Estate Broker, and a Florida State Licensed Private Investigator. He was licensed to carry a concealed weapon or firearm. After he passed away, my son kept all his firearms, expensive surveillance equipment, cameras, tripods, etc. in his closet. My husband, Dan Ortung, passed away on September 30, 2013, my daughter Patricia Lynne passed away on November 25, 2013. My eldest daughter Anne Marie passed away one year earlier on September 17, 2012. My husband and both my daughters were a total joy to my heart as my son is and always will be.

The Lake County Detention Center said the only way I could see my son was to write him a letter asking him to give them permission for me to visit him. This I did. On the fourth day of Robert's incarceration, a bail bondsman called and said, "Mrs. O'Hare, I'm here with your son. He is worried about you." He said he could have Robert out on bail and would come to my home for the payment of $13,500. I said, "Yes, come right over." When he arrived, he said, "I have an attorney you can hire for your son. He is one of the ten best criminal attorneys in the state of Florida. His name is Attorney XXXXXX. I told him I was hiring a former prosecutor with the state of Florida, who was coming to my home that evening. He said, "No, I'll call Attorney XXXXXX right now, and he will come to your home to see you."

Hours later, Attorney XXXXXX, came to my home and confirmed what the other three attorneys had said. "The deputies' forcing their way into your home was a violation of your son's 4th Amendment Rights, and their search and seizure without a warrant were illegal. Whatever they get, will be fruit from a poisonous tree, they cannot use it, because there was no legal reason for them to force their way into your home. There were no exigent circumstances present of any crime they could see, hear, or smell, and no contraband in plain view. Therefore, I'm confident they will be defeated on their violating your son's 4th Amendment Rights." Both the Attorney and the Bail Bondsman said they could have my son home that evening, and they did.

During Corporal XXXXXX's deposition taken on March 23, 2017, he testified that he could not view the inside of our home on October 5, 2015, because he could not see through the shutters on the front door. This confirms what Attorney XXXXXX said, "the deputies had no exigent circumstances to justify forcing their way into your home without a search warrant because they could not see, hear, or smell any crime being committed in order to exercise exigent circumstances." He repeated and said, "the deputies' forceful entry and the search and seizure of the laptop were 100% illegal and in violation of Robert's 4th Amendment Rights."

At 11:00 pm that evening, Attorney XXXXXX brought my son home and said, "I feel better about this case after meeting your son. He looks wholesome and is good looking and well mannered. He doesn't look like the charges the Deputies made against him!" I was more than elated to see my son after his being brutally beaten by the Deputies and in jail for 4 days. This was the first time in his 54 years of life he had ever been in jail. He had no prior criminal record, lived his life as a Christian, and was self-employed as a painter and also worked in our family's Real Estate Business. He never drank, smoked, or taken any drugs. My friends often told me how lucky I was to have such a close-knit family. I was proud of all three of my children. When Robert came home from the detention center, he said, "Mom, I prayed to God repeatedly for hours to let me come home and sleep in my own bed by 11:30 p.m. God answered my son's prayers, he was home and in his own bed by 11:30 p.m.

After bringing Robert home from the Lake County Detention Center, Attorney XXXXXX advised us to leave Mt. Dora immediately and go to our other home in Ft. Lauderdale, to be safe and away from any further harm from the Lake County Deputies. He knew of their reputation. We stayed at our home in Ft. Lauderdale for five months, and then returned to our 2nd home in Mt. Dora. I felt compelled to make a formal criminal complaint against the Sheriff's Deputies to the Lake County Internal Affairs in Tavares, Florida. I spoke with the Internal Affairs Investigator, XXXXXX, who was anxious to hear the details of my criminal complaint against the deputies. He wanted to see me as soon as I could meet with him at his office. I meant with him and his Supervisor, Corporal XXXXXX, the following day. After our meeting, they both wanted to interview my son as soon as possible. (Internal Affairs case #XXXXXXX)

The following morning, both the Investigator, Detective XXXXXX and, Corporal XXXXXX, arrived at our home. They asked Robert to tell them exactly what happened: Robert said, "Three (3) deputies came to our front door and asked if they could search our home. I asked if they had a search warrant? The deputy said, "No, we do not have a search warrant." I told them, to get a search warrant and I'll call my lawyer." "As I was closing the door, the 3 deputies forced the door open, entered our home, punched me in the stomach, knocked me to the floor, then one officer started kicking me repeatedly 10-12 times to my ribs and stomach on my left side, while another officer, on my right side, who was on his knee, was repeatedly cuffing me to my head, face, and eyes. I could not see out of my left eye. He blinded me! The third deputy, who was bald, was bodily holding down my ankles while the other two officers, on each side of me, kept beating me. I was in terrible pain. My mother walked into the room and was yelling at them to stop beating me. They wouldn't stop hitting and kicking me."

Before they left, my son asked the two investigators, "Can you take a polygraph test on them and me, so you know I am telling you the truth?" XXXXXX never gave the Deputies a polygraph test. Instead, months later the Lake County Sheriff said my criminal complaint against his deputies was "unfounded,"

Soon after Corporal XXXXXX blinded Robert, on October 5, 2015, he saw a Retina Macula specialist, Dr. XXXXXX, who surgically performed the removal of a scleral buckle in Robert's left eye. This buckle was surgically implanted one year earlier to secure a torn retina. Corporal XXXXXX's beating to his head and face with blunt blows to his eyes, caused the drum around the retina to wrinkle, leaving him not only blind but in unending pain from the dislodged drum.

Weeks later, Dr. XXXXXX from the Miami Eye Institute performed the 2nd surgery on Robert's left eye, after Surgeon XXXXXX removed the wrinkled buckle from his left eye. She wrote a letter stating, "Robert O'Hare's blindness was caused by a "trauma" to his left eye. Dr. XXXXXX's report is included in "Exhibit F" with the letter from eye surgeon, XXXXXX, MD.

Exhibit F: Eye surgeon's letter from XXXXXX, MD., and Dr. XXXXXX's procedure/operative report.

After the two unsuccessful surgeries to correct the blindness in Robert's left eye, the 2nd surgeon said, on August 2016, "I recommend a third operation within 90 days." Due to the Lake County Prosecutor, XXXXXX, filing his 2nd bogus arrest charges against Robert, on August 17, 2016, accusing Robert of delivering two (2) jukeboxes in 2011 or 2012 to a neighbor's house, and voyeurism, both of which he never did, this 3rd surgical procedure could not be performed to the date of this letter.

During Robert's first 13 months of incarceration, the Lake County Detention Center refused to give Robert any medical treatment for his blindness or treatment from a GI doctor for his pre-cancerous bleeding polyps as prescribed by Broward Health's medical report dated August 25, 2016. Copies of both reports were given to the Lake County Detention Center, the Lake County Sheriff, the State Attorney, XXXXXX, the Lake County medical staff, and the Lake County Warden. Attorney XXXXXX also made emergency Motions for a Medical Furlough to Judge XXXXXX for Robert to get outside medical treatment, because the Detention Center refused to give him any medical treatment for his colorectal bleeding cancer.

After thirteen months of incarceration, Judge XXXXXX only allowed Robert to see one outside GI Doctor, and only after he became critically ill and was bleeding like diarrhea from his colon. He was transported by two armed guards with chains around his hands, waist, and ankles to be examined by Doctor XXXXXX, a GI specialist who I hired and paid for. Doctor XXXXXX informed Robert he had pancreatic problems from an injury to his abdomen, which was from the Deputies beating. The Doctor said there was intestinal cancerous growth in his colon and he should have a colonoscopy and MRI immediately to see how extensive the cancer was. After this examination, the Lake County Detention Center contacted Doctor XXXXXX and said, "Do not treat Robert, the Doctor at the Detention Center will take over. I was informed of this by the Dr. XXXXXX's Head Nurse.

Several Days later, the Detention Center's Doctor gave Robert a colonoscopy and found he had malignant colon cancer with a 70% blockage in his colon. In medical terms, Robert was diagnosed with malignant neoplasm of the rectosigmoid junction, that requires immediate chemotherapy and surgery. The Doctor told Robert, this cancer was present in his colon for one year. He stated this on his Medical Report. This was the same period of time I was begging the Lake County Detention Center, the Lake County Sheriff, the Lake County Judicial System, and the Lake County State Attorney XXXXXX for emergency medical care and treatment for my son. On August 25, 2016, it was medically diagnosed as pre-cancerous bleeding polyps by the Broward Health Hospital in Ft. Lauderdale, FL. Now, over one year later, untreated by the Detention Center, my son has stage three (3) or stage four (4) Malignant Colon Cancer. The Doctor told Robert he did not know which stage it was in without taking more tests but thought it was stage 4. He also told Robert he had patients die within two months of having his size cancer in their colon.

The Lake County Detention Center did not give Robert any further tests for five months. Thereafter on January 28, 2018, he was given five radiation treatments.

Robert fell on his face repeatedly during his showers from being faint from weakness and anemia. The guard asked Robert when he came out of the shower because his face was all red, "did you fall again in the shower?" Robert answered, "yes." Other inmates told Robert, "you look really bad, you look like you're dying.

You have no color to your face; your skin is all gray." His Attorney XXXXXX told him the same thing, "Robert, you look God awful." Fearing for his client's life, his Attorneys made multiple emergency motions to Judge XXXXXX for Robert to receive outside urgently needed Medical treatment. All of which was to no avail. Judge XXXXXX denied all medical motions for outside medical treatment and a furlough. The monitored jail calls confirm all the above conversations I had with my son.

In addition to feeling nauseous and tired all the time, Robert lost a lot of weight in the Lake County Detention Center. For the first 2 ½ months, he was incarcerated in a cell 24/7 and only allowed out of his cell for a total of 3 hours a week. Shortly thereafter, he weighed in at 145 lbs. From his original weight of 190+ lbs. While on lockdown, Robert drank unfiltered water from his cell that had horrible taste and a foul odor. These conditions exacerbated his bowel and intestinal problems considerably. All of Robert's requests for medical care and hospitalization were denied for 17 months, as his health condition worsened daily while bleeding from his life-threatening malignant colon cancer.

The Lake County Detention Center was informed of Robert's original medical report dated August 25, 2016, from Broward County Health Hospital in Fort Lauderdale. Countless notifications were given thereafter of Robert's pre-cancerous bleeding polyps and his need for immediate medical treatment. This Medical Report instructed Robert to see a Gastroenterologist (GI) Doctor within three (3) days and have a colonoscopy because his pre-cancerous bleeding polyps were the beginning stage of colon cancer. Copies of this report and letters from two G. I. Doctors stating my son has life-threatening cancerous symptoms were given to the Lake County Detention Center, the Lake County Sheriff, the Lake County warden, the Lake County State Attorney,

XXXXXX, and urgently needed medical motions to the Lake County Judge XXXXXX

On or about December 15, 2017, the Lake County Detention Center brought a Waiver of Release to Robert's cell and asked him to sign it, so they would not be held liable if something happened to him. He refused to sign their Waiver.

The entire Lake County Judicial system failed to give Robert urgently needed medical treatment, hospitalization, surgery, chemotherapy for his malignant colon cancer for 17 months. From October 5, 2017, to January 1, 2018, my son informed me the only thing the detention center gave him was one iron pill a day for his anemia and a stool softener.

Finally, on or about January 28, 2018, Robert received for the first time since his incarceration on August 25, 2016, five radiation treatments. After his radiation treatments, he has not been given any follow up medical care from a Doctor or any medical supervision to the date of this letter, April 15, 2018.

In addition to no medical or hospital care, for 17 months, the Lake County Judicial System denied Robert's Motion to Suppress Hearing for close to eight (8) months. The Lake County Prosecutor canceled five of Robert's pre-scheduled Motions to Suppress hearing dates while keeping him incarcerated without any medical care or outside medical treatment for his malignant colon cancer. The Prosecutor, XXXXXX told Attorney XXXXXX he listens to all the monitored phone calls Robert had with me, which were almost daily. Therefore, the Prosecutor XXXXXX was fully aware of what postponing the Motion to Suppress Hearings five times was doing to Robert's health. Attorney XXXXXX told me the Prosecutor kept canceling the Hearing dates because he was afraid of losing his case against my son.

On November 8, 2017, Judge XXXXXX heard the sixth rescheduled Motion to Suppress Hearing. On his Order, Judge XXXXXX ruled that the Court found no justification for the Deputies Warrantless Entry into our home. He misinterpreted case law Rodriguez vs. State of Florida and put in his Order his own doctrine of Inevitable Discovery, which does not exist in this Supreme Court case law. The Supreme Court ruled that Inevitable discovery in Rodriguez vs. State of Florida (2015) is unlawful without a warrant. Judge XXXXXX knew the Lake County Deputies did not have a warrant in place upon their forced entry over the threshold of our home on October 5, 2018. He still chose to benefit the Deputies' unlawful actions with a doctrine of Inevitable Discovery that does not exist in Supreme Court Law.

To correct his error, Attorney XXXXXX filed a Motion for Reconsideration for Judge XXXXXX to correct his error on December 21, 2017. Days later, Judge XXXXXX denied the motion with no legal explanation. After these two shocking rulings by Judge XXXXXX, the Lawyers warned Robert not to go to trial. They said because of Judge XXXXXX bias, and not following the law, the Prosecutor's conspiracy with the Deputies, a trial would be lethal. They advised Robert to Plea "no contest," and Appeal in order to get Justice and be set free.

I submitted to the Dept. of Justice, on January 11, 2018, an updated criminal and civil complaint on Robert's medical condition and the ongoing deterioration of his health without being given any medical treatment by the Lake County Detention Center since August 25, 2016.

Exhibit G: Medical report from Broward Health Hospital dated August 25, 2016, which diagnosed Robert with pre-cancerous bleeding polyps, with instructions to see a GI Doctor and have a colonoscopy within three (3) days. A medical report from Dr. XXXXXX dated

September 5, 2017 stating Robert now has Malignant Colon Cancer with a 70% blockage and has had it for one year.

Upon receiving several notices of Robert needing urgent medical care, the Prosecutor, XXXXXX told Attorney XXXXXX, "I don't feel his health issues are serious." The Prosecutor, XXXXXX making false allegations against Robert to Judge XXXXXX, caused him to rule against Robert's Motions for a Medical Furlough or medical treatment for his life-threatening illness.

Robert's, civil, constitutional, and prisoner's rights were violated by the entire Lake County Judicial system. Prosecutor, XXXXXX told Attorney XXXXXX, "I'm going to put your client away for life." Such vindictiveness and bias statements are so egregious and violate Robert's constitutional rights and his due process of law.

The law clearly states a Prosecutor must remain neutral. An investigation of the court's electronic transcriptions will confirm that Prosecutor, XXXXXX was not neutral. The electronic transcription of the Bond Hearing will confirm the Prosecutor's conspiracy with the Deputies and their violations against Robert's 4th Amendment and Constitutional Rights. The Deputies criminal acts, which I fully outlined in my Internal Affairs Criminal Complaint in March-April 2016 were given to the Prosecutor, by the Investigator Detective XXXXXX of Lake County Internal Affairs. Despite the evidence of the Deputies Violations against Robert's 4th Amendment Rights and Federal Law Section 1983, he showed 100% partiality to the Deputies' violations, instead of his being neutral and seeking justice. Thereafter, he steadfastly supported the criminal actions of the Deputies and conspired with their giving even more false and damning sworn testimony against my son at hearings, which included the false and damning testimony made by Detective XXXXXX. Proof of this evidence is in their sworn testimony at Robert's Bond Hearing.

In Judge XXXXXX Order, to my son's Motion to Suppress he states:

"The Court observes that no justification was offered as to why police did not seek a warrant prior to approaching Defendant's house for the knock and talk. Had officers simply sought a warrant before entering Defendant's residence instead of afterward, they would have avoided an entirely unnecessary expenditure of both judicial and police resources. Separately from whether the tactics employed by police were legal, they were clearly unwise and unnecessary."

Judge XXXXXX ruled in his Order that the Deputies were not justified by the law in their warrantless entry into our home, nor were their tactics. Never the less, with this confirmation by the Judge who had been totally biased and ruled against every one of Robert's motions thus far, confirmed the Deputies violations against Robert's 4th Amendment Rights. Robert's Attorney said Judge Briggs gave Robert 95% of what his motion asked for. This made my son very pleased that Judge XXXXXX acknowledged the Deputies' violations and opened the door for him to appeal on the 5% of what the Judge made an error on, which was adding a doctrine of Inevitable Discovery that does not exist in the Supreme Court law. Robert's lawyers said Judge XXXXXX error could be overturned by doing a De Novo Appeal.

Prosecutor XXXXXX told Attorney XXXXXX multiple times he listened to all my monitored jail phone conversations with my son. He took those conversations out of context to alienate my relationship with my son's lawyers. On one occasion, Prosecutor XXXXXX told Attorney XXXXXX, "Mrs. O'Hare said she's going to fire you and replace you with another attorney." I told my son I was going to hire a civil rights attorney, not fire Attorney XXXXXX. I hired Attorney XXXXXX, a civil rights attorney, as my son's fourth (4th) attorney just for my son's Motion to Suppress Hearing. I did not intend to fire Attorney XXXXXX, as Prosecutor XXXXXX falsely stated to him.

After I hired Civil Rights Attorney XXXXXX, in June 2017, he said, "Robert's attorneys have done everything needed for your son's defense, and I cannot improve on their Motions to Suppress." He said my son's battle was against the Deputies and the Prosecutor who influenced Judge XXXXXX's motions by their bogus and lying testimony. He also told me, after reviewing my son's case and speaking with the other three lawyers, they all concluded that Judge XXXXXX was biased and was not following the law in his rulings on their motions for Robert. They all agreed Prosecutor XXXXXX was not only difficult to deal with but was totally uncooperative.

On one occasion, Attorney XXXXXX said, "The Prosecutor told me he let your Loch Leven neighbors listen to your conversations with your son, as well as the Deputies, who beat him up." He further stated, "The Prosecutor told me the deputies wanted him to put your son away for life and not lessen his offer of a sentence." This conspiracy between the Lake County Deputies, and the Lake County Prosecutor is egregious and 100% illegal. My son has not had his legal and constitutional rights upheld by the Lake County Judicial System, while the Prosecutor and the Deputies are negotiating my son's life sentence without his even having a jury trial. This is how justice is served in the Lake County Judicial System, with bias, corruption, conspiracy, and politics overruling the law and justice. This is the reason this Civil/Criminal Complaint is being made, seeking justice for my son and his civil and constitutional rights. Robert has suffered from undue and oppressive illegal tactics while trying to seek justice from a corrupt and bias judicial system. These violations against Robert's Prisoner's and Constitutional Rights have voided out any justice for him and his urgently needed medical treatment to save his life.

The platform of lies by the Prosecutor and the Deputies was poisonous to my son's chance for justice. By falsely stating to Judge XXXXXX that Robert was a flight risk, and a danger to the community, and falsely accusing him of delivering two (2) Jukeboxes to a neighbor in Loch Leven in 2011 or 2012, and again in 2016. These false and damning statements were difficult to defend in front of a biased Judge. To further support the Prosecutor's false arrest charge of Robert delivering two Jukeboxes in 2011 or 2012, he had Detective XXXXXX falsely testify at the Bond Hearing that he was told by Broward County Officer XXXXXX that Robert delivered two (2) jukeboxes to a family in Ft. Lauderdale in 2016. Robert never delivered any jute boxes in 2011-2012 or in 2016.

The Prosecutor's conspiracy with Detective XXXXXX to make this false and damaging statement, was lethal against my son and prevented him from receiving a fair ruling from Judge XXXXXX.

In order to get this evidence, I filed a formal complaint to Broward County Internal Affairs, to obtained proof that Officer XXXXXX never told Detective XXXXXX that Robert delivered two (2) Jukeboxes to a Broward County family in 2016. With this lethal evidence against Detective XXXXXX, I made a Formal Complaint against him to the Lake County Internal Affairs. In my complaint, I presented proof of statements made by Broward County Sargent XXXXXX and Internal Affairs Investigator, Detective XXXXXX that Officer XXXXXX never told Detective XXXXXX that Robert gave two jute boxes to a family in Broward. In addition to their statements, I presented the electronic transcription of the Bond Hearing and Broward Officer XXXXXX's filed Police Report. All this evidence confirmed that Officer XXXXXX never told Detective XXXXXX my son delivered two (2) Jukebox to a family in Broward County in 2016.

You can review **Exhibit A**, The Broward County Officer XXXXXX's Police Report #XXXXXXX. It proves there are no two (2) jukeboxes listed on this Police Report.

Lake County Investigator, Detective XXXXXX informed me that Internal Affairs was not going to take any action against Detective XXXXXX for lying under oath. At the end of this letter is an article on Detective XXXXXX's own arrest for indecent exposure of his private parts, and the Lake County Sheriff's office rehiring him back in their Cyber Sex Crime Unit. I also included this article in my Internal Affairs complaint. Detective XXXXXX was the same Investigator on Detective XXXXXX indecent charges, and again on my complaint against him as well.

All these false allegations against Robert postponed Justice and medical care for treatment of his malignant colon cancer and his case. After the Bond Hearing, Attorney XXXXXX instructed me to immediately hire a civil rights lawyer to sue the Lake County Detention Center, for denying Robert medical treatment for his malignant colon cancer. He also stated after he heard the electronic transcription of my son's Bond Hearing, "your son was set up by the Deputies and the Prosecutor." Such conspiracy and collusion between the Prosecutor and Deputies are 100% illegal!!! My son is paying for the Deputies criminal acts with his life.

Even though the Prosecutor admitted to the news media it was the neighbor who delivered the two (2)

Jukeboxes to their neighbor, in 2011 or 2012, he still charged my son for this delivery based solely on his "assumption" theory, in which he alleges Robert delivered two Jukeboxes to the wrong neighbor thinking the wrong neighbor would deliver the Jukeboxes to the right neighbor. He added another bogus charge against my son of voyeurism. These ridiculous and false charges were made up after I filed a criminal complaint against the Deputies on April 2016 to the Lake County Internal Affairs.

The news media spread Prosecutor XXXXXX's "assumption" theory, of my son's delivering two (2) Jukeboxes, all over the local and national news stations across the Country. Unfortunately, the Lake County Prosecutor XXXXXX's assumption theory against Robert is permanently recorded on the Internet. In fact, a former employee of mine, XXXXXX phoned me from Bermuda and said she was shocked in reading about those charges against my son on the internet. Knowing my son, she couldn't believe those charges. The harmful damages caused by Prosecutor, XXXXXX's false arrest charges is beyond being culpable and egregious.

I was present during the Bond Motion Hearing held on March 20, 2017, to reactivate Robert's $25,000 Bond, which the Prosecutor had previously revoked after Robert was falsely charged with resisting an officer during the Prosecutor's false 2nd arrest charges in Broward County, Fl. **Those false charges of resisting an officer were overturned by a Broward County Jury, who came back after less than 10 minutes of deliberation with a Not Guilty Verdict for Robert.**

The Prosecutor, XXXXXX gave his false assumptions to the press, which heightened public condemnation. Without a trial, the Prosecutor publicly had my son judged, by inciting public condemnation from the press. During our 17-year residency in Loch Leven, Mt. Dora,

Fl., and our 36-year residency in Ft. Lauderdale, FL, where we lived since 1979, my son never had any problems whatsoever as falsely alleged by Prosecutor, XXXXXX. Yet he gave these bogus charges to the news media which were based solely on his "assumption theory" without any evidence whatsoever.

According to State rules, Lake County Prosecutor, XXXXXX, is guilty of violating model rules 3.6 and 3.8 (f) the improper use of the media: "Cases are meant to be tried in court, based on evidence, not in the press. Rules broadly prohibit prosecutors from engaging in public communications that may prejudice the defendant's case or heighten public condemnation of the accused. Other than the basic details about a crime, most public communications about the defendant or defendant's case are improper and constitute prosecutorial misconduct." (see, e.g., aba model rules 3.6 and 3.8(f)).

"The U.S. Supreme Court has held that the constitutional guarantee of due process protects a defendant against prosecutorial vindictiveness, and, selective prosecution." XXXXXX's vindictiveness egregiously violated these rules of law against Robert.

The Prosecutor advertised his bogus charges against Robert throughout the news media, having no probable cause, and no evidence, just his "assumption" theory, which he stated to the news media. This bogus charge has caused my son to be incarcerated for 18 months while being denied his constitutional rights, a speedy trial, his due process of law, and urgently needed medical care and treatment. This miscarriage of justice is 100% illegal and also against Robert's 8th Amendment Rights which states: "Excessive bail shall not be required, nor excessive fines imposed, nor cruel and unusual punishments inflicted."

The Lake County Internal Affairs Investigator, Detective XXXXXX told me the Prosecutor XXXXXX used the same evidence collected from our home during the first arrest charges made on October 5, 2015, to make up his 2nd arrest charges on August 17, 2016. He said, "there was no new evidence against your son." Knowing we did not get a fair outcome from my criminal complaint from the Lake County Sheriff, who stated my complaint against his Deputies were "unfounded," XXXXXX said, "you can file your complaint with FDLE. I'll send you a copy of everything from my investigations with the deputies, and you can forward it to them." He wanted me to seek justice for justice sake for my son. He gave me the complete investigation report of the Deputies sworn statements from his Internal Affairs Report, which confirms the evidence of their violations to my son's constitutional rights.

Prosecutor XXXXXX had the entire file of my criminal complaint against the Deputies, from the Lake County Internal Affairs since March-April 2016. This criminal complaint detailed all the violations committed by the Deputies on October 5, 2015, when they forcefully and unlawfully entered our home without a warrant and did an illegal search and seizure. Both Captain XXXXXX and Corporal XXXXXX admitted, as recorded on my cell phone video, they did not have any probable cause when they forcefully entered our home on October 5, 2015, and no search warrant. Judge XXXXXX' Order to Robert's Motion to Suppress signed on December 4, 2017, confirmed the Deputies warrantless search was unlawful.

Even with the knowledge of the Deputies violations to my son's 4th Amendment Rights, and Federal Law 1983, the Prosecutor supported and conspired with the Deputies in making further bogus allegations against my son. These false allegations were sworn to in a court of law by the Lake County Deputies and prodded on during their sworn testimony by Prosecutor, XXXXXX. This fact is evidenced in the court's electronic transcription of these Hearings that attest to the Deputies giving false and inconsistent testimony against my son.

Lake County Prosecutor, XXXXXX, severely and egregiously violated the following rules:

Rule 3.8 (a, d, f): special responsibilities of a prosecutor. The prosecutor in a criminal case shall:

(a) "refrain from prosecuting a charge that the prosecutor knows is not supported by probable cause."

(d) "make timely disclosure to the defense of all evidence or information known to the prosecutor that tends to negate the guilt of the accused or mitigates the offense."

(f) "refrain from making extrajudicial comments that have a substantial likelihood of heightening public condemnation of the accused and exercise reasonable care to prevent investigators, law enforcement personnel, employees or other persons assisting or associated with the prosecutor in a criminal case from making an extrajudicial statement that the prosecutor would be prohibited from making under rule 3.6 or this rule."

It wasn't until the Prosecutor's 2nd arrest charges on Robert, 10 months after his first arrest charges, that the Prosecutor gave discovery of his forensic report to my son's defense attorneys. This was only after Attorney XXXXXX made two motions to Judge XXXXXX compelling the Prosecutor to do so. This is proof positive of Prosecutor XXXXXX's lack of cooperation with the defense attorney, to make timely disclosures as stated in Rule 3.8-d.

Exhibit H: Motion to Compel States discovery dated August 25, 2016, case #XXXXXXX. Prosecutor, XXXXXX waited 300 days before he would produce

State's Discovery to Defense Attorney XXXXXX and only after multiple requests and two court orders for him to do so. He waited until he made his 2nd bogus arrest charges on August 17, 2016, before turning over the States Discovery.

Due to the Prosecutor's misconduct, and denying Robert's constitutional rights, my son was forced to Plead no contest and take a stiff sentence of 20 years from a biased Judge. His Attorneys recommended Robert do this rather than go to trial against a Bias Judge and a Prosecutor who was conspiring with the Deputies against him. They said taking a Plea of "no contest" and doing the Appeal would free him from all the corruption and collusion in the Lake County Judicial System. They said Robert has an excellent chance of prevailing on the Appeal and being set free because Judge XXXXXX made an error in his ruling by adding a doctrine of Inevitable Discovery that does not exist in Supreme Court Law. This error made by Judge XXXXXX justified the Deputies unlawful warrantless search and seizure.

Defending my son's rights with these bogus charges and lies from the Prosecutor and Sheriff's Deputies has been an uphill battle for my son's defense attorneys to deal with. That's why this complaint is so crucial for you, Jeff Sessions, as our U. S. Attorney General to immediately investigate and intercede and protect my son's rights and life from all the corruption and conspiracy he is facing with the Lake County Judge, Prosecutor and Enforcement Officers. I sent a copy of the February 8, 2018, updated Criminal Complaint also to President Donald J. Trump, to bring this matter to his attention as well. President Trump responded and said he is turning this complaint about to the appropriate Federal Agency for further action.

A synopsis of damages caused by the Lake County Prosecutor XXXXXX's false 2nd arrest charges are inclusive herein:

On August 17, 2016, around 12:00 noon, my son, who was out on bond for 10 months, and I were leaving our home in Bay Colony, an upscale armed guard gated-waterfront community in Ft. Lauderdale, FL. As we were about to exit our street, a dark blue SUV started to tailgate us closely. Not knowing who this was, and in fear of the vehicle hitting us, I told Robert to drive down the next dead-end street to see if the vehicle would follow us. It not only followed us but drove past us and made a U-turn at the end of the cul-de-sac street, then sped head on towards our car. To avoid a head-on collision, my son immediately turned our car to the right side of the road and stopped just over the swale of our neighbor's lawn, to avoid a head-on collision because he feared I would get hurt. Just then, another vehicle came speeding down the street towards our stopped, parked car and smashed his large SUV into the passenger side of our vehicle. The driver jumped out of his vehicle, pointed his gun at us with his arms shaking nervously back and forth. Then, for no reason, he used a sharp iron instrument and smashed the rear window of our parked car, splattering glass all over the inside of the car. I made a formal complaint against this Broward County Officer to Internal Affairs Investigator, and spoke to his Supervisor, Sergeant XXXXXX as well. I was informed this Officer had only been employed one week prior to his crashing into my car.

Just then several other cars came onto the street, also unmarked with no lights or sirens. Then a voice command came from the first vehicle that was tailgating us, "put your hands up in the air." Robert immediately put up his left hand over his head, at the officer's command, while keeping his right hand on the stick shift trying to put it in a park position. The stick shift was stuck and difficult to put into park position due to the impact of the officer's large SUV driving onto the back wheel on the passenger's side of our car. I was later informed by a mechanic that the vehicle smashing into the rear tire bent the axle, which made it difficult for Robert to move the stick shift to the park position. Robert said, "the shift is stuck!" After several tries, Robert finally got it into the park position.

The officer told Robert to get out of the car and lie flat on the pavement. Robert unfastened his seat belt and laid face down on the hot pavement. When he did this, one of the officers abruptly pulled Robert's right arm up in the air, lifting him off the pavement bodily, then dropped him flat on his face on the concrete pavement. From this Officer's brutal act, Robert landed on the hot pavement with his left arm underneath his chest. Just then the other officer, who crashed his SUV into my car, laid bodily on Robert's left shoulder and said, "Put your hands behind your back." Robert put his right hand behind his back, but with the officer's full body weight laying on Robert's left shoulder, and his left arm underneath his chest it was difficult to do this. I heard the officer yelling, for no reason, "Stop resisting, stop resisting." Robert was not resisting! He was lying flat on the pavement. Despite the pain he was in, Robert forced his left hand from underneath his chest, with the weight of the officer still on his shoulder, causing his arm and hand to be scratched and bloody from the concrete pavement. He did this in order to comply with the officer's command. I took pictures on my cell phone that shows evidence of his cuts and bruises with blood on his arm, face, hand, and knees while complying with the officers' command to put his left arm behind his back. He never once resisted the officer as falsely charged.

After witnessing the Lake County deputies brutally

beating my son, on October 5, 2015, and falsely accusing him of resisting an officer without violence, and now watching another brutal police force being used on him was appalling to watch. I yelled and said, "He is not resisting!" "He can't get his hand behind his back with your 200 lbs. of body weight laying on his shoulder." "I'm going to sue you for using excessive force on my son and crashing into my car," I asked the U. S. Marshal if he had a copy of the arrest warrant, so I could see it. He said, "No, I don't have a copy of the warrant."

I immediately called Attorney XXXXXX and had him speak with the U.S. Marshal in charge. The Marshal told Mr. XXXXXX, **"We are charging Robert with resisting an officer without violence because we used force."** The officer admitted they were the ones who used force not Robert, yet they charged him with resisting an officer. Officer XXXXXX filed the false charge of resisting an officer without violence, in order to justify their using excessive police force on my son, and his smashing into my car, and breaking the back window. Attorney XXXXXX gave us a sworn affidavit of the U.S. Marshal's telling him because they used excessive force is why they charged Robert with resisting an officer without violence. This bogus charge of resisting an officer invalidated my son's bond in Lake County, which I had just paid $25,000 for, only four (4) days earlier.

The names of the Broward County Deputy Police Officers and the U.S. Marshals who used excessive physical police force on Robert and made a bogus charge of resisting an officer are:

1 U.S. Marshal, XXXXXX

2 Deputy U.S. Marshal, XXXXXX

3 Deputy U.S. Marshal, XXXXXX

4 Deputy U.S. Marshal, XXXXXX

Exhibit I: A Sworn affidavit from Attorney XXXXXX stating the U.S. Marshal told him they charged Robert with resisting an officer without violence because "they used force."

After they took my son away, one of the officers drove my car back to my home, because it was unsafe to drive with the back wheel being wobbly from the vehicle being hit by the officer's SUV. I had a mechanic pick up my car to repair the body damage. That's when I learned the rear axle was bent, and unsafe to drive. The expense of fixing the bent axle, caused me to trade down for a new less expensive vehicle. At 80 years of age, I feared driving an unsafe vehicle that had serious mechanical issues.

After this incident, I met with Attorney XXXXXX and the Bail bondsman in my Ft. Lauderdale home and paid him for Robert's 2nd bond of $25,000 and an additional legal fee of $13,000 to Attorney XXXXXX to represent my son on these new charges by the Lake County Prosecutor, XXXXXX.

Broward County Officers and the U.S. Marshals committed the following violations upon presenting the Lake County Prosecutor, XXXXXX's 2nd "BOGUS" arrest warrant on Robert:

On August 17, 2016, when the Broward County Officers and the U.S. Marshal falsely charged my son with resisting an officer without violence, the Lake County Prosecutor XXXXXX, issued another arrest warrant on August 25, 2016, to revoke my son's $25,000 bond, for the false charge of resisting an officer without violence. Robert was arrested by the same Officers who served their first arrest warrant. The U.S. Marshal stated to me, "this time we are not charging your son with resisting an officer."

Due to this bogus misdemeanor charge, my son

not only lost his original bond of $13,500 for his First arrest charges, but also the 2nd bond I had just paid $25,000 for only four days earlier. Charging this excessive bail on a bogus charge, violated Robert's 8th Amendment Rights which states: "Excessive bail shall not be required, nor excessive fines imposed, nor cruel and unusual punishments inflicted."

During the U.S. Marshal serving their 1st arrest warrant on August 17, 2016, Robert had severe intestinal pain, and colon bleeding after the U. S. Marshal pulled him up bodily from his lying down position on the pavement then dropped him down bodily on the concrete pavement. This exacerbated his already painful intestinal bleeding problems during bowel movements, caused initially from being repeatedly kicked to his ribs and abdomen by the Lake County Deputy XXXXXX on October 5, 2015. The U.S. Marshals took my son to the Emergency Room at the Broward Health Hospital in Ft. Lauderdale, FL For observation. The medical report stated my son had pre-cancerous bleeding polyps and should be seen by a GI Doctor within three (3) days and must have a colonoscopy.

Robert was transported to Lake County Detention Center and placed in protective custody. I have previously described in this letter the conditions he endured while incarcerated in Lake County Detention Center. He suffered from a great deal of pain while waiting for his Jury trial date in Broward County for the false charge of resisting an officer without violence. Robert spent approximately 1800 hours at the Lake County Detention Center, and only allowed out of his cell a total of 7½ hours during the 2 ½ months while in Protective Custody. This was maltreatment for any human being, especially one suffering from Robert's intestinal health issues, and not having any medical care or treatment.

Being confined in his cell for over 2 ½ months,

Robert lost over 40 lbs. He was bleeding heavily from his intestinal pre-cancerous polyps. During this time, my son's health continued on a downward spiral. Even with all of my countless requests for Robert to have medical treatment to the Lake County Detention Center, and the Lake County Sheriff, they steadfastly denied him medical treatment for over one year of his incarceration. The only water Robert could drink, while in lockdown 24/7 was from the sink in his cell that was not filtered and had a putrid smell of sewer and a bitter taste to it. The food was less than healthy for the type of nourishment and diet needed for his serious intestinal medical issues.

I hired a Broward County Attorney XXXXXX to represent Robert against the Broward County's U.S. Marshal's bogus charge of resisting an officer w/out violence. Robert refused to plea to the prosecutor's settlement offer for a reduced charge. He said, "I'm innocent of those charges. I never resisted the officers. I did exactly what they told me to do."

On November 9, 2016, Robert was transported from the Lake County Detention Center to the Broward County detention center while waiting for his Jury trial, to challenge the U.S. Marshal's bogus misdemeanor charge of resisting an officer without violence. After two trial dates were canceled, the third trial date was rescheduled for January 24, 2017. This new date for Robert's trial was just after being incarcerated for a total of five (5) months, 2 ½ months in Lake County Detention Center in protective custody 24/7, and 2 ½ months in Paul Rein Detention Center in Broward County, Florida, which was a far superior facility.

On, January 24, 2017, after a 2-day jury trial, **six Broward County Jurors found my son "NOT GUILTY" of the false "resisting" charges made up by the U.S. Marshals.** The 7th Alternate Juror came over to Robert after the trial and said, "I would have voted for you "NOT

GUILTY" if I were still on the Jury." Those Officers were lying through their teeth." He told me the same thing as we were leaving the courtroom.

After the trial, Robert was transported back to Lake County Detention Center in Tavares, FL., where he is currently incarcerated as of the date of this updated letter. During all this time, Robert has never had a trial, and five of his hearing dates for his Motion to Suppress were canceled by Prosecutor, XXXXXX. These postponed hearing dates prolonged my son's pain and suffering while being denied urgently needed medical treatment for his malignant colon cancer.

The false misdemeanor charge of resisting an officer by the U. S. Marshal in Broward County, Florida, not only caused Judge XXXXXX to revoke both of my son's bonds, $13,500 and $25,000 respectively but prevented him from having any outside medical care and treatment for his serious, life-threatening intestinal bleeding. The Lake County Detention Center not medically treating Robert for his pre-cancerous bleeding polyps, for over one year, allowed his condition to develop into stage 3 or 4 malignant colon cancer. The Doctor was not sure which stage his cancer was in without taking further tests, which the Lake County Detention Center has failed to do as of the date of this letter.

During the Hearing to Reinstate Robert's Bond held on January 26, 2017, the Prosecutor, XXXXXX and the three (3) deputies, Deputy XXXXXX, Corporal XXXXXX, and Deputy XXXXXX made false and damning statements against Robert, which caused Judge XXXXXX to deny reactivating Robert's $25,000 Bond. Judge XXXXXX ignored the fact that Robert won a "not guilty verdict" against the false charge of resisting an officer in Broward County, FL, and was legally entitled to have his Bond reinstated. Attorney XXXXXX was not present at the Bond Hearing but listened to the electronic court transcription, and said, "your son was set up at the Bond Hearing by XXXXXX and the Deputies."

This ruling caused a setback for Robert's health, and not being able to obtain outside Medical treatment. His health was rapidly deteriorating, without any medical treatment from the Lake County Detention Center. For over one solid year, since his August 25, 2016 incarceration, multiple requests for urgently needed medical care were made and denied by the entire Lake County Judicial system. This included the Warden, the Lake County Sheriff, the Lake County Detention Center, the Lake County State Attorney, XXXXXX, and the Lake County Judge XXXXXX. This denial of urgently needed medical care is a violation of my son's Civil, Constitutional, and Prisoner's Rights. On October 4th, 2017, Judge XXXXXX again denied Robert's Motion for a Medical Furlough for outside medical treatment for his stage 3 or 4 malignant colon cancer.

This is a detailed summary of events and violations by the Lake County Justice System:

During the first 2 ½ months in Lake County Detention Center, Robert was placed in lockdown 24/7 with a cellmate, XXXXXX, who was in the final stages of Hepatitis C and had s severe mental disorder. Thereafter, Robert was transported back to Ft. Lauderdale for a November 9, 2016 jury trial for the U. S. Marshal's bogus charge of resisting an officer without violence. The prospective jurors were totally biased against the Justice system, which caused both attorneys to block all the prospective jurors. The trial was rescheduled for November 29th, 2016. For his Thanksgiving meal, Robert was given 4 slices of white bread with baloney at the Paul Rein Detention Center, in Pompano Beach, FL. This was one of the regular meals on the inmate's lunch menu.

On the morning of November 29, 2016, I drove to the courthouse, anxious to see my son for the first time since he was incarcerated on August 25, 2016. I was blessed with a parking space right next to the courthouse building and had only a few minutes to get to the courtroom on the 4th floor before the trial began. When I stepped out of my car onto the sidewalk in front of the courthouse, I accidentally tripped on a broken protruding edge of the sidewalk and fell on my hands and knees with copies of legal papers for my son's trial flying everywhere from the severe gusty winds. Retrieving all the documents alone was impossible. The papers were blown in several different directions. Hurting badly from the fall, I got up and tried to get as many of the documents as I could. A lady and a man came to my rescue and ran to gather up every single document.

I hurried into the courthouse with my papers all disarranged, but every document back in my folder. I stopped in the restroom to clean my wounds before going into the courtroom. The Broward County Prosecutor, XXXXXX, came into the restroom and said, "Did your attorney call and tell you the trial has been canceled again and rescheduled. My heart sank, as I was trying to catch my breath after the fall and rushing to be on time for Robert's trial. Disappointed, I asked, "To when?" She said, "I don't want to tell you?" I asked, "please!" She said, "To January 24, 2017." I asked why. She said, "Because your attorney was too sick with the flu to try your son's case." I thought, "This cannot be happening!" I was bloody with bruises on my hands and knees, trying hard to hold back the sadness of not being able to see my son and dealing with the pain from the fall. The Prosecutor said, "Let's sit on a bench, in the hallway." We spoke for about a half hour. I asked her, "Why are you doing this to my son? You have all the evidence you need to prove my son was not resisting those officers. Those lying officers have caused my son to lose his Bond that I just paid $25,000 for!" Her answer was, "I'm just doing my job."

This delay meant I would spend Christmas and New Year's Eve alone without my son, the only living member left of my family. Two years prior to this, I had lost my husband and two daughters. Fortunately, friends invited me to celebrate the holidays with their family for lunch, and other friends invited me to dinner with their family members.

I spoke almost daily to my son during the 2 ½ months he was incarcerated at the Paul Rein Detention Center while waiting for his new trial date. On a positive side, Paul Rein Detention Center was a far superior facility, and more humane than the Lake County Detention Center. For one thing, there were no bars. This facility offered inmates sports activities, bible studies, and they were allowed to go out daily in the fenced yard. It was a very well operated facility. I met three times with the nursing administrator, to let her know of my son's pre-cancerous bleeding polyps to coordinate his medical treatments. She said their facility scored 100% by the State of Florida for the operation of their facility. After reviewing Robert's medical reports from Broward Health Hospital Report and two letters from two GI specialists, she said she would do everything she could to get Robert a GI Doctor as soon as possible. After winning the Jury Verdict in Broward County, Robert was transported back to the Lake County Detention Center, the day before he was scheduled to see the GI Doctor.

I prayed with my son daily during our monitored jail calls from the Paul Rein Detention Center. I regularly sent him whatever he needed, money for his commissary, which he always shared with the other inmates, who were less fortunate.

One night at 8:00 p.m. My son called and said, "Mom, put on your bathrobe, we're going for a walk down our street as we used to every night when I was home. Surprised and happy, I put my bathrobe over my nightgown and walked outside while talking with my son on my cell phone. I was blessed with our ongoing conversations, which were always on world events, especially current breaking news, and bible prophecy. Even though I walked alone down the street then back to our two-story colonial home, I could actually feel his presence being there with me even though we were only talking on the phone. Thereafter, we did this on a regular basis. These walks were truly a blessing and a joy for me to take while talking with him on the phone.

I used to take walks with my husband and daughters before they passed away. We never ran out of conversations. We all loved keeping abreast of world affairs and tying them together with Bible prophecy. One evening while we were talking on the phone, Robert asked me, while I was walking alone down our street, "mom, look up at the stars in the sky. Do you see the moon and the three bright stars next to it?" I said, "Yes, Rob, I do." That's good because I see the same from my third-floor cell window, the moon, and the three stars." Then he said, "Because it is New Year's Eve, "I want you to go to Pompano Isles Buffet tomorrow." My husband, Rob, and my daughters and I ate for years at that restaurant. Thankfully, dear friends invited me to their home on New Year's Day. The evening before, they called and said, "We changed our minds, we want to take you to Pompano Isles Buffet tomorrow instead." My son was happy to hear I went to our favorite restaurant and said, "Just because I'm suffering in here doesn't mean you have to as well." I asked him what he had for his holiday meal; he said, "I had 4 slices of white bread with baloney."

I put extra money for Robert in his commissary so he could buy what he needed and give to the other inmates who were not so fortunate. He did this on a regular basis. He told me how much they appreciated this because they did not have the funds to buy from the commissary, and were tired of eating the same meals, with no variations in the menu.

The U.S. Marshal's false charges of resisting an officer without violence, caused my son to go through all these dreadful experiences including being ostracized from our upscale gated community. The U.S. Marshal's arrest of Robert on August 17, 2016, was made in Bay Colony, an upscale armed guard gated waterfront community, where my son and I lived since 2011 with our family before they passed away. The U.S. Marshal filing a false and bogus charge of resisting an officer and falsely stated Robert fled on foot, led the lawyer for the homeowner's association to forbid my son to reside in our community because his arrest was considered a "nuisance," which is not allowed in the By-Laws.

This issue faded away immediately when my son was found innocent of the resisting charges by a Broward County Jury. In fact, the Captain of the Guards, said to me, "Virginia, with your faith in God, I know that Robert will be free and home with you soon. I'm praying for you both." The Association asked me to run for one of their offices that just became available. I declined in lieu of spending my time exonerating my son from those horrible bogus charges.

Exhibit J: Letter from our Home Owner's Association resulting from the U. S. Marshal's false charges on my son resisting an officer without violence and fleeing on foot down the street, which he never did. My cell phone pictures showed Robert lying face down on the pavement, only a couple of feet from the driver's side of our car.

Our family lived in the Landings and Bay Colony subdivisions since 1979. We never had any legal issues or problems. My son challenged the false charges in

Broward County and won a "not guilty" verdict, only 10 minutes after the Jurors deliberated. Robert said, "I will do the same in Lake County. On 1/28/2018, on our monitored call from the Jail, Robert said, "mom, I can now see the light through the tunnel." I can see this is God's plan and not Man's Laws. That's what you should name your book, God's Plan vs. Man's Laws. I was meant to go through this, so you could write your book." His words of wisdom deeply touched my heart!

The financial expense to defend the U. S. Marshal's false charge of resisting an officer without violence was not only costly but damning to my son's case in Lake County. It gave the Prosecutor XXXXXX a foothold to incarcerate my son not only for the 18 months thus far, but to revoke his bond, which cost $25,000, and his original bond of $13,500, and to cause him to be denied his Motion for a Medical Furlough, and to lose his Motion to Suppress.

The extra-legal fees for the Broward County Case were a total of $17,500, and the replacement cost of a new car was $15,000, plus the trade in. Worse of all, are the 18 months, to date, of torturous incarceration in Lake County Detention center Robert had to endure, with suffering, pain, bleeding from the colon cancer and being denied medical treatment for his life-threatening health issues. These are all violation to his constitutional rights. It wasn't until January 28th, 2018 that Robert was given five radiation treatments for his bleeding like diarrhea. To date, March 25, 2018, Robert has not received any follow up medical treatment not even a Doctor's visit after his five radiation treatments, which caused constant diarrhea 24/7, nausea, and weakness. The Detention Center is keeping Robert in lockdown 24/7 and only allow him out of his cell for one hour on Monday, Wednesday, and Friday.

Prior to my son's trial in Broward County Florida

to defend himself against the U. S. Marshal's false resisting charge, his attorney XXXXXX was in pre-trial negotiations with the Broward County Prosecutor to drop the charges. He said they were making headway towards the charges being dropped so Robert's $25,000 Bond could be reinstated in Lake County. Lake County Prosecutor, XXXXXX tried to vindictively sabotage my son's chance for having the charges dropped in Broward County by calling the Broward County Prosecutor XXXXXX. He told her my son was a flight risk and a danger to the community and would send her an audio recording she should listen to of my conversation with my son during one of our monitored jail calls.

Prosecutor XXXXXX said she wanted to meet with me before making her decision. Knowing the reinstatement of my son's bond was predicated upon her dropping those resisting charges in Broward County, I was more than pleased to have the opportunity to meet with her and give her my eyewitness account of the events of the U.S. Marshals' bogus resisting charges.

During this meeting, she told me she received a call from the Lake County Prosecutor, XXXXXX, who told her my son was a flight risk, and a danger to the community and wanted her to listen to an audio of my conversation with my son before making her decision to drop the charges. She said after she listened to his audio, she would let my attorney know of her decision. She said, "I heard you read some of the new book you're writing to your son while you spoke to him on the jail phone. "I wanted you to continue reading more of it. It sounded really interesting. You must have done a lot of research for the book. I want to purchase it when it comes out." She asked what the name of the book would be. I told her: ***Virginia O'Hare Documents God's Laws vs. Man's Laws***." She also wanted the name of the first book I had published a year earlier. I told her,

"*Virginia O'Hare's Trials, Triumphs, and Vision from God*." She said she wanted to purchase that book as well. I said both books were written and inspired by God's Holy Spirit, with divine warnings of disasters coming upon our generation, with the end of days just around the corner!

On the audiotape, she was given by Prosecutor XXXXXX; I was recorded as saying, "Robert, when this is over, we are going to travel around the world." Robert's response on one of our monitored jail calls was, "my preference to date is to ride my motorbike through the Blue Ridge Mountains." That audio tape was given to the Broward Prosecutor of my conversation with my son which was taken completely out of context. However, she opted to ignore all the prima facie evidence submitted to her during her pre-trial negotiations with Attorney XXXXXX and went with the Lake County Prosecutor's false characterization of Robert being a flight risk and a danger to the community. I told her, through tears, "you will lose this case when it goes to trial!" We went to trial, and she lost the case. Praise God for His Justice!

Writing this book was gut-wrenching as I detailed all the corruption I witnessed in the Lake County Judicial System against my son. I only got through the heart rendering details of the travesty of justice my son suffered through thus far, by being 100% inspired by God's Holy Spirit. I believe God is using my son's experience for me to write this book on God's Laws vs. Man's Laws, not only to expose the corruption my son which I witnessed in the Lake County Judicial System in Tavares, Florida, but for all to know God's laws, HIS Ten Commandments, are forever.

The 3rd rescheduled jury trial in Broward County commenced on January 24, 2017. Seeing my son for the first time, since his arrest on August 25, 2016, was heart-wrenching. He was led into the Courtroom with chains around his hands, waist, and ankles. His body looked thin, frail, and sickly. His cheekbones protruding from his face showed the excessive amount of weight he lost during his first and only time in his life of being incarcerated. As a mother, witnessing all this ongoing corruption in the Lake County Judicial System, and now my son facing these false charges made against him by Broward County Officers was disturbing to the core of my being.

During the two (2) day jury trial in Broward County, the three (3) U.S. Marshal's, I was told, nervously testified to their bogus and inconsistent stories to support their bogus charges of Robert resisting an officer without violence. The Broward County Prosecutor, XXXXXX, without any credible evidence tried to defend and support the three lying U.S. Marshal's testimony and their bogus charges. She was sorely losing the battle to convince the Jurors and the Judge. This Broward County Judge was honorable, decent and fair during the two-day trial. He followed the law to the "T." The Lake County Judge XXXXXX was just the opposite. He was biased, unfair in his rulings and did not follow the law.

When I took the stand and testified as an eyewitness that my son was not resisting the officer, and was only compliant, the Prosecutor, tried in vain to "impeach "my testimony. She took the evidence she received during the pre-trial negotiations with Robert's Lawyer to present it to the Judge. Attorney, XXXXXX, said according to the rule of law, it is not permissible to take evidence submitted during pretrial negotiations into a court of law. He added, "I'm surprised that she would do such a thing, she knows better."

The Judge overruled her Motion to Impeach my testimony. Despite over-ruling her and allowing my testimony to stand as an eye-witness for my son, she kept insisting I be impeached. She wanted the Judge to hear my taped conversation with my son, that was given to her by the Lake County Prosecutor, XXXXXX. The Judge dismissed the jurors and me from the courtroom and listened to the taped conversation. My son said after the Judge heard the taped conversation, he scolded her and said, 'Did you not hear what I said, "Overruled!" Stop badgering this 80-year-old woman. I'm not changing my ruling. You are not going to impeach her as a witness!"

I went back into the courtroom and finished my testimony as an eyewitness to the Officers false assertion that my son resisted an officer during their arrest. Thereafter, my son testified and told the Jurors exactly what happened, which was supported by all the prima facie evidence. Thereafter, the jurors left the courtroom for deliberation. During the 2-day trial, my son said the jurors carefully reviewed all the evidence presented to them, which included: (1). Testimony of the three (3) U.S. Marshals, (2). Robert's testimony, (3). My eyewitness testimony, (4). Pictures of the police inflicted wounds on my son's face, neck, arms hands, and body, (5). Pictures of the officer's SUV smashing into my car on the passenger's side, and breaking the back window on the passenger's side, (6). The cost of repairs and replacement for my damaged vehicle, and (7). Attorney XXXXXX's Sworn Affidavit of the U.S. Marshal's admission to him stating, "because we used force, that's why we charged Robert with resisting an officer without violence." With all this evidence, the jury returned after less than 10 minutes of deliberation, with a verdict in favor of my son, "Not guilty."

After the Broward County Jury came back with a "not guilty" verdict, the Prosecutor XXXXXX came over to me and said, "Congratulations! I wish you and your son peace; I know you both have been put through hell!" I deeply appreciated her kind and heartfelt words.

My son and I were elated over the verdict. I

thanked God, and complemented Attorney, XXXXXX, for a job well done. He said, "I didn't win this case for your son. Your son won his own case by telling the whole truth most thoroughly with all the details supported by the evidence. Your son was most eloquent!" I, too, was impressed and proud of Robert's testimony, and his incredible strength of character living through and triumphing over the false charges made by the three U.S. Marshals.

Only God could give such strength and endurance for Robert to live through all these serious violations committed against him by Law Enforcement Officers in both Lake and Broward Counties. Fortunately, my son had his day in Court in Broward County where the Judge and Jury ruled in his favor against the lying Officers.

Several months later, on July 31, 2017, I was in a restaurant called XXXXXX, on the Ft. Lauderdale intercoastal waterway. I was having lunch with my friend XXXXXX, a Senior Vice President of a local bank. We were enjoying our meal and celebrating our 30-year-old friendship, when the former Broward County Prosecutor, XXXXXX, came over to our table. She hugged me and said, "You don't know how often I think of you. In fact, I think about you all the time. I'm a mother of a son and can identify with what you are going through." She wanted to know how my son and I were doing. I told her, "keeping our faith in God!" She said, "I don't hug anyone, but I am hugging you." I reminded her, "I told you my son was going to win his case." My friend said, "Virginia sees things before they happen and is 100% accurate." We wished each other well. The meeting was a fine moment of closure for both of us.

After winning a "not guilty jury verdict" in Broward County on January 26, 2017, Robert's lawyers were hopeful Judge XXXXXX would now reinstate his

$25,000 bond in Lake County, because he had no legal reason not to.

Robert was transferred back to Lake County Detention Center awaiting his Motion to Reinstate his $25,000 Bond. During my son's Bond Hearing held on February 24, 2017, Prosecutor XXXXXX lied to Judge XXXXXX and said my son was a danger to the community and a flight risk, and his bond should not be reinstated. Judge XXXXXX asked me about this. I said, "Your honor, I told my son, when this is all over, I want us to travel around the world. This is something that I've always wanted to do but never did in my 80 years of life. Those were not Robert's words, but mine. I was trying to comfort my son. He is not a flight risk." The Prosecutor purposefully had taken our monitored jail calls completely out of context in front of Judge XXXXXX and never produced any evidence of any jail calls I had with my son to support his false allegations.

The Prosecutor didn't stop there with his character assassination on my son. He called as his witness, Deputy XXXXXX, the officer who brutally assaulted my son during his unlawful warrantless entry into our home on October 5, 2015. Prosecutor XXXXXX questioned him about listening to my conversations with my son on our monitored jail calls. Attorney XXXXXX objected to Deputy XXXXXX, giving a third-party hearsay testimony, without first producing the jail phone calls. The Judge ordered the Prosecutor to give a copy of the phone calls between my son and me to Attorney XXXXXX. The hearing was canceled and rescheduled for the following month. This delay caused my son to suffer still another month without any medical treatment for his intestinal bleeding. I looked over to my son, who was pale and sickly looking with the loss of weight showing on his face. He took a deep breath of disappointment that this would delay his medical treatment for yet another month.

When Deputy XXXXXX exited the courtroom, he walked past me; wearing the same beige shoes, he wore when he brutally and repeatedly kicked my son in his stomach and ribs. I thought, "Dear God, how do we fight against all this corruption, conspiracy, bias, and injustice against my son?" God's powerful words to my spirit were, "Virginia, no weapons forged against your son will prosper, and there will be a judgment on those who did this to him."

Prior to the next Bond Hearing held on March 20, 2017, Prosecutor XXXXXX told Attorney XXXXXX, "I'm going to put your client away for life." At the rescheduled Bond Hearing, Prosecutor XXXXXX never brought up the taped jail phone conversations between my son and me, because he knew he took our jail phone conversations out of context. He didn't have Deputy XXXXXX testify, but did have two neighbors in Loch Leven testify to the following: "I saw Robert taking walks at 9:00 pm with his mother on the street in front of their home. The other neighbor said, "I close my shades at night for privacy." With these two statements, the Prosecutor convinced Judge XXXXXX my son was a "danger" to our neighborhood. The Prosecutor, XXXXXX told Robert's Attorney, "I let Mrs. O'Hare's neighbors listen to her jail calls with her son."

The Prosecutor lead his next witness, Detective XXXXXX, with questions that were obviously rehearsed. Detective XXXXXX, under oath stated, "I was told by Broward County Officer XXXXXX that Robert O'Hare delivered two Jukeboxes to a family in Broward County, FL In 2016." I saw Robert, shaking his head in total disbelief at these false statements coming from Detective XXXXXX, to make my son look culpable and a danger to the community in front of Judge XXXXXX.

Seven months prior to Detective XXXXXX's testifying about two Jukeboxes, Prosecutor XXXXXX arrested and falsely accused my son of delivering two Jukeboxes in 2011-2012 to a neighbor and added the charge of voyeurism. Both charges were insane accusations without any evidence whatsoever because none existed. The Prosecutor told the news media he "assumed" Robert delivered two Jukeboxes in either 2011 or 2012 to the wrong neighbor thinking the wrong neighbor would deliver the Jukeboxes to the right neighbor. Prosecutor XXXXXX prodded Detective XXXXXX to not only make up another Jukebox Story, but this time gave the name of the Broward County Officer XXXXXX who told him this made-up story. This Broward County Officer just happened to be the same one who falsely accused my son of resisting an officer without violence and smashed his SUV into my car on August 17, 2016. I had filed a formal complaint against this Officer to Internal Affairs and to his Supervisor, Sargent XXXXXX.

When Attorney, XXXXXX, and I left the courtroom, I asked, "if we prove Detective XXXXXX lied about the Broward County Officer XXXXXX telling him that Robert gave two jukeboxes to a family in Broward County in 2016, what would that do?" The Attorney said, "If he lied about something like that under oath, that would be lethal against the Detective."

After being told that, I immediately phoned the Broward County Officer's Supervisor, Sargent XXXXXX, who I had spoken to previously on Robert's Broward County Resisting an Officer case that he won with a Jury Verdict on January 26, 2017. Sargent XXXXXX denied that any such statement was ever made by Officer XXXXXX to the Lake County Detective XXXXXX, of Robert giving two Jukeboxes to a family in Broward County in 2016. He further added, "We don't have any Jukeboxes on our police report as proof of this. You have a copy of that Police Report, you can see for yourself no Jukeboxes were reported. If that Jukebox story were true, it would have to be put on the Police Report. We just don't make up stories like that and put them in the Police Report. You should subpoena Officer XXXXXX to confirm this fact."

Instead, I went further and filed a formal complaint with Internal Affairs in Broward County, FL against Officer XXXXXX. The Internal Affairs Investigator XXXXXX upon his investigation, also confirmed what Sargent XXXXXX stated, "Officer XXXXXX did not say anything to Lake County Detective XXXXXX about two (2) Jukeboxes being delivered to a family in Broward County by Robert O'Hare." I have a copy of the police report, that confirms what Sargent XXXXXX confirmed. There was no mention whatsoever of any Jukeboxes being given by Robert to a Broward County family on the police report.

Unfortunately, the conspiracy between the Prosecutor XXXXXX and Detective XXXXXX worked, because Judge XXXXXX, on March 20, 2017, denied reinstating my son's $25,000 bond, and wrote on his Order that Robert would be a danger to the Loch Leven community if released on Bond. Judge XXXXXX stated in his ruling he used evidence submitted to him at the Bond Hearing by the witness, stating Robert would be a danger to Loch Leven if he reinstated his Bond. The witness was Deputy XXXXXX. Thereafter, Judge XXXXXX ruled against all of Robert's motions.

Exhibit K: $25,000 Bond revoked by Judge XXXXXX, due to false testimony by Detective XXXXXX, the Master Deputy XXXXXX, and Prosecutor XXXXXX.

We lived in Loch Leven Community since 1999, as the first homeowners in this newly developed waterfront community in Mt. Dora, FL For 17 years with no problems whatsoever. Robert was never a threat to any neighborhood or anyone for that matter in his entire life!

He is not a flight risk, and never ever delivered any Jukeboxes to any family in our neighborhood neither in 2011-2012 nor in 2016, as Prosecutor, XXXXXX, falsely stated to Judge XXXXXX. As further evidence of this Robert was out on Bond for 10 months from October 9, 2015 to August 25, 2016 and was not a flight risk then or any danger to any community we ever lived in.

Internal Affairs Investigator, XXXXXX confirmed the only evidence used in my son's second arrest charges by Prosecutor, XXXXXX, was what the Deputies took from my son's locked bedroom closet in the State's first arrest charges on October 5, 2015. XXXXXX said, "there was no new evidence against your son."

The only thing Robert ever gave to any family in Broward County, Florida, in 2016, was a picture frame with a gold police badge in it from Hawaii 5-0, which he gave to my tenant in Ft. Lauderdale, FL. I asked the tenant to return the picture frame, so I could present this as proof that this was the only thing my son ever gave to a family in Broward County in 2016, and not two (2) Jukeboxes, as falsely sworn to by Detective XXXXXX at the Bond Hearing.

After the Bond Hearing, when I made a formal complaint to Broward County's Internal Affairs against Officer XXXXXX, the Investigator, Detective XXXXXX wanted a copy of the Hawaii 5-0 picture frame, which I gave to him. Upon his Internal Affairs investigation of Officer XXXXXX, I was informed that Officer XXXXXX never told Detective XXXXXX that my son delivered two (2) jukeboxes to a family in Broward County, and he knew nothing about the picture frame. Officer XXXXXX's Supervisor, Sargent XXXXXX confirmed this fact as well. He stated, "as further proof of this, there was no jukebox story put on Officer XXXXXX's Police Report, you can depose Officer XXXXXX yourself, and he will tell you he never gave that story of two (2) jukeboxes to Lake

County Detective XXXXXX."

Exhibit L: A Picture frame with Hawaii 5-0 gold police badge, and not two (2) Jukeboxes as falsely stated by Detective XXXXXX, under oath, at the Bond Hearing to Judge XXXXXX:

Prosecutor XXXXXX canceled the Motion to Suppress five times over a period of close to eight months. The original date set on April 2017 was canceled and rescheduled for June 2017; canceled again and rescheduled for August 10, 2017; canceled again and rescheduled for September 5, 2017; canceled again and rescheduled for October 4, 2017; canceled again and rescheduled and finally held on November 8, 2017. These delays by Prosecutor XXXXXX were burdensome to my son's already failing health while being unjustly incarcerated without allowing Robert to have an outside Medical Furlough or reactivation of his bond. Attorney XXXXXX told me the Prosecutor's reason for postponing all the hearing dates was because he was afraid of losing his case against Robert's Motion to Suppress.

While waiting for the Motion to Suppress Hearing, Robert's Attorney made another motion to Judge XXXXXX for Robert's Emergency Furlough on October 4, 2017, for outside urgently needed medical treatment, hospitalization, and surgery! Judge XXXXXX denied that motion as well. For 17 months, the Lake County Detention Center continued to deny Robert his urgently needed medical treatment for his malignant colon cancer and allowed him to suffer from pain and bleeding from his cancer symptoms.

I received an email dated October 5, 2017, from attorney XXXXXX who stated: "We will continue to stand by what we've been saying…that the police overstepped and conducted an illegal search. You need to hire a civil rights attorney and commence a lawsuit immediately."

The Motion to Suppress was finally held on November 8,2017. Prosecutor XXXXXX failed to bring to the Hearing the defense's evidence to Judge XXXXXX, which was a Live Video of the Deputies violation to my son's 4th Amendment Rights, and Federal Law Section 1983. XXXXXX promised Attorney XXXXXX he would show Judge XXXXXX the Video pre-hearing and would bring the Video to the Motion to Suppress Hearing as well. He did neither, even though his office is right next door to Judge XXXXXX' office in the Court House Building in Tavares, Florida.

Fortunately, for Robert's vitally important evidence for his Motion to Suppress, Attorney XXXXXX had an extra copy of the Live Cell Phone Video with him at the Suppression Hearing and showed it to Judge XXXXXX from his laptop computer. During the hearing, Prosecutor XXXXXX lied to Judge XXXXXX again about a doctrine that does not exist in the Supreme Court Case Law. This caused XXXXXX to go over to him in front of Judge XXXXXX and say, "XXXXXX, if you lie to me one more time in Court, I will go after your Bar License." Attorney XXXXXX heard Judge XXXXXX say to XXXXXX, "you put me in a bad situation."

After previewing the Live Video, Prosecutor XXXXXX knew this evidence would benefit the defense and incriminate the Lake County Deputies. The Prosecutor's failure to present defense's evidence to Judge XXXXXX would prevent Robert from having a favorable ruling from his Motion to Suppress.

The Live Cell Phone Video was prima facie evidence against the Deputies, which showed their being unlawfully in our home on October 5, 2015, while conducting an unlawful warrantless search and seizure. The Video also showed the aftermath of their brutal beating to Robert, and Captain XXXXXX making an unlawful and threatening command to Robert while restraining him without a warrant for several hours. The Video proved, with unrefuted evidence, their violent and criminal violations against Robert's 4th Amendment Rights and Federal Law Section 1983. **XXXXXX's failure to bring this Video to the Motion to Suppress Hearing was not only intentional to avoid losing his case against my son but is further proof of his prosecutorial misconduct.** Upon previewing this Live Video, Prosecutor XXXXXX knew it would be beneficial to the defense, and lethal evidence against the Deputies and his case. This is another instance of Prosecutor XXXXXX being in violation of the law.

The Court's Electronic transcription of the Motion to Suppress Hearing confirms Prosecutor XXXXXX's misconduct and his conspiring with the Deputies to give false testimony before Judge XXXXXX. In his ruling, Judge XXXXXX added a doctrine of Inevitable Discovery that doesn't exist in Supreme Court law, Rodriguez vs. State of Florida. By Judge XXXXXX adding this non-existent doctrine to his Order supports the unlawful warrantless search and seizure of the Deputies. At the Motion to Suppress Hearing, Attorney XXXXXX presented a copy of the Supreme Court Case Law Rodriguez vs. State of Florida to Judge XXXXXX, after Prosecutor XXXXXX misquoted it to Judge XXXXXX. Upon reading it, the Judge knew the doctrine of Inevitable Discovery did not exist because the Deputies did not have a warrant. However, knowing this he still added this doctrine of Inevitable Discovery to his Order.

Judge XXXXXX misinterpreting a Supreme Court case law, Rodriguez vs. State of Florida (2015), in his ruling after Attorney XXXXXX presented him with a copy of this case law removes any probability of error for misinterpretation. Such bias, corruption, and collusion committed by the Lake County Judicial Officials have unjustly misrepresented Robert's legal rights instead of upholding them. Such violations of the law have been ongoing against Robert and are reflected in all of Judge XXXXXX adverse rulings, which the electronic transcriptions of all the proceedings will verify.

The Mt. Dora Real Estate Broker, XXXXXX, who sold our Mt. Dora home was at the Hearing, as was XXXXXX a long-time friend of 35 years of the family. Both observed Judge XXXXXX at the beginning of the Hearing. Both said Judge XXXXXX came into the courtroom with his mind made up against my son's Motion to Suppress before even hearing any evidence. They said his demeanor changed dramatically after he viewed the Live Video. In fact, my son said Judge XXXXXX looked right at him while previewing the Video. This Live Video showed the serious violations committed by Deputies, XXXXXX, XXXXXX, and XXXXXX, and Capt. XXXXXX with undeniable proof of their warrantless entry, search, seizure, and the aftermath of the three Deputies XXXXXX, XXXXXX and XXXXXX, brutally beating Robert.

During his testifying, Corporal XXXXXX had a problem keeping his stories straight and repeatedly said, "I don't recall." His body worn video camera/recorder added proof to their violations of staging a crime scene with the laptop computer they found in a locked bedroom closet several hours before obtaining a search warrant. Electronic transcription of this hearing was submitted as evidence to your office.

Before previewing the Video, Judge XXXXXX had previously denied Robert's 3rd Attorney XXXXXX's Motion to Suppress immediately after he finished his last sentence. His Motion to Suppress was based on Master Deputy XXXXXX's improper disclosure to the Magistrate Judge when he had him sign his warrant. The expert witness for the defense was a well-known Forensic Attorney, XXXXXX, who confirmed **the following disclo-**

sures on the search warrant were omitted:

1. Master Deputy XXXXXX left out what the reports showed. The screenshots show that between 11 to 29 people were on that wireless network at any given time. Dep. XXXXXX made it sound like my son was the only PC connected. This was wrong! He left out the fact that he had Robert's DL information. But never bothered to tell the court his DL ADDRESS was three (3) hours away.

2. Master Detective XXXXXX left out the fact that he had no idea how many of the 11 to 29 people connected to Wi-Fi were PC users versus other types of computers, which leads us to the next omission, he left out the fact that the software reports never told him the downloader was a PC, he merely "assumed" such without digital verification. There were ways to verify this, but Detective XXXXXX never did!

Robert's 3rd Attorney XXXXXX's email to me detailing Detective XXXXXX's omissions on the search warrant:

Dear Virginia,

Basically, Detective XXXXXX misled the Judge because he told the Judge that Robert was the only person in the coffee house using a PC. This was a lie. The FING reports show that there were several other PC users on XXXXXX public Wi-Fi at the time that child porn was being shared over the system. It was a lie on several levels because PC users were not the only folks who could have downloaded child porn via the system, the ARES software permits other users to download as well. Again, Detective XXXXXX never told the judge that other users could have done this—he never even told the judge that there were other users on the Wi-Fi! Sometimes, there were over 20 different devices on the system, yet he made it seem like only one person was on the system.

To make matters even worse, there were several common users at each of the times child porn was being downloaded. In other words, the first-time child porn was being downloaded Robert wasn't even on the Wi-Fi! The judge wasn't told this. The second and third time, Robert was on the Wi-Fi, but so were several other folks!

Very poor police work, for sure.

Kindly,

Attorney XXXXXX, Attorney At Law

Exhibit M: Motion to Suppress: by Attorney XXXXXX, who outlines serious omissions made by Master Deputy XXXXXX on his Search Warrant, which Judge XXXXXX immediately denied.

In Robert's Motion to Suppress, Judge XXXXXX correctly noted in his Order, Page 3 of 6 #2, "the Deputies had no justification whatsoever to make a warrantless entry, search and seizure in defendant's home." He further states, "the Deputies warrantless entry, search, and seizure, was unjustified, unwise, costly, and unnecessary."

However, Judge XXXXXX in error added to his Order a doctrine of Inevitable Discovery that does not exist in this Supreme Court case law, Rodriguez vs. State of Florida, does not allow an officer who breaks the law to benefit from the fruits from a "poisonous tree." This exclusionary rule is designed to exclude such evidence obtained in violation of a defendant's Fourth Amendment rights, which protects one's rights against unreasonable searches and seizures by law enforcement personnel.

Robert's lawyers made a Motion for Reconsideration for Judge XXXXXX to correct his error in misinterpreting Supreme Court Case Law Rodriguez vs. State of Florida. Several days later, Judge XXXXXX denied the Motion for Reconsideration, with no written legal explanation for his denial, because none existed. This opened the door for Robert to Appeal on the basis of Judge XXXXXX' error in misinterpreting this Supreme Court Case Law.

Robert's lawyers strongly recommended that he not go to trial but "Plead no contest," and Appeal, and be free from Judge XXXXXX' bias, politics, and unjust rulings and the Prosecutor's misconduct, and conspiracy and collusion with the Deputies. They all agreed that the Lake County Judicial System did not serve my son well legally, civilly, or constitutionally. After dealing 17 months with this corruption and now having Judge XXXXXX add a doctrine that does not exist in the law was like trying a case without law and justice. In Judge XXXXXX's Order to protect the Deputies violations and purposefully misinterpreting a Supreme Court Case law, then refusing to correct it, left no other option for Robert other than to Plea "no contest" and Appeal. Going to trial would only prolong Robert's health crisis, and under Judge XXXXXX unfair rulings, would not be on the side of justice or my son's constitutional rights. The only thing Robert could do to seek justice and save his life would be outside of the Lake County's Corrupt Judicial System, and through the Appellate Court.

All evidence submitted in this Civil and Criminal Complaint of egregious criminal acts, conspiracy, and bias committed by the Lake County Deputies, the Lake County Prosecutor, the Lake County Detention Center, the Lake County Sheriff, and the Lake County Judicial System, warrants a speedy and thorough investigation against their violating my son's civil, constitutional and prisoner's rights. The evidence provided herein supports the urgency for an immediate criminal investigation of these Government Employees.

Robert's faith in God, since childhood, is seeing him through these very challenging 18 months of pain, suffering, and injustice, while being imprisoned by this corrupt legal system that is denying him his civil and constitutional rights. The Detention Center's Doctor, after examining my son on October 2017 stated in his report, "Mr. O'Hare is a pleasant 55-year old gentleman." Robert is truly a gentleman. I am so proud of the God-given strength, and character Robert has exhibited and maintained as he is living through all this holocaust of injustice poured on him without measure by the Lake County Judicial System.

Due to the Lake County Sheriff's Deputies criminally assaulting my son, and causing him permanent bodily harm and disability, they also violated his constitutional rights, and Federal Law Section 1983 as well. Our home no longer was our homestead sanctuary, but a nightmare of terror. This caused me to sell our beautiful Mt. Dora, FL Home on November 16, 2017, with a great amount of sadness. All who ever stepped into our home, or viewed it online including the Broker, XXXXXX, who sold our home within four months for the full asking price, said, "this is a "WOW WOW HOME!" She said the home, which I designed and built, sold for the highest price in the Mt. Dora community, which was close to $1,000,000.

The video of my Mt. Dora home located on XXXXXX is on the Internet, and those that viewed it have told me the home is absolutely drop dead gorgeous! My son asked me on January 28, 2018, if I missed our home. Not wanting him to feel any remorse, I said, "God has something better for us, and our being reunited as a family with the spirit of Anne, Patty, and Dan with us is far more important than the home we had for 17 years." He agreed, and said, "Mom each home we've ever had was more beautiful. I thought our home in Poughkeepsie, N. Y. was the bomb, but each home we've had since has been even more beautiful!"

I have previously submitted to you in my letter dated December 27, 2017, my son's Motion to Suppress, and Judge XXXXXX' Order denying both the Motion to Suppress and the Motion for Reconsideration.

Attorney XXXXXX was not at the two Bond Hearings but heard the Court's Electronic CD Tapes of the two hearings, stated, "Your son was set up by the Prosecutor and Deputies at that hearing."

Attorney XXXXXX's Motion to Suppress was based on the legally deficient search warrant drawn up by Master Deputy XXXXXX. He stated: "If Judge XXXXXX goes by the law, in our Motion to Suppress, which is based solely on the law, your son will be free if he doesn't you son will appeal and most likely prevail at the Appellate level." Unfortunately, Judge XXXXXX did not rule according to the law and denied Attorney XXXXXX's Motion to Suppress. Judge XXXXXX did not rule according to the law on Attorney XXXXXX's Motion to Suppress as well, which was based on the law. In my son's instant case, there is **no law that exists which allows the unlawful warrantless violations committed by the Lake County Deputies. Their actions were 100% illegal and against Robert's 4th Amendment Rights.** The Deputies also violated Federal Law Section 1983 by using brutal police force on my son, which caused permanent bodily harm and disability.

A Central Florida Judge who read Judge XXXXXX Order to our Motion to Suppress, and case law of Rodriguez vs. State of Florida, said, "Judge XXXXXX made an error in his Order. He used the doctrine of Inevitable

Discovery that does not exist in Rodriguez vs. State of Florida. The Deputies did not have a warrant in place when they entered your home, and never applied for one. Therefore, the Doctrine of Inevitable Discovery is not applicable. **His ruling is wrong.** You can Motion for Reconsideration. If that doesn't work, your son can Plea and has an excellent chance on an Appeal."

Robert's four lawyers agreed that Judge XXXXXX should have granted his Motion to Suppress. They also stated Judge XXXXXX should have granted reinstatement of Robert's bond and allowed him to have a medical furlough. They said their Motion to Suppress was based 100% on the law. They told me their obvious conclusion was that Judge XXXXXX was biased against my son and would not grant Robert's Motion for Reconsideration to correct his error in misinterpreting the law. They were correct. Judge XXXXXX did not correct his error of adding a doctrine of Inevitable Discovery that does not exist in the Supreme Court case law, Rodriguez vs. State of Florida. Judge XXXXXX error was a monumental blow to my son's case and justice!

Robert's lawyers said they were preparing their Appeal Brief prior to Judge XXXXXX' final two rulings because they were positive he would not grant my son's motions due to his prior rulings that were not in compliance with the law but according to his extreme bias against Robert. They said the Appellate Court would correct Judge XXXXXX' inventing a doctrine of Inevitable Discover that does not exist in the law and Robert will be set free on a De Nova Appeal. A "De novo" appeal refers to an appeal in which the appellate court uses the trial court's record but reviews the evidence and law without yielding to the trial court's rulings. "De novo" is a standard of review that can be applied on appeal."

The Lawyers agreed that Robert going to trial with a biased Judge and the conspiracy between the Prosecutor and Deputies was lethal. To protect my son's life against any further unjust rulings by Judge XXXXXX, they had my son Plea "No Contest" so they can Appeal and get Robert the much-needed Justice and freedom he is legally entitled to as a US citizen.

Herein is a synopsis of violations committed against Robert O'Hare's civil, constitutional, and prisoner's rights by the lake county judicial system:

1   Upon Robert's incarceration, on August 25, 2016, the Lake County Detention Center placed him in protective custody for 2 1/2 months in an 8 x 13 cell. He was confined 24/7 in lockdown with up to five to six cellmates at one time. He was only let out of his cell for 1 hour on Monday, Wednesday, and Friday. One of Robert's cellmates, XXXXXX was in the final stages of a contagious liver disease, Hepatitis C, and had a severe mental disorder. This cellmate's disease was lethal exposure to Robert's already failing health, having just been diagnosed with a precancerous bleeding colon. During these 2 ½ months, his severe symptoms caused pain and suffering and his weight to plummet from 190+ lbs. Down to 140 lbs. During this time, I, and his lawyers made ongoing formal requests for Medical treatment for his pre-cancerous bleeding colon. All to no avail. The Detention Center denied giving Robert any medical care or medical treatment whatsoever, allowing him to suffer from symptoms of malignant colon cancer, which he was later diagnosed as having with a 70% blockage in his colon.

2   The Lake County Detention Center allowed Robert to suffer cruel and inhuman punishment, as his condition worsened daily. He was allowed to bleed and suffer without any medical care or treatment for seventeen (17) months during his incarcera-

tion. This was a Violation of his 8th Amendment, Civil, Constitutional, and Prisoner's Rights.

3   Attached to this complaint is a Notarized statement from a cellmate, XXXXXX, who witnessed Robert's pain and suffering and being denied medical care by the Lake County Detention Center. Another cellmate I spoke with during a monitored jail call with Robert stated to me Robert was very ill and the Detention Center refused to give him any medical care. He said the Nurse told Robert, "You can get your medical treatment when you get out."

4   Prosecutor, XXXXXX denied Robert his constitutional rights including his due process of law, which violated his 5th and 14th Amendment, during his entire period of incarceration.

5   The Lake County Prosecutor, the Lake County Sheriff, the Lake County State Attorney, XXXXXX, and the Lake County Judge XXXXXX, were formerly put on notice of the Lake County Deputies' criminal violations and the Lake County Detention Center denying Robert his urgently needed medical treatment. By doing nothing, and not taking any legal action, they sanctioned these violations against Robert's civil, constitutional and prisoner's rights.

6   The Prosecutor's Prosecutorial Misconduct includes the following: "courtroom misconduct, making improper remarks or improperly introducing evidence designed to prejudice the judge; hiding, destroying or tampering with evidence, case files or court records; failing to disclose evidence that might tend to exonerate the defendant, threatening, and presenting false or misleading evidence; selective or vindictive prosecution, denial

for a speedy trial, and the use of unreliable and untruthful witnesses."

7 In addition to the Lake County Prosecutor committing all the above unlawful acts of misconduct, my son was charged an excessive amount of bail of $13,500 for their false charge of resisting an officer, the laptop computer they took out of my son's locked bedroom closet where my deceased husband's firearm was also kept. The Prosecutor charged Robert with still another $25,000 Bond for their 2nd bogus charge of alleging in 2011 or 2012 that Robert delivered two jukeboxes with lenses in them to a wrong neighbor, thinking the wrong neighbor would deliver the boxes to the correct neighbor. Prosecutor XXXXXX stated his assumption theory to the news media that went viral all over the country.

8 The Deputies staged the laptop computer as a crime scene, after unlawfully removing the laptop's case and short barrel rifle from the locked bedroom closet without a search warrant. None of those items can be legally used against Robert, because of the Deputies unlawful warrantless search, which is against Robert's 4th Amendment Rights. The Deputies knowingly staged the crime scene to comply with the plain view doctrine, "If the police can see it, they can seize it without a warrant during a "lawful" observation." The Deputies placed the laptop computer on the floor and the case on the bed, then put on their police report it was in "plain view." This unlawful act was attested to and confirmed by Corporal XXXXXX's body-worn-camcorder video and in their Police Report. The Deputies did not qualify for the plain view doctrine because they made an unlawful warrantless entry into our home without any lawful

observation, which is in violation of Robert's 4th Amendment Rights. Judge XXXXXX confirmed the Deputies' unlawful entry without a warrant in his Order to Robert's Motion to Suppress.

9   Detective. XXXXXX from Lake County Internal Affairs confirmed to me there was no additional evidence Prosecutor XXXXXX had for his 2nd arrest charges on Robert. He said the Prosecutor used what was collected from the first charges which they found in my son's locked bedroom closet without a warrant to make their 2nd arrest charges. Yet Robert was charged $25,000 for his 2nd Bond, which Judge XXXXXX revoked after four days of receiving this payment, due to the Broward County Officer XXXXXXX filing a false Resisting an Officer Charge.

10   During Robert's 17 months of incarceration in Lake County Detention Center, he went without medical care and treatment, existed under inhuman conditions, drank unfiltered water (with a foul sewer odor) from his cell during his 2 ½ months of 24/7 lockdown. He had to deal with his now life-threatening malignant colon cancer, blindness in one eye caused by the Deputies' beating, physical, emotional, and mental pain and suffering without being treated by a Medical Doctor. In addition, Judge XXXXXX denied Robert all his Motions for an Emergency Medical Outside Furlough and was not given any urgently needed mandatory medical treatment by the Lake County Detention Center for his life-threatening malignant colon cancer. For over one year, he was not examined by a GI Doctor. He was not given medically required hospitalization, surgery, or chemotherapy. These are all clear violation of his civil, constitutional, and prisoner's rights as well as his 8th

Amendment rights.

11 Robert was denied "five" hearing dates for his Motion to Suppress for close to eight (8) months. This postponed going to trial and caused his detention to be over the six-month limit by law. The sixth Hearing was heard on November 8, 2017. In Judge XXXXXX' ruling, he confirmed on his Order that the Deputies had no justification for their warrantless entry into our home. The Live Video viewed by Judge XXXXXX during the Suppression Hearing, visually attested to the Deputies' criminal violations.

12 In Judge XXXXXX' Order on my son's Motion to Suppress, dated December 4, 2017, he gave the Deputies a doctrine of Inevitable Discovery that does not exist in the Supreme Court case law Rodriguez vs. State of Florida.

13 To correct Judge XXXXXX's error, Attorney XXXXXX filed a Motion for Reconsideration to give Judge XXXXXX an opportunity to correct his misinterpreting of case law Rodriguez vs. State of Florida. Instead of correcting his error he denied it, with no legal explanation. This caused Robert's lawyers to strongly advise him to Plead "No Contest" and Appeal rather than go to trial with a biased Judge who ruled against all his Motions, that were allowed by law.

14 Prosecutor XXXXXX's failed to bring Defendant's live Video to Judge XXXXXX prior to the Motion to Suppress Hearing and to the Hearing on November 8, 2017, as he promised Attorney XXXXXX he would. He intentionally did this with the knowledge that the Live Video would prove the Deputies' violations against Robert's constitutional rights and cause him to lose his case.

15 Robert's original diagnoses by the Broward County Health Hospital in Ft. Lauderdale, FL of pre-cancerous bleeding polyps made on August 25, 2016, during his ER visit to Broward County Health Hospital, was verified, as malignant colon cancer thirteen (13) months later, when he became critically ill. It was then that he was finally given a colonoscopy, which confirmed he has malignant colon cancer with a large 70% blockage in his colon. The Oncologist stated to Robert, "this cancer was present in your colon for one year." The Lake County Detention Center having Robert's Medical Report since August 25, 2016, and denying him urgently needed medical treatment for close to 17 months violated his 8th Amendment, constitutional and Prisoner's rights. It was not until January 28th, 2018 that he was given five (5) radiation treatments by the Detention Center, as he was regularly bleeding like diarrhea from his colon.

16 Prior to this treatment, the Lake County Detention Center asked Robert to sign a waiver of liability against the Detention center. When Robert refused to sign their release of liability, is when they gave him five radiation treatments without any follow up medical care from a doctor since the date of this updated letter on May 8th, 2018. They placed Robert in lockdown where he is currently and only allowed out of his cell for one hour on Monday, Wednesday, and Friday. One of his cellmates was a psych patient who refused to take a shower and lacked any form of hygiene.

Exhibit N: Medical Report from Broward County Health Hospital, on August 25, 2016, and letter from renowned Gastroenterologist Doctor stating, **"Patient, Robert O'Hare urgently needs to have a colonoscopy**

and treatment for his life-threatening illness:"

Robert's lawyer, XXXXXX, continued to make formal requests to the Lake County Sheriff's Legal Dept. for medical treatment for Robert. Their reply was, "There's nothing wrong with him." They made this statement to XXXXXX without a GI doctor or any medical doctor examining Robert for his life-threatening health issues since his incarceration on August 25, 2016, until his first medical exam and colonoscopy on September 5, 2017.

Exhibit O: Attorney XXXXXX's letter to the Lake County Sheriff's Legal Dept. Putting them on notice of Robert's health issue and a copy of the letter was sent to the Lake County Detention Center.

Some of the electronic equipment, which was taken by the Lake County Sheriff's Deputies, from our home on October 5, 2015, belonged to my deceased husband. As a Florida Licensed Private Investigator, my husband used electronics, in his line of work, tripods, cameras, firearms, and smaller electronics needed for surveillance. My husband also had a Florida license for a concealed weapon or firearm permit. Upon my husband's death on September 30, 2013, Robert kept all his surveillance equipment in his locked bedroom closet. One charge made by the Prosecutor against Robert was possession of a short barrel rifle the deputies found in Robert's locked bedroom closet stored with my husband's electronics. The deputies made this charge upon their unlawful warrantless entry without consent, without probable cause, and without any exigent circumstances.

Exhibit P: My husband's Florida License as a Private Investigator and licensed for a Concealed Weapon or Firearm:

Even though a Broward County Jury found Robert

"Not Guilty" of resisting an officer without violence, Judge XXXXXX still refused to reinstate Robert's Bond so he could receive outside medical treatment. He did not make his ruling on the law. He made his ruling based on his bias and false statements made by the Deputies and Prosecutor XXXXXX. They alleged Robert was a flight risk and a danger to the small subdivision community we lived in. These false and damaging statements made by the Prosecutor and Deputies were vindictive and false and denied justice for my son. Judge XXXXXX refused to honor any of my son's legally sufficient motions to date.

Exhibit Q: Robert O'Hare's was acquitted by a Broward County Jury with a verdict of "Not Guilty" of Resisting an Officer without violence on January 25, 2017.

Robert's cellmate, XXXXXX witnessed the Lake County Detention Center refusing to give him any medical treatment. On 10/4/2017, my Fort Lauderdale Maid, XXXXXX called and said her son, XXXXXX, was in the Lake County Detention Center for two weeks for a traffic ticket violation. She said he was in the same pod four cells away from my son. When XXXXXX came home, he told his mother about my son's pain and suffering and the Detention Center's refusal to give Robert any medical treatment. He signed this Notarized Statement, which I submitted to the Dept. Of Justice with my Exhibits A-Q.

This is XXXXXX's notarized statement:

XXXXXX said: "I hear Robert cry at night with pain. They refuse to give him any medicine for the pain from his cancer. Robert looks sickly and is very skinny. His hair has turned white. I feel very sorry for him they are killing him. He has cancer and is very ill. He is dying, and they are doing nothing to help him. He asks for medicine, and they refuse to give him any medicine. That place is horrible! He said, "Robert is a kind person and asked me when I left to give my mattress to one of his cellmates that sleeps above him on just an iron mattress. Even though Robert is very ill, he still thinks about helping others. He is a very kind and a very good person."

My maid showed her son a picture of my son before he was incarcerated and asked him, "is this Robert?" He said, "yes, but he looks really bad now, skinny, and sickly, his hair is all white.

Another cellmate of Robert's, a homeless man, brought Robert his peanut butter sandwich because he was too sick to raise his head off the bed. My son told me about this heartfelt event and said, "mom, here is this man who is homeless and was brought in for panhandling and helping me because I was too sick even to raise my head off the bed. He fed me his peanut butter sandwich. Here I had an affluent life, and this man sleeps under bridges and gives me his peanut butter sandwich. That deed got to my heart." I said, Robert, God is watching over you, and he will exonerate you and see you through all these unjust and bogus charges."

In my soon to be published book, *"Virginia O'Hare Documents God's Laws vs. Man's Laws,"* I've included this letter to you with a letter to President Donald J. Trump, and the FBI with a copy of all these three letters to Lake County State Attorney XXXXXX. This book will be published worldwide to bring attention to God's laws, and awareness of the corruption, injustice, bias, that my son has been subjected to while being incarcerated in the Lake County Judicial System in Tavares, Florida.

On January 29, 2018, the eve of Robert's supersedeas bond hearing in front of Judge XXXXXX, the prosecutor came up with still another bogus charge against Robert. He is being falsely accused of solicitation to kill Judge XXXXXX while he was talking to me on a monitored jail call. Attorney XXXXXX said the state wants me to be their ~~star~~ witness against my son. This false and outlandish charge was made up, in my opinion, because 95% of the charges against Robert were declared unlawful by Judge XXXXXX against the Lake County deputies in his order to Robert's Motion to Suppress. The 5% was Judge XXXXXX making a doctrine in error of Inevitable Discovery that does not exist in the Supreme Court case law Rodriguez vs. State of Florida. His error of misinterpreting the law made it possible for Robert's lawyers to do an appeal on his misrepresentation of the law.

I met with the Lead Attorney XXXXXX and spoke with the Trial Attorney XXXXXX, who both believe this charge is in retribution to the fact that Robert will be free upon his appeal. The lawyers made a Motion to Recuse the entire Judicial System in Lake County.

Update: The Motion to Recuse the entire Judicial System in Lake County was granted. Prior to this Order, the Lake County State Attorney had recused Judge XXXXXX from my son's case.

Deputy XXXXXX, the one who beat up my son and kicked him multiple times in the ribs and stomach on his forced entry into our home on October 5, 2015, is the one who did the investigation of these new charges against Robert, and is the State's star witness. He publicly alleged to the news media a falsehood against a family friend, XXXXXX, as being solicited to kill Judge XXXXXX. His name is, XX XXXXX. He is a 75-year-old senior citizen, blind in one eye and cataracts in the other eye with cancer in his body. He vehemently denies any affiliation with any such bogus allegations made up by the Lake County Prosecutor and stated so to this Deputy when he came to his home to question him. He said he told Deputy XXXXXX, "you are not going to do to my life what you did to Robert O'Hare, what I have left of it. You Deputies have a very bad reputation in this community and are the ones that should be locked up not the innocent people you go after." He also stated this to Robert's Lawyer XXXXXX and to the news media. He said he told Deputy XXXXXX, 'I was never solicited to kill a judge. I have known Virginia and Robert for 35 years, and they wouldn't hurt anyone." He told me he wants to sue Deputy XXXXXX and the Lake County Sheriff's office for smearing his name all over the news media.

My son said on our monitored phone call, "I can't believe they would come up with something like that. Judge XXXXXX did me a favor in my Motion to Suppress. If he were here, I would hug him and give him a kiss. He gave me 95% of what I asked for in my Motion to Suppress. He only misinterpreted the law, which I can win on the appeal."

These new false charges by the Sheriff's Office and the Prosecutor are their final attempt to try to wash away their own criminal violations by putting their final nail in my son's coffin by falsely accusing Robert of such a bogus charge on the eve of his supersedes bond hearing on January 30, 2018, so he could be released. This new charge kept my son from being released on a new bond.

Fear of my son being set free is the main purpose for these latest charges, and for Deputy XXXXXX coming to see Robert at the detention center on January 16, 2018, He wanted Robert to tell him where he was going to live when he gets out and to question him. Because Robert refused to talk with him without his lawyers being present. Deputy XXXXXX became angry and went into my son's cell and ransacked his belongings and left taking two bags of Robert's commissary food and one cookie. Right after this incident, a Security Officer

XXXXXX came over to talk to Robert and said, "I've been a guard here for 12 years and have never seen anything like this happen before to anyone. Robert, this deputy was really pissed at you."

This same Deputy XXXXXX drove from central Florida to my home in Ft. Lauderdale on January 11, 2018, and banged on my door and rang my doorbell repeatedly for three hours before finally leaving. He called me several times from his cell phone. I had Attorney XXXXXX verify his cell number as being registered to this Deputy. The captain of the guard where I live witnessed this incident and said, "that man is desperate and running scared."

Attorney XXXXXX said, "I have never seen a case like this before in my entire career. With all this corruption, I will file a Motion to Recuse the entire Lake County judicial system and defend these latest charges against Robert outside of the Lake County Judicial System." This motion was granted, and Robert was transferred out of Lake County Detention Center on May 24, 2018 to Marion County Jail in Ocala, Florida.

Every American citizen has their Civil and Constitutional Rights from the moment we take our first breath when we come out of the birth canal until we take our last breath when our spirit returns to God who gave it. No American citizen, rich or poor, black or white, young or old should never settle for injustice, corruption, conspiracy, and bias, from anyone employed by our Government that works in our Judicial System. Our constitutional rights are expressed in our Fifth Amendment guarantees that: "No person shall be deprived of life, liberty, or property, without due process of law." This applies to all states by the 14th Amendment.

These serious and egregious violations against my son Robert A. O'Hare, committed by Government Employees in Lake County, Tavares, Florida, who are under the Supervision of the Lake County State Attorney, XXXXXX, needs your immediate investigation and prosecution.

I will end this letter with a prayer to God that you will give this criminal complaint your immediate investigation and prosecution, so my son can receive the justice he is legally and constitutionally entitled to as an American citizen.

Respectfully Submitted,

____

VIRGINIA O'HARE

U. S. Department of Justice
Mail Referral Unit
Washington, D.C. 20530

April 9, 2018

Virginia O'Hare
XXXXXXXXXXXXXX
XXXXXXXXXXXXXX

Dear Friend:

Thank you for your letter dated April 5, 2018, to the Attorney General, Deputy Attorney General, or Associate Attorney General, which was received by the Department of Justice, Mail Referral Unit, on April 9, 2018, and assigned ID number XXXXXX.

Your letter will be reviewed, and if a response or an update is necessary, it will be sent to you within 60 business days. If you have any questions, please contact us at (301) 583-7350 and refer to your ID number XXXXXX when requesting any information concerning your correspondence.

Sincerely,

Mail Referral Unit

Department of Justice

U.S. Department of Justice
Criminal Section - PHB
950 Pennsylvania Ave, NW
Washington, DC 20530

June 1, 2018

Ms. Virginia O'Hare
XXXXXX
XXXXXXXXXXXXXXXXXXXXXX

Dear Ms. O'Hare:

This responds to your letter dated April 5, 2018, to the Attorney General, regarding your claim that your son, Mr. Robert O'Hare, was beaten by deputies of the Lake County Sheriff Department on October 5, 2015, at you home. You state your son was bruised in the face and was blinded in the left eye.

The Criminal Section of the Civil Rights Division is responsible for enforcing federal criminal civil rights statutes. Much of our enforcement activity relates to the investigation and prosecution of deprivations of civil rights under color of Jaw. These matters generally involve allegations of excessive physical force or sexual abuse by law enforcement officers.

The information you have provided to us does not give rise to a prosecutable violation of federal criminal civil rights statutes. We will consider your complaint further if you provide additional information concerning the beating incident by providing specific details such as the full names of the law enforcement officials; a detailed description of the sequence of events; copies of the medical records that describe Mr. O'Hare's injuries; and the names of neighbors who may have been eyewitnesses to the incident. Please send the additional information to us at the following address:

> United States Department of Justice
> Civil Rights Division
> Criminal Section
> 950 Pennsylvania Avenue
> Washington, D.C. 20530

You can be assured that if the documents you provide indicate a prosecutable violation of federal criminal civil rights statutes, appropriate action will be taken.

For your information, our office does not investigate or intervene in the Lake and Broward Counties Judicial systems. This office does not review the propriety of search warrant s or the sheriff's investigation of Mr. O'Hare. The Department of Justice does not have the authority to review and investigate your son's criminal proceedings.

Thank you for bringing this matter to our attention.

Sincerely,

XXXXXXX

July 13, 2018

United States Department of Justice
Civil Rights Division
Criminal Section
950 Pennsylvania Avenue
Washington, D.C. 20530

Dear XXXXXX

In response to your letter dated June 13, 2018, requesting the names of the three Lake County deputies' who brutally beat my son, Robert A. O'Hare after forcefully entering our home without a warrant or consent on October 5, 2015, are Corporal XXXXXX, Deputy XXXXXX, and Deputy XXXXXX. During the three deputies' altercation with my son, Captain XXXXXX and Deputy XXXXXX entered the home and were in concert with the three deputies' unlawful acts and violations. These deputies work for Lake County Sheriff XXXXXX, in Tavares Florida.

As per your request, herein are the detail descriptions of events that took place, with exhibits A-K as evidence:

On October 5, 2015, at around 11:15 am, three Lake County sheriff's deputies named above came to our home and asked Robert if they could come in and search his home without a warrant. Their purpose was to examine a laptop computer they allege may have child porn downloaded. This "used" laptop computer had been given to Robert from a childhood friend in Ft. Lauderdale, FL. Robert said his friend had downloaded child porn and other things in the laptop that he did not know was illegal when he was given the laptop. When the deputies informed Robert, they did not have a search warrant but wanted to search the home anyway, he told them to get a warrant and started to close the door. Corporal XXXXXX pushed open the door and unlawfully stepped over the threshold of my son's homestead property. The two deputies, XXXXXX and XXXXXX, followed after him over the threshold and began immediately beating Robert. I heard Robert cry out in pain and ran into the living room to witness their assault. I screamed for them to stop. When they wouldn't, I ran and got my cell phone video and taped them for 35 minutes until the cell phone video stopped recording.

Thereafter I took multiple pictures of their violations as they were roaming throughout all the rooms. I am enclosing both the video and pictures in **Exhibit A**. The video shows the deputies being unlawfully in our home, the aftermath of their brutal beating to Robert, and conducting an unlawful search of the home. This was done without consent, without probable cause, and without any exigent circumstances.

The deputies' life-threatening bodily assault caused blind-ness to Robert's left eye, and chronic pain and damage to his ribs, internal organs, including his intestines and pancreas,

Corporal XXXXXX was the first officer to enter our home. He admitted on tape the reason for their beating my son. He said, "This happened to your son because he would not allow us to come in and search your home (without a search warrant). I witnessed Corporal XXXXXX repeatedly hitting my son with blunt blows to his eyes, face, and head, which blinded Robert's left eye.

Deputy XXXXXX was just as aggressive in his brutal assault. He repeatedly kicked my son to his stomach and ribs 10-12 times, then alternately was punching him with his fists until he drew blood on his own left-hand knuckles and on Robert's body and torso. Deputy XXXXXX was sweating profusely during his brutal assault on my son as shown in the attached picture I took of him and also of his bloody knuckles which are in *Ex-*

hibit A. He tore Robert's t-shirt down below his chest, then lied on his police report stating the reason he tore Robert's t-shirt was because Robert was running towards the kitchen. My cell phone video and pictures in **Exhibit A** show Robert on the floor near the front entry door facing in the opposite direction to the kitchen.

Deputy XXXXXX held my son down bodily on the floor, laying over his legs while Dep. XXXXXX and Corporal XXXXXX brutally assaulted him. His cooperation with the two deputies' assault, and their doing an illegal search and seizure was unlawful.

Under our civil rights laws, "Officers have a duty to protect individuals from constitutional violations by fellow officers. Therefore, an officer who witnesses a fellow officer violating an individual's constitutional rights may be liable to the victim for failing to intervene." Deputy XXXXXX was fully aware that the two deputies, XXXXXX and XXXXXX, were breaking the law when they entered our home without a warrant and beat up my son. I was recently informed that he terminated his employment with the Sheriff's Department. He should be investigated to confirm the excessive and abusive police force used on my son and their illegally searching and seizing the laptop without a warrant and staging the laptop as a crime scene in my son's bedroom.

Captain XXXXXX entered our home during the three deputies' ensuing assault on my son was in concert with the three deputies. Captain XXXXXX made an unlawful command to Robert as he sat on the floor tightly handcuffed behind his back. In a beaten, traumatic and painful state. During their search of the home, the deputies could not find the laptop. The only place they had not searched was Robert's locked bedroom closet. Captain XXXXXX threatened Robert with an unlawful command, "If you don't give us the key to your locked bedroom closet to the count of 10, we will kick the door off its hinges. He started counting out loud, 1,2,3,4,5,6, 7, 8, etc. Out of fear and not consent, Robert told him where the key was.

The deputies unlocked the bedroom closet door, removed the laptop and a short barrel rifle, without a search warrant, without consent, without probable cause, and without any exigent circumstances. The deputies removed both items from the closet and staged the computer and rifle as a crime scene outside of the bedroom closet. They placed the laptop on the bedroom floor and the case on the bed. CSI was called in to take pictures of their staged crime scene. As proof of their doing this, the deputies were recorded on their police body worn camcorder video talking to each other about finding **the laptop in the locked bedroom closet**. The camcorder recorded the date and time of their conversation as being on October 5, 2015, @11:37 am. Their warrant was not signed by a magistrate judge until several hours later at 5:44 pm, and delivered to our home on 6:45 pm.

The deputy in charge, Detective XXXXXX called CSI to take pictures of their staged crime scene and filed a false police report stating the laptop and case were in plain view **after** they placed the laptop on the floor in the bedroom and **after** they placed the case on the bed. Master Deputy XXXXXX also put in his police report these items were in plain view and not locked up in a closet. The deputies had absolutely no plain view evidence of any contraband until they illegally removed the laptop and rifle from the closet and staged both inside the bedroom as a crime scene. **Then, called in CSI to take pictures of their staged crime scene.**

Master Deputy XXXXXX later testified at the bond hearing that he had to move clothes around in the back of the locked bedroom closet to get to the short barrel rifle. He stated this under oath, which was contrary to what he previously stated in his police report, that the rifle was in plain view. His false testimony can be verified in the court's electronic transcription of the bond proceedings and in his police report.

On October 5, 2015, Master Deputy XXXXXX filed a false arrest charge against Robert for resisting an officer without violence and arrested him before finding the laptop in the closet. According to Supreme Court and state law, "A law enforcement officer may not enter a person's home to arrest them for resisting an officer without violence, even if the crime is committed in his presence, regardless of whether the suspect is in the residence when he commits that crime or commits the crime outside the residence and then flees inside." The following case laws support this supreme court doctrine: M.J.R. v. State, 715 So.2d 1103 (Fla. 5th DCA 1998), Markus v. State, 160 So.3d 488 (Fla. 5th DCA 2015); Rodriguez v. State, 964 So.2d 833 (Fla. 2d DCA 2007), Connor v. State, 641 So.2d 143 (Fla. 4th DCA 1994), and Jackson v. State, 192 So.3d 541 (Fla. 4th DCA 2016). The above supreme court doctrine was copied from Robert's Appellate Attorney XXXXXX's answer brief which I include in this complaint as well as in **Exhibit F.** Therefore, the Lake County deputies' arresting Robert for resisting an officer in our home was 100% unlawful.

Exhibit A: Pictures and video of Robert, showing his bloody face, bruises, swollen eyes, and punch marks on his face, head, eyes, and upper torso.

> Robert suffered a lot of blows to his eyes, face, head, ribs, abdomen, and upper torso by the deputy's brutal beating, while on the floor in a submissive position. Corporal XXXXXX's blunt blows to Robert's eyes, caused the drum that was surgically implanted a year earlier to secure a torn

retina, become wrinkled around the retina. This dislodge drum caused Robert a severe amount of unending pain. Dr. XXXXXX from the Miami Eye Institute performed the 2nd surgery on Robert's left eye after surgeon XXXXXX removed the wrinkled buckle from his left eye. She wrote a letter stating, "Robert O'Hare's blindness was caused by a "trauma" to his left eye. Dr. XXXXXX's report is included in **Exhibit B** with the letter from the eye surgeon, XXXXXX, MD. Both eye surgeon's letter from XXXXXX, MD. and Dr. XXXXXX's procedure/operative report are included in Exhibit B.

After the two unsuccessful eye surgeries to correct the blindness in Robert's left eye, the 2nd surgeon said, on August 2016, "I recommend a third operation within 90 days." Due to the Lake County prosecutor, XXXXXX, filing his 2nd bogus arrest charges against Robert, on August 17, 2016, of falsely accusing Robert of delivering two (2) jukeboxes in 2011 or 2012 to a neighbor's house, and voyeurism, both of which he never did, this 3rd surgical procedure could not be performed to the date of this letter.

Dep. XXXXXX kicking Robert repeatedly to his abdomen and ribs 10-12 times caused a great deal of pain and rectal bleeding after bowel movements. After the beating, Robert had difficulty in eliminating his bowel movements and took enemas and stool softeners on a regular basis.

Exhibit B: Robert's surgical, medical reports on his left eye: several months after his beating, Robert's had two operations on his left eye by two different eye surgeons. One doctor removed the surgically implanted drum that became wrinkled from the blunt blows to his eyes by

Corporal XXXXXX, which caused Robert's blindness. Another eye surgeon operated on Robert's left eye to try to restore his vision. Both surgeries failed to restore Robert's vision. A letter attached herein is from one of the two eye surgeons stating Robert's blindness was caused from a blunt blow to his left eye. The doctor's letter is in **Exhibit B**.

> On August 25, 2016, while still out on his first bond, Prosecutor XXXXXX filed another set of bogus charges against Robert. He falsely accused Robert of delivering two jukeboxes in 2011 or 2012 with lenses in them to a neighbor for the purpose of voyeurism. Prosecutor XXXXXX admitted to the news media that this charge was based on his assumption theory. He said he thought Robert delivered two jukeboxes in either 2011 or 2012 to the wrong neighbor thinking the wrong neighbor would deliver the two jukeboxes to the right neighbor. This news report of Prosecutor XXXXXX's assumption theory went viral all over the world as well as local and national TV news stations across our country.

> On the basis of this illogical and ridiculous theory, which was drummed up by the prosecutor with no evidence whatsoever other than his assumption, he filed an arrest warrant and had the U.S. Marshals pick up Robert, which was just outside our Ft. Lauderdale guard gated residence. Robert was still suffering from a great deal of abdominal pain and the after effects of his two eye surgeries during this arrest. The U.S. Marshal took Robert immediately to Broward County Health Hospital as an ER patient for observation. He was medically diagnosed with pre-cancerous bleeding polyps and advised to see a GI doctor within 3 days and have a colonoscopy. Because the U.S. Marshals used

unnecessary excessive force on Robert during their arrest, they told Robert's lawyer, XXXXXX, they charged Robert with resisting an officer without violence. This false charge caused Robert's $25,000 bond in Lake County to be revoked by the prosecutor, XXXXXX.

Robert was transported back to Lake County Detention Center and placed in lockdown 24/7 for 2 ½ months while waiting for his trial date in Broward County to challenge the false charges of resisting an officer without violence. During this time, the Lake County Detention Center upon receiving Robert's medical records from Broward County Health Hospital refused to give Robert any medical treatment for his bleeding pre-cancerous polyps. After the 2 ½ months of incarceration without any medical care or treatment for his abdominal pain and bleeding polyps, Robert was transported back to Broward County for his trial. After a 2-day trial, the jury unanimously found Robert "not guilty" of resisting an officer without violence. The jury saw through the Marshal's false charge and their bogus testimony. After a two-day trial, the jurors took less than 10 minutes to make their decision that Robert was innocent! After the trial, the alternate juror came over to Robert and told him if he was still on the jury he would have voted in his favor. He said, "Those officers were lying through their teeth." He told me the same thing as we were exiting the courtroom.

After the trial, Robert was transported back to Lake County Detention Center on January 4, 2017, to have his $25,000 bond reinstated. Attorney XXXXXX made a motion to Judge XXXXXX to reinstate Robert's bond because he won his jury verdict in Broward County and there was no legal reason now for Judge XXXXXX to deny reinstatement of his bond.

On January 24, 2017, during the hearing, Judge XXXXXX postponed the hearing for another month because Prosecutor XXXXXX had Deputy XXXXXX (who severely kicked and beat Robert on October 5, 2015) testify to a third-party hearsay conversation without first giving this evidence to Attorney XXXXXX prior to the hearing. This third-party conversation was a jail call I had with my son in which I stated: "Robert, when this is all over we, are going to travel around the world." The Prosecutor took this conversation completely out of context and tried to have Deputy XXXXXX testifies to this hearsay conversation to convince Judge XXXXXX that Robert would be a flight risk if he were granted reinstatement of his bond. At the second rescheduled bond hearing, Prosecutor XXXXXX never brought up the jail calls but lied to Judge XXXXXX and said Robert was not only a flight risk but a danger to the community. Judge XXXXXX, relying on the false testimony from the Deputies and supported by the Prosecutor, refused to reinstate Robert's bond stating he would be a danger to the community and a flight risk. He wrote this on his order. Even though Robert was out on bond for 10 months on the first bogus charge, he was neither a danger to any community nor a flight risk. Judge XXXXXX ignored this evidence. His ruling caused Robert to lose reinstatement of his $25,000 bond and kept him incarcerated to the date of this letter, without ever having a trial or given his timely due process of law as outlined in this letter. His civil liberties and due process of law were egregiously violated by the Lake County Judicial System.

The Lake County Detention Center violated Robert's 8th amendment rights by refusing to give him medical care of treatment from the date of his incarceration on August 25, 2016, until one year later when Robert's illness became critical and life-threatening. On September 5, 2017, he was diagnosed with malignant colon cancer stage 3 or 4 by Dr. XXXXXX but was never medically treated with the prescribed chemotherapy, surgery, hospitalization, or any medical treatment until after 17 months of incarceration when he, for the first time, was given five radiation treatments on or about January 28, 2018. Before and after the five radiation treatments, Robert was never brought to a hospital. He was put into a lock-down cell 24/7, alone, suffering without any follow-up visit from a doctor. His medical report is attached herein. See **Exhibit C.**

Exhibit C: Attached herein are two medical reports, one from Broward County Health Hospital with a diagnosis of pre-cancerous bleeding polyps and one from Dr. XXXXXX, who diagnosed Robert with stage 3 or 4 malignant colon cancer with a 70% blockage to his colon. The Doctor's Medical Report states Robert had this cancer for one year.

Robert was denied his civil liberties of due process of law and his civil and constitutional rights by the Lake County Judicial System and the Lake County Detention Center:

Robert never received any medical treatment for his malignant colon cancer stage 3 or 4 until after 17 months of incarceration.

The Lake County Detention Center steadfastly refused to give Robert any hospitalization, medical treatment or medical care or medicine for 17 months. With full knowledge of his illness, the detention center allowed Robert to suffer from excruciating pain and anguish from stage 3 or 4 malignant colon cancer with a 70% blockage to his colon.

Knowing all these health issues and that Robert needed medical treatment, hospitalization, and treatment, the prosecutor canceled Robert's Motion to Suppress six times in eight months. Prosecutor XXXXXX falsely stated to Judge XXXXXX that Robert should not have reinstatement of his bond or his motions for a medical furlough for care, treatment, and hospitalization because he was a flight risk and a danger to the community. He made up these vindictive false and unproven allegations which can be proven by the electronic transcription of the courts hearing proceedings.

Prosecutor XXXXXX failed to give the states' discovery to the defense attorney, XXXXXX, for over 300 days. He gave this discovery only after the court compelled him twice to do so. Prosecutor XXXXXX's only motive was to win this case, conspire with the deputies, and do whatsoever he had to do to convict my son to protect the deputy's criminal violations and his 2nd false arrest charges against my son.

The prosecutor conspired with the deputies to lie under oath with false and damning statements against Robert's case and character. Their sole intent was to have Judge XXXXXX deny Robert's bond and medical motions and watch him die to cover over their own criminal violations. Their collusion worked. All of Robert's motions to date were denied by Judge XXXXXX. The electronic court transcriptions of the hearings confirm their conspiracy from their sworn testimony. Attorney XXXXXX said he heard the transcription recording of the two bond hearings and said, "Your son was set up by the prosecutor and deputies."

For 13 months Robert never went to trial, while waiting for his Motion to Suppress hearing, which was canceled by the prosecutor six times over a period of eight months. During which time the detention center refused to give Robert any medical treatment or medical care for over 12 months. From the day of his incarceration for the false charges of delivering 2 jukeboxes which prosecutor XXXXXX alleged happened in 2011 or 2012, I put multiple legal demands on the judicial system with lawyers, letters, and motions to Judge XXXXXX. All to no avail. For the first and only time, during Robert's entire 17 months of incarceration, Judge XXXXXX allowed me to hire and pay for only one doctor to examine Robert, which was after his one year of incarceration. This was with Doctor XXXXXX. He diagnosed Robert with colon cancer and inflammation of his pancreas and stated it was from an injury to his abdomen. After receiving that diagnoses, Robert said during one of our monitored jail calls, "This injury was from Deputy XXXXXX kicking me in my stomach." The Lake County Detention Center received Doctor XXXXXX's medical report. After Robert's first and only visit with Dr. XXXXXX, Dr. XXXXXX's nurse informed me they got a call from the Lake County Detention Center who informed Dr. XXXXXX they were terminated his services, because they were going to have their doctor from the Detention Center examine Robert.

Shortly thereafter, on or about September 5, 2017, the Lake County Detention Center had Dr.

XXXXXX examined Robert. He medically confirmed in his report what Dr. XXXXXX told Robert that he had malignant colon cancer. Dr. XXXXX told Robert he has stage 3 or 4 malignant colon cancer with a 70% blockage in his colon. Dr. XXXXXX also stated without further tests he could not tell which stage his cancer was in, but thought he had stage 4. He also told Robert he had the malignant colon cancer for over one year and did not know why the Lake County Detention Center didn't give him medical treatment before they called him in to diagnose Robert. He said, "Robert I have patients that have what you have, and they don't live beyond two months." He also put on Robert's medical report that Robert was a pleasant gentleman. See Dr. XXXXXX's medical report in **Exhibit B**.

Dr. XXXXXX recommended Robert immediately see General Surgeon Dr. XXXXXX. Thirteen days later, on September 18, 2017, at 1:30 pm Robert was diagnosed by Dr. XXXXXX with having a large growth in his colon that could not be removed safely. He said Robert needed chemotherapy immediately to reduce the size of the growth before he could safely remove it, which was now blocking his colon 70%. Knowing the severity of this surgery Doctor XXXXXX said he must have an MRI and chemotherapy immediately. No medical treatment was given by the detention center from August 25, 2016, until January 28, 2018 when Robert was given five radiation treatments. After his five radiation treatments, the detention center allowed Robert to suffer in unbearable pain with bleeding and diarrhea without giving him any follow up medical treatment by a medical doctor. This is a major violation of Robert's civil and constitutional rights against the Lake County Detention Center.

On one occasion, when Attorney XXXXXX went to visit Robert, he witnessed his poor health condition. He said, "Robert you look God awful." He made an emergency motion again to Judge XXXXXX for a medical furlough for Robert to be hospitalized. He gave the medical records from Dr. XXXXXX to Judge XXXXXX. The Prosecutor told Judge XXXXXX to deny Robert's motion stating again he was a flight risk and not that sick. Judge XXXXXX denied Robert's motion and said he could come back to see him in a month if the detention center didn't give him any medical treatment. Judge XXXXXX knew from prior motions that the detention center had not given Robert any medical treatment for his critical illness.

Why would Judge XXXXXX have Robert come back in another month when he had full documentation my son was critically ill with malignant colon cancer with a 70% blockage in his colon and in stage 3 or 4? After his hearing with Judge XXXXXX, Robert was taken back to his cell, sick, bleeding and in a great deal of unbearable pain and suffering. Now, he had to wait yet another month for another hearing in front of Judge XXXXXX! This can be verified by the electronic court records and Robert's lawyers.

After Dr. XXXXXX's diagnoses, the Lake County Detention Center did nothing for five months. They allowed Robert to suffer in pain and anguish. This was not only grossly inhumane but against his civil liberties and 8th amendment rights. The first and only treatment Robert received was on or about January 28, 2018 when he received five debilitating radiation treatments. After the radiation treatments were administered, no further treatments, no examination, no doctor's visit, no medication were given to Robert to the date of this letter.

No human being should have their legal rights violated as egregiously as my son's rights have been by the Lake County Judicial System. To leave anyone untreated with malignant colon cancer with a 70% blockage in ones' colon for 17 months without any medical care or treatment is inhumane and unconscionable. Judge XXXXXX denied all of Robert's motions for medical care and treatment for his malignant colon cancer. Untreated, he was left to suffer and die. This fact can be proven by the court's electronic transcriptions as well as his medical records at the Lake County Detention Center. Robert's life is uncertain without having proper medical care for his malignancy. With full knowledge of Robert's critical condition, the head of Lake County's Nursing Administration asked Robert to sign a waiver of release that if something happened to him, he would release them from any and all liability. Robert refused to sign their waiver of liability. Robert informed me of this on one of our jail calls around the beginning of 2018.

After the five radiation treatments were administered, Robert was kept in lockdown, in a small cell, 24/7, and only allowed out of his cell for 3 hours a week. The detention center never had any doctor examine Robert after his five radiation treatments, even after Robert asked multiple times to go to the hospital and see a medical doctor. When he asked for medication for his unbearable pain, he was given nothing. The detention center allowed Robert to suffer daily without any medical care or treatment. This was witnessed by his cellmates and two Security Guards who are documented as witnesses in this criminal complaint.

During our monitored jail calls, Robert said he was bleeding-like diarrhea and could not hold his bowels. He had lost over 40 lbs. He said he was eliminating from his bowels every five minutes. To go without medical treatment is inhumane treatment for anyone to undergo, and is against Robert's prisoner's rights, his 8th amendment rights, and his civil and constitutional rights.

Prior to the five radiation treatments, he suffered hourly with pain, intestinal bleeding, diarrhea and being confined with 5-6 other cellmates who told him he looked awful, like he was dying. They all said his skin was grey, and his bowel movements were foul smelling. Being confined to a small cell with 5-6 other cellmates sharing one toilet was beyond appalling, especially in Robert's critical health condition.

From the beginning of his incarceration on August 25, 2016, until his first medical treatment at the end of January 2018, he was medically untreated for his malignant colon cancer, by the Lake County Detention Center. According to Dr. XXXXXX, this untreated cancer existed in his body for over one year and caused the development and growth of his life-threatening malignant colon cancer to grow to a 70% blockage to his colon and was at stage 3 or 4. The Doctor told Robert, "I don't know why the Detention Center didn't treat you sooner than this. I've lost patients with your stage of cancer within two months."

I reported all this to the State Attorney, XXXXXX, who, to date, was non-responsive in giving my son any urgently needed medical care that he is legally and morally entitled to for this life-threatening illness. The State Attorney has not taken any actions against the criminal violations committed by the three deputies that are under his direct supervision, or the detention center for their gross neglect to Robert's urgently needed medical treatment.

Evidence of the deputies' egregious violations and their brutal beating caused all of Robert's health issues. Attorney XXXXXX's answer brief to the appellate court dated June 18, 2018 details their violations and the judge's misrepresentation of Supreme Court law. He cites 16 case laws that make warrantless searches in one's home unlawful. These case laws do not support any form of inevitable discovery or any plain view doctrine for an officer's lawless acts.

Exhibit D: The appellate brief outlines the laws the deputies violated and is supported with a total of 16 case laws.

When I got Robert out on bond on October 9, 2015, he was in a beaten state. Attorney XXXXXX told us to leave Mt. Dora immediately. He wanted us to be safely away from the Lake County deputies who viciously assaulted my son. He said, "I don't trust what they may do further to your son." This newly hired Lawyer and the Bail Bondsman knew of the Lake County Sheriff Deputies' reputation. The following morning, we went back to live in our home in Ft. Lauderdale. I watched Robert suffer daily from the after-effects of the deputies' beating with blindness, intestinal ailments, with much pain and suffering. After his beating, he couldn't lie on his left side or on his stomach for many months.

Five months later, we returned to our home in Mt. Dora. I was motivated, after witnessing my son's beating and suffering the ill effects of his brutal assault to file a formal criminal complaint to the Lake County Internal Affairs against the deputies' warrantless and illegal entry to our home, and inflicting physical harm and disability to my son. After the investigation, Detective XXXXXX presented me with a copy of his investigative report of the deputies' testimony, which I am enclosing herein as evidence of the deputies' criminal violations. Even though the outgoing Sheriff took no action against the deputies, the Investigator wanted me to seek justice for my son.   He gave me his entire investigated report to take further action against the deputies. *See Exhibit E.*

Exhibit E: Lake County's Internal Affairs investigative report dated April 1, 2016

The deputies were cognoscente of the following crimes they mutually agreed to commit on October 5, 2015:

The three deputies, XXXXXX, XXXXXX, and XXXXXX, were fully aware of their unlawful actions when they forcefully stepped over the threshold of our home without a search warrant, without probable cause, without consent, and without any exigent circumstances. Captain XXXXXX, who entered our home while the Deputies' altercation was going on with my son, admitted on the recorded video that he had no probable cause and no search warrant when he entered our home, but stated they were going to draw one up. The deputies testified to internal affairs during their criminal investigation stating, "We thought going in without a warrant would work like it did all the other times." In other words, these deputies made

it a practice of violating the people's 4th Amendment rights, whenever they can get away with it.

The deputies in unison brutally beat my son,
causing serious physical harm, including blindness, intestinal and pancreas damage which led to
his current disability. These health issues left untreated by the Lake County Detention Center for
almost 17 months, developed into life-threatening
malignant colon cancer with a 70% blockage in his
colon, which is either stage 3 or 4.

Upon forcefully entering our home on October 5,
2015, the deputies took full control of Robert and
me and held us both hostage while they commenced their illegal search and seizure and mutually staged a crime scene. The deputies kept
Robert handcuffed while they took several hours
to obtain a search warrant, and for over 10 hours
before they transported him to the Lake County
Detention Center.

Captain XXXXXX made a warrantless and unlawful command to my son demanding the key to his
locked bedroom closet with the threat of knocking
the hinges off the door if he didn't give him the
key. Robert out of fear, and not consent, told him
where the key was. Captain XXXXXX's unlawful
command and his unlawful threat was recorded
on my cell phone video. *See Exhibit A.*

Upon obtaining the key, the deputies unlocked
Robert's bedroom closet door, removed the laptop
and staged the laptop and case as a crime scene
in Robert's bedroom. This was confirmed at the
Motion to Suppress hearing when Corporal
XXXXXX's body-worn camcorder video was
played, and the voices of the deputies could be
heard talking about finding the laptop in the
closet.

After the deputies found the laptop in the locked bedroom closet, they removed the laptop from its black zippered case, placed the case on the bed and the laptop on the floor. Then called CSI to take pictures of their staged crime scene. CSI pictures of the staged crime scene can be obtained as evidence of the deputies' criminal staging, as well as Corporal XXXXXX's body-worn camcorder video, which was used as evidence at the Motion to Suppress hearing. The voices of the deputies can be heard on the camcorder video talking about finding the laptop in the bedroom closet. The camcorder recorded this event at 11:37 am. The deputy in charge, XXXXXX, obtained the search warrant, signed by a magistrate at 5:44 pm. He filed a false police report alleging the laptop and rifle, as being in plain view.

Exhibit F: Transcription of the Motion to Suppress hearing proceedings dated November 8, 2017.

The deputies not only falsified their police report to justify their criminal acts but gave false sworn testimony under oath to cover over their criminal acts. Electronic court transcriptions verify their lying under oath.

To justify their own illegal acts, the deputies knowingly filed a false charge against my son of resisted an officer without violence. According to Supreme Court Law and Florida State Law, "A law enforcement officer may not enter a person's home to arrest them for resisting an officer without violence, even if the crime is committed in his presence, regardless of whether the suspect is in the residence when he commits that crime or commits the crime outside the residence and then flees inside." The following case laws support this supreme court doctrine: M.J.R. v. State, 715 So.2d 1103 (Fla. 5th DCA 1998), Markus v. State, 160 So.3d 488 (Fla. 5th DCA 2015); Rodriguez v. State, 964 So.2d 833 (Fla. 2d DCA 2007), Connor v. State, 641 So.2d 143 (Fla. 4th DCA 1994), and Jackson v. State, 192 So.3d 541 (Fla. 4th DCA 2016).

Captain XXXXXX was recorded on my cell phone video admitting: "If we don't find the laptop, we are still going to arrest your son anyway for resisting an officer without violence." After he unlawfully entered our home, I asked Captain XXXXXX for his search warrant. He said, "We are going to draw up one." He also stated in the video; he did not have any probable cause. The cell phone video is in ***Exhibit A***.

Exhibit G: In addition to their false arrest charge against my son the deputies also violated my son's 4th amendment rights: **"The fourth amendment prohibits unreasonable seizure of any person or personal property without proper authorization, i.e., a warrant.** In legal terms, seizure of property is when there is significant interference by the government with an individual's possessions."** The deputies' violation of this statute was confirmed by Judge XXXXXX in his order to my son's Motion to Suppress. *See* **Exhibit F**.

Without a search warrant, the deputies held my son hostage and handcuffed him in his own home, which was titled in his name and declared as his legal homestead dwelling. **Their search warrant came several hours after they had conducted their warrantless search and seizure and removed the laptop from my son's locked bedroom closet and staged it as a crime scene.**

I witnessed the deputies' violations as well as recorded them on my cell phone video and took pictures of their warrantless, illegal acts. They are included in **Exhibit A** and are prima facie evidence to this complaint.

Exhibit H: Under civil rights laws and police misconduct: "A statute known as section 1983 is the primary civil rights law victims of police misconduct rely upon. This law was originally passed as part of the civil rights act of 1871, which was intended to curb oppressive conduct by government and private individuals participating in vigilante groups, such as the Ku Klux Klan. It is now called Section 1983 because that is where the law has been published, within Title 42 of the United States code. Section 1983 makes it unlawful for anyone acting under the authority of State Law to deprive another person of his or her rights under the constitution or Federal Law."

A primary purpose of the nation's civil rights laws is to protect citizens from abuses by the Government, including police officers, who breached my son's civil and constitutional rights as evidenced in the video, pictures, police camcorder, witnesses, and court documentation submitted herein in ***Exhibits A-L***.

Exhibit I: The following evidence and case law of the deputies' criminal violations are herein cited:

Under M.J.R. vs. State, Corporal XXXXXX's act of preventing the defendant, my son, from closing the front door and then forcing his way into the residence, under Davis, v. United States that any order for him to exit the residence to be arrested or detained was **a violation of the Fourth Amendment**. Any exigency which may have arisen after that would be an impermissibly officer-created exigency under King v. State, and thus could not be used to excuse the nonconsensual, warrantless entry. The deputies sweep of the entire home exceeded what was constitutionally permissible. This statement was included in Attorney XXXXXX's appellate brief to the 5th DCA, which I have included in this complaint as evidence in **Ex-hibit D**.

Corporal XXXXXX's body-worn camcorder video was played at the Motion to Suppress Hearing, which recorded the deputies talking about finding the laptop in the locked bedroom closet at 11:37 am. They didn't obtain a magistrate's signed search warrant until several hours later at 5:44 pm. **This was a violation of my son's 4th amendment rights.**

To cover over their serious criminal violations, the deputies conspired with Prosecutor XXXXXX to lie in a court of law, under oath, to convict my son of their false and damning made up allegations. Their goal was to put my son away for life in order to hide their own criminal violations from surfacing, which are now being exposed with prima facie evidence. This complaint has been submitted to Attorney General Jeff Sessions and President Donald J. Trump, whose response letter is attached herein.

Exhibit J: As further proof of a conspiracy between the Prosecutor and Deputies, Prosecutor XXXXXX made the following statements to Attorney XXXXXX, "I am going to put your client away for life. The deputies told me not to lessen the sentence on your client's life. I let the deputies and Mrs. O'Hare's neighbors listen to all her jail calls with her son." These conversations between the Prosecutor and the Deputies are evidence of their conspiracy and the Prosecutor's misconduct. These conversations can be verified by the Lead Attorney XXXXXXX and the Trial Attorney XXXXXX

During the Motion to Suppress hearing on November 8, 2017, Prosecutor XXXXXXX often lied in front of Judge XXXXXXX. This caused the Trial Attorney XXXXXXX to approach the Prosecutor in front of Judge XXXXXXX and state, "if you lie to me one more time in court, I'm going after your Florida Bar License." Lies and false statements from the Deputies and Prosecutor shows their unlawful collusion and conspiracy which pollutes our entire justice system. Both Attorney XXXXXXX and Attorney XXXXXXX can and will verify these and other statements made to them which proves the Prosecutor and Deputies unlawful collaborated conspiracy, which severely violates justice for my son and his civil and constitutional rights.

Another Lake County deputy who lied under oath at my son's reinstatement bond hearing was Detective XXXXXXX, who was in charge of the Cyber Sex Unit. He stated under oath, "I was told by Broward County Officer XXXXXXX that Robert O'Hare delivered two jukeboxes to a family in Broward County in 2016 with nothing in them." This lie was to support Prosecutor XXXXXXX's false arrest charges he made against Robert on August 17, 2016, stating Robert delivered two jukeboxes in 2011 or 2012 to a family in Mt. Dora with lenses in them for the purpose of voyeurism. He had no such evidence whatsoever of Robert making any such delivery, and stated so to the news media, who went viral with his assumption theory stating: "I **assume** that Robert O'Hare delivered two jukeboxes in either 2011 or 2012 to the wrong neighbor thinking the wrong neighbor would deliver the two jukeboxes to the right neighbor." This damning news story made up by the Prosecutor went viral all over the country.

Detective XXXXXXX conspired with Prosecutor XXXXXXX to give this false statement under oath in front of Judge XXXXXXX to support his false arrest charges against Robert of delivering two jukeboxes in 2011-2012. This lie had absolutely no credible evidence of any delivery made by Robert because none existed. However, Judge XXXXXXX believed this lie, which caused him to deny the reinstatement of my son's $25,000 bond on the basis that he would be a danger to the small community of Loch Leven we lived in, in Mt. Dora, FL For 17 years without ever having any problems whatsoever.

Exhibit K: A letter dated July 17, 2018, from Lake County Internal Affairs stating, "no misconduct was identified against Detective XXXXXX."

After Robert lost his Bond Motion, I asked Attorney XXXXXXX if I prove Detective XXXXXXX lied under oath what would this do to his false testimony. He said, "If you prove he lied under oath about something like that, it would be lethal against him. To prove Detective XXXXXXX lied against my son; I made a formal complaint to Internal Affairs against Broward Officer, XXXXXXX in Ft. Lauderdale, FL. The Broward County Officer XXXXXXX testified to the Internal Affairs Investigator, Detective XXXXX, and told his

Supervisor, Sergeant XXXXXXX, "I never made that statement to Detective XXXXXX that Robert gave two jukeboxes to a family in Broward County in 2016.

Upon receiving this information, I filed an Internal Affairs complaint in Lake County, Tavares, FL with the evidence against Detective XXXXXXX for lying under oath. On July 17, 2017, I received a letter stating: "According to my formal complaint filed on July 10, 2017, against Deputy XXXXXXX NO misconduct was identified."

Exhibit L: A letter from the White House – President Donald J. Trump.

With these multiple Exhibits, the United States Department of Justice has enough evidence to not only investigate these criminal charges but to prosecute the Deputies for willfully lying under oath, violating the law and tarnishing the very essence of justice that their official positions and our government must stand for. Prosecutor XXXXXX, Deputies, XXXXXX, XXXXXX, XXXXXX, XXXXXX, XXXXXX, and the Lake County Detention Center have all egregiously violated my son's civil liberties of due process of law, his 4th amendment rights, his 8th amendment rights, and his constitutional and prisoner's rights. This complaint is supported 100% with bonified prima facie evidence, including pictures, videos, camcorder, transcriptions of court proceedings, filed false police reports, pictures taken by CSI, and credible witnesses as outlined in this complaint, which is all detailed with evidence submitted herein in ***Exhibits A through L.***

The Prosecutor's misconduct and the illegal and ongoing violations committed by these Lake County Deputies to conceal their egregious violations were witnessed by Robert's three lawyers, XXXXXX, XXXXXX, and XXXXXX. The Lead Attorney XXXXXX was not at the two bond hearings but heard the court's electronic recordings of the two hearings. He emailed me stating, "Your son was set up by the Prosecutor and Deputies at the Bond hearing."

Robert's lawyers will testify to Judge XXXXXX' bias, the collusion and conspiracy between the Deputies and the Prosecutor and their multiple dishonest statements made under oath during Robert's hearings. This is why the lawyers counseled Robert to plead no contest and appeal, rather than go to trial and have to deal any further with all this corruption. Upon your investigation of all the evidence presented herein, you will conclude without any iota of doubt that all this evidence herein substantially proves 100% the validity of this criminal complaint, which calls out for justice for my son with convictions to all the officers who violated Federal and State Law ~~of the land~~ and my son's civil and constitutional rights as well. They not only tarnish their badges but are damaging the reputations of police officers everywhere.

After receiving my formal complaints about the Deputies' violations, their conspiracy with the Prosecutor, and the Judge's bias in favor of the Deputies and Prosecutor, the State Attorney on or about January 30, 2018, recused Judge XXXXXX from my son's case. However, this was too late. It was after my son pled no contest to avoid going to trial with a biased Judge, lying Deputies and the misconduct of the Prosecutor.

The Prosecutor and Deputies falsely testifying to Judge XXXXXX that my son was a flight risk and a danger to the community, was not only vindictive and without merit, but denied justice for my son in a court of law. A security guard witnessed Robert falling in the shower because he was too weak to stand up. Yet, Prosecutor XXXXXX falsely accused my son of being a flight risk, and told Attorney XXXXXX, "He is not that sick." The Prosecutor lying to Judge XXXXXX prevented Robert from obtaining his Motion for Reinstatement of his $25,000 bond and his urgently needed Motion for Medical Furlough so he could seek outside mandatory treatment for his malignant colon cancer

The collusion and conspiracy between the Deputies, the Prosecutor and the Judge's bias against Robert's legal rights, are fully documented in all the court's electronic transcriptions of Robert's Hearing Proceedings.

There was no legal reason for Judge XXXXXX to deny any of my son's motions, but he did at every hearing. Lies from the Prosecutor and Deputies took priority over my son's legal rights that supported all his motions.

Prosecutor XXXXXX's misconduct and the Deputy's criminal acts not only thwarted justice for my son but tarnished the image of the Lake County Judicial System. The rule of law is the principle that all people and institutions are subject to and accountable to the law that is fairly applied and enforced for everyone. The rule of law must prevail in order to preserve justice for all the people and government. No one should be above the law, including those who wear a badge. Everyone is legally entitled to have their civil, constitutional, and democratic rights upheld. Without the rule of law, our government would become a mobocracy instead of a democracy.

Our family lived in the same Mt. Dora community for 17 years without any legal problems whatsoever. Robert was never a danger to anyone or to any community we lived in during his 56 years of life. He never smoked, drank or took drugs and was raised in a devout Christian home. These false and damning allegations and false charges made by the deputies and prosecutor caused Judge XXXXXX to deny my son's bond and his urgently needed medical furlough for his life-threatening malignant colon cancer.

Immediately after the deputy's severe beating to my son on October 5, 2015, Robert had debilitating health issues which included: blindness in his left eye, severe pain on the left side of his ribs, abdominal pain with rectal bleeding, much difficulty in eliminating bowel movements. After his beating, Robert needed to take stool softeners and enemas. He had, understandably, panic attacks from the beating. The Lake County Detention Center was well aware of his illness as was the Prosecutor who listened to all our monitored jail calls. Robert's health crisis was so severe; he would go for 4 days at a time without moving his bowels. His cries of pain and suffering were heard but totally ignored. No one would help him at the Lake County Detention Center, or anyone from the Lake County Judicial System.

On September 5, 2017, when Robert became critically ill, the detention center, for the first time, called in Dr. XXXXXX to examine him. He diagnosed Robert with stage 3 or 4 malignant colon cancer with a 70% blockage to his colon. Dr. XXXXXX told Robert, "I have patients with this type of growth, and they die within two months. I do not understand why the detention center has not given you any medical treatment sooner. You had this cancer for over one year." Dr. XXXXXX recommended chemotherapy, an MRI, and surgery. It wasn't until the last week in January 2018 that the detention center gave Robert five radiation treatments with absolutely no follow up medical care to the date of this letter. Their medical records will verify this fact.

For over one year, Robert's lawyers and I, on multiple occasions, gave Robert's medical reports and requests for his urgent need for medical treatment to the Lake County Sheriff, to the Lake County

Detention Center, to the Lake County Warden, with motions to Lake County Judge XXXXXX, and to the Lake County State Attorney, XXXXXX. They all ignored giving Robert any medical treatment or medical care for 17 months of his incarceration. This was without question a severe violation to Robert's Civil, Constitutional, and Prisoner rights. Allowing Robert to go through unbearable pain and suffering violated his 8th Amendment rights as well.

Attach to this complaint is a notarized statement from an inmate, XXXXXX, who witnessed Robert's pain and suffering and watched him being denied medical treatment by the Lake County Detention Center as he was crying out for medical help. His cell was near to my son's cell for the 2 weeks he was incarcerated for a traffic violation. He heard my son crying out for medical help. He witnessed the Lake County Detention Center denying Robert medicine, medical treatment or care for his severe pain from his malignant colon cancer.

This is the inmate's notarized statement: "I hear Robert cry at night with pain. They refuse to give him any medicine for the pain from his cancer. Robert looks sickly and is very skinny. His hair has turned all white. I feel very sorry for him they are killing him. He has cancer and is very ill. He is dying, and they are doing nothing to help him. He asks for medicine, and they refuse to give him medicine. That place is horrible! He said, "Robert is a kind person and asked me when I left to give my mattress to one of his cellmates that sleeps above him on just an iron mattress. Even though Robert is very ill, he still thinks about helping others. He is a very kind and a very good person."

This inmate was my Ft. Lauderdale maid's son. When he got out, my maid showed her son a picture of my son and asked him, "Is this Robert?" He said, "Yes. But he looks really bad now, skinny, and sickly; his hair is all white."

Another inmate I spoke with during a monitored jail call with Robert was XXXXXX. He stated to me, "Robert was very ill, and the detention center refused to give him any medical care." He said the nurse told Robert, "You can get your medical treatment when you get out, and Robert said, I will pay for it." This inmate said he could be contacted as a witness for what he heard and saw.

Another inmate, a homeless man, brought Robert a peanut butter sandwich, and hand fed him the sandwich because he was too sick even to raise his head off the mattress to eat by himself. Robert told me, "Mom, here is this homeless man who was brought in for panhandling. He was helping me because I was too sick even to raise my head off the bed to eat. He hand fed me his peanut butter sandwich. Here, I had an affluent life, and this man sleeps under bridges and gives me his peanut butter sandwich. His deed got to my heart." I said, "Robert, God is watching over you. He will exonerate you and see you through all these bogus charges." This monitored jail call from Robert can be verified as well as all the other conversations I've had with my son to date, which I have detailed in this complaint.

Judge XXXXXX stated on his order to Robert's Motion to Suppress that the deputies made an unlawful warrantless entry into our home on October 5, 2015. On addendum #2 at the bottom of page 3 of 6 of my son's Motion to Suppress order, which was held on November 8, 2017, Judge XXXXXX confirmed that the deputies violated Robert's 4th amendment rights.

Judge XXXXXX' order: "The court observes that no justification was offered as to why police did not seek a warrant prior to approaching the defendant's house for the knock and talk. Had officers simply sought a warrant before entering the defendant's residence instead of afterward, they would

have avoided an entirely unnecessary expenditure of both judicial and police resources. Separately from whether the tactics employed by police were legal, they were clearly unwise and unnecessary."

In his Order, Judge XXXXXX added a doctrine of Inevitable Discovery that does not exist in Supreme Court Case Law, Rodriguez vs. State of Florida. His error in adding the doctrine of Inevitable Discovery exonerated the Deputies' unlawful search and seizure, but opened the door for Robert's current appeal with the Florida 5th DCA.

Robert's lawyers filed a Motion for Reconsideration for Judge XXXXXX to correct his error on his order, which he also denied with no legal explanation. The lawyers told Robert with all of Judge XXXXXX' bias shown in his rulings, and the conspiracy between the Prosecutor and Deputies he should plead no contest and appeal on the basis of Judge XXXXXX misinterpretation of the law. They warned Robert that with Judge XXXXXX' bias, he would give him a stiff sentence but that he would be free on the Appeal. Judge XXXXXX' stiff sentence was 20 years.

Robert's three lawyers witnessed the following: (1) Unlawful conspiracy against my son by the Prosecutor, XXXXXX with the Lake County Deputies. (2) The Lake County Detention Center's denying Robert urgently needed medical treatment and care. (3) Judge XXXXXX bias against my son's legal rights, including his denying Robert any medical furlough to obtain urgently needed medical care and treatment, his Motion to Reinstate his bond, his Motion to Suppress, and his Motion for Reconsideration.

After the deputies originally filed a false arrest charge against Robert for resisting an officer without violence, on October 5, 2015, Robert was out on bail four days later on October 9, 2015. During the 10 months,

Robert was out on bond; he was not a flight risk. He was not a danger to any community as falsely alleged by Prosecutor XXXXXX to Judge XXXXXX during Robert's Motion to Reinstate his Bond and, thereafter, his Motion a Medical Furlough. Despite this fact, the Prosecutor came up with even more bogus lies and charges. He accused Robert on August 17, 2016, of delivering two Jukeboxes to a neighbor in 2011 or 2012 with lenses in them for the purpose of voyeurism. The Prosecutor wasn't sure which year this was in and had no evidence whatsoever of such delivery. He told the news media he assumed Robert O'Hare delivered two jukeboxes in either 2011 or 2012 to the wrong neighbor so the wrong neighbor would deliver the two jukeboxes to the correct neighbor. He wasn't even sure which year this delivery was in.

In one of our monitored phone calls, at the on January 28, 2018, my son said, **"Mom, they are slowing murdering me."** This call can be verified through the monitored jail calls at the lake county detention center.

The Lake County Detention Center refused to give my son any urgently needed medical care or hospitalization for close to 17 months. Two guards, Officer XXXXXX, and Officer XXXXXX both witnessed Robert asking the nurses for medical help and their refusal to do so. These two guards witnessed Robert lying on the floor, sick with bleeding-like diarrhea and asking for medical help and hospitalization, with the nursing staff refusing to help him. **Officer XXXXXX said, "Robert, it's bad the way they are treating you." Officer XXXXXX was present and agreed**. Knowing he was dying, the Lake County Detention Center asked Robert to sign their waiver of release so if he died they would not be liable. Robert refused to sign the waiver of liability.

After seventeen months of incarceration without any medical treatment, Robert said he was passing away and could not hold on any longer. That's when the detention center allowed Robert to have his first and only medical treatment for his malignant colon cancer. He received five radiation treatments to his colon on about January 28, 2018. Thereafter, they gave him no follow up care or treatment, and he was left to suffer the after-effects of the five radiation treatments alone in a 24/7 lockdown cell and only allowed out of his cell 3 hours a week. His legal rights were egregiously violated as he suffered cruel and unusual punishment and was not given any medical care or treatment. His due process rights were totally non-existent and 100% abolished by the Lake County Detention Center. His lack of medical care from the Lake County Detention Center was appalling. He was left to suffer pain and anguish without his civil liberties, and constitutional rights being upheld.

Robert was weak, frail and dying. A guard questioned Robert when he came out from taking his shower, and his face was all red and bruised. He said, "Robert did you fall again" Robert admitted to the guard he fell again on his face because he was so weak, he couldn't stand up. He told me of this incident on one of our monitored phone calls. He said, "I could not stand up and was crying out for medical treatment and help, while they all ignored me. One nurse told me," You will get medical treatment when you get out." Another guard told me, "If you complain one more time I will put you in a box." Those conversations are recorded on Robert's monitored jail calls with me.

During Robert's hearings for his motions for urgently needed medical treatment and care, Prosecutor XXXXXX repeatedly lied to Judge XXXXXX and said my son was a flight risk and a danger to the community. This can be verified on the electronic court transcriptions of the hearing proceedings. Believing this lie, Judge XXXXXX denied all of Robert's motions for a medical furlough and reinstatement of his $25,000 bond. To kill my son was the intent of the Prosecutor and Deputies and they came close to accomplishing just that until God stepped in and as of today, my son is still alive and breathing. He called me on July 9, 2017, and said, "Mom, both guards XXXXXX, and XXXXXX saw me suffering, bleeding and in pain, they said, "Why are they letting you suffer like this." He asked me, "Do I have any legal rights because they are attempting to murder me." I told him I am making this complaint with the Federal Government's U. S. Dept. of Justice to protect him from this happening.

Prosecutor XXXXXX told Attorney XXXXXX at one of my son's motions before Judge XXXXXX for medical treatment, "Your client is not sick. I'm going to put him away for life!" Attorney XXXXXX can verify these and other vindictive statements the Prosecutor made to purposefully have Robert's Motion for a Reinstatement of his Bond and his Medical Furlough denied. In the Lake County Judicial System, all of Robert's constitutional liberties for medical treatment and his due process of law were egregiously violated by the Lake County Prosecutor, the Lake County Deputies, Judge XXXXXX, and the Lake County Detention Center.

All these major criminal violations committed by the Lake County Deputies, the Lake County Detention Center, the Lake County Prosecutor, XXXXXX, and

the Lake County Judicial System cry out for justice for my son.

Fearing for our lives, I sold our home in Mt. Dora, FL on November 16, 2017, and went back to our home in Fort Lauderdale, Florida. Our beautiful Mt. Dora homestead became tarnished after the Sheriff's Deputies' criminal violations and their brutally assaulting my son inside our home. On January 11, 2018, this same Deputy, who kicked and punched my son in his stomach, on October 5, 2015, came to my home in Ft. Lauderdale and commenced banging on my front door and ringing the doorbell multiple times from 3:35 to 6:45 pm. I looked from my two-story Colonial home at this angry Deputy banging repeatedly on my front door, while he kept calling my cell phone several times. Being 81 years old and living alone, I feared for my life! I called Attorney XXXXXX, who verified that the number on my caller ID was registered to this Deputy. This man was not only frightening but very dangerous. After witnessing his punching and kicking my son on October 5, 2015, his presence at my front door made me fear for my life.

As if it weren't enough torture for my son to go through this Deputy, on January 16th, 2018, went to see my son at the Lake County Detention Center. He asked Robert, "I want to talk to you and ask you some questions. Where are you going to live when you get out?" My son said, "I don't want to talk with you." Deputy XXXXXX angrily demanded my son go into his cell while he ransacked through all his belongings. He took two bags of Robert's commissary food and one cookie and left angry. After Deputy XXXXXX left, the guard, Officer XXXXXX, came over to Robert and said, "I've been a guard here for 12 years and have never seen anything like this happen before to anyone! Robert, that deputy was really pissed at you."

Officer XXXXXX witnessed this incident, and both he and the other Officer XXXXXX witnessed the medical staff refusing to give Robert any medical care while Robert laid on the floor bleeding, with unbearable pain and suffering, and crying out for medical help! These two incidents can be verified from the monitored jail calls I had with my son and interviewing both of these Security Officers XXXXXX and XXXXXX.

Please immediately investigate this criminal complaint as my son's life is at stake.

Respectfully submitted,

____

VIRGINIA O'HARE

CORRESPONDENCE TO THE FEDERAL BUREAU OF INVESTIGATION

April 24, 2018

Federal Bureau of Investigation

444 Seabreeze Blvd. Suite 300

Daytona Beach, FL 32118

To: FBI Unit in Daytona Beach, Florida

This updated correspondence is to be added to my criminal complaint which was submitted to your office on March 5, 2018, for an investigation of government employees who violated my son, Robert O'Hare's civil, constitutional and prisoner's rights. This includes the Lake County Judge XXXXXX, the Lake County Prosecutor XXXXXX, Lake County Sheriff's Deputies, Corporal XXXXXX, Deputy XXXXXX, Deputy XXXXXX, Captain XXXXXX, Detective XXXXXX, the Lake County Detention Center, the Lake County Sheriff XXXXXX, and the Lake County State Attorney XXXXXX.

On October 5, 2015, at approximately 11:15 am, three Lake County Sheriff's Deputies came to our home and asked my son Robert if they could come in and search our home for a laptop computer they allege may have child porn on it. They informed Robert they did not have a warrant. He told them to get a warrant and started to close the door. Corporal XXXXXX forcefully pushed open the door and unlawfully stepped over the threshold of our home with Deputy XXXXXX, and Deputy XXXXXX.

The three deputies immediately commenced brutally assaulting Robert in rapid succession; I witnessed this with a great deal of fear and consternation. After ripping Robert's t-shirt down below his chest, Deputy XXXXXX started kicking my son repeatedly, 10-12 times soccer ball style, to his ribs and abdomen, as he laid helpless on the floor crying out in severe pain with every hard blow to his face, eyes, head, and body. Corporal XXXXXX was kneeling on Robert's right side, thrusting his fist with blunt blows to Robert's face, eyes, and head. The third Deputy XXXXXX laid bodily over Robert's legs, while the other two deputies viciously beat him causing blood, bruises and cuts, to break out on his body, head, face, and eyes.

I kept screaming for them to stop. When they wouldn't, I ran into my bedroom, retrieved my cell phone and started to videotape them. That's when they stopped and tightly hand-cuffed Robert's hands behind his back. Corporal XXXXXX said, "this happened to your son because he wouldn't let us come in and search your home. Robert said, "they didn't have a search warrant. I said, "without a search warrant, I don't blame him!"

During the ensuing assault on my son, Captain XXXXXX came into our home with two other deputies, and said, "If we don't find the laptop we are looking for, we are going to arrest your son anyway." I asked, "For what?" He said, "For resisting an officer without violence." Pictures of Robert's abuse and the cell phone video of the above conversations were mailed to your office on March 5, 2018, with my criminal complaint.

While unlawfully searching our home without a warrant, the deputies kept me and Robert captive by the front door. I was in fear the deputies would do further harm to my son. I sorrowfully witnessed the physical beating that left my son with cuts, bruises and blood on his face and body while in a beaten traumatized state. I asked the deputy to please loosen the handcuffs because it was cutting off blood circulation to Robert's hands. Out of spite, the deputy made the notch tighter.

The deputies commenced an extensive warrantless search of our home and could not find the laptop computer. The only place the deputies had not searched in our home was in my son's locked bedroom closet. Captain XXXXXX knew he was unlawfully in our home without a search warrant, without consent, without probable cause, and without any exigent circumstances. Yet, he threatened Robert with an unlawful command, "If you don't tell me where the key is to your locked bedroom closet, at the count of 10, I will have the deputies kick the door off its hinges." My son, being in a beaten and fearful state, still on the floor with his hands tightly handcuffed behind his back told him where the key was, without giving his consent. The deputies unlocked the closet door, found the laptop computer and a short barrel rifle. They charged Robert with possession of both, plus resisting an officer without violence.

According to the Master Deputy XXXXXX's police report, the court's electronic transcriptions, and Corporal XXXXXX's body-worn camcorder video, the following violations were revealed: the deputies removed the laptop computer from the locked bedroom closet, unzipped the black case, placed the laptop on the bedroom floor and the laptop's case on the bed. Then called in CSI to take pictures of their staged crime scene to satisfy the plain view doctrine, "if police can see it, they can seize it during a lawful observation." Master Deputy XXXXXX filed a false account of their unlawful entry, search, and seizure while conspiring to stage a bogus crime scene with the other deputies.

Seven hours before obtaining the search warrant, the deputies committed multiple violations of my son's civil and constitutional rights. I fully detailed these criminal acts in an updated criminal complaint sent to the Department of Justice, Attorney General Jeff Sessions on 4/24/2018 with a faxed copy sent to your office the same day.

Thereafter, the nightmare of corruption that ensued from the Lake County Judicial System plagued Robert with their multiple violations of his civil, constitutional, and prisoner's rights. Prosecutor XXXXXX orchestrated multiple prosecutorial acts of misconduct against Robert's constitutional due process of his legal rights. One of which was making false and bogus allegations during hearings and filing additional charges against Robert without any bona fide evidence. He based his bogus charges solely on his assumptions and to cover up the deputies' unlawful violations while they were in our home.

Prosecutor XXXXXX committed the following acts of prosecutorial misconduct which is detailed herein:

1 Prosecutor XXXXXX postponed Robert's Motion to Suppress five times in almost eight months while keeping him incarcerated and in critical ill health, while denying him reactivation of his bail. The prosecutor denied Robert his due process of law by created months of delays and postponements of his motions for justice which were all based on his legal rights

2 The Prosecutor objected to Robert's Motion for a Medical Furlough, several times, which prevented him from receiving urgently needed medical treat-

ment for his stage 3 or 4 malignant colon cancer. During the hearings, the Prosecutor convinced Judge XXXXXX that Robert was a flight risk and a danger to the Loch Leven community. Our family lived in that community since 1999 without any incidents and were in very good standing with our neighbors, and those on the Homeowner's Association. The bogus lies convinced Judge XXXXXX to rule against all of Robert's motions.

3   The Lake County Detention Center refused to give Robert any medical treatment for 17 months for his life-threatening illness, even after being put on notice of his medical condition since August 25, 2016. On that date, Robert was diagnosed with precancerous bleeding polyps. This condition, untreated by the Lake County Detention Center has developed into stage 3 or 4 malignant colon cancer with a 70% blockage to his colon. The doctor told Robert he was not sure which stage his cancer was in without taking further tests. To date, the Lake County Detention Center has failed to give Robert any of the required medical tests. For the first time during Robert's incarceration of almost 18 months, he was given five radiation treatments to his colon, on or about January 28, 2018. As of the date of this correspondence, April 24, 2018, Robert has not received any follow-up care or had any follow-up exam by a doctor.

4   The Prosecutor not only lied to Judge XXXXXX during court hearings but to the Trial Attorney XXXXXX as well. During the Motion to Suppress, Attorney XXXXXX, in front of Judge XXXXXX, stated to the Prosecutor, "if you lie to me one more time in court, I will go after your bar license." Attor-

ney XXXXXX can attest to the Prosecutor XXXXXX lying during court proceedings. Attorney XXXXXX told me he heard Judge XXXXXX tell the Prosecutor, "You put me in a very bad position."

5   I made a formal criminal complaint to the Lake County Internal Affairs on March 2016 against the Deputies' unlawful entry and beating of my son on October 5, 2015. A full investigative Lake County Internal Affairs report was given to the Prosecutor for his review. Instead of acknowledging the evidence in the report against the deputies' criminal violations to Robert's 4th Amendment rights and Federal Law Section 1983, he ignored all this evidence from the Lake County Internal Affairs criminal investigation report and conspired with the deputies to create even more damning lies and bogus allegations against Robert to cover up his prosecutorial misconduct and the deputies' violations. He ignored the legal fact that any evidence obtained by the deputies unlawfully could not be used in a court of law against Robert. Consistent with his conspiracy with the deputies, Prosecutor XXXXXX failed to bring to Judge XXXXXX during my son's suppression hearing, my son's live video, which was prima facie evidence against the deputies' violations to his 4th amendment rights, even though he had a legal obligation to do so.

6   The deputies committed unlawful acts while in our home against my son's 4th Amendment rights, and Federal Law Section 1983. Immediately thereafter, at all the hearings the deputies made false and damning sworn testimony against Robert's character to cover over their own serious violations. Evidence of this is in the court's electronic

transcriptions of the hearing proceedings.

7   In Master Deputy XXXXXX's police report, he made up several false statements. One being they found the laptop on the floor in "plain view," with the case on the bed and a short barrel rifle in "plain view." During a court hearing, Deputy XXXXXX contradicted himself and said when he went into the closet there were clothes in front of the rifle, and he had to move clothes around to get to it. Another false statement he made on his police report was he came through a front door by the garage and yelled twice, "Sheriff's office, Sheriff's office." He also falsely stated he heard the deputies saying twice, "Stop resisting, stop resisting." When all this time I have a live video of him by the front entry door laying over my son's legs talking to me. He never went through the front door by the garage because that door was padlocked. No one could come through that door unless they knocked it down. He fabricated his police report with those and other lies. I saw Master Deputy XXXXXX come through the front door.

8   My deceased husband, Daniel R. Ortung was a Florida licensed private investigator, licensed to carry a gun and firearm. After his passing, my son was given these items, which he kept locked in his bedroom closet.

9   Corporal XXXXXX's body-worn camcorder video was played at the Motion to Suppress hearing on December 8, 2018. It recorded the deputies talking about finding the laptop at around 11:37 am on October 5, 2015, in the closet. Their warrant wasn't obtained and signed by a Magistrate Judge until 5:44 pm and delivered to our home at 6:45 pm that

evening. Clearly, this was an illegal warrantless search and seizure, and against Robert's 4th Amendment rights.

10 Master Deputy XXXXXX put in his police report that they found the laptop on the bedroom floor and the case on the bed. After staging this as a crime scene, they called in CSI to take pictures of the laptop and case as being in plain view to satisfy the plain view doctrine which is, "if the police can see It, they can seize it during a lawful observation." This staging of a crime scene by the deputies is 100% illegal.

11 The deputies' beating caused permanent harm and bodily damage to Robert, blinding him in his left eye and damage to his pancreas and intestines which caused constant bleeding and severe bowel problems, with nausea, weakness, and loss of weight. This condition untreated by the Lake County Detention Center for over one year developed into malignant colon cancer, stage three or four. The doctor told Robert further tests are needed to determine which stage the cancer is in, which has not been done by the detention center to the date of this letter.

12 During Robert's seventeen months of incarceration, his constitutional and prisoner's rights were egregiously violated. He was denied urgently needed medical care and treatment from August 25, 2016 when he was first diagnosed with precancerous bleeding polyps to January 28, 2018, when, he was given his first medical treatment of five radiation treatments, which was almost five (5) months after being diagnosed by Dr. XXXXXX on September 5, 2017, with malignant colon cancer.

13 Prior to receiving the five radiation treatments, the Lake County Detention Center, knowing the seriousness of Robert's condition, asked Robert to sign a release of liability. He refused to sign their waiver of liability.

14 On September 5, 2016, after Dr. XXXXXX confirmed Robert has stage three or stage four malignant colon cancer; he said, "Robert, this growth has been in your colon for one year. We need to take an MRI immediately, so I can see how large this growth is before we operate." The detention center was informed by Dr. XXXXXX's nurse that Robert needed to have an MRI immediately. The detention center waited several weeks before allowing Robert to have an MRI. When an MRI was finally taken, it showed Robert had a 70% blockage in his colon.

15 Robert has never had a trial. He was consistently denied his constitutional due process by Prosecutor XXXXXX, who committed the following additional acts of misconduct:

16 Prosecutor XXXXXX objected to Robert's Motion for a Medical Furlough by falsely alleging Robert was a flight risk and a danger to the community we lived in. This prevented Robert from being given urgently needed outside medical treatment for his malignant colon cancer in preparation for surgery.

17 Prosecutor XXXXXX purposefully misquoted case law at the Motion to Suppress hearing on November 8, 2017, in order to benefit the illegal acts of the deputies. He lied several times in court which caused Trial Attorney XXXXXX to warn the Prosecutor, "if you lie to me one more time in court, I will

go after your bar license."

18 Prosecutor XXXXXX postponed Robert's Motion to Suppress five (5) times for over a period of close to eight (8) months while keeping him incarcerated without any medical treatment for his malignant colon cancer.

19 Prosecutor XXXXXX convinced Judge XXXXXX to deny reactivation of Robert's $25,000 bond by falsely alleging that Robert was a flight risk and a danger to the community. He made these false allegations without having any evidence of this to show the court.

20 The $25,000 bond was an excessive amount to be charged according to Robert's 8th amendment rights because this was in addition to paying $13,500 for his first charge. The 2nd bogus charge was made up by the Prosecutor based solely on his assumption, which he admitted to the news media because he had no evidence to support the validity of his charges. He charged Robert with delivering two jukeboxes to a family in 2011 or 2012 and wasn't even sure what year his false allegations of delivery were in. The Prosecutor admitted to the news media it was a neighbor, not Robert, who delivered the jukeboxes to their neighbor.

21 I was informed by Detective. XXXXXX of Internal Affairs who told me, "The Prosecutor did not have any new evidence for his 2nd charges. The 2nd charges were made from the same evidence he had from your son's closet when the Prosecutor made their 1st charges."

22 Prosecutor XXXXXX vindictively stated to Attorney

XXXXXX, "I am going to put your client away for life." He said this without my son having a trial or for his lawyers providing his defense in a court of law. The Prosecutor's goal wasn't to seek justice but to have a conviction at any cost.

23 Robert was out on bond on the Prosecutor's first bogus charges for 10 months, and never once was a flight risk, and never once was a danger to any community as falsely alleged by the Prosecutor. Nor was there ever any evidence of this during Robert's entire 56 years of life!

24 Prosecutor XXXXXX informed the news media that he made his 2nd arrest charges based on his "assumption." He told the news media he "assumed" Robert delivered two (2) jukeboxes with lenses in them in either 2011 or 2012 to a wrong neighbor thinking the wrong neighbor would deliver the two (2) jukeboxes to the right neighbor. Then falsely charged Robert with voyeurism. He told the news media he wasn't sure which year this was in. This ridiculous made-up bogus charge had no proof or any evidence whatsoever of Robert making any such delivery several years ago. His charge was based solely on his "assumption."

25 Robert was medically diagnosed with pre-cancerous bleeding polyps, by the Broward County Health Hospital in Ft. Lauderdale, FL, the same day the prosecutor made his 2nd arrest charge against him on August 25, 2016. I gave Robert's medical report several times during the course of several weeks to the Lake County Detention Center, the Lake County Sheriff, the Lake County Warden, and later to the State Attorney XXXXXX. They all ignored my no-

tices to them of Robert's medical report.

26 My son's lawyers made several motions to the Lake County Judge XXXXXX requesting an emergency furlough for Robert to have urgently needed medical treatment, which he wasn't getting at the detention center. Judge XXXXXX denied multiple motions for an outside medical furlough.

27 In his 17 months of incarceration without a trial, the judge only allowed Robert to see one doctor, and only when Robert became critically ill. This outside doctor, Dr. XXXXXX discovered Robert's colon cancer and said he also had pancreas inflammation from an injury. That injury was caused by Deputy XXXXXX repeatedly kicking Robert in his abdomen and ribs with brute force, during his unlawful entry to our home on October 5, 2015. Robert's bleeding from his colon and bowel problems commenced right after this beating.

28 All formal requests for medical treatments were given to the Lake County State Attorney XXXXXX. He continued to ignore Robert's medical needs, and the violations committed against his constitutional rights. The detention center allowed Robert to undergo unbearable pain and suffering, as his weight plummeted, losing over 40 lbs. While his health and body degenerated rapidly before their eyes.

29 Robert informed me that his cellmates made numerous comments to him of his gray color skin, and said he looked like he was dying because he was! The Lake County Detention Center's medical neglect violated his 8th amendment and prisoner's rights which caused his pre-cancerous bleeding polyps to

develop into malignant colon cancer stage three or four with a 70% blockage in his colon. The doctor was not sure which stage of cancer Robert had without further tests. To date, 17-months later, the detention center has refused to give Robert these necessary tests.

On October 4, 2017, my Fort Lauderdale maid, XXXXXX called and said, her son, XXXXXX, was in the Lake County Detention Center for two weeks for a traffic ticket violation. She said, her son was in the same pod with my son. When her son, XXXXXX, came home, he told his mother about my son's pain and suffering, and the detention center's refusal to give Robert any medical treatment.

Her son gave the following notarized statement:

"I hear Robert cry at night with pain. They refuse to give him any medicine for the pain from his cancer. Robert looks sickly and is very skinny. His hair has turned all white. I feel very sorry for him; they are killing him. He has cancer and is very ill. He is dying, and they are doing nothing to help him. He asks for medicine, and they refuse to give him medicine. That place is horrible! Robert is a kind person and asked me when I left to give my mattress to one of his cellmates that sleeps above him on just an iron mattress. Even though Robert is very ill, he still thinks about helping others. He is a very kind and a very good person."

My maid, XXXXXX said she showed her son a picture of my son before he was incarcerated and asked him, "Is this Robert?" He said, "Yes, but he looks really bad now, skinny, and sickly; his hair is all white."

When I was told this, I cried hysterically. She said,

"I didn't mean to upset you."

Another cellmate, a homeless man, brought Robert a peanut butter sandwich because he was too sick to raise his head off the bed to eat on his own. My son told me about this heart rendering event. He said, "Mom, here is this man who is homeless and was brought in for panhandling and helping me because I was too sick even to raise my head off the bed to eat. He fed me his peanut butter sandwich. Here, I had an affluent life, and this man sleeps under bridges and gives me his peanut butter sandwich. His deed got to my heart." I said, Robert God is watching over you, and he will exonerate you and see you through all these unjust and bogus charges." This monitored call from the detention center can be verified like all the monitored conversations I've had with my son to date.

A guard asked Robert if he fell again in the shower because his face was all red when he came out. Robert admitted to the guard he fell on his face again because he was so weak, he couldn't stand up. Robert told me of this incident on one of our monitored phone calls. He said, "I could not stand up and was crying out for medical treatment and help, while they all ignored me. One nurse told me," You will get medical treatment when you get out." Another guard told me, "If you complain one more time I will put you in a box."

The detention center allowed Robert to suffer needlessly with severe pain, bleeding-like diarrhea for over one year before one doctor examined him and diagnosed Robert with life-threatening malignant colon cancer with a 70% blockage in his colon. This growth made it difficult and painful for Robert to empty his bowels. Robert said he would go up to four (4) days without a bowel movement. This painful and aggressively spreading colon cancer should have been medically treated by the Lake County Detention Center and not allow him to go untreated for 17 months.

On or about January 28, 2018, was the first time Robert was given five radiation treatments. Dr. XXXXXX informed Robert on September 5, 2017; his colon cancer was present in him for one year. He told Robert he did not know why the Detention Center did not treat his cancer earlier.

The Lake County Detention Center asked Robert to sign a waiver of release of liability, which would exonerate them from any liability if something happened to him. He refused to sign their waiver. This was just before they gave him the five radiation treatments.

While my son was crying out in unbearable pain and suffering for medical treatment, the three deputies were conspiring with each other and with the Prosecutor to prevent my son from having medical treatment and justice. With their lies, they convinced Judge XXXXXX not to reactivate Robert's bond motion or any of his medical motions. The three deputies that beat up Robert, XXXXXX, XXXXXX, and XXXXXX testified under oath at Robert's hearings, with false, and damaging allegations to convince Judge XXXXXX not to reinstate Robert's $25,000 bond or to give him a medical furlough. They said Robert was a flight risk and a danger to the Loch Leven community. This is where our family lived in good standing for seventeen (17) years with absolutely no problems, and no incidents whatsoever.

During my son's entire life, he never had any legal problems, didn't drink or smoke, had a spotless record. Despite my son's legally clean record, Judge XXXXXX ruled in favor of the deputy's false sworn testimony and the Prosecutor's lies against my son's character. Judge XXXXXX did this even though the deputies did not produce any evidence whatsoever of their false and bogus allegations,

The Prosecutor told Attorney XXXXXX, "I'm going to put your client away for life." This vindictive statement made by the prosecutor was carried out by using every form of prosecutorial misconduct he could to destroy my son's quest for justice.

More importantly, Judge XXXXXX not only denied Robert's motion to reactivate his $25,000 bond, which he was legally entitled to, he also denied his emergency medical furlough motions for urgently needed outside medical care. The judge also denied Robert's Motion to Suppress which was based 100% on the law with prima facie evidence of pictures and a live video of the deputies violating his 4th amendment rights. The Motion to Suppress is based on constitutional grounds and on ones' 4th, 5th, and 14th Amendments that protect citizens from unreasonable search and seizure, self-incrimination and due process.

In Judge XXXXXX's Order to Robert's Motion to Suppress, he did acknowledge the deputy's unlawful warrantless entry into our home which is against Robert's 4th amendment rights. But he added a doctrine of Inevitable Discovery that does not exist in the Supreme Court case law, Rodriguez vs. State of Florida. This doctrine was made in error by Judge XXXXXX which exonerated the criminal violations of the deputies warrantless and unlawful entry, illegal search, and seizure while in our home.

Robert's lawyers made a Motion for Reconsideration

for Judge XXXXXX to correct his error in misinterpreting the Supreme Court case law in adding a doctrine of Inevitable Discovery that does not exist in the law. Instead of correcting his error, Judge XXXXXX denied the Motion for Reconsideration without giving a legal reason for his denial.

After making rulings that did not comply with the law, Robert's lawyers advised, "Robert with all the bias and corruption we witness against your legal rights, going to trial with a biased judge, and conspiracy between the prosecutor and the deputies would be lethal. You should plead no contest and appeal because Judge XXXXXX does not follow the law. This is the only chance we can see for you to have justice and be set free. With Judge XXXXXX' bias against you, he will give you a stiff sentence, but we will do a De Nova Appeal to find justice for you and for you to be set free. Your appeal will be based solely on Judge XXXXXX misinterpreting the law. We all suspected he would do this and this is why we are preparing in advance your appeal brief."

Robert's lawyers rightly advised him, because going to trial would be filled with the Judge's bias, the Prosecutor and the Deputies' collusion, conspiracy, and corruption. The fact that Judge XXXXXX did not follow the Supreme Court case law, Rodriguez vs. State of Florida, and did not follow the law in his previous rulings, was a major red flag to Robert's lawyers that corruption, conspiracy and politics would triumph over justice for Robert if he went to trial.

The eve of Robert supersedeas bond hearing, which was to be held on January 30, 2018, the State Attorney came up with another bogus charge against Robert. They falsely allege that Robert gave me, his 81-year-old mother, during our monitored jail phone call, a code asking me to give a piece of paper to a longtime family friend to kill the Judge. This longtime family friend, XXXXXX, told me he was approached by the Deputy, who beat up my son in our home and questioned him if I gave him a piece of paper to kill the judge. He said he told Deputy XXXXXX "No she never gave me a piece of paper and told me to kill anyone. This is all bull shit; you are not going to do to me what you did to Robert O'Hare. What years I have left (he is 75 years old) you are not going to take away from me. I've known Virginia and Robert for 35 years, and they never hurt anyone or asked me to kill anyone. I haven't spoken to Virginia or Robert for six months. The last time I saw Virginia was on her 81st birthday on November 13, 2017, when I took her to lunch. This is all bull shit!" He also spoke with Robert's Attorney, XXXXXX, and told him the same thing. This bogus false charge was investigated by Deputy XXXXXX and given to the news media by the Lake County Prosecutor, making this a smear campaign against my son and the family friend.

Another Lake County deputy lying under oath against my son was Detective XXXXXX at Robert's Bond Motion to Reinstate his $25,000 bond. Detective XXXXXX falsely stated: "The Broward County Officer XXXXXX told me Robert delivered two jukeboxes to a family in Broward County Florida in 2016." Detective XXXXXX told this bogus story under oath, so Prosecutor's 2nd false arrest charge of alleging Robert delivered two jukeboxes to a Mt. Dora neighbor in 2011 or 2012 would stand and convince Judge XXXXXX my son was a danger to the community.

After the bond hearing, I called Broward County Officer XXXXXX's Supervisor Sargent XXXXXX, and also Internal Affairs investigator, Detective XXXXXX and told them both what Detective XXXXXX testified to at the bond hearing, stating that Officer XXXXXX told him Robert delivered two jukeboxes to a family in Broward County in 2016. They both questioned officer XXXXXX and informed me that Officer XXXXXX never told Detective XXXXXX that Robert delivered two jukeboxes to a family in Broward County in 2016. They said as further proof of this; no jukeboxes were ever put on their police report. They said if this story were true it would have to be put in the police report, and it wasn't. Upon confirmation of this, I submitted a formal complaint to the Lake County Internal Affairs Department against Detective XXXXXX lying under oath at Robert's Bond Hearing. The Lake County Internal Affairs Investigator, Detective XXXXXX chose to take no action against Detective XXXXXX and closed out the complaint against him.

My son never delivered two jukeboxes in 2011-2012 or in 2016 as falsely alleged by the Prosecutor and Detective XXXXXX. This false and conspired testimony during the bond hearing motion was made up by the Prosecutor and Detective XXXXXX to have Judge XXXXXX deny my son's bond on the premise he would be a threat to the community. Their conspiracy worked. Judge XXXXXX denied my son's bond and stated on his order that my son was a danger to the Loch Leven waterfront community, where we lived for 17 years without any such threat to the community. He stated in his Order that he made his decision from the witness testimony, which was from Detective XXXXXX lying under oath . Robert's lead Attorney XXXXXX was not at this bond hearing but heard the court's electronic transcription of the hearing. He said, "Your son, Robert, was set up by the deputies and the prosecutor."

Collusion in a court of law between a judge, a prosecutor, and deputies is a very powerful force for any defense lawyer to overcome, or for anyone seeking justice. Such criminal conspiracy destroys the lives of innocent people. In my son's case, I have prima facie evidence, of their collusion and conspiracy with evidence in depositions, pictures, live video, police body worn camcorder video, electronic transcriptions of the court proceedings, and testimony from Robert's three lawyers. They witnessed Judge XXXXXX being biased and not following the law, and the prosecutor's conspiracy with the deputies, with their lying under oath; and the detention center denying Robert his urgently needed medical treatment for his malignant colon cancer.

All of this evidence is fully documented and recorded on the electronic transcriptions of court proceedings. This criminal complaint was also mailed to the United States Dept. of Justice, Attorney General, Jeff Sessions, and President Donald J. Trump. President Donald J. Trump has turned this criminal complaint over to their federal agency for further action. The Dept. of Justice has opened a file on this criminal complaint as well.

Judge XXXXXX denying all my son's motions, even those for an emergency medical furlough to receive outside urgently needed medical treatment for his malignant colon cancer is a travesty of justice.

For the record, I can't stress enough that any enforcement officer doing the unconscionable must be stopped by our federal government. They are plaguing our justice system and should be prosecuted to the full extent of the law. These officers of the law who did this to my son are 100% guilty with irrefutable evidence of their serious criminal violations. There is no question that Deputy XXXXXX caused my son's current life-threatening disability by beating him during his unlawful warrantless entry into our home on October 5, 2015. There is irrefutable evidence that Robert's blindness was caused by Corporal XXXXXX's severe beating to Robert's face, head, and eyes. Beatings by these deputies is a violation against Federal Law Section 1983. They should all be immediately arrested and prosecuted to the full extent of the law! No officer should be allowed to serve the public while violating the citizen's constitutional rights and committing all the criminal acts these enforcement officers have against my son.

Pictures and live video of the deputy's malicious beating of Robert were submitted to your office on March 5th, 2018. Our federal government has the responsibility and the obligation to the people of not allowing such criminal violations by officers of the law to prevail over its citizens. Officers of the law who violate the people's constitutional rights which destroys the very foundation of our justice system. These offending officers are replacing our democracy with anarchy and mobocracy.

The final stab against the heart of justice occurred at the Motion to Suppress hearing held on November 8, 2017. Prosecutor, XXXXXX, failed to bring my son's live video pre-hearing to the judge or to the hearing, as he promised he would to defense Attorney XXXXXX. Upon the Prosecutor reviewing the live video, he knew it would be lethal evidence against his case and against the deputies. So, he chose not to show the video to Judge XXXXXX pre-hearing and did not bring the video to the hearing as well. Due to the fact that his office is right next door to the judge's office in the courthouse building, there was no logistical excuse for not showing this video to Judge XXXXXX. This act of prosecutorial misconduct was purely 100% intentional!

Suspecting that Prosecutor XXXXXX would not bring the video to Judge XXXXXX as he promised, Attorney XXXXXX had an extra copy of the live video and showed it to Judge XXXXXX on his laptop computer. This left the Judge little or no chance to ignore the horrendous unlawful acts of the deputies.

During the suppression hearing, Prosecutor XXXXXX misinterpreted a Supreme Court case law which makes it unlawful for warrantless searches. He lied intentionally to support the three deputies' warrantless entry, and their illegal search and seizure.

The video is proof positive of the Lake County deputies' violations against Robert's 4th Amendment rights, which the Supreme Court case law Rodriguez vs. State of Florida (2015) confirms. This law states that all warrantless entry is illegal, and the doctrine of Inevitable Discovery does not exist without a warrant being first in place. The three deputies had no warrant in place. Therefore, they all violated Robert's 4th Amendment rights. Judge XXXXXX erroneously gave the deputies a doctrine of Inevitable Discovery that does not exist in the Florida Supreme Court Case Law, Rodriguez vs. State of Florida. His misruling prevented justice for my son. Attorney XXXXXX prepared a Motion for Reconsideration to give Judge XXXXXX the opportunity to correct his error of misinterpreting the law. Judge XXXXXX without any legal explanation denied that motion as well.

Prosecutor XXXXXX's lying to the Judge and his conspiracy with the Sheriff's Deputies was successful in preventing justice for my son again. The court's electronic transcriptions of the hearing proceedings will attest to their conspiracy.

Prosecutor XXXXXX committed the following acts of misconduct on Robert's case.

1 The Prosecutor lying about Robert's character prevented his $25,000 bond from being reinstated, which he was legally entitled to. My payment for the $25,000 bond was lost due to the Prosecutor's lying in a court of law and nothing my son did or said.

2 The Prosecutor lying about Robert being a flight risk and a danger to the community prevented Robert from having a medical furlough for outside medical treatment for his malignant colon cancer, which caused his pre-cancerous bleeding polyps to grow into malignant colon cancer.

3 During the Motion to Suppress hearing, the Prosecutor misquoting case law, and lying to the judge and Attorney XXXXXX caused Attorney XXXXXX to walk over to the Prosecutor and say in front of Judge XXXXXX, "XXXX if you lie to me one more time in court, I will go after your bar license." Attorney XXXXXX told me he heard Judge XXXXXX tell the Prosecutor, "you put me in a bad situation."

The court's electronic transcriptions of all the hearings confirm conspiracy, collusion, bias, and false sworn testimony by Lake County Officers of the law and the Prosecutor. Hearings included are the Motion for Reinstatement of the $25,000 bond, the Motion(s) for Medical Furlough, Motion to Suppress, and Motion for Reconsideration. I submitted to your office the entire transcription of the Motion to Suppress proceedings along with my formal criminal complaint on March 5, 2018.

Judge XXXXXX noted in his order of denial on Robert's Motion to Suppress, on page 3 of 6 par. Addendum #2 that there was no justification for the deputies to enter our home on October 5, 2015, without a search warrant. However, the judge reversed their illegal warrantless entry, search and seizure, by making up a doctrine of Inevitable Discovery that does not exist in the Supreme Court case law, Rodriguez vs. State of Florida. Judge XXXXXX erroneously adding this doctrine of Inevitable Discovery to his order, which justified the deputy's illegal warrantless entry into our home along with all their illegal violations.

In order for Judge XXXXXX to correct his error in misinterpreting the law in his ruling, Robert's lawyers filed a Motion for Reconsideration, which he denied without any legal explanation. Due to all of Judge XXXXXX adverse rulings which were made contrary to the law, speaks volumes of his bias against my son and being bias to the Prosecutor and the Deputies.

A day before Robert's Supersedeas Bond Hearing that was scheduled for January 30, 2018, the Lake County State Attorney recused Judge XXXXXX from my son's case. Eight months prior to recusing Judge XXXXXX, I personally spoke with the Lake County State Attorney, XXXXXX in May 2017. I informed him of all the violations committed by his employees that were under his supervision. He asked me to send him a detailed account of what happened to my son, which I did with all the evidence, including medical reports, depositions to prove their violations.

Thereafter I kept the State Attorney updated on all the additional violations against my son's constitutional and prisoner's rights that were violated by the Sheriff's Deputies, XXXXXX, XXXXXX, XXXXXX, Captain XXXXXX, Detective XXXXXX, the Lake County Detention

Center, Judge XXXXXX and Prosecutor XXXXXX. Despite all the evidence I submitted to him of these serious violations, he allowed them to continue, unabated, and without any form of retribution.

After the Bond Hearing, I filed a formal complaint against Detective XXXXXX to Lake County Internal Affairs, for falsely stating under oath that the Broward County Officer XXXXXX told him Robert gave two jukeboxes to a family in Broward County in 2016. I presented documented evidence from both Sargent XXXXXX and Detective XXXXXX of Broward County Internal Affairs who both stated Officer XXXXXX never told Detective XXXXXX that Robert gave two jukeboxes to a family in Broward County in 2016. They both added, "as proof of this, it was not in our police report."

I also submitted a copy of the Broward County Police Report in my formal complaint to the Lake County Internal Affairs investigator, Detective XXXXXX. He ignored all the evidence I submitted against Detective XXXXXX and closed out my complaint with no written explanation. This was the same Lake County Investigator who had Investigated Detective XXXXXX when he was arrested in Baltimore in 2012 for exposing his private parts in public. The Sheriff's Dept. rehired Detective XXXXXX back and employed him in their Cyber Sex Unit as Supervisor. I've attached the article of Detective's arrest to this complaint.

The Lake County Prosecutor XXXXXX's major and egregious prosecutorial misconduct and his collusion with the deputies is fully documented herein in this complaint with supporting evidence from the court's electronic transcriptions of the proceedings, as well as Robert's three lawyers.

In Summary:

The live video presented to Judge XXXXXX, at the Motion to Suppress hearing, verified the Deputies' unlawful entry, illegal search and seizure, and the aftermath of their severe beating to Robert. This vitally important evidence was the basis of which Robert's Motion to Suppress was based on and was prima facie evidence of the Deputies' violations of his 4th Amendment rights. Prosecutor XXXXXX knowing this live video would benefit Robert in prevailing legally for his Motion to Suppress, never gave it to Judge XXXXXX prehearing or at the hearing as he promised Attorney XXXXXX he would. This was an intentional act of prosecutorial misconduct.

Fortunately, suspecting this would happen, Attorney XXXXXX had an extra copy of the live video and played it before Judge XXXXXX on his laptop computer. Despite all this evidence, Judge XXXXXX put in his order a doctrine of Inevitable Discovery, that does not exist in the Supreme Court law, Rodriguez vs. State of Florida. This doctrine of Inevitable Discovery, that was put in the Judges' Order in error, exonerated the deputies warrantless search and seizure and caused Robert to lose his Motion to Suppress unjustly.

Judge XXXXXX was given a copy of this case law by Attorney XXXXXX during the Suppression Hearing, which states in black and white that the doctrine of Inevitable Discovery does not exist in a warrantless search. Despite this fact, Judge XXXXXX' bias against my son caused him to ignore the law and put in his order a doctrine of Inevitable Discovery. Attorney XXXXXX filed a Motion for Reconsideration for Judge XXXXXX to correct his error. Instead, Judge XXXXXX denied it without adding any legal explanation. This was the last ruling Judge XXXXXX made for my son before he was recused by the Lake County State Attorney XXXXXX.

There's undeniable evidence that the Prosecutor XXXXXX conspired with the deputies to give false and damning character assassinations and false allegations against Robert to Judge XXXXXX, which adversely influenced his rulings. In Robert's Motion to Reactivate his bond, which he was legally entitled to, and his Motion(s) for a Medical Furlough were only denied due to the Prosecutor and Deputies falsely stating Robert was a danger to the Loch Leven community and a flight risk. There was no credible evidence shown to the court of either of these false allegations. However, Judge XXXXXX chose to believe the testimony from the deputies and statements made by the Prosecutor without their presenting any viable evidence. They never did, because there was none.

The evidence of collusion, conspiracy, corruption, and bias by Lake County's Judicial Officers are outlined herein:

Prosecutor XXXXXX had all the evidence of the deputies, XXXXXX, XXXXXX and XXXXXX's, violations of their sworn statements to Internal Affairs from my criminal complaint made in March 2016. The Prosecutor knew from all the evidence that was presented on this criminal complaint to Internal Affairs that the Deputies violated Robert's 4th Amendment rights, and Federal Law Section 1983. Evidence of their 4th Amendment violations were substantiated by their own sworn statements to Internal Affairs Investigator XXXXXX. They all admitted to their warrantless and unlawful search and seizure and stated regarding their warrantless entry: "we thought this would work like it did all the other times, and O'Hara would let us come in to search his home."

The Prosecutor knew or should have known the three deputies violated my son's 4th Amendment rights and that all the evidence received could not be used in a court of law. Instead of acknowledging their unlawful warrantless violations, Prosecutor XXXXXX conspired with the deputies to commit even more egregious violations and charges against Robert's legal rights by lying and making false, damning and vile allegations against his character at hearings. To compound their errors, the Prosecutor made these damning statements to the news media as well.

The deputies jointly conspired to break the law in order to cover over their unlawful entry and ~~their~~ maliciously and brutally beating my son in our own home. They staged a crime scene in our home, made up a false police report to support their criminal violations, falsely charged Robert with resisting an officer without violence, and delivering two jukeboxes in 2011 or 2012 and again in 2016. The Judge made his rulings based on the prosecutor and deputies' bogus stories and lies and not on the defense's evidence or the law.

The lawyers wanted to save Robert from drowning in the cesspool of such corruption but were helpless in doing so. Their having to deal with the conspiracy between the Prosecutor and Deputies, and Judge XXXXXX' unjust rulings and his not following the law, was legally impossible to deal with. Therefore, they warned Robert that going to a trial with these judicial officials would be lethal. The only alternative for Robert to seek justice and be set free was to plead no contest and appeal.

Robert's lawyers filed the Appeal Brief with Florida 5th DCA on 2/8/2018. They feel confident Robert will win the appeal and be set free because the appeal is based 100% on the law.

Deputy XXXXXX, has done everything in his power to keep my son incarcerated in order to keep his own criminal violations from surfacing. On January 11, 2018, I viewed him from my 2nd story Colonial home when he came to my home in Ft. Lauderdale and banged his fist repeatedly on my front door for three (3) hours and kept calling me on my cell phone from 3:35 to 6:45 pm until he finally left. I called Attorney XXXXXX and gave him the cell number on my caller ID. He verified that the number was registered to this Deputy. This Deputy is dangerous! He almost killed my son when he repeatedly kicked him in his stomach and ribs after he forced his way into our home without a search warrant on October 5, 2015. Being true to character, he consistently manipulated the law, using his position with the Sheriff's Office to destroy our lives to cover up his own criminal violations. His plan to discredit the character of my son and keep him unjustly incarcerated will not succeed. God's justice and his judgment will prevail over all this corruption that has been poured without measure upon my son by the Lake County Judicial System in Tavares, Florida.

A few days after coming to my home, Dep. XXXXXX went to my son's cell on January 16, 2018, and wanted to know where my son was going to live when he gets out. When my son refused to talk with him without his lawyers being present, he became angry and ordered my son back into his cell. He ransacked my son's cell, took two bags of his commissary food and one cookie then left being angry. The guard on duty, Officer XXXXXX, told Robert, "I've been a guard here for 12 years. This is the first time I've ever seen anything like this happen before to anyone. Robert, that deputy was really pissed at you."

Prosecutor XXXXXX told Robert's lead Attorney XXXXXX, "The deputies told me to give Robert the longest sentence possible." He also said, "I am going to put your client away for life!" The Prosecutor also stated, "I allowed Mrs. O'Hare's neighbors in Loch Leven to listen to her monitored conversations with her son." Those neighbors used our conversations for the purpose of gossip throughout our neighborhood. Other vindictive statements made by the Prosecutor to Robert's Attorneys can be verified with them.

The Judge's Order to Robert's Motion to Suppress states:

"The court observes that no justification was offered as to why police (i.e., Dep. XXXXXX, Dep. XXXXXX, and Dep. XXXXXX) did not seek a warrant prior to approaching defendant's house for the knock and talk. Multiple search warrants had already been granted in the course of the investigation, nor does there appear to have been any particular time constraint. Had officers simply sought a warrant before entering the defendant's residence instead of afterward, they would have avoided an entirely unnecessary expenditure of both judicial and police resources. Separately from whether the tactics employed by police were legal, they were clearly unwise and unnecessary."

After reading Judge XXXXXX' ruling dated December 4, 2017, to Robert, he was thrilled that all the deputies' violations against his 4th Amendment rights were acknowledged by the court and that all the charges against my son would go away upon winning the appeal. Robert said on the monitor jail phone, "I would like to give Judge XXXXXX a big hug and kiss because he ruled in my favor when he put in his order what these deputies did to me was illegal. They blinded me and caused me to have this intestinal bleeding." This conversation and all the other monitored jail calls mentioned herein can be verified.

Robert's lawyers counseled him not to go to trial with a biased judge, a corrupt prosecutor, and the lying deputies. The Lawyers all stated that the Judge 's ruling gave Robert 95% of what their motion asked for, and the 5% was Judge XXXXXX' misrepresentation of a Supreme Court Case Law which can be reversed on an appeal. This is why my son took a plea of "no contest," because he has malignant colon cancer and wants to clear his name and win the appeal before anything happens to him

Please immediately investigate the following violations committed by the Lake County government employees:

1 Three Lake County Sheriff's Deputies, XXXXXX, XXXXXX, and XXXXXX, who violated Robert's 4th amendment rights and federal law section 1983.

2 Lake County Judge, XXXXXX' rule on Robert's Motion to Suppress with a doctrine of Inevitable Discovery that does not exist in Supreme Court Law. Then, when this error was brought to his attention in a Motion for Reconsideration, he refused to make the correction. This error if it were intentional, and not a misrepresentation by this judge, affects the life of my son.

3 The Lake County Detention Center denying Robert his urgently needed medical care and treatment for 17 months, has caused his pre-cancerous bleeding polyps to develop into stage 3 or 4 malignant colon cancer. By having full knowledge of Robert's major health issues since his incarceration date on August 25, 2016, the Lake County Detention Center vio-

lated Robert's 8th amendment and prisoner's rights in denying him urgently needed medical care and treatment for his life-threatening malignant colon cancer. For 17 months, they allowed him to undergo extreme pain and suffering without giving him any medical treatment for his cancer. It wasn't until death was looming over my son's life that on or about January 28, 2018, the Lake County Detention Center finally gave Robert his one and only cancer treatment, of five consecutive doses of radiation. Since the five radiation treatments, to the date of this letter, they have not given Robert any follow-up tests or care from a physician.

4   Detective XXXXXX lied under oath at Robert's hearing Motion to Reactivate his Bond. He falsely stated he was told by Broward County Officer XXXXXX that in 2016 Robert delivered two jukeboxes to a family in Broward County. Knowing this was a lie, the Trial Attorney asked the Detective, under cross examination, "what was in the two Jukeboxes?" After squirming in his seat and hesitating, he said, "Nothing." This was the same Broward Officer who smashed into my car with his SUV and falsely charged Robert with Resisting an officer without violence on August 17, 2016. I had filed a formal complaint against this Broward Officer to his Supervisor, Sergeant XXXXXXX and to the Investigator, Detective XXXXXX of Internal Affairs. I called and spoke with his Sergeant, XXXXXX and Internal Affairs Investigator, Detective XXXXXX and told them what Detective XXXXXX had said about the Broward Officer telling him the story under oath of Robert delivering two Jukeboxes to a family in Ft. Lauderdale in 2016. They both confirmed, after

speaking with the Broward Officer that he stated, "I never told Detective XXXXXX that Robert delivered two Jukeboxes to a family in 2016." Both Sergeant XXXXXX and Detective XXXXXX stated, "As proof of this, it was not on Officer XXXXXX's police report." This police report was submitted as evidence to the U.S. Dept. of Justice to Attorney General Jeff Sessions.

5   Detective XXXXXX made up this bogus story to support Prosecutor XXXXXX's false arrest charges on Robert that were made on August 16, 2016, where he, too, falsely charged Robert with delivering two jukeboxes to a family in Mt. Dora in 2011 or 2012. The Prosecutor wasn't even sure which year his bogus story of the two jukeboxes was in. Prosecutor XXXXXX, not Detective XXXXXX had more to gain by lying under oath about this made-up story of the two jukeboxes. Without any question, this proves collusion and conspiracy between the Prosecutor XXXXXX and Detective XXXXXX. Nevertheless, these false statements sworn under oath by Detective XXXXXX caused Judge XXXXXX to rule against reactivating Robert's $25,000 bond.   Detective XXXXXX lying under oath caused Robert to lose his $25,000 Bond.

6   Captain XXXXXX who unlawfully entered our home on October 5, 2015, without a search warrant and made an unlawful command to my son by threatening to kick my son's locked bedroom closet door off its hinges if he didn't give him the key to his locked bedroom closet, should be investigated for his unlawful conduct. His unlawful command is recorded on the live video, which was sent to your office with my March 5, 2018, criminal complaint.

7   Prosecutor, XXXXXX, committed multiple acts of prosecutorial misconduct against Robert which includes his filing of false arrest charges, lying in a court of law, conspiring with the deputies against my son's motions, and presenting false, damning, and vindictive statements in a court of law and to the news media. Robert's Attorneys are witness to all the above.

8   The Lake County State Attorney XXXXXX and the Lake County Sheriff XXXXXX were informed of the deputies' violations, the Judge's bias, and the detention center's refusal to give my son his urgently needed medical care. Both ignored taking any action of their violations. This left the Judge, Prosecutor, Deputies, and the Detention Center with a free reign to make even more ongoing violations against my son's civil, constitutional and prisoner's rights. I've outlined these violations with exhibits sent to the U.S. Dept. of Justice, to Attorney General, Jeff Sessions, with a copy of an updated correspondence faxed to your office on March 5, 2018.

Wanting justice for my son is what prompted me to write to our President, Donald J. Trump, who reviewed this complaint and is forwarding it over to a federal agency for further action. Attorney General, Jeff Sessions also reviewed this complaint. Thank God, both are taking Federal action!!! I want the FBI to investigate this criminal complaint as well. This has to be a unified and joint effort to seek justice for my son who has suffered unmercifully under the corrupt Lake County Judicial System in Tavares, Florida by these government employees. **<u>Such egregious corruption pollutes our Justice System to its very core</u>**.

Your prompt investigation of this criminal complaint is urgently needed for my son to see justice before anything further happens to him. In one of our monitored phone calls, at the end of January 2018, my son said, "Mom, they are slowing murdering me." This call can be verified through the monitored jail calls at the Lake County Detention Center.

One witness to my son's suffering was my maid's son, who gave me a notarized statement. Her son's cell was next to my son's cell during the 2 weeks, he was incarcerated for a traffic violation; he heard my son crying at night with pain and suffering while being denied medical treatment by the Lake County Detention Center.

He states: "I hear Robert cry at night with pain. They refuse to give him any medicine for the pain from his cancer. Robert looks sickly and is very skinny. His hair has turned all white. I feel very sorry for him they are killing him. He has cancer and is very ill. He is dying, and they are doing nothing to help him. He asks for medicine, and they refuse to give him medicine. That place is horrible! Robert is a kind person and asked me when I left to give my mattress to one of his cellmates that sleeps above him on just an iron mattress. Even though Robert is very ill, he still thinks about helping others. He is a very kind and a very good person."

My maid showed her son a picture of my son before he was incarcerated and asked him, "is this Robert?" He said, "Yes, but he looks really bad now, skinny, and sickly; his hair is all white."

Another cellmate, XXXXXX spoke to me during one of Robert's calls to me. He said, "Your son Robert is very ill, and the detention center refuses to give him any medical treatment for his colon cancer. He is in a lot of pain."

Another cellmate, a homeless man, brought Robert a peanut butter sandwich because he was too sick to raise his head off the mattress to eat. My son told me about this heart rendering event. He said, "mom, here is this man who is homeless and was brought in for panhandling, helping me because I was too sick even to raise my head off the bed to eat. He hand fed me his peanut butter sandwich. Here, I had an affluent life, and this man sleeps under bridges and gives me his peanut butter sandwich. His deed got to my heart." I said, "Robert God is watching over you. He will exonerate you and see you through all these bogus charges." This monitored call from the detention center can be verified as well as all the other conversations I've had with my son to date, which I outlined in this complaint.

On or about January 28th, 2018, Robert was given his first medical treatment from the Lake County Detention Center since his incarceration on August 25, 2016. He received five (5) radiation treatments which he says caused him to lose control of his bowels 24/7 and was going every five minutes while suffering from the painful after-effects of the radiation treatments. The detention center never once gave Robert any follow-up care from a doctor since his five (5) radiation treatments on January 28, 2018 to the date of this letter April 24, 2018.

Since his five (5) radiation treatments, the detention center placed Robert in lockdown 24/7 with a cellmate who has a severe mental disorder. Robert was only allowed out of his cell three (3) hours a week to bathe, phone me and walk around. He is coping with the painful, life-threatening illness of stage three or four malignant colon cancer and has had no follow up medical treatment from a doctor since his five radiation treatments. This inhuman treatment is in violation of Robert's civil, constitutional and prisoner's rights.

Robert was forced to plead no contest just to avoid a trial that would have been filled with continued conspiracy bias, lies, and corruption from Judge XXXXXX, Prosecutor XXXXXX, Deputy XXXXXX, Corporal XXXXXX, Deputy XXXXXX, Detective XXXXXX, and Captain XXXXXX.

Time is of the essence for your criminal investigation to commence to save my son from being slowly murdered by these corrupt Lake County officials, who are under your jurisdiction.

Thank God, the criminal complaint I submitted to President Donald J. Trump and Attorney General Jeff Sessions have been acknowledged in writing. President Trump is turning this over to the appropriate federal agency for further action. The U.S. Department of Justice is now reviewing this criminal complaint. I'm requesting FBI to conduct a timely investigation as well. Every American citizen wants our Government to uphold our democratic and human rights as well as our U.S. civil, constitutional and prisoner's rights!

Respectfully submitted,

VIRGINIA O'HARE

APPENDIX - B

APPELLATE COURT
FILINGS
DISTRICT COURT OF
APPEAL
OF FLORIDA
FIFTH DISTRICT

APPELLATE BRIEF

IN THE DISTRICT COURT OF APPEAL OF FLORIDA
FIFTH DISTRICT

CASE NO.: XXXXXX

LOWER TRIBUNAL NO.: XXXXXX

ROBERT O'HARE.

Appellant,

v.

STATE OF FLORIDA,

Appellee.

On Appeal From the Circuit Court

of the Fifth Judicial Circuit

In and For Lake County

Reply Brief of Appellant

TABLE OF CONTENTS

TABLE OF CITATIONS

CASES

PRELIMINARY STATEMENT

Appellant, Robert O'Hare, was the Defendant in the trial proceedings and will hereinafter be referred to as "Appellant." The State of Florida was the prosecuting authority in the trial court and will hereinafter be referred to as the "State."

This is an appeal from the judgment and sentence issued by the Circuit Court of the Fifth Judicial Circuit in and for Lake County as well as from that Court's order in the above-styled case denying Appellant's Motion to Suppress.

The record in this case was transcribed in one volume. References to the record will be denoted by "R." followed by the appropriate page of the record. Additionally, the record includes a media exhibit entered into evidence during the hearing on the Motion to Suppress. The exhibit is an audio recording of the entry into the home from an officer-worn recording device entered as Defense Exhibit 4. References to this audio recording will be denoted "AR." followed by the appropriate time stamp.

References to Appellee's Answer Brief will be denoted by "A.B." followed by the appropriate page number. References to Appellant's Initial Brief will be denoted "I.B." followed by the appropriate page number.

ARGUMENT IN RESPONSE

I. THE FLORIDA SUPREME COURT'S RULING IN <u>RODRIGUEZ V. STATE</u>, 187 So.3d 841 (FLA.2015) IS CONTROLLING IN THIS CASE.

In its answer brief, Appellee repeatedly asserts that <u>Rodriguez v. State</u>, 187 So.3d 841 (Fla.2015) stands for the proposition that the inevitable discovery doctrine will apply, even in the context of a warrantless search of a home, as long as there was an investigation underway prior to any police misconduct. Thus, Appellee attempts, as did the lower court, to distinguish <u>Rodriguez</u> and argue that the facts of the current case are more akin to those in <u>Fitzpatrick v. State</u>, 900 So.2d 495 (Fla.2005). This misconstrues the Court's plain ruling, which it states numerous times throughout its opinion in <u>Rodriguez</u>; namely, that the inevitable discovery doctrine is inapplicable, and the exclusionary rule will apply, in cases where law enforcement conducts a warrantless search of a home, even while clearly possessing probable cause, when the police were not at least in the process of securing a search warrant. <u>Rodriguez v. State</u>, 187 So.3d 841 (Fla.2015).

In fact, the Court itself spelled out in no uncertain terms exactly what question was before it and what its holding was:

> "The question before this Court is whether the inevitable discovery rule requires the prosecution to demonstrate that the police were in the process of obtaining a warrant prior to the misconduct or whether the prosecution need only establish that a warrant could have been obtained with information available prior to the misconduct. We conclude that permitting warrantless searches without the prosecution demonstrating that the police were in pursuit of a warrant is not a proper application of the inevitable discovery rule."
>
> <u>Rodriguez</u> at 849.

Appellee's citations to the Court's discussion of cases such as <u>Fitzpatrick v. State</u>, 900 So.2d 495 (Fla.2005) and <u>Nix v. Williams</u>, 467 U.S. 431 (1984) concerning the importance of a preceding investigation to the application of the inevitable discovery doctrine is misleading for four reasons. First, **all** such references occur during the part of the opinion wherein the Court is summarizing the evolution of the law in this area. It should be noted that **no** such discussion is found after the Court's clear holding, quoted above.

Second, Appellee omits any mention of the majority of the Court's analysis wherein it discusses numerous opinions, both state and federal, requiring that law enforcement be in pursuit of a warrant for inevitable discovery to apply. <u>Rodriguez v. State</u>, 187 So.3d 841, 846-848 (Fla.2015). Again, it is worth noting that this discussion occurs immediately after the Court's recitation of the holdings in <u>Fitzpatrick v. State</u>, 900 So.2d 495 (Fla.2005) and <u>Nix v. Williams</u>, 467 U.S. 431 (1984).

For example, the Court began this discussion with Judge Hawkes dissent in <u>McDonnell v. State</u>, 981 So.2d 585 (Fla. 1st DCA 2008), noting that "Judge Hawkes would have ruled that probable cause is not sufficient when there has been no attempt to obtain a warrant prior to contact with the Defendant." <u>Rodriguez v. State</u>, 187 So.3d 841, 846 (Fla.2015) (*citing* <u>McDonnell</u>, 981 So.2d at 594 (Hawkes, J., dissenting). The Court then went on to cite both <u>Rowell v. State</u>, 83 So.3d 990, 993 (Fla. 4th DCA 2012) and <u>King v. State</u>, 79 So.3d 236, 238 (Fla. 1st DCA 2012), in which both courts agreed with Judge Hawke's logic and held that inevitable discovery requires that officers be in the process of obtaining a warrant at the time of the misconduct.

The Court then went on to cite numerous federal cases also requiring a requirement that police be pursing a warrant at the time of misconduct in order for inevitable discovery to apply. *See* <u>Rodriquez</u> at 847-848 (*citing* <u>United States v. Quinney</u>, 583 F.3d 891, 894 (6th Cir.2009); <u>United States v. Virden</u>, 488 F.3d, 1317, 1322 (11th Cir.2007); <u>United States v. Mejia</u>, 69 F.3d 309, 320 (9th Cir.1995); <u>United States v. Echegoyen</u>, 799 F.2d 1271, 1280 n. 7 (9th Cir.1986); <u>United States v. Silvestri</u>, 787 F.2d 736, 746 (1st Cir.1986); and <u>United States v. Cherry</u>, 759 F.2d 1196 (5th Cir.1985)).

Third, the Court specifically distinguished both <u>Fitzpatrick</u> and <u>Moody</u>, on the ground that they did not involve warrantless searches of the home, as was the case in <u>Rodriguez</u>, and as is the case in this appeal. The Court held,

> "Furthermore, neither *Moody* nor *Fitzpatrick* involves warrantless searches of home, as seen here. As recently affirmed by the United States Supreme Court, "when it comes to the Fourth Amendment, the home is first among equals. At the Amendment's 'very core' stands 'the right of a man to retreat into his own home and there be free from unreasonable government intrusion.' " *Florida v. Jardines*, —-U.S.—-, 133 S.Ct 1409, 1414, 185 L.Ed.2d 495 (2013) (quoting *Silverman v. United States*, 365 U.S. 505, 81 S.Ct. 69, 5 L.Ed.2d 734 (1961)). As such, we must hold firm the protections of the Fourth Amendment and find the actions here unreasonable."

<u>Rodriguez</u> at 848.

Fourth, the Appellee ignores the Court's treatment of the First District Court of Appeal's decision in <u>McDonnell v. State</u>, 981 So.2d 585 (Fla. 1st DCA 2012), **in which both courts agreed with Judge Hawkes and held that inevitable discovery requires that officers be in the process of obtaining a warrant at the time of the mis-**

conduct, and the Third District Court of Appeal's decision in <u>Rodriguez v. State</u>, 129 So.3d 1135 (Fla. 1st DCA 2013) (*decision quashed by* <u>Rodriguez v. State</u>, 187 So.3d 841 (Fla. 2015)) in light of the contents of those lower appellate court opinions. A reading of the <u>McDonnell</u> opinion reveals that in that case there was an investigation ***prior*** to the officers' warrantless entry. <u>McDonnell v. State</u>, 981 So.2d 585, 587-588 (Fla. 1st DCA 2008). Thus, <u>McDonnell</u> puts forth the very situation the Appellee urges that the Court held in <u>Rodriguez</u> would allow for inevitable discovery to apply; specifically, in situations where there was an active investigation prior to a warrantless entry where no warrant was sought prior to the misconduct. However, the Court declined to follow <u>McDonnell</u> in <u>Rodriguez</u>.

In <u>Rodriguez v. State</u>, 129 So.3d 1135 (Fla. 1st DCA 2013), the decision on appeal and quashed by the Florida Supreme Court in <u>Rodriguez v. State</u>, 187 So.3d 841 (Fla. 2015), the First District Court of Appeal commented that "the case must be in such a posture that the facts already in possession of the police would have led to this evidence notwithstanding the police misconduct. *Fitzpatrick v.*

State, 900 So.2d 495, 515 (Fla.2005). The Supreme Court of Florida has not imposed a more specific requirement that law enforcement must also be in the process of applying for a warrant in such a case." <u>Rodriguez v. State</u>, 129 So.3d 1135 (Fla. 1st DCA 2013) (*decision quashed by* <u>Rodriguez v. State</u>, 187 So.3d 841 (Fla. 2015)). Given that this was the posture in which the Florida Supreme Court addressed and quashed that decision, it can scarcely be argued that the Court has not now imposed that very requirement.

II. NOTHING IN <u>RODRIGUEZ V. STATE</u>, 187 SO.3D 841 (FLA.2015) CHANGED THE LAW REGARDING THE ILLEGALITY OF THE INITIAL ENTRY, SO THE EXCLUSIONARY RULE SHOULD APPLY.

Appellee also argues that because the Florida Supreme Court did not issue its ruling in <u>Rodriquez</u> until after the illegal entry and search in this case that "[l]aw enforcement cannot be said to have ignored long standing (sic) precedent in this case," and application of the exclusionary rule would serve no purpose. (A.B. 9). However, nothing in <u>Rodriguez</u> modified the long-standing constitutional prohibition against law enforcement entering a person's home without either a warrant or exigent circumstances. *See* <u>Payton v. New York</u>, 445 U.S. 573 (1980); <u>Saavedra v. State</u>, 622 So.2d 952 (Fla.1993). It is worth noting that the lower court held, and Appellee does not contest, that law enforcement violated this prohibition, which has been well-settled law now for 38 years. (A.B. 6, FN1); (R. 281-283). It is the disregard for such well-established law, untouched by the Court's decision in <u>Rodriquez</u>, that compels exclusion. Application of the exclusionary rule is particularly necessary in this case for the same reasons the Florida Supreme Court felt that is was in <u>Rodriguez</u>:

> "Further, this case involves the sanctity of the home – a bedrock of the Fourth Amendment and an area where a person should enjoy the highest reasonable expectation of privacy. The constitutional guarantee to freedom from warrantless searches is not an inconvenience to be dismissed in favor of claims for police and prosecutorial efficiency. While it is true that here police were already in possession of the information leading to the evidence before the misconduct, they failed to pursue a legal means to attain this evidence."

<u>Rodriguez</u> at 849.

<u>Rodriguez</u> addressed only the application of a savings doctrine to the exclusionary rule, and not to any law defining the legal bounds of police conduct and simply did not involve the type of legal change that would warrant application of the good faith doctrine, such as was the case in <u>Davis v. United States</u>, 564 U.S 229 (2011) (addressing law enforcement's good faith reliance on <u>Belton</u> in cases "in the pipeline" when <u>Gant</u> was decided). Rather, unlike that situation, where law enforcement was **relying** on search and seizure law that had been well-settled for over 30 years, in the present case, law enforcement **violated** search and seizure law that has been well-settled for over 30 years. *See* <u>Payton v. New York</u>, 445 U.S. 573 (1980).

CONCLUSION

If there were any debate about the Florida Supreme Court's holding in <u>Rodriguez v. State</u>, 187 So.3d 841 (Fla.2015), the application of that holding to the present case, or to the necessity of applying exclusionary rule upon such facts, it was laid to rest in the penultimate paragraph of the majority's opinion in that case:

> "Because the exclusionary rule works to deter police misconduct by ensuring that the prosecution is not in a better position as a result of the misconduct, the rule cannot be expanded to allow application where there is only probable cause and no pursuit of a warrant. If the prosecution were allowed to benefit in this way, police misconduct would be encouraged instead of deterred, and the rationale behind the exclusionary rule would be eviscerated. Where the prosecution has made no showing that a search warrant was being actively pursued prior to the occurrence of the illegal conduct, application of the inevitable discovery rule would effectively nullify the requirement of a search warrant under the Fourth Amendment. [...] Accordingly, the officers' failure to seek a search warrant precludes the application of the inevitable discovery doctrine in this case."

> <u>Rodriguez</u> at 849-850.

Based on the above-cited authorities and reasoning, the Appellant respectfully requests this Court reverse his judgment of conviction and sentence and remand this cause to the lower court with instructions to grant the Appellant's Motion to Suppress.

APPELLATE COURT ORDER

IN THE DISTRICT COURT OF APPEAL
OF THE STATE OF FLORIDA
FIFTH DISTRICT

ROBERT O'HARE,

        Appellant,

v.   CASE NO. XXXX-XXXX

STATE OF FLORIDA,

        Appellee.

DATE: November 20, 2018

BY ORDER OF THE COURT:

        ORDERED that the parties are given fifteen days from the date of this order to file supplemental briefs on the issue of whether the independent source doctrine provides an alternative basis to affirm the order on appeal under the "Tipsy Coachman" doctrine. A party's supplemental brief shall not exceed twenty pages.

Panel: Judges XXXXXX, XXXXXX, and XXXXXX

cc:

Office of Attorney General   XXXXXX   XXXXXX

SUPPLEMENTAL
BRIEF

IN THE DISTRICT COURT OF APPEAL OF FLORIDA
FIFTH DISTRICT

CASE NO.: XXXXXX

LOWER TRIBUNAL NO.: XXXXXX

ROBERT O'HARE.

Appellant,

v.

STATE OF FLORIDA,

Appellee.

On Appeal From the Circuit Court
of the Fifth Judicial Circuit
In and For Lake County

Supplemental Brief of Appellant

TABLE OF CONTENTS

TABLE OF CITATIONS

PRELIMINARY STATEMENT

Appellant, Robert O'Hare, was the Defendant in the trial court proceedings and will hereinafter be referred to as "Appellant." The State of Florida was the prosecuting authority in the trial court and will hereinafter be referred to as the "State."

The record in this case was transcribed in one volume. References to the record will be denoted by "R." followed by the appropriate page of the record. Additionally, the record includes a media exhibit entered into evidence during the hearing on the motion to suppress. The exhibit is an audio recording of the entry into the home from an officer-worn recording device entered as Defense Exhibit 4. References to this audio recording will be denoted "AR." followed by the appropriate time stamp. This is a Supplemental Brief filed pursuant to an Order of this Court dated November 20, 2018 requesting the Parties submit briefs on the issue of whether the independent source doctrine provides grounds to affirm the lower court's ruling under the "Tipsy Coachman" doctrine.

ARGUMENT

In order for the independent source doctrine to apply, the State has to show that the illegally-obtained evidence was also obtained by "means wholly independent of any constitutional violation." Jackson v. State, 1 So.3d 273 (Fla. 1st DCA 2009) (quoting Nix v. Williams, 467 U.S. 431 (1984)). The evidence must also be discovered independent of the illegal activity through lawful investigation that is "untainted by the initial illegality." Id. (quoting Murray v. U.S., 487 U.S. 533 (1988)). A search warrant is not a genuinely independent source if (1) law enforcement's decision to seek the warrant was prompted by observations made during an illegal search or (2) if information obtained during an illegal search was presented to the judge that issued the warrant and affected his decision to do so. Murray v. U.S., 487 U.S. 533 (1988).

The record in the current case, however, reveals ample evidence that law enforcement's decision to obtain the search warrant was prompted by observations they made during the illegal protective sweep. Law enforcement did not know they would find digital devices containing child pornography at Appellant's residence until after finding the Toshiba laptop during the illegal search. This is because the only device that law enforcement had ever purported connected John@Ares, JOHN-SMITH-PC, the illicit internet activity through the IP address at One Flight Up, and Appellant was that Toshiba. They had observed Appellant using that device at One Flight Up on prior occasions while illicit files were being accessed at that location. (R.213-217).

On the date of the illegal search, however, when law enforcement responded to One Flight Up after receiving notice that illicit online activity was again occurring, that activity had already ceased, and all they saw Appellant with was a black "computer type bag." (R.217). They did not see the actual Toshiba laptop, which was the key to their investigation. If they executed a search warrant on the house at a time when that specific Toshiba laptop was not present – the only device they had any indication might contain evidence of child pornography – their entire investigation would have been undone.

Law enforcement needed to confirm that the Toshiba was in the residence before executing a search warrant, or risk the entire investigation. As such, no search warrant was applied for until the detectives confirmed the Toshiba was in the residence during their purported protective sweep. The Court need look no further for evidence that this was not only the reason for the illegal search, but why application for the warrant was delayed until law enforcement had confirmed the Toshiba was in the residence, than Corporal Harmon's own statements, captured by his very own audio recorder.

During the illegal search – when detectives purport to have been sweeping only for the presence of other persons in the residence – Corporal Harmon asks if they had "found the laptop bag." (A.R. 11:32-11:35). His audio recorder also captures him asking a fellow officer involved in the search, "is this the Toshiba?". (A.R. 11:42-11:43). After this, he is recorded stating, "yup, that's it; that's the one right there." (A.R. 11:44-11:46). The recording then captures a conversation between Corporal Harmon and the other law enforcement officer about whether Appellant would have had time to remove the laptop from the case they had seen him enter with and plug it in before they entered. (A.R. 11:47-11:52).

The last exchange is particularly important to whether detectives entered the house for the purpose of confirming that the Toshiba was there as a precondition to seeking a warrant. Corporal Harmon's question indicates that he was trying to determine whether it was possible that the Toshiba was actually in the bag Appellant was seen with at One Flight Up earlier that day. It demonstrates that law enforcement did not know, prior to the illegal search, that Appellant had the Toshiba that day at One Flight Up, and that they would "find it" at his house on that particular day. Only after this confirmation was the application made for the search warrant.

Additionally, the record reflects that observations from the illegal entry and search were included in the affidavit for search warrant. Detective Hart testified at the suppression hearing that he included information about Appellant's resistance following law enforcement's illegal entry into his home in the application for the search warrant. (R.455) (R.457) (R.218). Thus, the record clearly contains evidence regarding both prongs of the Murray test, demonstrating that the search warrant was not truly independent of the initial illegal search.

However, this Court conducting an independent source analysis is preconditioned on the applicability of the "tipsy coachman" doctrine in this case.

While the "tipsy coachman" doctrine permits an appellate court to affirm a trial court that "reaches the right result, but for the wrong reasons" so long as "there is any basis which would support the judgment in the record[,]" "[t]he key to the application of this doctrine of appellate efficiency is that there must have been support for the alternative theory or principle of law in the record before the trial court." Robertson v. State, 829 So.2d 901 (Fla.2002) (quoting Dade County School Bd. v. Radio Station WQBA, 731 So.2d 638 (Fla.1999)).

Even where a record does exist, the "tipsy coachman" doctrine is inapplicable when factual determinations necessary for application of the alternative theory were not made by the trial court. State v. Gerry, 855 So.2d 157, FN5 (Fla. 5th DCA 2003);

Powell v. State, 120 So.3d 577 (Fla. 1st DCA 2013); Harris v. State, 238 So.3d 396 (Fla. 3d DCA 2018); Bueno v. Workman, 20 So.3d 993 (Fla. 4th DCA 2009). This is particularly true when the record reveals conflicting evidence regarding the un-resolved factual issue. Mohan v. Orlando Health, Inc., 163 So.3d 1231 (Fla. 5th DCA 2015); Tarver v. State, 961 So.2d 1094 (Fla. 2d DCA 2007).

As discussed above, the record in this case clearly contains evidence that (1) law enforcement's observations during the il-legal search prompted them to seek the subsequent warrant, and (2) the observations made during that search (namely Ap-pellant's resistance) were included in the application for that search warrant. What the record does not contain are factual findings from the lower court as to whether the officers' obser-vations actually did contribute to prompting them to seek the subsequent warrant or as to whether the impermissibly ob-tained information included in the affidavit for search warrant contributed to the issuing judge's decision. Both findings are necessary to establish the applicability of the independent source doctrine in this case. As such, application of the "tipsy coachman" doctrine on this record is not proper. State v. Gerry, 855 So.2d 157, FN5 (Fla. 5th DCA 2003); Powell v. State, 120 So.3d 577 (Fla. 1st DCA 2013); Harris v. State, 238 So.3d 396 (Fla. 3d DCA 2018); Bueno v. Workman, 20 So.3d 993 (Fla. 4th DCA 2009); Mohan v. Orlando Health, Inc., 163 So.3d 1231 (Fla. 5th DCA 2015); Tarver v. State, 961 So.2d 1094 (Fla. 2d DCA 2007).

Furthermore, this is not a case where remand for determination of such questions is appropriate, because, unlike in most cases where the doctrine has been applied, the alternative theory of independent source was actually presented to the lower court at the suppression hearing. (R.478-480). In fact, it was counsel for Appellant that raised the issue to apprise the lower court of it and to explain why it does not apply in this case. Here, the record does not conclusively establish the warrant was an independent source, findings necessary to the application of said doctrine were not made by the lower court, and the lower court was fully apprised of the issue and its inapplicability on these facts at the suppression hearing. Certainly, if the lower court did not make a finding that the independent source doctrine applied, even after being apprised of its potential applicability by Appellant and hearing argument as to why it does not apply here, it would be reasonable to infer that he concluded it did not apply.

CONCLUSION

Based on the above-cited authorities and reasoning, the Appellant respectfully requests this Court reverse his judgment of conviction and sentence and remand this cause to the lower court with instructions to grant the Appellant's Motion to Suppress.

APPENDIX - C

JUDICIAL COMPLAINT
TO THE
STATE OF FLORIDA
JUDICIAL
QUALIFICATIONS
COMMISSION

November 1, 2018

State of Florida
Judicial Qualifications Commission
Post Office Box 14106
Tallahassee, Florida 32317

Re: Judicial Misconduct of Judge XXXXXX

<u>Please investigate the judicial misconduct of Judge XXXXXX, which is detailed herein:</u>

Judge XXXXXX showed egregious judicial misconduct and bias during all of my son's, (Robert A. O'Hare) hearings. He was denied his lawful motions which were made according to State, Federal, and Supreme Court Precedence. A formal criminal complaint was submitted against Lake County Judge XXXXXX, the Lake County Sheriff's Department, and the Lake County Detention Center, to President Donald J. Trump, Attorney General, Jeff Sessions, the FBI, and to Florida State Attorney XXXXXX.

EXHIBIT A - Attached are pages from my manuscript titled: *"Virginia O'Hare Documents God's Laws vs. Man's Laws"* containing letters to the Federal Government and their response. These letters outline the egregious acts and violations committed by these government employees.

Judge XXXXXX was viewed by all of my son's attorneys as being biased, and not following the law. All the court room electronic transcriptions of my son's hearings and proceedings with Judge XXXXXX will attest to his bias, collusion, and conspiracy with the Prosecutor XXXXXX, the Lake County Sheriff's Deputies, Corporal XXXXXX , Deputy XXXXXX , Master Deputy XXXXXX, Deputy XXXXXX, Captain XXXXXX, and Detective XXXXXX. The corruption, criminal violations, bias, collusion, conspiracy, and politics in this case are being published world-wide.

Your immediate investigation is hereby requested as my son's life depends upon receiving justice and enforcing his U. S. Civil and Constitutional rights. <u>Today is my son's 57th birthday. This formal judicial misconduct complaint is my birthday gift to him to expose the corruption that was unjustly poured upon him.</u>

Due to Judge XXXXXX's extreme bias, our motion to remove him and the entire judicial system from my son's case was granted. A guard who was in Judge XXXXXX's chambers, said that he and Prosecutor XXXXXX discuss cases before the trial and the Judge makes his decision before trying the case. He said Judge XXXXXX always rules on the side of the Prosecutor and the Sheriff's Deputies and not for the Defendants. The Defendants just don't have a chance.

My son witnessed this travesty of justice first hand and that's why I am making this complaint.

The Prosecutor made another malicious charge against my son. The State accused my chronically ill son of asking me, his 81-year-old mother to give a piece of paper to a friend, asking him to kill Judge XXXXXX. In the name of Jesus, **this never happened!** This friend, XXXXXX, refutes these allegations as well and states: "I was never solicited by either Virginia or Robert to kill the Judge. I haven't seen either one of them for several months. This is all bull shit. The Sheriff's Office put my name all over the news that I was a Rabbi hired to kill Judge XXXXXX. I am not a Rabbi and I wasn't hired to kill anyone. I've known Virginia and Robert for 35 years. They wouldn't hurt anyone. When Deputy XXXXXX came to my home, I told him that he is not going to do to me what you did to Robert O'Hare. What time I have left, you are not going to take it from me." XXXXXX is a 75 years old gentleman, has had skin cancer, is blind in one eye and the other eye has cataracts. He is in fragile health and has a pacemaker. He does not need these erroneous allegations made up against him during these twilight moments of his life.

Deputy XXXXXX, who went to his residence, was the same one who unlawfully entered our home on October 5, 2015 and kicked my son 10-12 times as he laid defenseless and in a submissive and prone position on the floor. He is the State's star witness against my son in this case.

I'm 81 years of age, I'll be 82 on November 13, 2018, a Christian woman who has dedicated her entire life to God, and raising three wonderful children. My husband of 45 years and two daughters have gone home to be with the Lord a few years ago. My only living heir is my son, Robert, who is being murdered, physically, emotionally, and mentally by the corrupt Lake County Judicial System and the Lake County Detention Center. He is being denied his civil, constitutional and prisoner's rights and needs medical treatment for his malignant colon cancer, surgery and hospitalization to save his life. <u>Judge XXXXXX denied all his motions for medical treatment of his cancer.</u>

It's a known fact that being diagnosed with cancer, which Robert was on September 5, 2017, affects ones' emotional health, causes feelings of depression, anxiety and fear. These are the most common and normal responses to this life-changing disease. On top of all this, Robert, has to deal with the overwhelming bias from Judge XXXXXX, corruption and conspiracy by the Sheriff's Deputies, and false charges and prosecutorial misconduct by Prosecutor XXXXXX.

In addition, he was denied urgently needed medical treatment and care for his malignant cancer for the first 18 months of his incarceration by the Lake County Detention Center. Their inaction forced him to go through unbearable pain and suffering, which I outlined in my letters to the Federal Government. This is not only against God's laws, man's laws, and our U.S. Constitutional rights, but denying medical treatment to anyone in my son's critical medical condition is 100% inhumane.

Judge XXXXXX, Prosecutor XXXXXX, and the Sheriff's Deputies are all guilty of violating my son's civil and constitutional rights. They work under the direct supervision of State Attorney XXXXXX, who I have made aware of all these violations. To date, I have not received a response letter from State Attorney XXXXXX, but I have from the President of the United States, the U.S. Attorney General and the U.S. Dept. of Justice. I am hopeful that I will from the Commissioner on this Judicial Misconduct Complaint as well.

On August 17, 2016, the Prosecutor, XXXXXX made a false charge against my son, accusing him of delivering two jukeboxes in 2011 or 2012, for the purpose of spying. The prosecutor explains his theory to the press, "I <u>assume</u> O'Hare delivered two juke boxes in either 2011 or 2012, to the wrong neighbor thinking the wrong neighbor would deliver the two juke-boxes to the correct neighbor, for the purpose of spying. I'm not sure which year this was in." His statement went viral all over the news media and the internet.

Several months later, during a hearing to reinstate my son's bond, the prosecutor, XXXXXX, conspired with Lake County Detective, XXXXXX, to falsely testify under oath that he was told by Broward County Police Officer, XXXXXX, that my son delivered two "<u>empty</u>" juke boxes to a family in Ft. Lauderdale, Florida in 2016. This false and damning testimony, sworn to under oath, by Detective XXXXXX was to support the Prosecutor's false arrest charge against my son on August 17, 2016, which has kept him unjustly incarcerated to date.

During Detective XXXXXX's cross examination by Attorney XXXXXX, he literally squirmed in his chair, when asked what was in the two (toy) jukeboxes. He stammered, not knowing what to say, and blurted out, "Nothing." Detective XXXXXX's testimony was apparently coached and led by the Prosecutor XXXXXX. This outrageous story was to support the Prosecutor's false charges made months earlier against Robert of delivering two jukeboxes in 2011 or 2012. When Attorney XXXXXX informed me, "If you can prove Detective XXXXXX lied under oath about the two jukeboxes, this would be lethal against him."

I immediately filed an Internal Affairs complaint against Broward County Officer XXXXXX and was informed by Broward County Internal Affairs Investigator, XXXXXX that Officer XXXXXX <u>never</u> stated this jukebox story to Detective XXXXXX about my son. Officer XXXXXX's supervisor, Sergeant XXXXXX, confirmed this to me personally as well. He stated, "If this story were true, it would have to be put on the Police Report, and it wasn't. You have a copy of the Police Report, you can see for yourself there is no jukebox story on the Police Report. You can depose Officer XXXXXX yourself and he will tell you the same thing."

With all this evidence, I filed a formal complaint with the Lake County Internal Affairs Department against Detective XXXXXX for lying under oath. I presented proof from the Broward County Officer, his Supervisor, the Investigator of Broward County's Internal Affairs Department, and Officer XXXXXX's Police Report. Upon submitting all this evidence, the Lake County investigator found no fault in Detective XXXXXX's false sworn testimony at my son's Bond Hearing. The electronic court transcriptions of this Bond Hearing and all the Hearings my son had with Judge XXXXXX are available for your review.

As a result of Detective XXXXXX's false testimony, Judge XXXXXX denied reinstatement of my son's $25,000 bond, which Robert was legally entitled to. Judge XXXXXX further stated on his order, "From the witness testimony of the jukeboxes, Robert is a danger to the community of Mt. Dora." We lived for 17 years in that community with absolutely no problems whatsoever. We owned two homes, one in Mt. Dora and one in Ft. Lauderdale, where we lived for a total of over 40 years. During those 40 some years we lived in harmony with our family, friends and neighbors and never had any legal problems whatsoever.

Tragedy encompassed our lives on October 5, 2015, when my son was physically assaulted in our own Mt. Dora home by three Lake County Deputies, Corporal XXXXXX, Deputy XXXXXX, and Deputy XXXXXX. They unlawfully forced their way into our home, **without a search warrant, without probable cause, without consent, and without any exigent circumstances.**

They beat my son, blinded him in his left eye, kicked him, soccer ball style, in the stomach 10-12 times, which caused intestinal bleeding and difficulties in moving his bowels. After their assault, they falsely charged Robert with resisting an officer without violence. The Deputies made this false arrest charge against my son who I witnessed lying face down on the floor, in a submissive prone position while being unmercifully beaten to a pulp by these three Deputies. This horrible beating caused internal and external bleeding to his head, face and body. Proof of this assault and the Deputies' criminal violations are recorded on my cell phone video. I also took multiple pictures, and acquired several medical reports attesting to his severe injuries and his current physical disability.

The Sheriff's Deputies were looking for a laptop they allege had child porn on it. This used laptop was given to my son by XXXXXX, a friend from Ft. Lauderdale. My son was not aware that his friend's downloads were illegal. The Deputies never found any such pictures in Robert's bedroom other than one pencil drawing of Jesus on the Cross with the Face of God hovering over His Son. This picture

<u>is attached herein to this complaint</u>.

Judge XXXXXX denied all my son's motions that were in compliance to civil and Constitutional laws. One being to have urgently needed medical treatment for his stage 3 or 4 malignant colon cancer, with a 70% blockage to his colon. This condition developed after deputy XXXXXX repeatedly kicked Robert in his abdomen 10-12 times. This beating caused Robert to bleed internally with chronic bowel problems, which he still has to this day.

The Deputy's false allegations made during court hearings and Judge XXXXXX's biased rulings, kept Robert incarcerated for 18 months at the Lake County Detention Center without any medical treatment until he almost died in January 2018. In fact, the Lake County Detention Center asked Robert to sign a Waiver of Liability, in case he died. When he refused to sign, they gave him their one and only cancer treatment, 5 radiation treatments and left him to suffer in lock down with no follow up medical treatment or care from a doctor thereafter.

I have medical reports which confirms my son's blindness, and malignant colon cancer with a 70% blockage in his colon. The doctor stated on his report dated September 5, 2017, that this cancer was present in Robert's body for one year. This would be when my son was incarcerated on August 25, 2016. From the date of his incarceration until his first cancer treatment on January 20, 2018, the Lake County Detention Center allowed Robert to suffer with this life-threatening cancer in his body and refused to give him any medical care, treatment, surgery, or hospitalization that the doctor said was mandatory.

Due to Judge XXXXXX's extreme bias against my son, he ignored all the medical reports that Robert's three attorneys submitted to him for a medical furlough. Robert's motions were based solely on his Constitutional rights for urgently needed medical care and treatment.

Judge XXXXXX's bias for the Prosecutor, XXXXXX and the Deputies, were reflected in his unjust and unlawful rulings. This was so obvious to Robert's lawyers, they warned Robert and me of what they were dealing with. The court's electronic transcriptions of Judge XXXXXX's proceedings will attest to his bias and judicial misconduct.

Letters to President Donald J. Trump, the U.S. Department of Justice, the FBI, and their current investigation of these egregious acts against my son by Lake County Judge, XXXXXX, Prosecutor XXXXXX, the Lake County Deputies, and the Lake County Detention Center, were fully detailed and attached to those criminal complaints.

This complaint to you is specifically against the Judicial Misconduct of Judge XXXXXX. I can supply any further evidence you may need, including videos, pictures, depositions, and medical reports required for your investigation of Judge XXXXXX's major Judicial Misconduct.

The following evidence was presented to Judge XXXXXX during my son's Motion to Suppress:

A video showing Lake County Sheriff's Deputies presence in our home after their forceful warrantless entry and the aftermath of their brutal beating to Robert.

Captain XXXXXX's unlawful command and threat to Robert, in his beaten traumatic state: "If you don't tell us where the key to your bedroom closet is, I will have the deputy kick the door off its hinges."

Corporal XXXXXX's body worn camcorder video played at the Motion to Suppress Hearing, on which the voices of the Deputies could be heard while illegally confiscating the laptop computer from my son's locked bedroom closet. The Deputies mutually agreed to stage a crime scene of the encased laptop computer. Evidence shows the Deputies unzipped the laptop black case and placed the laptop computer on the floor with its case on the bed. Then called CSI to take pictures of their "staged" crime scene.

Deputy XXXXXX made a false police report of their entire unlawful entry, search and seizure, and their staged crime scene.

Attorney XXXXXX presented a motion on the Deputies' unlawful warrant that was issued by Master Deputy XXXXXX who had a Magistrate Judge sign the search warrant without disclosing mandatory documentation. Attorney XXXXXX, a forensic analyst was the expert witness who testified against the legitimacy of Detective XXXXXX's warrant. This Motion to Suppress was based 100% on the law. Judge XXXXXX denied Attorney XXXXXX's Motion to Suppress as soon as he finished his last sentence right there in his courtroom. The judge never investigated this evidence that was legally documented and required by law as outlined in Attorney XXXXXX's Motion to Suppress. Judge XXXXXX again allowed the Sheriff's Deputy non-compliance to the law be exempt.

The live cell phone video of the aftermath of the Deputies beating to Robert, causing blindness in his left eye and intestinal bleeding, which led to Robert's disability and his malignant colon cancer.

Summary:

During the Motion to Suppress, Judge XXXXXX viewed the camcorder video and heard the deputies talking on Corporal XXXXXX's body worn camcorder video of their finding the laptop in the locked bedroom closet at 11:37 am. Their warrant wasn't signed by a magistrate judge until 5:45 pm, several hours later.

Judge XXXXXX also listened to my 35-minute live video of the corruption and violations committed by the Deputies while they were unlawfully in our home. He saw pictures of my son's beaten bloody face after the Deputies assaulted him on his body and face, head, and eyes. Judge XXXXXX was also given multiple pictures of the Deputies assault on my son.

Prior to the Motion to Suppress proceedings, the live cell phone video was given to Prosecutor XXXXXX by Attorney XXXXXX to give to Judge XXXXXX, pre-hearing. The Prosecutor never showed this video to Judge XXXXXX pre-hearing or at the hearing.

Fortunately, Attorney XXXXXX suspecting the Prosecutor would do this, due to his prior dealings with him, brought an extra copy of the video to the Suppression Hearing and showed it to the Judge. A Mount Dora Real Estate Broker, and a family friend both stated that the judge came into the court room with his mind made up to deny my son's Motion to Suppress. When he viewed the video, they said his demeaner changed. I will send this video to you upon request.

Judge XXXXXX ignored all this evidence in support of Robert's Motion to Suppress, which was based 100% on the law. The Judge made an error on his order by adding a Doctrine of Inevitable Discovery that does not exist in the Florida Supreme Court ruling, Rodriguez vs. State of Florida.

His ruling of Inevitable Discovery violates Supreme Court Precedence and supports the criminal acts of the Deputies. The Lake County Judicial System corruption was so powerful, Robert's three competent lawyers could not penetrate the wall of conspiracy between the Judge, Prosecutor and Deputies. Their united pack was more powerful than the U.S. Constitution, the State and Federal laws and all the prima facie evidence put together and presented to Judge XXXXXX during all of my son's motions.

<u>Judge XXXXXX put his bias, politics, and conspiracy with the Prosecutor and Deputies above the law, which caused his unjust rulings and major Judicial Misconduct.</u>

Judge XXXXXX added this Doctrine of Inevitable Discovery <u>after</u> Attorney XXXXXX presented him with a copy of the Florida Supreme Court ruling, Rodriguez vs. State of Florida in black in white so he would not make a mistake in his ruling, which he did anyway. Attorney XXXXXX made a Motion for Reconsideration, for Judge XXXXXX to correct his error. He denied this motion without any legal explanation, because there was none!

During this hearing, the Prosecutor lied in front of Judge XXXXXX about this case law to protect the criminal acts of the Deputies. This caused Attorney XXXXXX to go over to the Prosecutor, XXXXXX, and say, in front of Judge XXXXXX, "If you lie to me one more time during court proceedings, I will go after your bar license."

All the prima facie evidence that was presented to Judge XXXXXX was ignored. His bias and politics, which was crystal clear to the lawyers, and everyone in his courtroom, took priority over justice for Robert. He ruled on the side of State Attorney, XXXXXX's office and not on the U.S. Constitution.

Just recently, a Marion County Judge, XXXXXX confirmed in an article recently published by the Ocala Post that "State Attorney XXXXXX wants me to rule in their Suppression Hearings for his office and not the Constitution of the United States of America." This is why my son, Robert, lost his Motion to Suppress. Judge XXXXXX honored the State Attorney's office and politics, and not the law. He is guilty of major Judicial Misconduct.

EXHIBIT B - Attached to this complaint is a copy

of Marion County Judge XXXXXX's statement to Ocala Post.

All three of my son's lawyers advised him against going to trial with Judge XXXXXX's bias, and the Prosecutor's conspiracy with the Deputies. They advised Robert to plead no contest and appeal Judge XXXXXX's misinterpretation of Florida Supreme Court case law, Rodriguez vs. State of Florida. Being true to his bias and judicial misconduct Judge XXXXXX gave my son a very harsh sentence of 20 years for his plea of no contest.

Judge XXXXXX egregiously denied all my son's motions, including his emergency motions for urgently needed medical treatment and care to save his life from stage 3-4 malignant colon cancer. His ruling was 100% inhumane and proves his bias and Judicial Misconduct in not following the law and the U.S. Constitution. His unjust rulings even violated my son's Prisoner's Right to urgently needed medical care and treatment.

Attorney XXXXXX's Appeal Answer Brief which is supported by the U.S. Constitution, Florida Supreme Court case law, Rodriguez vs. State of Florida, and 16 additional Court rulings, confirms that Judge XXXXXX's order was in error by adding a Doctrine of Inevitable Discovery that does not exist in the Florida Supreme Court case law. My son's civil and constitutional rights and justice were not honored by Judge XXXXXX's rulings due to his extreme bias and Judicial Misconduct against my son.

Robert's Lead Attorney XXXXXX said, "Virginia, I don't think Judge XXXXXX misinterpreted the law, I think it was intentional and due to politics. I will make a Motion to Recuse him and the entire Lake County Judicial System from Robert's case. I also think this latest charge against Robert is due to their fear that if Robert is free, they will all be exposed."

<u>EXHIBIT C</u> - Attached are pages from my manuscript with Attorney XXXXXX's Answer Brief for my son's De Nova Appeal. He clarifies my son's appeal is based on Florida Supreme Court case law, which Judge XXXXXX misinterpreted in his order to Robert's Motion to Suppress.

Due to Judge XXXXXX's Judicial Misconduct and the proven conspiracy with the Prosecutor and the Sheriff's Deputies, as recorded on all the courtroom electronic transcriptions, Robert's Attorneys made a Motion to Transfer Robert out of the Lake County Judicial System. On May 24, 2018, Robert was transferred to the Marion County Detention Center, and was recently placed in a medical pod as of one week ago. Robert is suffering with horrible symptoms from the malignant colon cancer.

There is no Judge in the world, except Judge XXXXXX, who would deny any human being urgently needed medical treatment for stage 3-4 malignant colon cancer. Especially one with a 70% blockage in their colon, and difficulty in eliminating their bowels.

<u>If all the above is not Judicial Misconduct by Judge XXXXXX, please tell me what is?</u>

My son said, "Mom, they are slowly murdering me." Whatever action or inaction is taken to this complaint will be placed in my book that will be read all over the world.

Respectfully Submitted:

____

Virginia O'Hare

APPENDIX - D

PHOTOGRAPHS

"The Scene of the Crime"

Our beautiful home in Mt. Dora, FL. For more than ten years, it represented a family refuge for peace and tranquility. That peace was forever **SHATTERED** on the morning of October 5, 2015 as three Lake County Sheriff's Deputies illegally forced their way through the front door, without a Warrant or any Exigent Circumstances, and proceeded to savagely beat Robert, causing his physical disability.

Just inside the front door of our Mt. Dora, FL home as it was moments before the Lake County Sherriff's Deputies pushed through the door after **Robert legally declined their request to search the house WITHOUT A SEARCH WARRANT!** This photo also clearly shows that with the shutters closed, as they were on October 5, 2015, no one, including the police, could see through the doors or windows to claim they had "Exigent Circumstances" to forcefully enter the home.

It was on this very floor, just a few feet from the door, that Robert was beaten, bloodied, and blinded by the three Deputies from the Lake County Sherriff's Department as he laid face down on the floor, in a submissive, prone position.

Robert's Bedroom – On the left side of the picture you can see the closet door that was locked when the Deputies unlawfully entered the house. They threatened to kick the door off its hinges if Robert did not give them the key. This is the room in which they staged the *"Crime* Scene" to make it appear as if the laptop was ***"in plain view."***

On the right side of the photo above you can see a framed picture hanging on the wall. The picture is a beautiful pencil sketch, "The Face of God." That is the only picture or photograph ***"in plain view"* when the Deputies entered Robert's bedroom.**

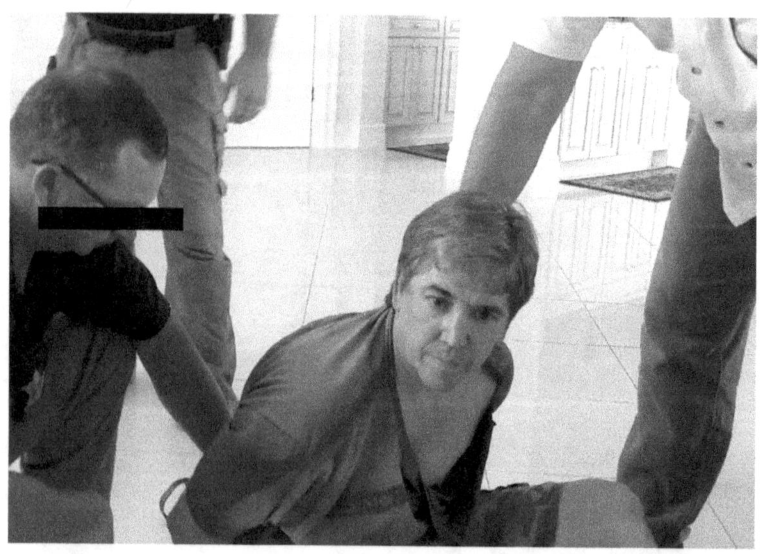

Above, Deputies swarm around Robert, already in handcuffs, as the punching and kicking stops and he is pulled into a sitting position, **the very moment I started to record their unlawful beating.**

Below, Robert, clearly frightened, tries to understand what is happening inside our home!

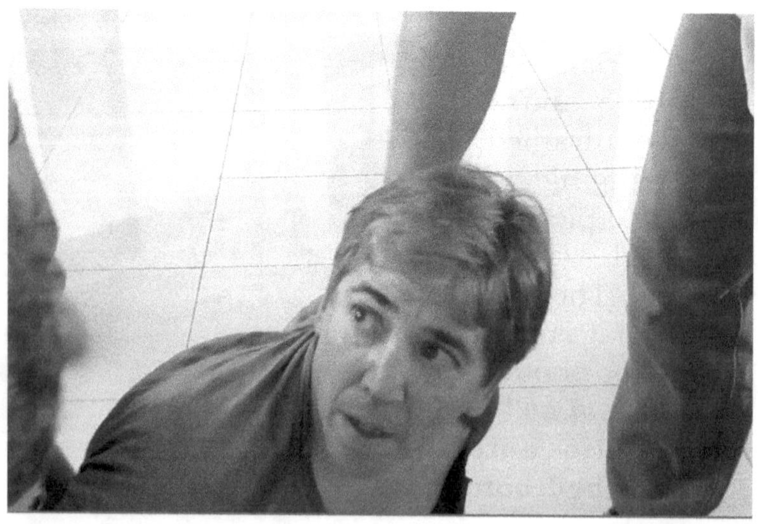

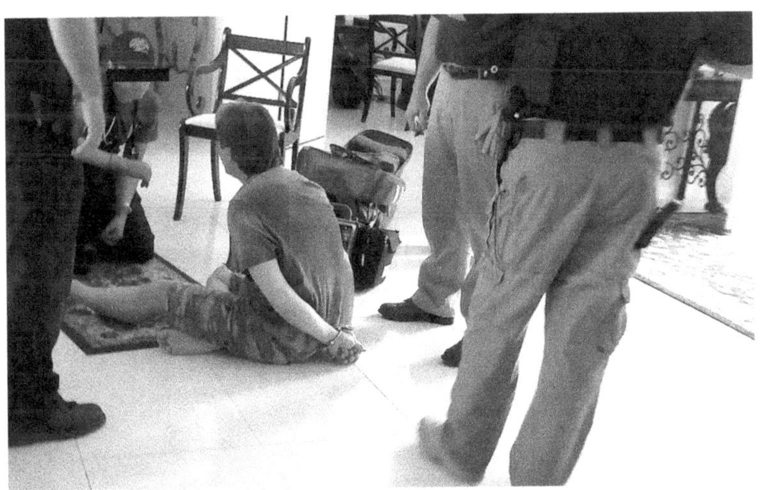

Above, Deputies continue to stand in a tight perimeter around Robert, even though he is sitting cross-legged, and handcuffed on the floor, receiving treatment from the EMTs for injuries caused by the Deputies beating.

Below, with his t-shirt ripped down the front, the cuts and bruises from the brutal assault by law enforcement officers, are very visible.

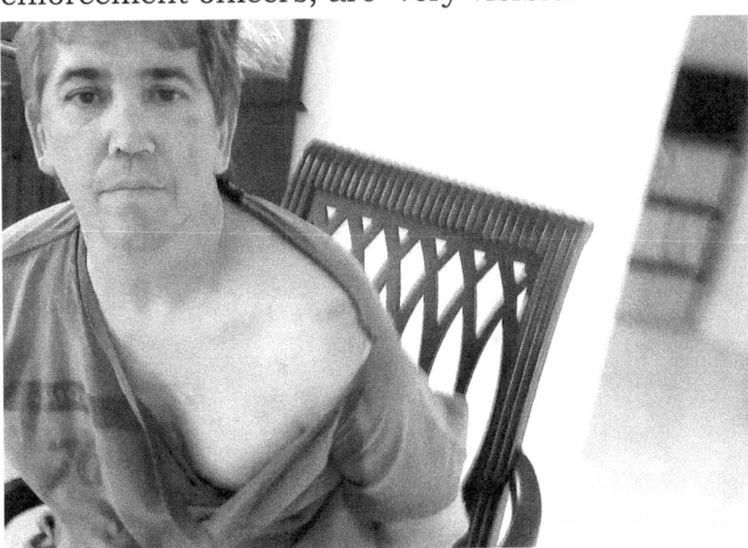

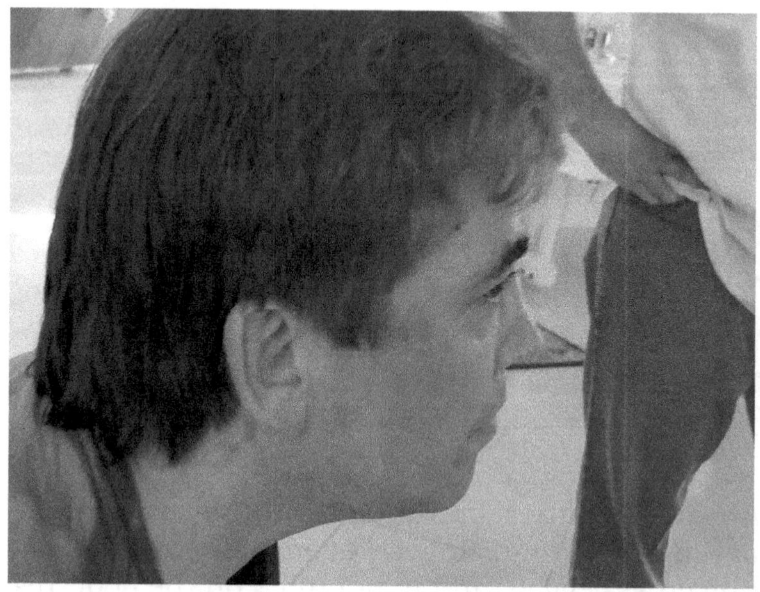

Above and below: The cuts and bruises from the injuries Robert sustained during the vicious bashing from the Sherriff's Deputies to his head and face are clearly visible.

Right, Robert's Official Booking Photo taken the night of October 5, 2015 at the Lake County Detention Center. He was finally transferred there after being forced to endure 10+ hours of agonizing pain from the injuries, extra-tight handcuffs and being denied any food and water.

Robert was finally released on Bond on October 9, 2015. In the weeks that followed, he and I would spend virtually every minute together, both for his safety and mine. This picture to the right was taken shortly after his release. As you can see, the contusions around his eyes have now fully formed, as the tiny blood vessels, called capillaries, burst from the trauma of his beating and the blood pooling just under the skin.

The Second False Arrest

Shortly after the incident at our Mt. Dora FL home, Robert and I returned to **our second home in Ft. Lauderdale, FL.** (above) On the morning of August 17, 2016, we left home as usual, to run a few errands and have a quiet lunch together. As soon as we were out of the driveway, I noticed a big dark-blue SUV following us very closely. I asked Robert to turn down the next street, but the SUV continued to follow us. Robert stopped the car near the curb. Just then, **the SUV SPED UP and smashed into the passenger side of our car!** Several seconds later, several other un-marked cars completely encircled us.

A voice from a police megaphone ordered Robert to raise his hands, exit the vehicle and lay flat on the cement road.

After Robert complied, an officer lifted him up and bodily dropped him face down on the hot cement pavement. Just then, another officer fell with his full body weight on Robert's left shoulder yelling, "Stop Resisting! Stop Resisting!" He was not resisting, but in a submissive, prone position, ready to be handcuffed. Such physical brutality caused Robert abdominal pain and intestinal bleeding. After this officer filed a false resisting charge, a Broward County Jury exonerated Robert from those false resisting charges.

This totally unnecessary collision was so severe that it bent the rear axle of my car, rendering it unsafe to drive. I replaced it with a **brand new Honda CRV**.

Additional Scenes from the Second False Arrest

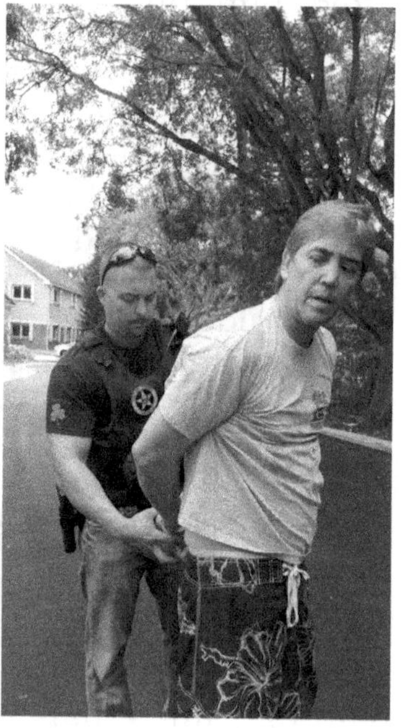

For the second time in ten months, Robert is beaten and physically abused by law enforcement officials and led away in handcuffs.

This time, the new injuries compounded the previous injuries and Robert was taken to the Broward Health Medical Center in Ft. Lauderdale, FL. for observation. He was diagnosed on August 25, 2016 with pre-cancerous bleeding polyps.

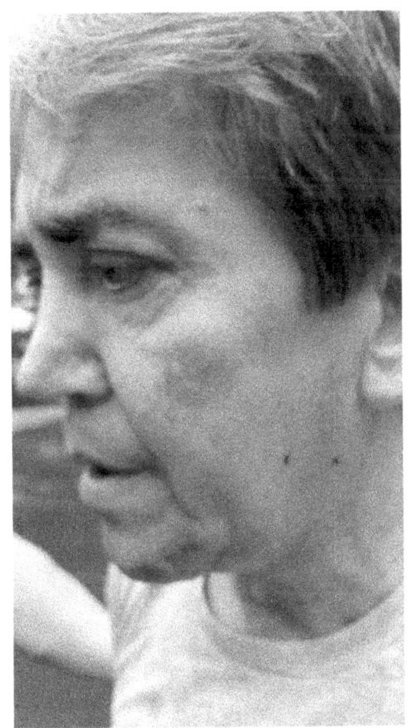
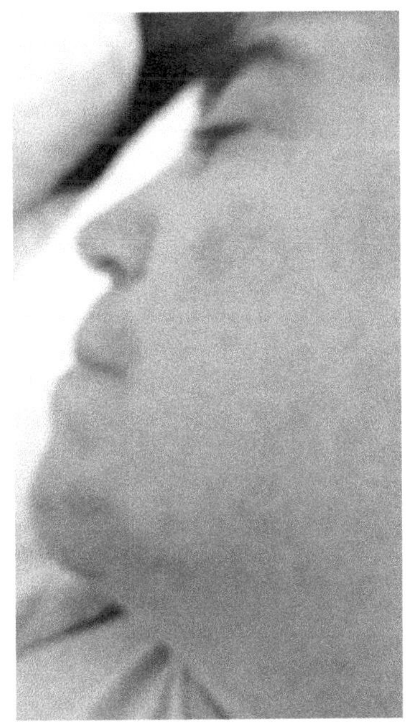

New injuries add even more pain for Robert!

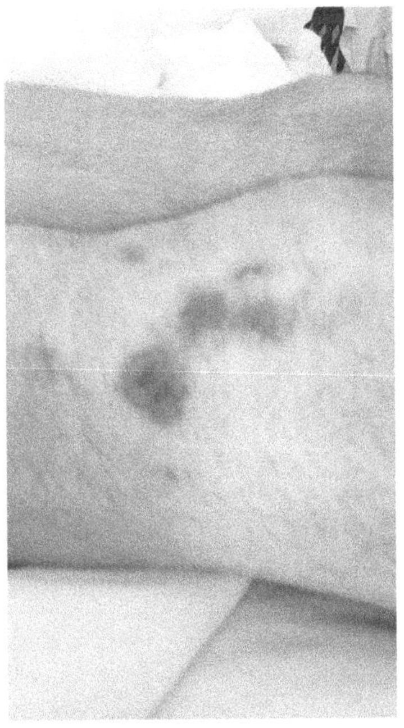
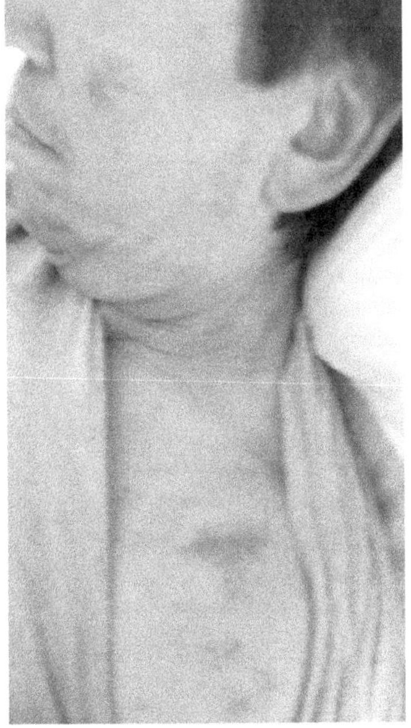

A Blessed Life

Robert Anthony O'Hare was born November 1, 1961, in Elmira, NY. He was a beautiful baby brother to his two older sisters, Anne Marie, 3 and Patty Lynne, 2. My greatest earthly blessing was being their mother.

As a young boy, growing-up in Elmira, NY, Robert was always fascinated with adventure.He loved reading books and stories of great explorers, and treasure hunters. He was also very interested in science and mechanics. He was constantly experimenting with the way things worked and how he could make them even better. As a young man, Robert created several inventions. Above all, Robert loved God and treasured his family.

Chickamauga Battlefield
Visitor Center

Above: My two priceless gems, Anne Marie *(r)* and Patty Lynne *(l)* were incredible, and well disciplined daughters God blessed me with.

Below: Family Thanksgiving 1985.

Dan, and I spent 45 wonderful years together with Anne Marie, Patty Lynne and Robert Anthony. Our life together as a family was filled with loving, caring, and fun filled memories. On September 30, 2013 Dan joined Anne Marie who had passed away a year earlier on September 17, 2012, and Patty Lynne joined them both on November 24, 2013.